50% OFF
Online TSI Prep Course!

By Mometrix

Dear Customer,

We consider it an honor and a privilege that you chose our TSI Study Guide. As a way of showing our appreciation and to help us better serve you, we are offering **50% off our online TSI Prep Course**. Many TSI courses are needlessly expensive and don't deliver enough value. With our course, you get access to the best TSI prep material, and **you only pay half price**.

We have structured our online course to perfectly complement your printed study guide. The TSI Prep Course contains **in-depth lessons** that cover all the most important topics, **150+ video reviews** that explain difficult concepts, over **1,050 practice questions** to ensure you feel prepared, and over **300 digital flashcards**, so you can study while you're on the go.

Online TSI Prep Course

Topics Covered:

- Mathematics
  - *Elementary Algebra and Functions*
  - *Intermediate Algebra and Functions*
  - *Geometry and Measurement*
  - *Data Analysis, Statistics, and Probability*
- Reading
  - *Literary Analysis*
  - *Main Idea and Supporting Details*
  - *Inferences in a Text or Texts*
  - *Author's Use of Language*
- Writing
  - *Foundations of Grammar and Punctuation*
  - *Essay Revision and Sentence Logic*
  - *Agreement and Sentence Structure*

Course Features:

- TSI Study Guide
  - Get content that complements our best-selling study guide.
- 9 Full-Length Practice Tests
  - With over 1050 practice questions, you can test yourself again and again.
- Mobile Friendly
  - If you need to study on the go, the course is easily accessible from your mobile device.
- TSI Flashcards
  - Our course includes a flashcard mode consisting of over 300 content cards to help you study.

To receive this discount, simply head to our website at mometrix.com/university/tsi or simply scan this QR code with your smartphone. At the checkout page, enter the discount code: **tsi50off**

If you have any questions or concerns, please contact us at support@mometrix.com.

Sincerely,

FREE Study Skills Videos/DVD Offer

Dear Customer,

Thank you for your purchase from Mometrix! We consider it an honor and a privilege that you have purchased our product and we want to ensure your satisfaction.

As part of our ongoing effort to meet the needs of test takers, we have developed a set of Study Skills Videos that we would like to give you for FREE. These videos cover our *best practices* for getting ready for your exam, from how to use our study materials to how to best prepare for the day of the test.

All that we ask is that you email us with feedback that would describe your experience so far with our product. Good, bad, or indifferent, we want to know what you think!

To get your FREE Study Skills Videos, you can use the **QR code** below, or send us an **email** at studyvideos@mometrix.com with *FREE VIDEOS* in the subject line and the following information in the body of the email:

- The name of the product you purchased.
- Your product rating on a scale of 1-5, with 5 being the highest rating.
- Your feedback. It can be long, short, or anything in between. We just want to know your impressions and experience so far with our product. (Good feedback might include how our study material met your needs and ways we might be able to make it even better. You could highlight features that you found helpful or features that you think we should add.)

If you have any questions or concerns, please don't hesitate to contact me directly.

Thanks again!

Sincerely,

Jay Willis
Vice President
jay.willis@mometrix.com
1-800-673-8175

TSI Assessment SECRETS

Study Guide

Your Key to Exam Success

Written and edited by the Mometrix College Placement Test Team

Printed in the United States of America

This paper meets the requirements of ANSI/NISO Z39.48-1992 (Permanence of Paper).

Paperback
ISBN 13: 978-1-63094-531-2
ISBN 10: 1-63094-531-5

Ebook
ISBN 13: 978-1-5167-0300-5
ISBN 10: 1-5167-0300-6

Hardback
ISBN 13: 978-1-5167-0539-9
ISBN 10: 1-5167-0539-4

DEAR FUTURE EXAM SUCCESS STORY

First of all, **THANK YOU** for purchasing Mometrix study materials!

Second, congratulations! You are one of the few determined test-takers who are committed to doing whatever it takes to excel on your exam. **You have come to the right place.** We developed these study materials with one goal in mind: to deliver you the information you need in a format that's concise and easy to use.

In addition to optimizing your guide for the content of the test, we've outlined our recommended steps for breaking down the preparation process into small, attainable goals so you can make sure you stay on track.

We've also analyzed the entire test-taking process, identifying the most common pitfalls and showing how you can overcome them and be ready for any curveball the test throws you.

Standardized testing is one of the biggest obstacles on your road to success, which only increases the importance of doing well in the high-pressure, high-stakes environment of test day. Your results on this test could have a significant impact on your future, and this guide provides the information and practical advice to help you achieve your full potential on test day.

Your success is our success

We would love to hear from you! If you would like to share the story of your exam success or if you have any questions or comments in regard to our products, please contact us at **800-673-8175** or **support@mometrix.com**.

Thanks again for your business and we wish you continued success!

Sincerely,
The Mometrix Test Preparation Team

Need more help? Check out our flashcards at:
http://MometrixFlashcards.com/TSI

TABLE OF CONTENTS

INTRODUCTION 1

SECRET KEY #1 – PLAN BIG, STUDY SMALL 2

SECRET KEY #2 – MAKE YOUR STUDYING COUNT 3

SECRET KEY #3 – PRACTICE THE RIGHT WAY 4

SECRET KEY #4 – HAVE A PLAN FOR GUESSING 5

TEST-TAKING STRATEGIES 8

THREE-WEEK TSI STUDY PLAN 12
- WEEK 1: MATHEMATICS 13
- WEEK 2: READING AND WRITING 14
- WEEK 3: ESSAY 15

MATHEMATICS 17
- QUANTITATIVE REASONING 17
- ALGEBRAIC REASONING 57
- GEOMETRIC AND SPATIAL REASONING 78
- PROBABILISTIC AND STATISTICAL REASONING 107

READING 121
- LITERARY TEXT ANALYSIS 121
- LITERARY TEXT ANALYSIS CHAPTER QUIZ 126
- INFORMATIONAL TEXT ANALYSIS 127
- INFORMATIONAL TEXT ANALYSIS CHAPTER QUIZ 130
- INFERENCES 131
- INFERENCES CHAPTER QUIZ 134
- AUTHOR'S CRAFT 135
- AUTHOR'S CRAFT CHAPTER QUIZ 142
- ARGUMENTATION 143
- ARGUMENTATION CHAPTER QUIZ 146
- VOCABULARY 147
- VOCABULARY CHAPTER QUIZ 150

WRITING 151
- CONVENTIONS OF GRAMMAR AND USAGE 151
- CONVENTIONS OF GRAMMAR AND USAGE CHAPTER QUIZ 175
- CONVENTIONS OF PUNCTUATION 176
- CONVENTIONS OF PUNCTUATION CHAPTER QUIZ 183
- CONVENTIONS OF SPELLING 184
- CONVENTIONS OF SPELLING CHAPTER QUIZ 193
- ESSAY REVISION AND EDITING 194
- ESSAY REVISION AND EDITING CHAPTER QUIZ 198

ESSAY 199

CHAPTER QUIZ ANSWER KEY 202

Literary Text Analysis — 202
Informational Text Analysis — 203
Inferences — 204
Author's Craft — 205
Argumentation — 206
Vocabulary — 207
Conventions of Grammar and Usage — 208
Conventions of Punctuation — 209
Conventions of Spelling — 210
Essay Revision and Editing — 211

TSI Practice Test #1 — 212
Math — 212
English Language Arts and Reading — 217
Essay — 228

Answers and Explanations for Test #1 — 229
Math — 229
English Language Arts and Reading — 232

TSI Practice Test #2 — 236
Math — 236
English Language Arts and Reading — 241
Essay — 250

Answers and Explanations for Test #2 — 251
Math — 251
English Language Arts and Reading — 255

TSI Practice Test #3 — 259
Math — 259
English Language Arts and Reading — 263
Essay — 272

Answers and Explanations for Test #3 — 273
Math — 273
English Language Arts and Reading — 276

TSI Practice Test #4 — 280
Math — 280
English Language Arts and Reading — 285
Essay — 294

Answers and Explanations for Test #4 — 295
Math — 295
English Language Arts and Reading — 298

TSI Practice Test #5 — 302
Math — 302
English Language Arts and Reading — 307
Essay — 317

Answers and Explanations for Test #5 — 318
Math — 318

English Language Arts and Reading 321

How to Overcome Test Anxiety 325

Causes of Test Anxiety 325

Elements of Test Anxiety 326

Effects of Test Anxiety 326

Physical Steps for Beating Test Anxiety 327

Mental Steps for Beating Test Anxiety 328

Study Strategy 329

Test Tips 331

Important Qualification 332

How to Overcome Your Fear of Math 333

What Is Math Anxiety? 333

Debunking Math Myths 336

Tips and Strategies for Overcoming Math Anxiety 337

Remember, You Can Do This! 339

Tell Us Your Story 340

Additional Bonus Material 341

Introduction

Thank you for purchasing this resource! You have made the choice to prepare yourself for a test that could have a huge impact on your future, and this guide is designed to help you be fully ready for test day. Obviously, it's important to have a solid understanding of the test material, but you also need to be prepared for the unique environment and stressors of the test, so that you can perform to the best of your abilities.

For this purpose, the first section that appears in this guide is the **Secret Keys**. We've devoted countless hours to meticulously researching what works and what doesn't, and we've boiled down our findings to the four most impactful steps you can take to improve your performance on the test. We start at the beginning with study planning and move through the preparation process, all the way to the testing strategies that will help you get the most out of what you know when you're finally sitting in front of the test.

We recommend that you start preparing for your test as far in advance as possible. However, if you've bought this guide as a last-minute study resource and only have a few days before your test, we recommend that you skip over the first two Secret Keys since they address a long-term study plan.

If you struggle with **test anxiety**, we strongly encourage you to check out our recommendations for how you can overcome it. Test anxiety is a formidable foe, but it can be beaten, and we want to make sure you have the tools you need to defeat it.

Secret Key #1 – Plan Big, Study Small

There's a lot riding on your performance. If you want to ace this test, you're going to need to keep your skills sharp and the material fresh in your mind. You need a plan that lets you review everything you need to know while still fitting in your schedule. We'll break this strategy down into three categories.

Information Organization

Start with the information you already have: the official test outline. From this, you can make a complete list of all the concepts you need to cover before the test. Organize these concepts into groups that can be studied together, and create a list of any related vocabulary you need to learn so you can brush up on any difficult terms. You'll want to keep this vocabulary list handy once you actually start studying since you may need to add to it along the way.

Time Management

Once you have your set of study concepts, decide how to spread them out over the time you have left before the test. Break your study plan into small, clear goals so you have a manageable task for each day and know exactly what you're doing. Then just focus on one small step at a time. When you manage your time this way, you don't need to spend hours at a time studying. Studying a small block of content for a short period each day helps you retain information better and avoid stressing over how much you have left to do. You can relax knowing that you have a plan to cover everything in time. In order for this strategy to be effective though, you have to start studying early and stick to your schedule. Avoid the exhaustion and futility that comes from last-minute cramming!

Study Environment

The environment you study in has a big impact on your learning. Studying in a coffee shop, while probably more enjoyable, is not likely to be as fruitful as studying in a quiet room. It's important to keep distractions to a minimum. You're only planning to study for a short block of time, so make the most of it. Don't pause to check your phone or get up to find a snack. It's also important to **avoid multitasking**. Research has consistently shown that multitasking will make your studying dramatically less effective. Your study area should also be comfortable and well-lit so you don't have the distraction of straining your eyes or sitting on an uncomfortable chair.

The time of day you study is also important. You want to be rested and alert. Don't wait until just before bedtime. Study when you'll be most likely to comprehend and remember. Even better, if you know what time of day your test will be, set that time aside for study. That way your brain will be used to working on that subject at that specific time and you'll have a better chance of recalling information.

Finally, it can be helpful to team up with others who are studying for the same test. Your actual studying should be done in as isolated an environment as possible, but the work of organizing the information and setting up the study plan can be divided up. In between study sessions, you can discuss with your teammates the concepts that you're all studying and quiz each other on the details. Just be sure that your teammates are as serious about the test as you are. If you find that your study time is being replaced with social time, you might need to find a new team.

Secret Key #2 – Make Your Studying Count

You're devoting a lot of time and effort to preparing for this test, so you want to be absolutely certain it will pay off. This means doing more than just reading the content and hoping you can remember it on test day. It's important to make every minute of study count. There are two main areas you can focus on to make your studying count.

Retention

It doesn't matter how much time you study if you can't remember the material. You need to make sure you are retaining the concepts. To check your retention of the information you're learning, try recalling it at later times with minimal prompting. Try carrying around flashcards and glance at one or two from time to time or ask a friend who's also studying for the test to quiz you.

To enhance your retention, look for ways to put the information into practice so that you can apply it rather than simply recalling it. If you're using the information in practical ways, it will be much easier to remember. Similarly, it helps to solidify a concept in your mind if you're not only reading it to yourself but also explaining it to someone else. Ask a friend to let you teach them about a concept you're a little shaky on (or speak aloud to an imaginary audience if necessary). As you try to summarize, define, give examples, and answer your friend's questions, you'll understand the concepts better and they will stay with you longer. Finally, step back for a big picture view and ask yourself how each piece of information fits with the whole subject. When you link the different concepts together and see them working together as a whole, it's easier to remember the individual components.

Finally, practice showing your work on any multi-step problems, even if you're just studying. Writing out each step you take to solve a problem will help solidify the process in your mind, and you'll be more likely to remember it during the test.

Modality

Modality simply refers to the means or method by which you study. Choosing a study modality that fits your own individual learning style is crucial. No two people learn best in exactly the same way, so it's important to know your strengths and use them to your advantage.

For example, if you learn best by visualization, focus on visualizing a concept in your mind and draw an image or a diagram. Try color-coding your notes, illustrating them, or creating symbols that will trigger your mind to recall a learned concept. If you learn best by hearing or discussing information, find a study partner who learns the same way or read aloud to yourself. Think about how to put the information in your own words. Imagine that you are giving a lecture on the topic and record yourself so you can listen to it later.

For any learning style, flashcards can be helpful. Organize the information so you can take advantage of spare moments to review. Underline key words or phrases. Use different colors for different categories. Mnemonic devices (such as creating a short list in which every item starts with the same letter) can also help with retention. Find what works best for you and use it to store the information in your mind most effectively and easily.

Secret Key #3 – Practice the Right Way

Your success on test day depends not only on how many hours you put into preparing, but also on whether you prepared the right way. It's good to check along the way to see if your studying is paying off. One of the most effective ways to do this is by taking practice tests to evaluate your progress. Practice tests are useful because they show exactly where you need to improve. Every time you take a practice test, pay special attention to these three groups of questions:

- The questions you got wrong
- The questions you had to guess on, even if you guessed right
- The questions you found difficult or slow to work through

This will show you exactly what your weak areas are, and where you need to devote more study time. Ask yourself why each of these questions gave you trouble. Was it because you didn't understand the material? Was it because you didn't remember the vocabulary? Do you need more repetitions on this type of question to build speed and confidence? Dig into those questions and figure out how you can strengthen your weak areas as you go back to review the material.

Additionally, many practice tests have a section explaining the answer choices. It can be tempting to read the explanation and think that you now have a good understanding of the concept. However, an explanation likely only covers part of the question's broader context. Even if the explanation makes perfect sense, **go back and investigate** every concept related to the question until you're positive you have a thorough understanding.

As you go along, keep in mind that the practice test is just that: practice. Memorizing these questions and answers will not be very helpful on the actual test because it is unlikely to have any of the same exact questions. If you only know the right answers to the sample questions, you won't be prepared for the real thing. **Study the concepts** until you understand them fully, and then you'll be able to answer any question that shows up on the test.

It's important to wait on the practice tests until you're ready. If you take a test on your first day of study, you may be overwhelmed by the amount of material covered and how much you need to learn. Work up to it gradually.

On test day, you'll need to be prepared for answering questions, managing your time, and using the test-taking strategies you've learned. It's a lot to balance, like a mental marathon that will have a big impact on your future. Like training for a marathon, you'll need to start slowly and work your way up. When test day arrives, you'll be ready.

Start with the strategies you've read in the first two Secret Keys—plan your course and study in the way that works best for you. If you have time, consider using multiple study resources to get different approaches to the same concepts. It can be helpful to see difficult concepts from more than one angle. Then find a good source for practice tests. Many times, the test website will suggest potential study resources or provide sample tests.

Secret Key #4 – Have a Plan for Guessing

When you're taking the test, you may find yourself stuck on a question. Some of the answer choices seem better than others, but you don't see the one answer choice that is obviously correct. What do you do?

The scenario described above is very common, yet most test takers have not effectively prepared for it. Developing and practicing a plan for guessing may be one of the single most effective uses of your time as you get ready for the exam.

In developing your plan for guessing, there are three questions to address:

- When should you start the guessing process?
- How should you narrow down the choices?
- Which answer should you choose?

When to Start the Guessing Process

Unless your plan for guessing is to select C every time (which, despite its merits, is not what we recommend), you need to leave yourself enough time to apply your answer elimination strategies. Since you have a limited amount of time for each question, that means that if you're going to give yourself the best shot at guessing correctly, you have to decide quickly whether or not you will guess.

Of course, the best-case scenario is that you don't have to guess at all, so first, see if you can answer the question based on your knowledge of the subject and basic reasoning skills. Focus on the key words in the question and try to jog your memory of related topics. Give yourself a chance to bring the knowledge to mind, but once you realize that you don't have (or you can't access) the knowledge you need to answer the question, it's time to start the guessing process.

It's almost always better to start the guessing process too early than too late. It only takes a few seconds to remember something and answer the question from knowledge. Carefully eliminating wrong answer choices takes longer. Plus, going through the process of eliminating answer choices can actually help jog your memory.

Summary: Start the guessing process as soon as you decide that you can't answer the question based on your knowledge.

How to Narrow Down the Choices

The next chapter in this book (**Test-Taking Strategies**) includes a wide range of strategies for how to approach questions and how to look for answer choices to eliminate. You will definitely want to read those carefully, practice them, and figure out which ones work best for you. Here though, we're going to address a mindset rather than a particular strategy.

Your odds of guessing an answer correctly depend on how many options you are choosing from.

Number of options left	5	4	3	2	1
Odds of guessing correctly	20%	25%	33%	50%	100%

You can see from this chart just how valuable it is to be able to eliminate incorrect answers and make an educated guess, but there are two things that many test takers do that cause them to miss out on the benefits of guessing:

- Accidentally eliminating the correct answer
- Selecting an answer based on an impression

We'll look at the first one here, and the second one in the next section.

To avoid accidentally eliminating the correct answer, we recommend a thought exercise called **the $5 challenge**. In this challenge, you only eliminate an answer choice from contention if you are willing to bet $5 on it being wrong. Why $5? Five dollars is a small but not insignificant amount of money. It's an amount you could afford to lose but wouldn't want to throw away. And while losing $5 once might not hurt too much, doing it twenty times will set you back $100. In the same way, each small decision you make—eliminating a choice here, guessing on a question there—won't by itself impact your score very much, but when you put them all together, they can make a big difference. By holding each answer choice elimination decision to a higher standard, you can reduce the risk of accidentally eliminating the correct answer.

The $5 challenge can also be applied in a positive sense: If you are willing to bet $5 that an answer choice *is* correct, go ahead and mark it as correct.

Summary: Only eliminate an answer choice if you are willing to bet $5 that it is wrong.

Which Answer to Choose

You're taking the test. You've run into a hard question and decided you'll have to guess. You've eliminated all the answer choices you're willing to bet $5 on. Now you have to pick an answer. Why do we even need to talk about this? Why can't you just pick whichever one you feel like when the time comes?

The answer to these questions is that if you don't come into the test with a plan, you'll rely on your impression to select an answer choice, and if you do that, you risk falling into a trap. The test writers know that everyone who takes their test will be guessing on some of the questions, so they intentionally write wrong answer choices to seem plausible. You still have to pick an answer though, and if the wrong answer choices are designed to look right, how can you ever be sure that you're not falling for their trap? The best solution we've found to this dilemma is to take the decision out of your hands entirely. Here is the process we recommend:

Once you've eliminated any choices that you are confident (willing to bet $5) are wrong, select the first remaining choice as your answer.

Whether you choose to select the first remaining choice, the second, or the last, the important thing is that you use some preselected standard. Using this approach guarantees that you will not be enticed into selecting an answer choice that looks right, because you are not basing your decision on how the answer choices look.

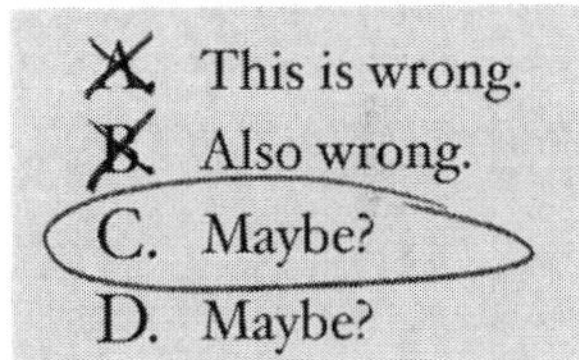

This is not meant to make you question your knowledge. Instead, it is to help you recognize the difference between your knowledge and your impressions. There's a huge difference between thinking an answer is right because of what you know, and thinking an answer is right because it looks or sounds like it should be right.

Summary: To ensure that your selection is appropriately random, make a predetermined selection from among all answer choices you have not eliminated.

Test-Taking Strategies

This section contains a list of test-taking strategies that you may find helpful as you work through the test. By taking what you know and applying logical thought, you can maximize your chances of answering any question correctly!

It is very important to realize that every question is different and every person is different: no single strategy will work on every question, and no single strategy will work for every person. That's why we've included all of them here, so you can try them out and determine which ones work best for different types of questions and which ones work best for you.

Question Strategies

✅ Read Carefully

Read the question and the answer choices carefully. Don't miss the question because you misread the terms. You have plenty of time to read each question thoroughly and make sure you understand what is being asked. Yet a happy medium must be attained, so don't waste too much time. You must read carefully and efficiently.

✅ Contextual Clues

Look for contextual clues. If the question includes a word you are not familiar with, look at the immediate context for some indication of what the word might mean. Contextual clues can often give you all the information you need to decipher the meaning of an unfamiliar word. Even if you can't determine the meaning, you may be able to narrow down the possibilities enough to make a solid guess at the answer to the question.

✅ Prefixes

If you're having trouble with a word in the question or answer choices, try dissecting it. Take advantage of every clue that the word might include. Prefixes can be a huge help. Usually, they allow you to determine a basic meaning. *Pre-* means before, *post-* means after, *pro-* is positive, *de-* is negative. From prefixes, you can get an idea of the general meaning of the word and try to put it into context.

✅ Hedge Words

Watch out for critical hedge words, such as *likely, may, can, sometimes, often, almost, mostly, usually, generally, rarely,* and *sometimes.* Question writers insert these hedge phrases to cover every possibility. Often an answer choice will be wrong simply because it leaves no room for exception. Be on guard for answer choices that have definitive words such as *exactly* and *always.*

✅ Switchback Words

Stay alert for *switchbacks.* These are the words and phrases frequently used to alert you to shifts in thought. The most common switchback words are *but, although,* and *however.* Others include *nevertheless, on the other hand, even though, while, in spite of, despite,* and *regardless of.* Switchback words are important to catch because they can change the direction of the question or an answer choice.

✓ Face Value

When in doubt, use common sense. Accept the situation in the problem at face value. Don't read too much into it. These problems will not require you to make wild assumptions. If you have to go beyond creativity and warp time or space in order to have an answer choice fit the question, then you should move on and consider the other answer choices. These are normal problems rooted in reality. The applicable relationship or explanation may not be readily apparent, but it is there for you to figure out. Use your common sense to interpret anything that isn't clear.

Answer Choice Strategies

✓ Answer Selection

The most thorough way to pick an answer choice is to identify and eliminate wrong answers until only one is left, then confirm it is the correct answer. Sometimes an answer choice may immediately seem right, but be careful. The test writers will usually put more than one reasonable answer choice on each question, so take a second to read all of them and make sure that the other choices are not equally obvious. As long as you have time left, it is better to read every answer choice than to pick the first one that looks right without checking the others.

✓ Answer Choice Families

An answer choice family consists of two (in rare cases, three) answer choices that are very similar in construction and cannot all be true at the same time. If you see two answer choices that are direct opposites or parallels, one of them is usually the correct answer. For instance, if one answer choice says that quantity x increases and another either says that quantity x decreases (opposite) or says that quantity y increases (parallel), then those answer choices would fall into the same family. An answer choice that doesn't match the construction of the answer choice family is more likely to be incorrect. Most questions will not have answer choice families, but when they do appear, you should be prepared to recognize them.

✓ Eliminate Answers

Eliminate answer choices as soon as you realize they are wrong, but make sure you consider all possibilities. If you are eliminating answer choices and realize that the last one you are left with is also wrong, don't panic. Start over and consider each choice again. There may be something you missed the first time that you will realize on the second pass.

✓ Avoid Fact Traps

Don't be distracted by an answer choice that is factually true but doesn't answer the question. You are looking for the choice that answers the question. Stay focused on what the question is asking for so you don't accidentally pick an answer that is true but incorrect. Always go back to the question and make sure the answer choice you've selected actually answers the question and is not merely a true statement.

✓ Extreme Statements

In general, you should avoid answers that put forth extreme actions as standard practice or proclaim controversial ideas as established fact. An answer choice that states the "process should be used in certain situations, if…" is much more likely to be correct than one that states the "process should be discontinued completely." The first is a calm rational statement and doesn't even make a definitive, uncompromising stance, using a hedge word *if* to provide wiggle room, whereas the second choice is far more extreme.

✓ Benchmark

As you read through the answer choices and you come across one that seems to answer the question well, mentally select that answer choice. This is not your final answer, but it's the one that will help you evaluate the other answer choices. The one that you selected is your benchmark or standard for judging each of the other answer choices. Every other answer choice must be compared to your benchmark. That choice is correct until proven otherwise by another answer choice beating it. If you find a better answer, then that one becomes your new benchmark. Once you've decided that no other choice answers the question as well as your benchmark, you have your final answer.

✓ Predict the Answer

Before you even start looking at the answer choices, it is often best to try to predict the answer. When you come up with the answer on your own, it is easier to avoid distractions and traps because you will know exactly what to look for. The right answer choice is unlikely to be word-for-word what you came up with, but it should be a close match. Even if you are confident that you have the right answer, you should still take the time to read each option before moving on.

General Strategies

✓ Tough Questions

If you are stumped on a problem or it appears too hard or too difficult, don't waste time. Move on! Remember though, if you can quickly check for obviously incorrect answer choices, your chances of guessing correctly are greatly improved. Before you completely give up, at least try to knock out a couple of possible answers. Eliminate what you can and then guess at the remaining answer choices before moving on.

✓ Check Your Work

Since you will probably not know every term listed and the answer to every question, it is important that you get credit for the ones that you do know. Don't miss any questions through careless mistakes. If at all possible, try to take a second to look back over your answer selection and make sure you've selected the correct answer choice and haven't made a costly careless mistake (such as marking an answer choice that you didn't mean to mark). This quick double check should more than pay for itself in caught mistakes for the time it costs.

✓ Don't Rush

It is very easy to make errors when you are in a hurry. Maintaining a fast pace in answering questions is pointless if it makes you miss questions that you would have gotten right otherwise. Test writers like to include distracting information and wrong answers that seem right. Taking a little extra time to avoid careless mistakes can make all the difference in your test score. Find a pace that allows you to be confident in the answers that you select.

✓ Keep Moving

Panicking will not help you pass the test, so do your best to stay calm and keep moving. Taking deep breaths and going through the answer elimination steps you practiced can help to break through a stress barrier and keep your pace.

Final Notes

The combination of a solid foundation of content knowledge and the confidence that comes from practicing your plan for applying that knowledge is the key to maximizing your performance on test day. As your foundation of content knowledge is built up and strengthened, you'll find that the strategies included in this chapter become more and more effective in helping you quickly sift through the distractions and traps of the test to isolate the correct answer.

Now that you're preparing to move forward into the test content chapters of this book, be sure to keep your goal in mind. As you read, think about how you will be able to apply this information on the test. If you've already seen sample questions for the test and you have an idea of the question format and style, try to come up with questions of your own that you can answer based on what you're reading. This will give you valuable practice applying your knowledge in the same ways you can expect to on test day.

Good luck and good studying!

Three-Week TSI Study Plan

On the next few pages, we've provided an optional study plan to help you use this study guide to its fullest potential over the course of three weeks. If you have six weeks available and want to spread it out more, spend two weeks on each section of the plan.

Below is a quick summary of the subjects covered in each week of the plan.

- Week 1: Mathematics
- Week 2: Reading and Writing
- Week 3: Essay

Please note that not all subjects will take the same amount of time to work through.

Five full-length practice tests are included in this study guide. We recommend saving practice tests 3-5 for after you've completed the study plan. Take these practice tests without any reference materials a day or two before the real thing as practice runs to get you in the mode of answering questions at a good pace.

Week 1: Mathematics

Instructional Content

First, read carefully through the Mathematics chapter in this book, checking off your progress as you go:

- ❑ Quantitative Reasoning
- ❑ Algebraic Reasoning
- ❑ Geometric and Spatial Reasoning
- ❑ Probabilistic and Statistical Reasoning

As you read, do the following:

- Highlight any sections, terms, or concepts you think are important
- Draw an asterisk (*) next to any areas you are struggling with
- Watch the review videos to gain more understanding of a particular topic
- Take notes in your notebook or in the margins of this book

After you've read through everything, go back and review any sections that you highlighted or that you drew an asterisk next to, referencing your notes along the way.

Practice Test #1

Now that you've read over the instructional content, it's time to take a practice test. Complete the Math section of Practice Test #1. Take this test with **no time constraints**, and feel free to reference the applicable sections of this guide as you go. Once you've finished, check your answers against the provided answer key. For any questions you answered incorrectly, review the answer rationale, and then **go back and review** the applicable sections of the book. The goal in this stage is to understand why you answered the question incorrectly, and make sure that the next time you see a similar question, you will get it right.

Practice Test #2

Next, take the Math section of Practice Test #2. The TSI isn't timed, so go at your own pace, but try to minimize how often you have to refer to the study guide. Once you've finished, check your answers against the provided answer key and as before, review the answer rationale for any that you answered incorrectly and go back and review the associated instructional content. Your goal is still to increase understanding of the content but also to get used to not having any references for when you have to take the real test.

Week 2: Reading and Writing

Instructional Content

First, read carefully through the Reading and Writing chapters in this book, checking off your progress as you go:

- ❑ Literary Text Analysis
- ❑ Informational Text Analysis
- ❑ Inferences
- ❑ Author's Craft
- ❑ Argumentation
- ❑ Vocabulary
- ❑ Conventions of Grammar and Usage
- ❑ Conventions of Punctuation
- ❑ Conventions of Spelling

As you read, do the following:

- Highlight any sections, terms, or concepts you think are important
- Draw an asterisk (*) next to any areas you are struggling with
- Watch the review videos to gain more understanding of a particular topic
- Take notes in your notebook or in the margins of this book

After you've read through everything, go back and review any sections that you highlighted or that you drew an asterisk next to, referencing your notes along the way.

Practice Test #1

Now that you've read over the instructional content, it's time to take a practice test. Complete the English Language Arts and Reading section of Practice Test #1. Take this test with **no time constraints**, and feel free to reference the applicable sections of this guide as you go. Once you've finished, check your answers against the provided answer key. For any questions you answered incorrectly, review the answer rationale, and then **go back and review** the applicable sections of the book. The goal in this stage is to understand why you answered the question incorrectly, and make sure that the next time you see a similar question, you will get it right.

Practice Test #2

Next, take the English Language Arts and Reading section of Practice Test #2. The TSI isn't timed, so go at your own pace, but try to minimize how often you have to refer to the study guide. Once you've finished, check your answers against the provided answer key and as before, review the answer rationale for any that you answered incorrectly and go back and review the associated instructional content. Your goal is still to increase understanding of the content but also to get used to not having any references for when you have to take the real test.

Week 3: Essay

Instructional Content

First, read carefully through the Essay chapter in this book, checking off your progress as you go:

- ❑ Introduction
- ❑ Paragraphs
- ❑ Paragraph Length
- ❑ Coherent Paragraphs

As you read, do the following:

- Highlight any sections, terms, or concepts you think are important
- Draw an asterisk (*) next to any areas you are struggling with
- Watch the review videos to gain more understanding of a particular topic
- Take notes in your notebook or in the margins of this book

After you've read through everything, go back and review any sections that you highlighted or that you drew an asterisk next to, referencing your notes along the way.

Practice Test #1

Now that you've read over the instructional content, it's time to take a practice test. Complete the Essay section of Practice Test #1. Take this test with **no time constraints**, and feel free to reference the applicable sections of this guide as you go. Once you've finished, check your essay against the provided guide to make sure you have included all of the components of a well-constructed essay.

Practice Test #2

Next, complete the Essay section of Practice Test #2. The TSI isn't timed, so go at your own pace, but try to minimize how often you have to refer to the study guide. Once you've finished, check your essay against the provided guide to make sure you have included all of the components of a well-constructed essay. Your goal is still to increase understanding of the content but also to get used to not having any references for when you have to take the real test.

Mathematics

Quantitative Reasoning

NUMBERS

CLASSIFICATIONS OF NUMBERS

Numbers are the basic building blocks of mathematics. Specific features of numbers are identified by the following terms:

Integer – any positive or negative whole number, including zero. Integers do not include fractions $\left(\frac{1}{3}\right)$, decimals (0.56), or mixed numbers $\left(7\frac{3}{4}\right)$.

Prime number – any whole number greater than 1 that has only two factors, itself and 1; that is, a number that can be divided evenly only by 1 and itself.

Composite number – any whole number greater than 1 that has more than two different factors; in other words, any whole number that is not a prime number. For example: The composite number 8 has the factors of 1, 2, 4, and 8.

Even number – any integer that can be divided by 2 without leaving a remainder. For example: 2, 4, 6, 8, and so on.

Odd number – any integer that cannot be divided evenly by 2. For example: 3, 5, 7, 9, and so on.

Decimal number – any number that uses a decimal point to show the part of the number that is less than one. Example: 1.234.

Decimal point – a symbol used to separate the ones place from the tenths place in decimals or dollars from cents in currency.

Decimal place – the position of a number to the right of the decimal point. In the decimal 0.123, the 1 is in the first place to the right of the decimal point, indicating tenths; the 2 is in the second place, indicating hundredths; and the 3 is in the third place, indicating thousandths.

The **decimal**, or base 10, system is a number system that uses ten different digits (0, 1, 2, 3, 4, 5, 6, 7, 8, 9). An example of a number system that uses something other than ten digits is the **binary**, or base 2, number system, used by computers, which uses only the numbers 0 and 1. It is thought that the decimal system originated because people had only their 10 fingers for counting.

Rational numbers include all integers, decimals, and fractions. Any terminating or repeating decimal number is a rational number.

Irrational numbers cannot be written as fractions or decimals because the number of decimal places is infinite and there is no recurring pattern of digits within the number. For example, pi (π) begins with 3.141592 and continues without terminating or repeating, so pi is an irrational number.

Real numbers are the set of all rational and irrational numbers.

> **Review Video: Numbers and Their Classifications**
> Visit mometrix.com/academy and enter code: 461071
>
> **Review Video: Rational and Irrational Numbers**
> Visit mometrix.com/academy and enter code: 280645
>
> **Review Video: Prime and Composite Numbers**
> Visit mometrix.com/academy and enter code: 565581
>
> **Review Video: Irrational Numbers on a Number Line**
> Visit mometrix.com/academy and enter code: 433866

The Number Line

A number line is a graph to see the distance between numbers. Basically, this graph shows the relationship between numbers. So a number line may have a point for zero and may show negative numbers on the left side of the line. Any positive numbers are placed on the right side of the line. For example, consider the points labeled on the following number line:

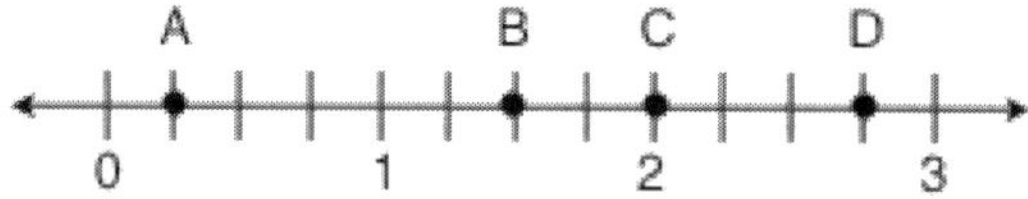

We can use the dashed lines on the number line to identify each point. Each dashed line between two whole numbers is $\frac{1}{4}$. The line halfway between two numbers is $\frac{1}{2}$.

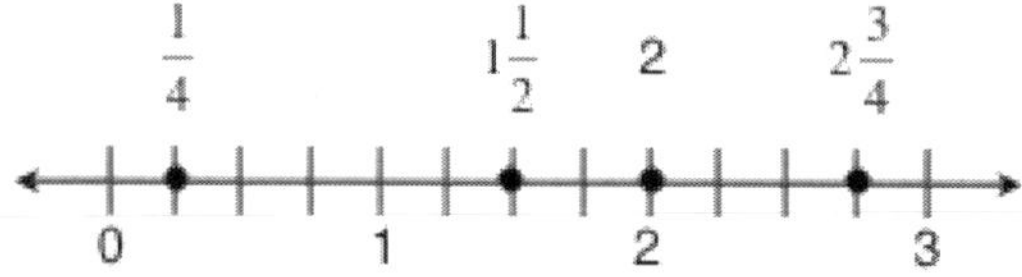

> **Review Video: Negative and Positive Number Line**
> Visit mometrix.com/academy and enter code: 816439

Numbers in Word Form and Place Value

When writing numbers out in word form or translating word form to numbers, it is essential to understand how a place value system works. In the decimal or base-10 system, each digit of a number represents how many of the corresponding place value – a specific factor of 10 – are contained in the number being represented. To make reading numbers easier, every three digits to the left of the decimal place is preceded by a comma. The following table demonstrates some of the place values:

Power of 10	10^3	10^2	10^1	10^0	10^{-1}	10^{-2}	10^{-3}
Value	1,000	100	10	1	0.1	0.01	0.001
Place	thousands	hundreds	tens	ones	tenths	hundredths	thousandths

For example, consider the number 4,546.09, which can be separated into each place value like this:

4: thousands
5: hundreds
4: tens
6: ones
0: tenths
9: hundredths

This number in word form would be *four thousand five hundred forty-six and nine hundredths.*

Review Video: Place Value
Visit mometrix.com/academy and enter code: 205433

Absolute Value

A precursor to working with negative numbers is understanding what **absolute values** are. A number's absolute value is simply the distance away from zero a number is on the number line. The absolute value of a number is always positive and is written $|x|$. For example, the absolute value of 3, written as $|3|$, is 3 because the distance between 0 and 3 on a number line is three units. Likewise, the absolute value of -3, written as $|-3|$, is 3 because the distance between 0 and -3 on a number line is three units. So $|3| = |-3|$.

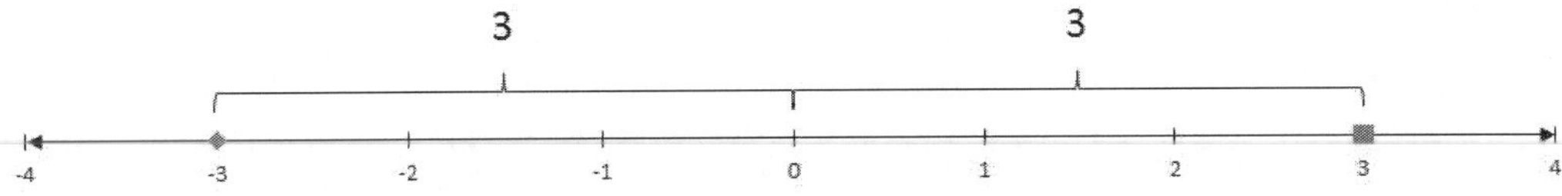

Review Video: Absolute Value
Visit mometrix.com/academy and enter code: 314669

Practice

P1. Write the place value of each digit in 14,059.826

P2. Write out each of the following in words:

(a) 29
(b) 478
(c) 98,542
(d) 0.06
(e) 13.113

P3. Write each of the following in numbers:

(a) nine thousand four hundred thirty-five
(b) three hundred two thousand eight hundred seventy-six
(c) nine hundred one thousandths
(d) nineteen thousandths
(e) seven thousand one hundred forty-two and eighty-five hundredths

Practice Solutions

P1. The place value for each digit would be as follows:

Digit	Place Value
1	ten-thousands
4	thousands
0	hundreds
5	tens
9	ones
8	tenths
2	hundredths
6	thousandths

P2. Each written out in words would be:

(a) twenty-nine
(b) four hundred seventy-eight
(c) ninety-eight thousand five hundred forty-two
(d) six hundredths
(e) thirteen and one hundred thirteen thousandths

P3. Each in numeric form would be:

(a) 9,435
(b) 302876
(c) 0.901
(d) 0.019
(e) 7,142.85

Operations

An **operation** is simply a mathematical process that takes some value(s) as input(s) and produces an output. Elementary operations are often written in the following form: *value operation value*. For instance, in the expression $1 + 2$ the values are 1 and 2 and the operation is addition. Performing the operation gives the output of 3. In this way we can say that $1 + 2$ and 3 are equal, or $1 + 2 = 3$.

Addition

Addition increases the value of one quantity by the value of another quantity (both called **addends**). For example, $2 + 4 = 6; 8 + 9 = 17$. The result is called the **sum**. With addition, the order does not matter, $4 + 2 = 2 + 4$.

When adding signed numbers, if the signs are the same simply add the absolute values of the addends and apply the original sign to the sum. For example, $(+4) + (+8) = +12$ and $(-4) + (-8) = -12$. When the original signs are different, take the absolute values of the addends and subtract the smaller value from the larger value, then apply the original sign of the larger value to the difference. For instance, $(+4) + (-8) = -4$ and $(-4) + (+8) = +4$.

Subtraction

Subtraction is the opposite operation to addition; it decreases the value of one quantity (the **minuend**) by the value of another quantity (the **subtrahend**). For example, $6 - 4 = 2; 17 - 8 = 9$. The result is called the **difference**. Note that with subtraction, the order does matter, $6 - 4 \neq 4 - 6$.

For subtracting signed numbers, change the sign of the subtrahend and then follow the same rules used for addition. For example, $(+4) - (+8) = (+4) + (-8) = -4$.

Multiplication

Multiplication can be thought of as repeated addition. One number (the **multiplier**) indicates how many times to add the other number (the **multiplicand**) to itself. For example, 3×2 (three times two) $= 2 + 2 + 2 = 6$. With multiplication, the order does not matter: $2 \times 3 = 3 \times 2$ or $3 + 3 = 2 + 2 + 2$, either way the result (the **product**) is the same.

If the signs are the same, the product is positive when multiplying signed numbers. For example, $(+4) \times (+8) = +32$ and $(-4) \times (-8) = +32$. If the signs are opposite, the product is negative. For example, $(+4) \times (-8) = -32$ and $(-4) \times (+8) = -32$. When more than two factors are multiplied together, the sign of the product is determined by how many negative factors are present. If there are an odd number of negative factors then the product is negative, whereas an even number of negative factors indicates a positive product. For instance, $(+4) \times (-8) \times (-2) = +64$ and $(-4) \times (-8) \times (-2) = -64$.

Division

Division is the opposite operation to multiplication; one number (the **divisor**) tells us how many parts to divide the other number (the **dividend**) into. The result of division is called the **quotient**. For example, $20 \div 4 = 5$; if 20 is split into 4 equal parts, each part is 5. With division, the order of the numbers does matter, $20 \div 4 \neq 4 \div 20$.

The rules for dividing signed numbers are similar to multiplying signed numbers. If the dividend and divisor have the same sign, the quotient is positive. If the dividend and divisor have opposite signs, the quotient is negative. For example, $(-4) \div (+8) = -0.5$.

Review Video: Mathematical Operations
Visit mometrix.com/academy and enter code: 208095

Parentheses

Parentheses are used to designate which operations should be done first when there are multiple operations. Example: $4 - (2 + 1) = 1$; the parentheses tell us that we must add 2 and 1, and then subtract the sum from 4, rather than subtracting 2 from 4 and then adding 1 (this would give us an answer of 3).

Review Video: Mathematical Parentheses
Visit mometrix.com/academy and enter code: 978600

Exponents

An **exponent** is a superscript number placed next to another number at the top right. It indicates how many times the base number is to be multiplied by itself. Exponents provide a shorthand way to write what would be a longer mathematical expression, for example: $2^4 = 2 \times 2 \times 2 \times 2$. A number with an exponent of 2 is said to be "squared," while a number with an exponent of 3 is said to be "cubed." The value of a number raised to an exponent is called its power. So 8^4 is read as "8 to the 4th power," or "8 raised to the power of 4."

The properties of exponents are as follows:

Property	Description
$a^1 = a$	Any number to the power of 1 is equal to itself
$1^n = 1$	The number 1 raised to any power is equal to 1
$a^0 = 1$	Any number raised to the power of 0 is equal to 1
$a^n \times a^m = a^{n+m}$	Add exponents to multiply powers of the same base number
$a^n \div a^m = a^{n-m}$	Subtract exponents to divide powers of the same base number
$(a^n)^m = a^{n \times m}$	When a power is raised to a power, the exponents are multiplied
$(a \times b)^n = a^n \times b^n$ $(a \div b)^n = a^n \div b^n$	Multiplication and division operations inside parentheses can be raised to a power. This is the same as each term being raised to that power.
$a^{-n} = \frac{1}{a^n}$	A negative exponent is the same as the reciprocal of a positive exponent

Note that exponents do not have to be integers. Fractional or decimal exponents follow all the rules above as well. Example: $5^{\frac{1}{4}} \times 5^{\frac{3}{4}} = 5^{\frac{1}{4}+\frac{3}{4}} = 5^1 = 5$.

Review Video: Exponents
Visit mometrix.com/academy and enter code: 600998

Review Video: Laws of Exponents
Visit mometrix.com/academy and enter code: 532558

Roots

A **root**, such as a square root, is another way of writing a fractional exponent. Instead of using a superscript, roots use the radical symbol ($\sqrt{\ }$) to indicate the operation. A radical will have a number underneath the bar, and may sometimes have a number in the upper left: $\sqrt[n]{a}$, read as "the nth root of a." The relationship between radical notation and exponent notation can be described by this equation: $\sqrt[n]{a} = a^{\frac{1}{n}}$. The two special cases of $n = 2$ and $n = 3$ are called square roots and cube roots. If there is no number to the upper left, the radical is understood to be a square root ($n = 2$). Nearly all of the roots you encounter will be square roots. A square root is the same as a number raised to the one-half power. When we say that a is the square root of b ($a = \sqrt{b}$), we mean that a multiplied by itself equals b: ($a \times a = b$).

A **perfect square** is a number that has an integer for its square root. There are 10 perfect squares from 1 to 100: 1, 4, 9, 16, 25, 36, 49, 64, 81, 100 (the squares of integers 1 through 10).

Review Video: Roots
Visit mometrix.com/academy and enter code: 795655

Order of Operations

The **order of operations** is a set of rules that dictates the order in which we must perform each operation in an expression so that we will evaluate it accurately. If we have an expression that includes multiple different operations, the order of operations tells us which operations to do first. The most common mnemonic for the order of operations is **PEMDAS**, or "Please Excuse My Dear Aunt Sally." PEMDAS stands for parentheses, exponents, multiplication, division, addition, and subtraction. It is important to understand that multiplication and division have equal precedence, as do addition and subtraction, so those pairs of operations are simply worked from left to right in order.

For example, evaluating the expression $5 + 20 \div 4 \times (2 + 3) - 6$ using the correct order of operations would be done like this:

- **P:** Perform the operations inside the parentheses: $(2 + 3) = 5$
- **E:** Simplify the exponents.
    - The equation now looks like this: $5 + 20 \div 4 \times 5 - 6$
- **MD:** Perform multiplication and division from left to right: $20 \div 4 = 5$; then $5 \times 5 = 25$
    - The equation now looks like this: $5 + 25 - 6$
- **AS:** Perform addition and subtraction from left to right: $5 + 25 = 30$; then $30 - 6 = 24$

> **Review Video: Order of Operations**
> Visit mometrix.com/academy and enter code: 259675

SUBTRACTION WITH REGROUPING

A great way to make use of some of the features built into the decimal system would be regrouping when attempting longform subtraction operations. When subtracting within a place value, sometimes the minuend is smaller than the subtrahend, **regrouping** enables you to 'borrow' a unit from a place value to the left in order to get a positive difference. For example, consider subtracting 189 from 525 with regrouping.

> **Review Video: Subtracting Large Numbers**
> Visit mometrix.com/academy and enter code: 603350

First, set up the subtraction problem in vertical form:

$$\begin{array}{r} 525 \\ -\ 189 \\ \hline \end{array}$$

Notice that the numbers in the ones and tens columns of 525 are smaller than the numbers in the ones and tens columns of 189. This means you will need to use regrouping to perform subtraction:

$$\begin{array}{rrrr} & 5 & 2 & 5 \\ - & 1 & 8 & 9 \\ \hline \end{array}$$

To subtract 9 from 5 in the ones column you will need to borrow from the 2 in the ten's columns:

$$\begin{array}{rrrr} & 5 & 1 & 15 \\ - & 1 & 8 & 9 \\ \hline & & & 6 \end{array}$$

Next, to subtract 8 from 1 in the tens column you will need to borrow from the 5 in the hundred's column:

$$\begin{array}{rrrr} & 4 & 11 & 15 \\ - & 1 & 8 & 9 \\ \hline & & 3 & 6 \end{array}$$

Last, subtract the 1 from the 4 in the hundred's column:

$$\begin{array}{rrrr} & 4 & 11 & 15 \\ - & 1 & 8 & 9 \\ \hline & 3 & 3 & 6 \end{array}$$

PRACTICE

P1. Demonstrate how to subtract 477 from 620 using regrouping.

P2. Simplify the following expressions with exponents:

(a) 37^0
(b) 1^{30}
(c) $2^3 \times 2^4 \times 2^x$
(d) $(3^x)^3$
(e) $(12 \div 3)^2$

PRACTICE SOLUTIONS

P1. First, set up the subtraction problem in vertical form:

$$\begin{array}{rrrr} & 6 & 2 & 0 \\ - & 4 & 7 & 7 \\ \hline \end{array}$$

To subtract 7 from 0 in the ones column you will need to borrow from the 2 in the tens column:

$$\begin{array}{rrrr} & 6 & 1 & 10 \\ - & 4 & 7 & 7 \\ \hline & & & 3 \end{array}$$

Next, to subtract 7 from the 1 that's still in the tens column you will need to borrow from the 6 in the hundreds column:

$$\begin{array}{rrrr} & 5 & 11 & 10 \\ - & 4 & 7 & 7 \\ \hline & & 4 & 3 \end{array}$$

Lastly, subtract 4 from the 5 remaining in the hundreds column:

$$\begin{array}{rrrr} & 5 & 11 & 10 \\ - & 4 & 7 & 7 \\ \hline & 1 & 4 & 3 \end{array}$$

P2. Using the properties of exponents and the proper order of operations:

(a) Any number raised to the power of 0 is equal to 1: $37^0 = 1$
(b) The number 1 raised to any power is equal to 1: $1^{30} = 1$
(c) Add exponents to multiply powers of the same base: $2^3 \times 2^4 \times 2^x = 2^{(3+4+x)} = 2^{(7+x)}$
(d) When a power is raised to a power, the exponents are multiplied: $(3^x)^3 = 3^{3x}$
(e) Perform the operation inside the parentheses first: $(12 \div 3)^2 = 4^2 = 16$

FACTORING

FACTORS AND GREATEST COMMON FACTOR

Factors are numbers that are multiplied together to obtain a **product**. For example, in the equation $2 \times 3 = 6$, the numbers 2 and 3 are factors. A **prime number** has only two factors (1 and itself), but other numbers can have many factors.

A **common factor** is a number that divides exactly into two or more other numbers. For example, the factors of 12 are 1, 2, 3, 4, 6, and 12, while the factors of 15 are 1, 3, 5, and 15. The common factors of 12 and 15 are 1 and 3.

A **prime factor** is also a prime number. Therefore, the prime factors of 12 are 2 and 3. For 15, the prime factors are 3 and 5.

The **greatest common factor** (**GCF**) is the largest number that is a factor of two or more numbers. For example, the factors of 15 are 1, 3, 5, and 15; the factors of 35 are 1, 5, 7, and 35. Therefore, the greatest common factor of 15 and 35 is 5.

Review Video: Factors
Visit mometrix.com/academy and enter code: 920086

Review Video: GCF and LCM
Visit mometrix.com/academy and enter code: 838699

MULTIPLES AND LEAST COMMON MULTIPLE

Often listed out in multiplication tables, **multiples** are integer increments of a given factor. In other words, dividing a multiple by the factor will result in an integer. For example, the multiples of 7 include: $1 \times 7 = 7$, $2 \times 7 = 14$, $3 \times 7 = 21$, $4 \times 7 = 28$, $5 \times 7 = 35$. Dividing 7, 14, 21, 28, or 35 by 7 will result in the integers 1, 2, 3, 4, and 5, respectively.

The least common multiple (**LCM**) is the smallest number that is a multiple of two or more numbers. For example, the multiples of 3 include 3, 6, 9, 12, 15, etc.; the multiples of 5 include 5, 10, 15, 20, etc. Therefore, the least common multiple of 3 and 5 is 15.

Review Video: Multiples
Visit mometrix.com/academy and enter code: 626738

RATIONAL NUMBERS

FRACTIONS

A **fraction** is a number that is expressed as one integer written above another integer, with a dividing line between them $\left(\frac{x}{y}\right)$. It represents the **quotient** of the two numbers "*x* divided by *y*." It can also be thought of as *x* out of *y* equal parts.

The top number of a fraction is called the **numerator**, and it represents the number of parts under consideration. The 1 in $\frac{1}{4}$ means that 1 part out of the whole is being considered in the calculation. The bottom number of a fraction is called the **denominator**, and it represents the total number of equal parts. The 4 in $\frac{1}{4}$ means that the whole consists of 4 equal parts. A fraction cannot have a denominator of zero; this is referred to as "*undefined.*"

Fractions can be manipulated, without changing the value of the fraction, by multiplying or dividing (but not adding or subtracting) both the numerator and denominator by the same number. If you divide both numbers by a common factor, you are **reducing** or simplifying the fraction. Two fractions that have the same value but are expressed differently are known as **equivalent fractions**. For example, $\frac{2}{10}, \frac{3}{15}, \frac{4}{20}$, and $\frac{5}{25}$ are all equivalent fractions. They can also all be reduced or simplified to $\frac{1}{5}$.

When two fractions are manipulated so that they have the same denominator, this is known as finding a **common denominator**. The number chosen to be that common denominator should be the least common multiple of the two original denominators. Example: $\frac{3}{4}$ and $\frac{5}{6}$; the least common multiple of 4 and 6 is 12. Manipulating to achieve the common denominator: $\frac{3}{4} = \frac{9}{12}; \frac{5}{6} = \frac{10}{12}$.

Proper Fractions and Mixed Numbers

A fraction whose denominator is greater than its numerator is known as a **proper fraction**, while a fraction whose numerator is greater than its denominator is known as an **improper fraction**. Proper fractions have values *less than one* and improper fractions have values *greater than one.*

A **mixed number** is a number that contains both an integer and a fraction. Any improper fraction can be rewritten as a mixed number. Example: $\frac{8}{3} = \frac{6}{3} + \frac{2}{3} = 2 + \frac{2}{3} = 2\frac{2}{3}$. Similarly, any mixed number can be rewritten as an improper fraction. Example: $1\frac{3}{5} = 1 + \frac{3}{5} = \frac{5}{5} + \frac{3}{5} = \frac{8}{5}$.

Review Video: Improper Fractions and Mixed Numbers
Visit mometrix.com/academy and enter code: 211077

Review Video: Fractions
Visit mometrix.com/academy and enter code: 262335

Adding and Subtracting Fractions

If two fractions have a common denominator, they can be added or subtracted simply by adding or subtracting the two numerators and retaining the same denominator. If the two fractions do not already have the same denominator, one or both of them must be manipulated to achieve a common denominator before they can be added or subtracted. Example: $\frac{1}{2} + \frac{1}{4} = \frac{2}{4} + \frac{1}{4} = \frac{3}{4}$.

Review Video: Adding and Subtracting Fractions
Visit mometrix.com/academy and enter code: 378080

Multiplying Fractions

Two fractions can be multiplied by multiplying the two numerators to find the new numerator and the two denominators to find the new denominator. Example: $\frac{1}{3} \times \frac{2}{3} = \frac{1\times2}{3\times3} = \frac{2}{9}$.

Dividing Fractions

Two fractions can be divided by flipping the numerator and denominator of the second fraction and then proceeding as though it were a multiplication problem. Example: $\frac{2}{3} \div \frac{3}{4} = \frac{2}{3} \times \frac{4}{3} = \frac{8}{9}$.

Review Video: Multiplying and Dividing Fractions
Visit mometrix.com/academy and enter code: 473632

Multiplying a Mixed Number by a Whole Number or a Decimal

When multiplying a mixed number by something, it is usually best to convert it to an improper fraction first. Additionally, if the multiplicand is a decimal, it is most often simplest to convert it to a fraction. For instance, to multiply $4\frac{3}{8}$ by 3.5, begin by rewriting each quantity as a whole number plus a proper fraction. Remember, a mixed number is a fraction added to a whole number and a decimal is a representation of the sum of fractions, specifically tenths, hundredths, thousandths, and so on:

$$4\frac{3}{8} \times 3.5 = \left(4 + \frac{3}{8}\right) \times \left(3 + \frac{1}{2}\right)$$

Next, the quantities being added need to be expressed with the same denominator. This is achieved by multiplying and dividing the whole number by the denominator of the fraction. Recall that a whole number is equivalent to that number divided by 1:

$$= \left(\frac{4}{1} \times \frac{8}{8} + \frac{3}{8}\right) \times \left(\frac{3}{1} \times \frac{2}{2} + \frac{1}{2}\right)$$

When multiplying fractions, remember to multiply the numerators and denominators separately:

$$= \left(\frac{4 \times 8}{1 \times 8} + \frac{3}{8}\right) \times \left(\frac{3 \times 2}{1 \times 2} + \frac{1}{2}\right)$$
$$= \left(\frac{32}{8} + \frac{3}{8}\right) \times \left(\frac{6}{2} + \frac{1}{2}\right)$$

Now that the fractions have the same denominators, they can be added:

$$= \frac{35}{8} \times \frac{7}{2}$$

Finally, perform the last multiplication and then simplify:

$$= \frac{35 \times 7}{8 \times 2} = \frac{245}{16} = \frac{240}{16} + \frac{5}{16} = 15\frac{5}{16}$$

Decimals

Decimals are one way to represent parts of a whole. Using the place value system, each digit to the right of a decimal point denotes the number of units of a corresponding *negative* power of ten. For example, consider the decimal 0.24. We can use a model to represent the decimal. Since a dime is worth one-tenth of a dollar and a penny is worth one-hundredth of a dollar, one possible model to represent this fraction is to have 2 dimes representing the 2 in the tenths place and 4 pennies representing the 4 in the hundredths place:

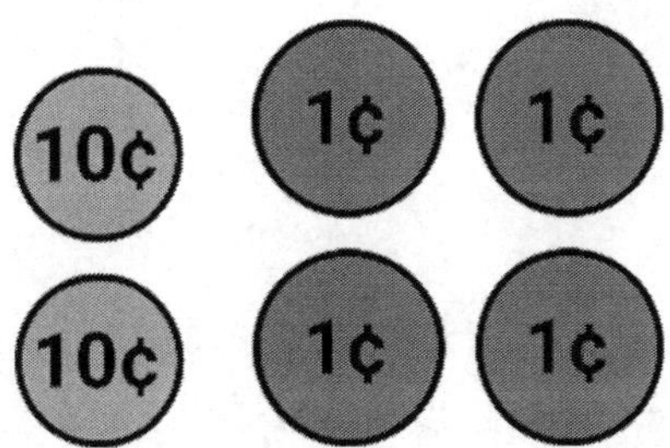

To write the decimal as a fraction, put the decimal in the numerator with 1 in the denominator. Multiply the numerator and denominator by tens until there are no more decimal places. Then simplify the fraction to lowest terms. For example, converting 0.24 to a fraction:

$$0.24 = \frac{0.24}{1} = \frac{0.24 \times 100}{1 \times 100} = \frac{24}{100} = \frac{6}{25}$$

Review Video: Decimals
Visit mometrix.com/academy and enter code: 837268

Adding and Subtracting Decimals

When adding and subtracting decimals, the decimal points must always be aligned. Adding decimals is just like adding regular whole numbers. Example: $4.5 + 2.0 = 6.5$.

If the problem-solver does not properly align the decimal points, an incorrect answer of 4.7 may result. An easy way to add decimals is to align all of the decimal points in a vertical column visually. This will allow you to see exactly where the decimal should be placed in the final answer. Begin adding from right to left. Add each column in turn, making sure to carry the number to the left if a column adds up to more than 9. The same rules apply to the subtraction of decimals.

Review Video: Adding and Subtracting Decimals
Visit mometrix.com/academy and enter code: 381101

Multiplying Decimals

A simple multiplication problem has two components: a **multiplicand** and a **multiplier**. When multiplying decimals, work as though the numbers were whole rather than decimals. Once the final product is calculated, count the number of places to the right of the decimal in both the multiplicand and the multiplier. Then, count that number of places from the right of the product and place the decimal in that position.

For example, 12.3×2.56 has a total of three places to the right of the respective decimals. Multiply 123×256 to get 31,488. Now, beginning on the right, count three places to the left and insert the decimal. The final product will be 31.488.

Review Video: Multiplying Decimals
Visit mometrix.com/academy and enter code: 731574

Dividing Decimals

Every division problem has a **divisor** and a **dividend**. The dividend is the number that is being divided. In the problem $14 \div 7$, 14 is the dividend and 7 is the divisor. In a division problem with decimals, the divisor must be converted into a whole number. Begin by moving the decimal in the divisor to the right until a whole number is created. Next, move the decimal in the dividend the same number of spaces to the right. For example, 4.9 into 24.5 would become 49 into 245. The decimal was moved one space to the right to create a whole number in the divisor, and then the same was done for the dividend. Once the whole numbers are created, the problem is carried out normally: $245 \div 49 = 5$.

Review Video: Dividing Decimals
Visit mometrix.com/academy and enter code: 560690

PERCENTAGES

Percentages can be thought of as fractions that are based on a whole of 100; that is, one whole is equal to 100%. The word **percent** means "per hundred." Percentage problems are often presented in three main ways:

- Find what percentage of some number another number is.
  - Example: What percentage of 40 is 8?
- Find what number is some percentage of a given number.
  - Example: What number is 20% of 40?
- Find what number another number is a given percentage of.
  - Example: What number is 8 20% of?

There are three components in each of these cases: a **whole** (W), a **part** (P), and a **percentage** (%). These are related by the equation: $P = W \times \%$. This can easily be rearranged into other forms that may suit different questions better: $\% = \frac{P}{W}$ and $W = \frac{P}{\%}$. Percentage problems are often also word problems. As such, a large part of solving them is figuring out which quantities are what. For example, consider the following word problem:

In a school cafeteria, 7 students choose pizza, 9 choose hamburgers, and 4 choose tacos. What percentage of student choose tacos?

To find the whole, you must first add all of the parts: $7 + 9 + 4 = 20$. The percentage can then be found by dividing the part by the whole ($\% = \frac{P}{W}$): $\frac{4}{20} = \frac{20}{100} = 20\%$.

Review Video: Computation with Percentages
Visit mometrix.com/academy and enter code: 693099

CONVERTING BETWEEN PERCENTAGES, FRACTIONS, AND DECIMALS

Converting decimals to percentages and percentages to decimals is as simple as moving the decimal point. To *convert from a decimal to a percentage*, move the decimal point **two places to the right**. To *convert from a percentage to a decimal*, move it **two places to the left**. It may be helpful to remember that the percentage number will always be larger than the equivalent decimal number. For example:

$$0.23 = 23\% \qquad 5.34 = 534\% \qquad 0.007 = 0.7\%$$
$$700\% = 7.00 \qquad 86\% = 0.86 \qquad 0.15\% = 0.0015$$

To convert a fraction to a decimal, simply divide the numerator by the denominator in the fraction. To convert a decimal to a fraction, put the decimal in the numerator with 1 in the denominator. Multiply the numerator and denominator by tens until there are no more decimal places. Then simplify the fraction to lowest terms. For example, converting 0.24 to a fraction:

$$0.24 = \frac{0.24}{1} = \frac{0.24 \times 100}{1 \times 100} = \frac{24}{100} = \frac{6}{25}$$

Fractions can be converted to a percentage by finding equivalent fractions with a denominator of 100. For example,

$$\frac{7}{10} = \frac{70}{100} = 70\% \quad \frac{1}{4} = \frac{25}{100} = 25\%$$

To convert a percentage to a fraction, divide the percentage number by 100 and reduce the fraction to its simplest possible terms. For example,

$$60\% = \frac{60}{100} = \frac{3}{5} \quad 96\% = \frac{96}{100} = \frac{24}{25}$$

Review Video: Converting Fractions to Percentages and Decimals
Visit mometrix.com/academy and enter code: 306233

Review Video: Converting Percentages to Decimals and Fractions
Visit mometrix.com/academy and enter code: 287297

Rational Numbers

The term **rational** means that the number can be expressed as a ratio or fraction. That is, a number, r, is rational if and only if it can be represented by a fraction $\frac{a}{b}$ where a and b are integers and b does not equal 0. The set of rational numbers includes integers and decimals. If there is no finite way to represent a value with a fraction of integers, then the number is **irrational**. Common examples of irrational numbers include: $\sqrt{5}$, $(1 + \sqrt{2})$, and π.

Review Video: Rational and Irrational Numbers
Visit mometrix.com/academy and enter code: 280645

Practice

P1. What is 30% of 120?

P2. What is 150% of 20?

P3. What is 14.5% of 96?

P4. Simplify the following expressions:

(a) $\left(\frac{2}{5}\right)/\left(\frac{4}{7}\right)$
(b) $\frac{7}{8} - \frac{8}{16}$
(c) $\frac{1}{2} + \left(3\left(\frac{3}{4}\right) - 2\right) + 4$
(d) $0.22 + 0.5 - (5.5 + 3.3 \div 3)$
(e) $\frac{3}{2} + (4(0.5) - 0.75) + 2$

P5. Convert the following to a fraction and to a decimal: **(a)** 15%; **(b)** 24.36%

P6. Convert the following to a decimal and to a percentage. **(a)** 4/5; **(b)** $3\frac{2}{5}$

P7. A woman's age is thirteen more than half of 60. How old is the woman?

P8. A patient was given pain medicine at a dosage of 0.22 grams. The patient's dosage was then increased to 0.80 grams. By how much was the patient's dosage increased?

P9. At a hotel, $\frac{3}{4}$ of the 100 rooms are occupied today. Yesterday, $\frac{4}{5}$ of the 100 rooms were occupied. On which day were more of the rooms occupied and by how much more?

P10. At a school, 40% of the teachers teach English. If 20 teachers teach English, how many teachers work at the school?

P11. A patient was given blood pressure medicine at a dosage of 2 grams. The patient's dosage was then decreased to 0.45 grams. By how much was the patient's dosage decreased?

P12. Two weeks ago, $\frac{2}{3}$ of the 60 customers at a skate shop were male. Last week, $\frac{3}{6}$ of the 80 customers were male. During which week were there more male customers?

P13. Jane ate lunch at a local restaurant. She ordered a $4.99 appetizer, a $12.50 entrée, and a $1.25 soda. If she wants to tip her server 20%, how much money will she spend in all?

P14. According to a survey, about 82% of engineers were highly satisfied with their job. If 145 engineers were surveyed, how many reported that they were highly satisfied?

P15. A patient was given 40 mg of a certain medicine. Later, the patient's dosage was increased to 45 mg. What was the percent increase in his medication?

P16. Order the following rational numbers from least to greatest: 0.55, 17%, $\sqrt{25}$, $\frac{64}{4}$, $\frac{25}{50}$, 3.

P17. Order the following rational numbers from greatest to least: 0.3, 27%, $\sqrt{100}$, $\frac{72}{9}$, $\frac{1}{9}$, 4.5

P18. Perform the following multiplication. Write each answer as a mixed number.

(a) $\left(1\frac{11}{16}\right) \times 4$
(b) $\left(12\frac{1}{3}\right) \times 1.1$
(c) $3.71 \times \left(6\frac{1}{5}\right)$

P19. Suppose you are making doughnuts and you want to triple the recipe you have. If the following list is the original amounts for the ingredients, what would be the amounts for the tripled recipe?

$1\,{}^3/_4$	cup	Flour
$1\,{}^1/_4$	tsp	Baking powder
${}^3/_4$	tsp	Salt
${}^3/_8$	cup	Sugar
$1\,{}^1/_2$	Tbsp	Butter
2	large	Eggs
${}^3/_4$	tsp	Vanilla extract
${}^3/_8$	cup	Sour cream

PRACTICE SOLUTIONS

P1. The word *of* indicates multiplication, so 30% of 120 is found by multiplying 120 by 30%. Change 30% to a decimal, then multiply: $120 \times 0.3 = 36$

P2. The word *of* indicates multiplication, so 150% of 20 is found by multiplying 20 by 150%. Change 150% to a decimal, then multiply: $20 \times 1.5 = 30$

P3. Change 14.5% to a decimal before multiplying. $0.145 \times 96 = 13.92$.

P4. Follow the order of operations and utilize properties of fractions to solve each:

(a) Rewrite the problem as a multiplication problem: $\frac{2}{5} \times \frac{7}{4} = \frac{2\times 7}{5\times 4} = \frac{14}{20}$. Make sure the fraction is reduced to lowest terms. Both 14 and 20 can be divided by 2.

$$\frac{14}{20} = \frac{14 \div 2}{20 \div 2} = \frac{7}{10}$$

(b) The denominators of $\frac{7}{8}$ and $\frac{8}{16}$ are 8 and 16, respectively. The lowest common denominator of 8 and 16 is 16 because 16 is the least common multiple of 8 and 16. Convert the first fraction to its equivalent with the newly found common denominator of 16: $\frac{7 \times 2}{8 \times 2} = \frac{14}{16}$. Now that the fractions have the same denominator, you can subtract them.

$$\frac{14}{16} - \frac{8}{16} = \frac{6}{16} = \frac{3}{8}$$

(c) When simplifying expressions, first perform operations within groups. Within the set of parentheses are multiplication and subtraction operations. Perform the multiplication first to get $\frac{1}{2} + \left(\frac{9}{4} - 2\right) + 4$. Then, subtract two to obtain $\frac{1}{2} + \frac{1}{4} + 4$. Finally, perform addition from left to right:

$$\frac{1}{2} + \frac{1}{4} + 4 = \frac{2}{4} + \frac{1}{4} + \frac{16}{4} = \frac{19}{4} = 4\frac{3}{4}$$

(d) First, evaluate the terms in the parentheses $(5.5 + 3.3 \div 3)$ using order of operations. $3.3 \div 3 = 1.1$, and $5.5 + 1.1 = 6.6$. Next, rewrite the problem: $0.22 + 0.5 - 6.6$. Finally, add and subtract from left to right: $0.22 + 0.5 = 0.72$; $0.72 - 6.6 = -5.88$. The answer is -5.88.

(e) First, simplify within the parentheses, then change the fraction to a decimal and perform addition from left to right:

$$\frac{3}{2} + (2 - 0.75) + 2 =$$
$$\frac{3}{2} + 1.25 + 2 =$$
$$1.5 + 1.25 + 2 = 4.75$$

P5. (a) 15% can be written as $\frac{15}{100}$. Both 15 and 100 can be divided by 5: $\frac{15 \div 5}{100 \div 5} = \frac{3}{20}$

When converting from a percentage to a decimal, drop the percent sign and move the decimal point two places to the left: $15\% = 0.15$

(b) 24.36% written as a fraction is $\frac{24.36}{100}$, or $\frac{2436}{10,000}$, which reduces to $\frac{609}{2500}$. 24.36% written as a decimal is 0.2436. Recall that dividing by 100 moves the decimal two places to the left.

P6. (a) Recall that in the decimal system the first decimal place is one tenth: $\frac{4 \times 2}{5 \times 2} = \frac{8}{10} = 0.8$

Percent means "per hundred." $\frac{4 \times 20}{5 \times 20} = \frac{80}{100} = 80\%$

(b) The mixed number $3\frac{2}{5}$ has a whole number and a fractional part. The fractional part $\frac{2}{5}$ can be written as a decimal by dividing 5 into 2, which gives 0.4. Adding the whole to the part gives 3.4.

To find the equivalent percentage, multiply the decimal by 100. $3.4(100) = 340\%$. Notice that this percentage is greater than 100%. This makes sense because the original mixed number $3\frac{2}{5}$ is greater than 1.

P7. "More than" indicates addition, and "of" indicates multiplication. The expression can be written as $\frac{1}{2}(60) + 13$. So the woman's age is equal to $\frac{1}{2}(60) + 13 = 30 + 13 = 43$. The woman is 43 years old.

P8. The first step is to determine what operation (addition, subtraction, multiplication, or division) the problem requires. Notice the keywords and phrases "by how much" and "increased." "Increased" means that you go from a smaller amount to a larger amount. This change can be found by subtracting the smaller amount from the larger amount: 0.80 grams– 0.22 grams = 0.58 grams.

Remember to line up the decimal when subtracting:

$$\begin{array}{r} 0.80 \\ -\ 0.22 \\ \hline 0.58 \end{array}$$

P9. First, find the number of rooms occupied each day. To do so, multiply the fraction of rooms occupied by the number of rooms available:

$$\text{Number occupied} = \text{Fraction occupied} \times \text{Total number}$$

$$\text{Number of rooms occupied today} = \frac{3}{4} \times 100 = 75$$

$$\text{Number of rooms occupied} = \frac{4}{5} \times 100 = 80$$

The difference in the number of rooms occupied is: $80 - 75 = 5$ rooms

P10. To answer this problem, first think about the number of teachers that work at the school. Will it be more or less than the number of teachers who work in a specific department such as English? More teachers work at the school, so the number you find to answer this question will be greater than 20.

40% of the teachers are English teachers. "Of" indicates multiplication, and words like "is" and "are" indicate equivalence. Translating the problem into a mathematical sentence gives $40\% \times t = 20$, where t represents the total number of teachers. Solving for t gives $t = \frac{20}{40\%} = \frac{20}{0.40} = 50$. Fifty teachers work at the school.

P11. The decrease is represented by the difference between the two amounts:

$$2 \text{ grams} - 0.45 \text{ grams} = 1.55 \text{ grams}.$$

Remember to line up the decimal point before subtracting.

$$\begin{array}{r} 2.00 \\ -\ 0.45 \\ \hline 1.55 \end{array}$$

P12. First, you need to find the number of male customers that were in the skate shop each week. You are given this amount in terms of fractions. To find the actual number of male customers, multiply the fraction of male customers by the number of customers in the store.

$$\begin{aligned} \text{Actual number of male customers} &= \text{fraction of male customers} \times \text{total customers} \\ \text{Number of male customers two weeks ago} &= \frac{2}{3} \times 60 = \frac{120}{3} = 40 \\ \text{Number of male customers last week} &= \frac{3}{6} \times 80 = \frac{1}{2} \times 80 = \frac{80}{2} = 40 \end{aligned}$$

The number of male customers was the same both weeks.

P13. To find total amount, first find the sum of the items she ordered from the menu and then add 20% of this sum to the total.

$$\$4.99 + \$12.50 + \$1.25 = \$18.74$$

$$\$18.74 \times 20\% = (0.20)(\$18.74) = \$3.748 \approx \$3.75$$

$$\text{Total} = \$18.74 + \$3.75 = \$22.49$$

P14. 82% of 145 is $0.82 \times 145 = 118.9$. Because you can't have 0.9 of a person, we must round up to say that 119 engineers reported that they were highly satisfied with their jobs.

P15. To find the percent increase, first compare the original and increased amounts. The original amount was 40 mg, and the increased amount is 45 mg, so the dosage of medication was increased by 5 mg ($45 - 40 = 5$). Note, however, that the question asks not by how much the dosage increased but by what percentage it increased.

$$\begin{aligned} \text{Percent increase} &= \frac{\text{new amount} - \text{original amount}}{\text{original amount}} \times 100\% \\ &= \frac{45 \text{ mg} - 40 \text{ mg}}{40 \text{ mg}} \times 100\% = \frac{5}{40} \times 100\% = 0.125 \times 100\% = 12.5\% \end{aligned}$$

P16. Recall that the term rational simply means that the number can be expressed as a ratio or fraction. Notice that each of the numbers in the problem can be written as a decimal or integer:

$$17\% = 0.1717$$
$$\sqrt{25} = 5$$
$$\frac{64}{4} = 16$$
$$\frac{25}{50} = \frac{1}{2} = 0.5$$

So, the answer is $17\%, \frac{25}{50}, 0.55, 3, \sqrt{25}, \frac{64}{4}$.

P17. Converting all the numbers to integers and decimals makes it easier to compare the values:

$$27\% = 0.27$$
$$\sqrt{100} = 10$$
$$\frac{72}{9} = 8$$
$$\frac{1}{9} \approx 0.11$$

So, the answer is $\sqrt{100}, \frac{72}{9}, 4.5, 0.3, 27\%, \frac{1}{9}$.

Review Video: Ordering Rational Numbers
Visit mometrix.com/academy and enter code: 419578

P18. For each, convert improper fractions, adjust to a common denominator, perform the operations, and then simplify:

(a) Sometimes, you can skip converting the denominator and just distribute the multiplication.

$$\begin{aligned}\left(1\frac{11}{16}\right) \times 4 &= \left(1 + \frac{11}{16}\right) \times 4 \\ &= 1 \times 4 + \frac{11}{16} \times 4 \\ &= 4 + \frac{11}{16} \times \frac{4}{1} \\ &= 4 + \frac{44}{16} = 4 + \frac{11}{4} = 4 + 2\frac{3}{4} = 6\frac{3}{4}\end{aligned}$$

(b)

$$\begin{aligned}\left(12\frac{1}{3}\right)\times 1.1 &= \left(12+\frac{1}{3}\right)\times\left(1+\frac{1}{10}\right)\\ &= \left(\frac{12}{1}\times\frac{3}{3}+\frac{1}{3}\right)\times\left(\frac{10}{10}+\frac{1}{10}\right)\\ &= \left(\frac{36}{3}+\frac{1}{3}\right)\times\frac{11}{10}\\ &= \frac{37}{3}\times\frac{11}{10}\\ &= \frac{407}{30}=\frac{390}{30}+\frac{17}{30}=13\frac{17}{30}\end{aligned}$$

(c)

$$\begin{aligned}3.71\times\left(6\frac{1}{5}\right) &= \left(3+\frac{71}{100}\right)\times\left(6+\frac{1}{5}\right)\\ &= \left(\frac{300}{100}+\frac{71}{100}\right)\times\left(\frac{6}{1}\times\frac{5}{5}+\frac{1}{5}\right)\\ &= \frac{371}{100}\times\left(\frac{30}{5}+\frac{1}{5}\right)\\ &= \frac{371}{100}\times\frac{31}{5}\\ &= \frac{11501}{500}=\frac{11500}{500}+\frac{1}{500}=23\frac{1}{500}\end{aligned}$$

P19. Fortunately, some of the amounts are duplicated, so we do not need to figure out every amount.

$$\begin{aligned}1\frac{3}{4}\times 3 &= (1\times 3)+\left(\frac{3}{4}\times 3\right)\\ &= 3+\frac{9}{4}\\ &= 3+2\frac{1}{4}\\ &= 5\frac{1}{4}\end{aligned}$$

$$\begin{aligned}1\frac{1}{4}\times 3 &= (1\times 3)+\left(\frac{1}{4}\times 3\right)\\ &= 3+\frac{3}{4}\\ &= 3\frac{3}{4}\end{aligned}$$

$$\begin{aligned}\frac{3}{4}\times 3 &= \frac{3}{4}\times 3\\ &= \frac{9}{4}\\ &= 2\frac{1}{4}\end{aligned}$$

$$\begin{aligned}\frac{3}{8}\times 3 &= \frac{3}{8}\times 3\\ &= \frac{9}{8}\\ &= 1\frac{1}{8}\end{aligned}$$

$$\begin{aligned}1\frac{1}{2}\times 3 &= 1\times 3+\frac{1}{2}\times 3\\ &= 3+\frac{3}{2}\\ &= 3+1\frac{1}{2}\\ &= 4\frac{1}{2}\end{aligned}$$

$$2\times 3 = 6$$

So, the result for the triple recipe is:

$5\,^{1}/_{4}$	cup	Flour
$3\,^{3}/_{4}$	tsp	Baking powder
$2\,^{1}/_{4}$	tsp	Salt
$1\,^{1}/_{8}$	cup	Sugar
$4\,^{1}/_{2}$	Tbsp	Butter
6	large	Eggs
$2\,^{1}/_{4}$	tsp	Vanilla extract
$1\,^{1}/_{8}$	cup	Sour cream

Measurement Principles

Rounding and Estimation

Rounding is reducing the digits in a number while still trying to keep the value similar. The result will be less accurate but in a simpler form and easier to use. Whole numbers can be rounded to the nearest ten, hundred, or thousand.

When you are asked to estimate the solution to a problem, you will need to provide only an approximate figure or **estimation** for your answer. In this situation, you will need to round each number in the calculation to the level indicated (nearest hundred, nearest thousand, etc.) or to a level that makes sense for the numbers involved. When estimating a sum **all numbers must be rounded to the same level**. You cannot round one number to the nearest thousand while rounding another to the nearest hundred.

Review Video: Rounding and Estimation
Visit mometrix.com/academy and enter code: 126243

Practice

P1. Round each number to the indicated degree:

(a) Round to the nearest ten: 11; 47; 118

(b) Round to the nearest hundred: 78; 980; 248

(c) Round each number to the nearest thousand: 302; 1274; 3756

P2. Estimate the solution to 345,932 + 96,369 by rounding each number to the nearest ten thousand.

P3. A runner's heart beats 422 times over the course of six minutes. About how many times did the runner's heart beat during each minute?

Practice Solutions

P1. (a) When rounding to the nearest ten, anything ending in 5 or greater rounds up. So, 11 rounds to 10, 47 rounds to 50, and 118 rounds to 120.

(b) When rounding to the nearest hundred, anything ending in 50 or greater rounds up. So, 78 rounds to 100, 980 rounds to 1000, and 248 rounds to 200.

(c) When rounding to the nearest thousand, anything ending in 500 or greater rounds up. So, 302 rounds to 0, 1274 rounds to 1000, and 3756 rounds to 4000.

P2. Start by rounding each number to the nearest ten thousand: 345,932 becomes 350,000, and 96,369 becomes 100,000. Then, add the rounded numbers: $350{,}000 + 100{,}000 = 450{,}000$. So, the answer is approximately 450,000. The exact answer would be $345{,}932 + 96{,}369 = 442{,}301$. So, the estimate of 450,000 is a similar value to the exact answer.

P3. "About how many" indicates that you need to estimate the solution. In this case, look at the numbers you are given. 422 can be rounded down to 420, which is easily divisible by 6. A good estimate is $420 \div 6 = 70$ beats per minute. More accurately, the patient's heart rate was just over 70 beats per minute since his heart actually beat a little more than 420 times in six minutes.

Proportions and Ratios

Proportions

A proportion is a relationship between two quantities that dictates how one changes when the other changes. A **direct proportion** describes a relationship in which a quantity increases by a set amount for every increase in the other quantity, or decreases by that same amount for every decrease in the other quantity. Example: Assuming a constant driving speed, the time required for a car trip increases as the distance of the trip increases. The distance to be traveled and the time required to travel are directly proportional.

An **inverse proportion** is a relationship in which an increase in one quantity is accompanied by a decrease in the other, or vice versa. Example: the time required for a car trip decreases as the speed increases and increases as the speed decreases, so the time required is inversely proportional to the speed of the car.

Review Video: Proportions
Visit mometrix.com/academy and enter code: 505355

Ratios

A **ratio** is a comparison of two quantities in a particular order. Example: If there are 14 computers in a lab, and the class has 20 students, there is a student to computer ratio of 20 to 14, commonly written as 20:14. Ratios are normally reduced to their smallest whole number representation, so 20:14 would be reduced to 10:7 by dividing both sides by 2.

Review Video: Ratios
Visit mometrix.com/academy and enter code: 996914

Constant of Proportionality

When two quantities have a proportional relationship, there exists a **constant of proportionality** between the quantities. The product of this constant and one of the quantities is equal to the other quantity. For example, if one lemon costs \$0.25, two lemons cost \$0.50, and three lemons cost \$0.75, there is a proportional relationship between the total cost of lemons and the number of lemons purchased. The constant of proportionality is the **unit price**, namely \$0.25/lemon. Notice that the total price of lemons, t, can be found by multiplying the unit price of lemons, p, and the number of lemons, n: $t = pn$.

WORK/UNIT RATE

Unit rate expresses a quantity of one thing in terms of one unit of another. For example, if you travel 30 miles every two hours, a unit rate expresses this comparison in terms of one hour: in one hour you travel 15 miles, so your unit rate is 15 miles per hour. Other examples are how much one ounce of food costs (price per ounce) or figuring out how much one egg costs out of the dozen (price per 1 egg, instead of price per 12 eggs). The denominator of a unit rate is always 1. Unit rates are used to compare different situations to solve problems. For example, to make sure you get the best deal when deciding which kind of soda to buy, you can find the unit rate of each. If soda #1 costs $1.50 for a 1-liter bottle, and soda #2 costs $2.75 for a 2-liter bottle, it would be a better deal to buy soda #2, because its unit rate is only $1.375 per 1-liter, which is cheaper than soda #1. Unit rates can also help determine the length of time a given event will take. For example, if you can paint 2 rooms in 4.5 hours, you can determine how long it will take you to paint 5 rooms by solving for the unit rate per room and then multiplying that by 5.

> **Review Video: Rates and Unit Rates**
> Visit mometrix.com/academy and enter code: 185363

SLOPE

On a graph with two points, (x_1, y_1) and (x_2, y_2), the **slope** is found with the formula $m = \frac{y_2 - y_1}{x_2 - x_1}$; where $x_1 \neq x_2$ and m stands for slope. If the value of the slope is **positive**, the line has an *upward direction* from left to right. If the value of the slope is **negative**, the line has a *downward direction* from left to right. Consider the following example:

A new book goes on sale in bookstores and online stores. In the first month, 5,000 copies of the book are sold. Over time, the book continues to grow in popularity. The data for the number of copies sold is in the table below.

# of Months on Sale	1	2	3	4	5
# of Copies Sold (In Thousands)	5	10	15	20	25

So, the number of copies that are sold and the time that the book is on sale is a proportional relationship. In this example, an equation can be used to show the data: $y = 5x$, where x is the number of months that the book is on sale, and y is the number of copies sold. So the slope of the corresponding line is $\frac{\text{rise}}{\text{run}} = \frac{5}{1} = 5$.

> **Review Video: Finding the Slope of a Line**
> Visit mometrix.com/academy and enter code: 766664

FINDING AN UNKNOWN IN EQUIVALENT EXPRESSIONS

It is often necessary to apply information given about a rate or proportion to a new scenario. For example, if you know that Jedha can run a marathon (26 miles) in 3 hours, how long would it take her to run 10 miles at the same pace? Start by setting up equivalent expressions:

$$\frac{26 \text{ mi}}{3 \text{ hr}} = \frac{10 \text{ mi}}{x \text{ hr}}$$

Now, cross multiply and solve for x:

$$26x = 30$$
$$x = \frac{30}{26} = \frac{15}{13}$$
$$x \cong 1.15 \text{ hrs } or \text{ 1 hr 9 min}$$

So, at this pace, Jedha could run 10 miles in about 1.15 hours or about 1 hour and 9 minutes.

Review Video: Cross Multiply Fractions
Visit mometrix.com/academy and enter code: 893904

PRACTICE

P1. Solve the following for x.

(a) $\frac{45}{12} = \frac{15}{x}$

(b) $\frac{0.50}{2} = \frac{1.50}{x}$

(c) $\frac{40}{8} = \frac{x}{24}$

P2. At a school, for every 20 female students there are 15 male students. This same student ratio happens to exist at another school. If there are 100 female students at the second school, how many male students are there?

P3. In a hospital emergency room, there are 4 nurses for every 12 patients. What is the ratio of nurses to patients? If the nurse-to-patient ratio remains constant, how many nurses must be present to care for 24 patients?

P4. In a bank, the banker-to-customer ratio is 1:2. If seven bankers are on duty, how many customers are currently in the bank?

P5. Janice made $40 during the first 5 hours she spent babysitting. She will continue to earn money at this rate until she finishes babysitting in 3 more hours. Find how much money Janice earns per hour and the total she earned babysitting.

P6. The McDonalds are taking a family road trip, driving 300 miles to their cabin. It took them 2 hours to drive the first 120 miles. They will drive at the same speed all the way to their cabin. Find the speed at which the McDonalds are driving and how much longer it will take them to get to their cabin.

P7. It takes Andy 10 minutes to read 6 pages of his book. He has already read 150 pages in his book that is 210 pages long. Find how long it takes Andy to read 1 page and also find how long it will take him to finish his book if he continues to read at the same speed.

PRACTICE SOLUTIONS

P1. Cross multiply, then solve for *x*:

(a) $45x = 12 \times 15$
$45x = 180$
$x = \frac{180}{45} = 4$

(b) $0.5x = 1.5 \times 2$
$0.5x = 3$
$x = \frac{3}{0.5} = 6$

(c) $8x = 40 \times 24$
$8x = 960$
$x = \frac{960}{8} = 120$

P2. One way to find the number of male students is to set up and solve a proportion.

$$\frac{\text{number of female students}}{\text{number of male students}} = \frac{20}{15} = \frac{100}{\text{number of male students}}$$

Represent the unknown number of male students as the variable x: $\frac{20}{15} = \frac{100}{x}$

Cross multiply and then solve for *x*:

$$20x = 15 \times 100$$
$$x = \frac{1500}{20}$$
$$x = 75$$

P3. The ratio of nurses to patients can be written as 4 to 12, 4:12, or $\frac{4}{12}$. Because four and twelve have a common factor of four, the ratio should be reduced to 1:3, which means that there is one nurse present for every three patients. If this ratio remains constant, there must be eight nurses present to care for 24 patients.

P4. Use proportional reasoning or set up a proportion to solve. Because there are twice as many customers as bankers, there must be fourteen customers when seven bankers are on duty. Setting up and solving a proportion gives the same result:

$$\frac{\text{number of bankers}}{\text{number of customers}} = \frac{1}{2} = \frac{7}{\text{number of customers}}$$

Represent the unknown number of customers as the variable *x*: $\frac{1}{2} = \frac{7}{x}$.

To solve for *x*, cross multiply: $1 \times x = 7 \times 2$, so $x = 14$.

P5. Janice earns \$8 per hour. This can be found by taking her initial amount earned, \$40, and dividing it by the number of hours worked, 5. Since $\frac{40}{5} = 8$, Janice makes \$8 in one hour. This can also be found by finding the unit rate, money earned per hour: $\frac{40}{5} = \frac{x}{1}$. Since cross multiplying yields $5x = 40$, and division by 5 shows that $x = 8$, Janice earns \$8 per hour.

Janice will earn \$64 babysitting in her 8 total hours (adding the first 5 hours to the remaining 3 gives the 8-hour total). Since Janice earns \$8 per hour and she worked 8 hours, $\frac{\$8}{\text{hr}} \times 8 \text{ hrs} = \$64$. This can also be found by setting up a proportion comparing money earned to babysitting hours. Since she earns \$40 for 5 hours and since the rate is constant, she will earn a proportional amount in 8 hours: $\frac{40}{5} = \frac{x}{8}$. Cross multiplying will yield $5x = 320$, and division by 5 shows that $x = 64$.

P6. The McDonalds are driving 60 miles per hour. This can be found by setting up a proportion to find the unit rate, the number of miles they drive per one hour: $\frac{120}{2} = \frac{x}{1}$. Cross multiplying yields $2x = 120$ and division by 2 shows that $x = 60$.

Since the McDonalds will drive this same speed for the remaining miles, it will take them another 3 hours to get to their cabin. This can be found by first finding how many miles the McDonalds have left to drive, which is $300 - 120 = 180$. The McDonalds are driving at 60 miles per hour, so a proportion can be set up to determine how many hours it will take them to drive 180 miles: $\frac{180}{x} = \frac{60}{1}$. Cross multiplying yields $60x = 180$, and division by 60 shows that $x = 3$. This can also be found by using the formula $D = r \times t$ (or distance = rate × time), where $180 = 60 \times t$, and division by 60 shows that $t = 3$.

P7. It takes Andy 10 minutes to read 6 pages, $\frac{10}{6} = 1\frac{2}{3}$ minutes, which is 1 minute and 40 seconds.

Next, determine how many pages Andy has left to read, $210 - 150 = 60$. Since it is now known that it takes him $1\frac{2}{3}$ minutes to read each page, that rate must be multiplied by however many pages he has left to read (60) to find the time he'll need: $60 \times 1\frac{2}{3} = 100$, so it will take him 100 minutes, or 1 hour and 40 minutes, to read the rest of his book.

Expressions and Equations

Terms and Coefficients

Mathematical expressions consist of a combination of one or more values arranged in terms that are added together. As such, an expression could be just a single number, including zero. A **variable term** is the product of a real number, also called a **coefficient**, and one or more variables, each of which may be raised to an exponent. Expressions may also include numbers without a variable, called **constants** or **constant terms**. The expression $6s^2$, for example, is a single term where the coefficient is the real number 6 and the variable term is s^2. Note that if a term is written as simply a variable to some exponent, like t^2, then the coefficient is 1, because $t^2 = 1t^2$.

Linear Expressions

A **single variable linear expression** is the sum of a single variable term, where the variable has no exponent, and a constant, which may be zero. For instance, the expression $2w + 7$ has $2w$ as the variable term and 7 as the constant term. It is important to realize that terms are separated by addition or subtraction. Since an expression is a sum of terms, expressions such as $5x - 3$ can be written as $5x + (-3)$ to emphasize that the constant term is negative. A real-world example of a single variable linear expression is the perimeter of a square, four times the side length, often expressed: $4s$.

In general, a **linear expression** is the sum of any number of variable terms so long as none of the variables have an exponent. For example, $3m + 8n - \frac{1}{4}p + 5.5q - 1$ is a linear expression, but $3y^3$ is not. In the same way, the expression for the perimeter of a general triangle, the sum of the side lengths $(a + b + c)$ is considered to be linear, but the expression for the area of a square, the side length squared (s^2) is not.

LINEAR EQUATIONS

Equations that can be written as $ax + b = 0$, where $a \neq 0$, are referred to as **one variable linear equations**. A solution to such an equation is called a **root**. In the case where we have the equation $5x + 10 = 0$, if we solve for x we get a solution of $x = -2$. In other words, the root of the equation is -2. This is found by first subtracting 10 from both sides, which gives $5x = -10$. Next, simply divide both sides by the coefficient of the variable, in this case 5, to get $x = -2$. This can be checked by plugging -2 back into the original equation $(5)(-2) + 10 = -10 + 10 = 0$.

The **solution set** is the set of all solutions of an equation. In our example, the solution set would simply be -2. If there were more solutions (there usually are in multivariable equations) then they would also be included in the solution set. When an equation has no true solutions, it is referred to as an **empty set**. Equations with identical solution sets are **equivalent equations**. An **identity** is a term whose value or determinant is equal to 1.

Review Video: Linear Equations Basics
Visit mometrix.com/academy and enter code: 793005

Linear equations can be written many ways. Below is a list of some forms linear equations can take:

- **Standard Form**: $Ax + By = C$; the slope is $\frac{-A}{B}$ and the y-intercept is $\frac{C}{B}$
- **Slope Intercept Form**: $y = mx + b$, where m is the slope and b is the y-intercept
- **Point-Slope Form**: $y - y_1 = m(x - x_1)$, where m is the slope and (x_1, y_1) is a point on the line
- **Two-Point Form**: $\frac{y-y_1}{x-x_1} = \frac{y_2-y_1}{x_2-x_1}$, where (x_1, y_1) and (x_2, y_2) are two points on the given line
- **Intercept Form**: $\frac{x}{x_1} + \frac{y}{y_1} = 1$, where $(x_1, 0)$ is the point at which a line intersects the x-axis, and $(0, y_1)$ is the point at which the same line intersects the y-axis

Review Video: Slope-Intercept and Point-Slope Forms
Visit mometrix.com/academy and enter code: 113216

SOLVING ONE-VARIABLE LINEAR EQUATIONS

Multiply all terms by the lowest common denominator to eliminate any fractions. Look for addition or subtraction to undo so you can isolate the variable on one side of the equal sign. Divide both sides by the coefficient of the variable. When you have a value for the variable, substitute this value into the original equation to make sure you have a true equation. Consider the following example:

Kim's savings are represented by the table below. Represent her savings, using an equation.

X (Months)	Y (Total Savings)
2	\$1300
5	\$2050
9	\$3050
11	\$3550
16	\$4800

The table shows a function with a constant rate of change, or slope, of 250. Given the points on the table, the slopes can be calculated as $(2050 - 1300)/(5 - 2)$, $(3050 - 2050)/(9 - 5)$, $(3550 - 3050)/(11 - 9)$, and $(4800 - 3550)/(16 - 11)$, each of which equals 250. Thus, the table shows a constant rate of change, indicating a linear function. The slope-intercept form of a linear equation is written as $y = mx + b$, where m represents the slope and b represents the y-intercept. Substituting the slope into this form gives $y = 250x + b$. Substituting corresponding x- and y-values from any point into this equation will give the y-intercept, or b. Using the point, (2, 1300), gives $1300 = 250(2) + b$, which simplifies as b = 800. Thus, her savings may be represented by the equation, $y = 250x + 800$.

Rules for Manipulating Equations

Like Terms

Like terms are terms in an equation that have the same variable, regardless of whether or not they also have the same coefficient. This includes terms that *lack* a variable; all constants (i.e. numbers without variables) are considered like terms. If the equation involves terms with a variable raised to different powers, the like terms are those that have the variable raised to the same power.

For example, consider the equation $x^2 + 3x + 2 = 2x^2 + x - 7 + 2x$. In this equation, 2 and -7 are like terms; they are both constants. $3x$, x, and $2x$ are like terms, they all include the variable x raised to the first power. x^2 and $2x^2$ are like terms, they both include the variable x, raised to the second power. $2x$ and $2x^2$ are not like terms; although they both involve the variable x, the variable is not raised to the same power in both terms. The fact that they have the same coefficient, 2, is not relevant.

Carrying Out the Same Operation on Both Sides of an Equation

When solving an equation, the general procedure is to carry out a series of operations on both sides of an equation, choosing operations that will tend to simplify the equation when doing so. The reason why the same operation must be carried out on both sides of the equation is because that leaves the meaning of the equation unchanged, and yields a result that is equivalent to the original equation. This would not be the case if we carried out an operation on one side of an equation and not the other. Consider what an equation means: it is a statement that two values or expressions are equal. If we carry out the same operation on both sides of the equation—add 3 to both sides, for example—then the two sides of the equation are changed in the same way, and so remain equal. If we do that to only one side of the equation—add 3 to one side but not the other—then that wouldn't be true; if we change one side of the equation but not the other then the two sides are no longer equal.

Advantage of Combining Like Terms

Combining like terms refers to adding or subtracting like terms—terms with the same variable—and therefore reducing sets of like terms to a single term. The main advantage of doing this is that it simplifies the equation. Often, combining like terms can be done as the first step in solving an equation, though it can also be done later, such as after distributing terms in a product.

For example, consider the equation $2(x + 3) + 3(2 + x + 3) = -4$. The 2 and the 3 in the second set of parentheses are like terms, and we can combine them, yielding $2(x + 3) + 3(x + 5) = -4$. Now we can carry out the multiplications implied by the parentheses, distributing the outer 2 and 3 accordingly: $2x + 6 + 3x + 15 = -4$. The $2x$ and the $3x$ are like terms, and we can add them together: $5x + 6 + 15 = -4$. Now, the constants 6, 15, and -4 are also like terms, and we can combine them as well: subtracting 6 and 15 from both sides of the equation, we get $5x = -4 - 6 - 15$, or $5x = -25$, which simplifies further to $x = -5$.

Review Video: Simplifying Equations by Combining Like Terms
Visit mometrix.com/academy and enter code: 668506

Canceling Terms on Opposite Sides of an Equation

Two terms on opposite sides of an equation can be canceled if and only if they *exactly* match each other. They must have the same variable raised to the same power and the same coefficient. For example, in the equation $3x + 2x^2 + 6 = 2x^2 - 6$, $2x^2$ appears on both sides of the equation and can be canceled, leaving $3x + 6 = -6$. The 6 on each side of the equation *cannot* be canceled, because it is added on one side of the equation and subtracted on the other. While they cannot be canceled, however, the 6 and −6 are like terms and can be combined, yielding $3x = -12$, which simplifies further to $x = -4$.

It's also important to note that the terms to be canceled must be independent terms and cannot be part of a larger term. For example, consider the equation $2(x + 6) = 3(x + 4) + 1$. We cannot cancel the x's, because even though they match each other they are part of the larger terms $2(x + 6)$ and $3(x + 4)$. We must first distribute the 2 and 3, yielding $2x + 12 = 3x + 12 + 1$. Now we see that the terms with the x's do not match, but the 12s do, and can be canceled, leaving $2x = 3x + 1$, which simplifies to $x = -1$.

Process for Manipulating Equations

Isolating Variables

To **isolate a variable** means to manipulate the equation so that the variable appears by itself on one side of the equation, and does not appear at all on the other side. Generally, an equation or inequality is considered to be solved once the variable is isolated and the other side of the equation or inequality is simplified as much as possible. In the case of a two-variable equation or inequality, only one variable needs to be isolated; it will not usually be possible to simultaneously isolate both variables.

For a linear equation—an equation in which the variable only appears raised to the first power—isolating a variable can be done by first moving all the terms with the variable to one side of the equation and all other terms to the other side. (*Moving* a term really means adding the inverse of the term to both sides; when a term is *moved* to the other side of the equation its sign is flipped.) Then combine like terms on each side. Finally, divide both sides by the coefficient of the variable, if applicable. The steps need not necessarily be done in this order, but this order will always work.

Review Video: Solving Equations with Variables on Both Sides
Visit mometrix.com/academy and enter code: 402497

Equations with More Than One Solution

Some types of non-linear equations, such as equations involving squares of variables, may have more than one solution. For example, the equation $x^2 = 4$ has two solutions: 2 and −2. Equations with absolute values can also have multiple solutions: $|x| = 1$ has the solutions $x = 1$ and $x = -1$.

It is also possible for a linear equation to have more than one solution, but only if the equation is true regardless of the value of the variable. In this case, the equation is considered to have infinitely many solutions, because any possible value of the variable is a solution. We know a linear equation has infinitely many solutions if when we combine like terms the variables cancel, leaving a true statement. For example, consider the equation $2(3x + 5) = x + 5(x + 2)$. Distributing, we get $6x +$

$10 = x + 5x + 10$; combining like terms gives $6x + 10 = 6x + 10$, and the $6x$ terms cancel to leave $10 = 10$. This is clearly true, so the original equation is true for any value of x. We could also have canceled the 10s leaving $0 = 0$, but again this is clearly true—in general if both sides of the equation match exactly, it has infinitely many solutions.

EQUATIONS WITH NO SOLUTION

Some types of non-linear equations, such as equations involving squares of variables, may have no solution. For example, the equation $x^2 = -2$ has no solutions in the real numbers, because the square of any real number must be positive. Similarly, $|x| = -1$ has no solution, because the absolute value of a number is always positive.

It is also possible for an equation to have no solution even if does not involve any powers greater than one, absolute values, or other special functions. For example, the equation $2(x + 3) + x = 3x$ has no solution. We can see that if we try to solve it. First, we distribute, leaving $2x + 6 + x = 3x$. But now if we try to combine all the terms with the variable, we find that they cancel: we have $3x$ on the left and $3x$ on the right, canceling to leave us with $6 = 0$. This is clearly false. In general, whenever the variable terms in an equation cancel leaving different constants on both sides, it means that the equation has no solution. (If we are left with the *same* constant on both sides, the equation has infinitely many solutions instead.)

FEATURES OF EQUATIONS THAT REQUIRE SPECIAL TREATMENT

LINEAR EQUATIONS

A linear equation is an equation in which variables only appear by themselves; they are not multiplied together, not with exponents other than one, and not inside absolute value signs or any other functions. For example, the equation $x + 1 - 3x = 5 - x$ is a linear equation; while x appears multiple times, it never appears with an exponent other than one, or inside any function. The two-variable equation $2x - 3y = 5 + 2x$ is also a linear equation. In contrast, the equation $x^2 - 5 = 3x$ is *not* a linear equation, because it involves the term x^2. $\sqrt{x} = 5$ is not a linear equation, because it involves a square root. $(x - 1)^2 = 4$ is not a linear equation because even though there's no exponent on the x directly, it appears as part of an expression that is squared. The two-variable equation $x + xy - y = 5$ is not a linear equation because it includes the term xy, where two variables are multiplied together.

Linear equations can always be solved (or shown to have no solution) by combining like terms and performing simple operations on both sides of the equation. Some non-linear equations can be solved by similar methods, but others may require more advanced methods of solution, if they can be solved analytically at all.

SOLVING EQUATIONS INVOLVING ROOTS

In an equation involving roots, the first step is to isolate the term with the root, if possible, and then raise both sides of the equation to the appropriate power to eliminate it. Consider an example equation, $2\sqrt{x + 1} - 1 = 3$. In this case, begin by adding 1 to both sides, yielding $2\sqrt{x + 1} = 4$, and then dividing both sides by 2, yielding $\sqrt{x + 1} = 2$. Now square both sides, yielding $x + 1 = 4$. Finally, subtracting 1 from both sides yields $x = 3$.

Squaring both sides of an equation may, however, yield a spurious solution—a solution to the squared equation that is *not* a solution of the original equation. It's therefore necessary to plug the solution back into the original equation to make sure it works. In this case, it does: $2\sqrt{3 + 1} - 1 = 2\sqrt{4} - 1 = 2(2) - 1 = 4 - 1 = 3$.

The same procedure applies for other roots as well. For example, given the equation $3 + \sqrt[3]{2x} = 5$, we can first subtract 3 from both sides, yielding $\sqrt[3]{2x} = 2$ and isolating the root. Raising both sides to the third power yields $2x = 2^3$, i.e. $2x = 8$. We can now divide both sides by 2 to get $x = 4$.

> **Review Video: Solving Equations Involving Roots**
> Visit mometrix.com/academy and enter code: 297670

Solving Equations with Exponents

To solve an equation involving an exponent, the first step is to isolate the variable with the exponent. We can then take the appropriate root of both sides to eliminate the exponent. For instance, for the equation $2x^3 + 17 = 5x^3 - 7$, we can subtract $5x^3$ from both sides to get $-3x^3 + 17 = -7$, and then subtract 17 from both sides to get $-3x^3 = -24$. Finally, we can divide both sides by -3 to get $x^3 = 8$. Finally, we can take the cube root of both sides to get $x = \sqrt[3]{8} = 2$.

One important but often overlooked point is that equations with an exponent greater than 1 may have more than one answer. The solution to $x^2 = 9$ isn't simply $x = 3$; it's $x = \pm 3$ (that is, $x = 3$ or $x = -3$). For a slightly more complicated example, consider the equation $(x - 1)^2 - 1 = 3$. Adding 1 to both sides yields $(x - 1)^2 = 4$; taking the square root of both sides yields $x - 1 = 2$. We can then add 1 to both sides to get $x = 3$. However, there's a second solution. We also have the possibility that $x - 1 = -2$, in which case $x = -1$. Both $x = 3$ and $x = -1$ are valid solutions, as can be verified by substituting them both into the original equation.

> **Review Video: Solving Equations with Exponents**
> Visit mometrix.com/academy and enter code: 514557

Solving Equations with Absolute Values

When solving an equation with an absolute value, the first step is to isolate the absolute value term. We then consider two possibilities: when the expression inside the absolute value is positive or when it is negative. In the former case, the expression in the absolute value equals the expression on the other side of the equation; in the latter, it equals the additive inverse of that expression—the expression times negative one. We consider each case separately and finally check for spurious solutions.

For instance, consider solving $|2x - 1| + x = 5$ for x. We can first isolate the absolute value by moving the x to the other side: $|2x - 1| = -x + 5$. Now, we have two possibilities. First, that $2x - 1$ is positive, and hence $2x - 1 = -x + 5$. Rearranging and combining like terms yields $3x = 6$, and hence $x = 2$. The other possibility is that $2x - 1$ is negative, and hence $2x - 1 = -(-x + 5) = x - 5$. In this case, rearranging and combining like terms yields $x = -4$. Substituting $x = 2$ and $x = -4$ back into the original equation, we see that they are both valid solutions.

Note that the absolute value of a sum or difference applies to the sum or difference as a whole, not to the individual terms; in general, $|2x - 1|$ is not equal to $|2x + 1|$ or to $|2x| - 1$.

Spurious Solutions

A **spurious solution** may arise when we square both sides of an equation as a step in solving it or under certain other operations on the equation. It is a solution to the squared or otherwise modified equation that is *not* a solution of the original equation. To identify a spurious solution, it's useful when you solve an equation involving roots or absolute values to plug the solution back into the original equation to make sure it's valid.

Choosing Which Variable to Isolate in Two-Variable Equations

Similar to methods for a one-variable equation, solving a two-variable equation involves isolating a variable: manipulating the equation so that a variable appears by itself on one side of the equation, and not at all on the other side. However, in a two-variable equation, you will usually only be able to isolate one of the variables; the other variable may appear on the other side along with constant terms, or with exponents or other functions.

Often one variable will be much more easily isolated than the other, and therefore that's the variable you should choose. If one variable appears with various exponents, and the other is only raised to the first power, the latter variable is the one to isolate: given the equation $a^2 + 2b = a^3 + b + 3$, the b only appears to the first power, whereas a appears squared and cubed, so b is the variable that can be solved for: combining like terms and isolating the b on the left side of the equation, we get $b = a^3 - a^2 + 3$. If both variables are equally easy to isolate, then it's best to isolate the independent variable, if one is defined; if the two variables are x and y, the convention is that y is the independent variable.

Practice

P1. Seeing the equation $2x + 4 = 4x + 7$, a student divides the first terms on each side by 2, yielding $x + 4 = 2x + 7$, and then combines like terms to get $x = -3$. However, this is incorrect, as can be seen by substituting –3 into the original equation. Explain what is wrong with the student's reasoning.

P2. Describe the steps necessary to solve the equation $2x + 1 - x = 4 + 3x + 7$.

P3. Describe the steps necessary to solve the equation $2(x + 5) = 7(4 - x)$.

P4. Find all real solutions to the equation $1 - \sqrt{x} = 2$.

P5. Find all real solutions to the equation $|x + 1| = 2x + 5$.

P6. Solve for x: $-x + 2\sqrt{x + 5} + 1 = 3$.

P7. Ray earns \$10 an hour at his job. Write an equation for his earnings as a function of time spent working. Determine how long Ray has to work in order to earn \$360.

P8. Simplify the following: $3x + 2 + 2y = 5y - 7 + |2x - 1|$

Practice Solutions

P1. As stated, it's easy to verify that the student's solution is incorrect: $2(-3) + 4 = -2$ and $4(-3) + 7 = -5$; clearly $-2 \neq -5$. The mistake was in the first step, which illustrates a common type of error in solving equations. The student tried to simplify the two variable terms by dividing them by 2. However, it's not valid to multiply or divide only one term on each side of an equation by a number; when multiplying or dividing, the operation must be applied to *every* term in the equation. So, dividing by 2 would yield not $x + 4 = 2x + 7$, but $x + 2 = 2x + \frac{7}{2}$. While this is now valid, that fraction is inconvenient to work with, so this may not be the best first step in solving the equation. Rather, it may have been better to first combine like terms. Subtracting $4x$ from both sides yields $-2x + 4 = 7$; subtracting 4 from both sides yields $-2x = 3$; *now* we can divide both sides by –2 to get $x = -\frac{3}{2}$.

P2. Our ultimate goal is to isolate the variable, x. To that end we first move all the terms containing x to the left side of the equation, and all the constant terms to the right side. Note that when we move a term to the other side of the equation its sign changes. We are therefore now left with $2x - x - 3x = 4 + 7 - 1$.

Next, we combine the like terms on each side of the equation, adding and subtracting the terms as appropriate. This leaves us with $-2x = 10$.

At this point, we're almost done; all that remains is to divide both sides by -2 to leave the x by itself. We now have our solution, $x = -5$. We can verify that this is a correct solution by substituting it back into the original equation.

P3. Generally, in equations that have a sum or difference of terms multiplied by another value or expression, the first step is to multiply those terms, distributing as necessary: $2(x + 5) = 2(x) + 2(5) = 2x + 10$, and $7(4 - x) = 7(4) - 7(x) = 28 - 7x$. So, the equation becomes $2x + 10 = 28 - 7x$. We can now add $7x$ to both sides to eliminate the variable from the right-hand side: $9x + 10 = 28$. Similarly, we can subtract 10 from both sides to move all the constants to the right: $9x = 18$. Finally, we can divide both sides by 9, yielding the final answer, $x = 2$.

P4. It's not hard to isolate the root: subtract one from both sides, yielding $-\sqrt{x} = 1$. Finally, multiply both sides by –1, yielding $\sqrt{x} = -1$. Squaring both sides of the equation yields $x = 1$. However, if we plug this back into the original equation, we get $1 - \sqrt{1} = 2$, which is false. Therefore $x = 1$ is a spurious solution, and the equation has no real solutions.

P5. This equation has two possibilities: $x + 1 = 2x + 5$, which simplifies to $x = -4$; or $x + 1 = -(2x + 5) = -2x - 5$, which simplifies to $x = -2$. However, if we try substituting both values back into the original equation, we see that only $x = -2$ yields a true statement. $x = -4$ is a spurious solution; $x = -2$ is the only valid solution to the equation.

P6. Start by isolating the term with the root. We can do that by moving the $-x$ and the 1 to the other side, yielding $2\sqrt{x + 5} = 3 + x - 1$, or $2\sqrt{x + 5} = x + 2$. Dividing both sides of the equation by 2 would give us a fractional term that could be messy to deal with, so we won't do that for now. Instead, we square both sides of the equation; note that on the left-hand side the 2 is outside the square root sign, so we have to square it. As a result, we get $4(x + 5) = (x + 2)^2$. Expanding both sides gives us $4x + 20 = x^2 + 4x + 4$. In this case, we see that we have $4x$ on both sides, so we can cancel the $4x$ (which is what allows us to solve this equation despite the different powers of x). We now have $20 = x^2 + 4$, or $x^2 = 16$. Since the variable is raised to an even power, we need to take the positive and negative roots, so $x = \pm 4$: that is, $x = 4$ or $x = -4$. Substituting both values into the original equation, we see that $x = 4$ satisfies the equation but $x = -4$ does not; hence $x = -4$ is a spurious solution, and the only solution to the equation is $x = 4$.

P7. The number of dollars that Ray earns is dependent on the number of hours he works, so earnings will be represented by the dependent variable y and hours worked will be represented by the independent variable x. He earns 10 dollars per hour worked, so his earnings can be calculated as $y = 10x$. To calculate the number of hours Ray must work in order to earn \$360, plug in 360 for y and solve for x:

$$360 = 10x$$
$$x = \frac{360}{10} = 36$$

P8. To simplify this equation, we must isolate one of its variables on one side of the equation. In this case, the x appears under an absolute value sign, which makes it difficult to isolate. The y, on the other hand, only appears without an exponent—the equation is linear in y. We will therefore choose to isolate the y. The first step, then, is to move all the terms with y to the left side of the equation, which we can do by subtracting $5y$ from both sides:

$$3x + 2 - 3y = -7 + |2x - 1|$$

We can then move all the terms that do *not* include y to the right side of the equation, by subtracting $3x$ and 2 from both sides of the equation:

$$-3y = -3x - 9 + |2x - 1|$$

Finally, we can isolate the y by dividing both sides by -3.

$$y = x + 3 - \frac{1}{3}|2x - 1|$$

This is as far as we can simplify the equation; we cannot combine the terms inside and outside the absolute value sign. We can therefore consider the equation to be solved.

INEQUALITIES

WORKING WITH INEQUALITIES

Commonly in algebra and other upper-level fields of math you find yourself working with mathematical expressions that do not equal each other. The statement comparing such expressions with symbols such as < (less than) or > (greater than) is called an *inequality*. An example of an inequality is $7x > 5$. To solve for x, simply divide both sides by 7 and the solution is shown to be $x > \frac{5}{7}$. Graphs of the solution set of inequalities are represented on a number line. Open circles are used to show that an expression approaches a number but is never quite equal to that number.

Review Video: Solving Multi-Step Inequalities
Visit mometrix.com/academy and enter code: 347842

Conditional inequalities are those with certain values for the variable that will make the condition true and other values for the variable where the condition will be false. **Absolute inequalities** can have any real number as the value for the variable to make the condition true, while there is no real number value for the variable that will make the condition false. Solving inequalities is done by following the same rules for solving equations with the exception that when multiplying or dividing by a negative number the direction of the inequality sign must be flipped or reversed. **Double inequalities** are situations where two inequality statements apply to the same variable expression. An example of this is $-c < ax + b < c$.

Review Video: Conditional and Absolute Inequalities
Visit mometrix.com/academy and enter code: 980164

DETERMINING SOLUTIONS TO INEQUALITIES

To determine whether a coordinate is a solution of an inequality, you can substitute the values of the coordinate into the inequality, simplify, and check whether the resulting statement holds true. For instance, to determine whether $(-2,4)$ is a solution of the inequality $y \geq -2x + 3$, substitute the values into the inequality, $4 \geq -2(-2) + 3$. Simplify the right side of the inequality and the result is $4 \geq 7$, which is a false statement. Therefore, the coordinate is not a solution of the inequality. You can also use this method to determine which part of the graph of an inequality is shaded. The graph of $y \geq -2x + 3$ includes the solid line $y = -2x + 3$ and, since it excludes the point $(-2,4)$ to the left of the line, it is shaded to the right of the line.

Flipping Inequality Signs

When given an inequality, we can always turn the entire inequality around, swapping the two sides of the inequality and changing the inequality sign. For instance, $x + 2 > 2x - 3$ is equivalent to $2x - 3 < x + 2$. Aside from that, normally the inequality does not change if we carry out the same operation on both sides of the inequality. There is, however, one principal exception: if we *multiply* or *divide* both sides of the inequality by a *negative number*, the inequality is flipped. For example, if we take the inequality $-2x < 6$ and divide both sides by -2, the inequality flips and we are left with $x > -3$. This *only* applies to multiplication and division, and only with negative numbers. Multiplying or dividing both sides by a positive number, or adding or subtracting any number regardless of sign, does not flip the inequality.

Compound Inequalities

A **compound inequality** is an equality that consists of two inequalities combined with *and* or *or*. The two components of a proper compound inequality must be of opposite type: that is, one must be greater than (or greater than or equal to), the other less than (or less than or equal to). For instance, "$x + 1 < 2$ or $x + 1 > 3$" is a compound inequality, as is "$2x \geq 4$ and $2x \leq 6$." An *and* inequality can be written more compactly by having one inequality on each side of the common part: "$2x \geq 1$ and $2x \leq 6$," can also be written as $1 \leq 2x \leq 6$.

In order for the compound inequality to be meaningful, the two parts of an *and* inequality must overlap; otherwise no numbers satisfy the inequality. On the other hand, if the two parts of an *or* inequality overlap, then *all* numbers satisfy the inequality and as such the inequality is usually not meaningful.

Solving a compound inequality requires solving each part separately. For example, given the compound inequality "$x + 1 < 2$ or $x + 1 > 3$," the first inequality, $x + 1 < 2$, reduces to $x < 1$, and the second part, $x + 1 > 3$, reduces to $x > 2$, so the whole compound inequality can be written as "$x < 1$ or $x > 2$." Similarly, $1 \leq 2x \leq 6$ can be solved by dividing each term by 2, yielding $\frac{1}{2} \leq x \leq 3$.

Review Video: Compound Inequalities
Visit mometrix.com/academy and enter code: 786318

Solving Inequalities Involving Absolute Values

To solve an inequality involving an absolute value, first isolate the term with the absolute value. Then proceed to treat the two cases separately as with an absolute value equation, but flipping the inequality in the case where the expression in the absolute value is negative (since that essentially involves multiplying both sides by -1.) The two cases are then combined into a compound inequality; if the absolute value is on the greater side of the inequality, then it is an *or* compound inequality, if on the lesser side, then it's an *and*.

Consider the inequality $2 + |x - 1| \geq 3$. We can isolate the absolute value term by subtracting 2 from both sides: $|x - 1| \geq 1$. Now, we're left with the two cases $x - 1 \geq 1$ or $x - 1 \leq -1$: note that in the latter, negative case, the inequality is flipped. $x - 1 \geq 1$ reduces to $x \geq 2$, and $x - 1 \leq -1$ reduces to $x \leq 0$. Since in the inequality $|x - 1| \geq 1$ the absolute value is on the greater side, the two cases combine into an *or* compound inequality, so the final, solved inequality is "$x \leq 0$ or $x \geq 2$."

> **Review Video: Solving Absolute Value Inequalities**
> Visit mometrix.com/academy and enter code: 997008

SOLVING INEQUALITIES INVOLVING SQUARE ROOTS

Solving an inequality with a square root involves two parts. First, we solve the inequality as if it were an equation, isolating the square root and then squaring both sides of the equation. Second, we restrict the solution to the set of values of x for which the value inside the square root sign is non-negative.

For example, in the inequality, $\sqrt{x-2}+1<5$, we can isolate the square root by subtracting 1 from both sides, yielding $\sqrt{x-2}<4$. Squaring both sides of the inequality yields $x-2<16$, so $x<18$. Since we can't take the square root of a negative number, we also require the part inside the square root to be non-negative. In this case, that means $x-2 \geq 0$. Adding 2 to both sides of the inequality yields $x \geq 2$. Our final answer is a compound inequality combining the two simple inequalities: $x \geq 2$ and $x<18$, or $2 \leq x < 18$.

Note that we only get a compound inequality if the two simple inequalities are in opposite directions; otherwise we take the one that is more restrictive.

The same technique can be used for other even roots, such as fourth roots. It is *not*, however, used for cube roots or other odd roots—negative numbers *do* have cube roots, so the condition that the quantity inside the root sign cannot be negative does not apply.

> **Review Video: Solving Inequalities Involving Square Roots**
> Visit mometrix.com/academy and enter code: 800288

SPECIAL CIRCUMSTANCES

Sometimes an inequality involving an absolute value or an even exponent is true for all values of x, and we don't need to do any further work to solve it. This is true if the inequality, once the absolute value or exponent term is isolated, says that term is greater than a negative number (or greater than or equal to zero). Since an absolute value or a number raised to an even exponent is *always* non-negative, this inequality is always true.

GRAPHICAL SOLUTIONS TO EQUATIONS AND INEQUALITIES

When equations are shown graphically, they are usually shown on a **Cartesian coordinate plane**. The Cartesian coordinate plane consists of two number lines placed perpendicular to each other and intersecting at the zero point, also known as the origin. The horizontal number line is known as the x-axis, with positive values to the right of the origin, and negative values to the left of the origin. The vertical number line is known as the y-axis, with positive values above the origin, and negative values below the origin. Any point on the plane can be identified by an ordered pair in the form (x, y), called coordinates. The x-value of the coordinate is called the abscissa, and the y-value of the coordinate is called the ordinate. The two number lines divide the plane into **four quadrants**: I, II, III, and IV.

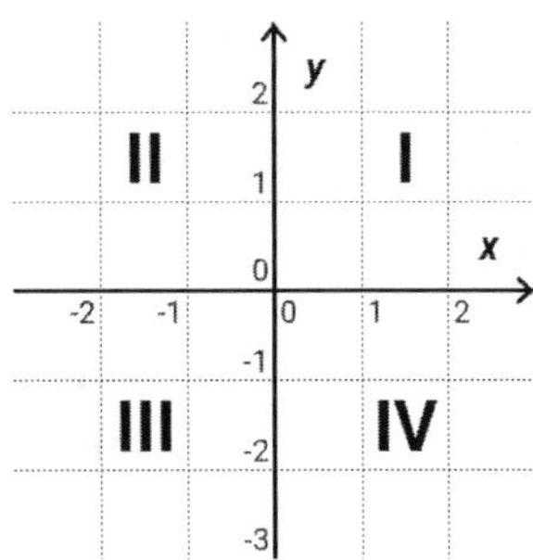

Note that in quadrant I $x > 0$ and $y > 0$, in quadrant II $x < 0$ and $y > 0$, in quadrant III $x < 0$ and $y < 0$, and in quadrant IV $x > 0$ and $y < 0$.

Recall that if the value of the slope of a line is positive, the line slopes upward from left to right. If the value of the slope is negative, the line slopes downward from left to right. If the y-coordinates are the same for two points on a line, the slope is 0 and the line is a **horizontal line**. If the x-coordinates are the same for two points on a line, there is no slope and the line is a **vertical line**. Two or more lines that have equivalent slopes are **parallel lines**. **Perpendicular lines** have slopes that are negative reciprocals of each other, such as $\frac{a}{b}$ and $\frac{-b}{a}$.

Graphing Simple Inequalities

To graph a simple inequality, we first mark on the number line the value that signifies the end point of the inequality. If the inequality is strict (involves a less than or greater than), we use a hollow circle; if it is not strict (less than or equal to or greater than or equal to), we use a solid circle. We then fill in the part of the number line that satisfies the inequality: to the left of the marked point for less than (or less than or equal to), to the right for greater than (or greater than or equal to).

For example, we would graph the inequality $x < 5$ by putting a hollow circle at 5 and filling in the part of the line to the left:

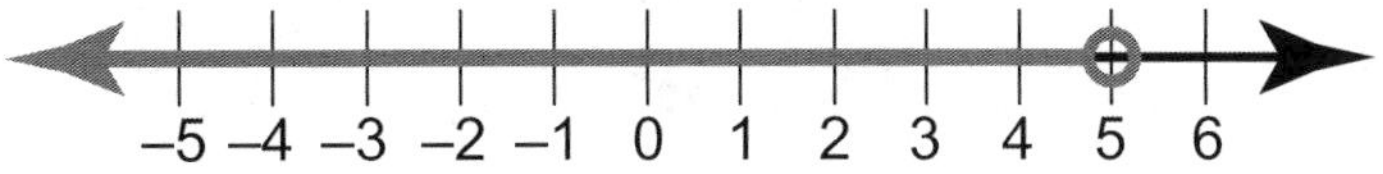

Graphing Compound Inequalities

To graph a compound inequality, we fill in both parts of the inequality for an *or* inequality, or the overlap between them for an *and* inequality. More specifically, we start by plotting the endpoints of each inequality on the number line. For an *or* inequality, we then fill in the appropriate side of the line for each inequality. Typically, the two component inequalities do not overlap, which means the shaded part is *outside* the two points. For an *and* inequality, we instead fill in the part of the line that meets both inequalities.

For the inequality "$x \leq -3$ or $x > 4$," we first put a solid circle at –3 and a hollow circle at 4. We then fill the parts of the line *outside* these circles:

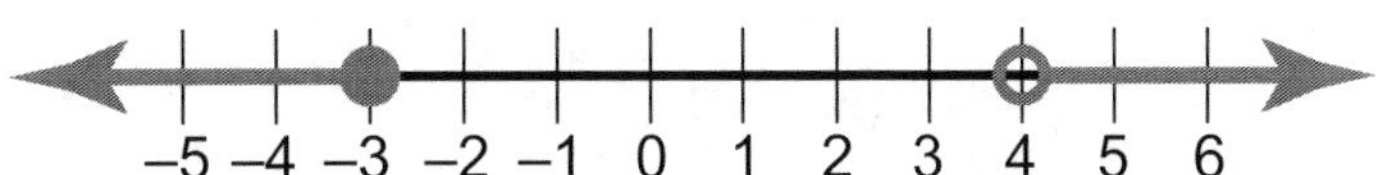

Graphing Inequalities Including Absolute Values

An inequality with an absolute value can be converted to a compound inequality. To graph the inequality, first convert it to a compound inequality, and then graph that normally. If the absolute value is on the greater side of the inequality, we end up with an *or* inequality; we plot the endpoints of the inequality on the number line and fill in the part of the line *outside* those points. If the absolute value is on the smaller side of the inequality, we end up with an *and* inequality; we plot the endpoints of the inequality on the number line and fill in the part of the line *between* those points.

For example, the inequality $|x+1| \geq 4$ can be rewritten as $x \geq 3$ or $x \leq -5$. We place solid circles at the points 3 and -5 and fill in the part of the line *outside* them:

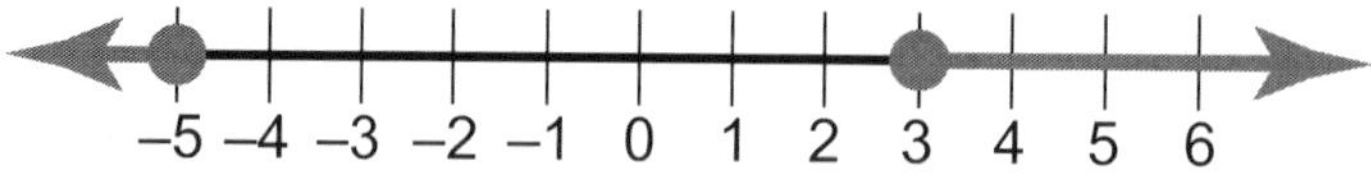

Graphing Equations in Two Variables

One way of graphing an equation in two variables is to plot enough points to get an idea for its shape and then draw the appropriate curve through those points. A point can be plotted by substituting in a value for one variable and solving for the other. If the equation is linear, we only need two points and can then draw a straight line between them.

For example, consider the equation $y = 2x - 1$. This is a linear equation—both variables only appear raised to the first power—so we only need two points. When $x = 0$, $y = 2(0) - 1 = -1$. When $x = 2$, $y = 2(2) - 1 = 3$. We can therefore choose the points $(0, -1)$ and $(2, 3)$, and draw a line between them:

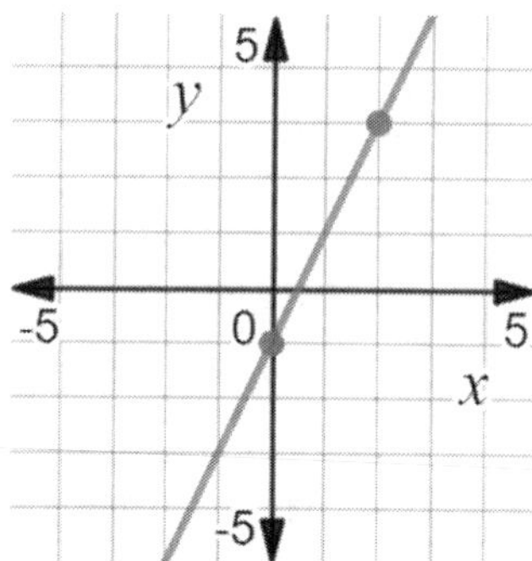

Graphing Inequalities in Two Variables

To graph an inequality in two variables, we first graph the border of the inequality. This means graphing the equation that we get if we replace the inequality sign with an equals sign. If the inequality is strict (> or <), we graph the border with a dashed or dotted line; if it is not strict (≥ or ≤), we use a solid line. We can then test any point not on the border to see if it satisfies the inequality. If it does, we shade in that side of the border; if not, we shade in the other side. As an example, consider $y > 2x + 2$. To graph this inequality, we first graph the border, $y = 2x + 2$. Since it is a strict inequality, we use a dashed line. Then, we choose a test point. This can be any point not on the border; in this case, we will choose the origin, (0,0). (This makes the calculation easy and is generally a good choice unless the border passes through the origin.) Putting this into the original inequality, we get $0 > 2(0) + 2$, i.e. $0 > 2$. This is *not* true, so we shade in the side of the border that does *not* include the point (0,0):

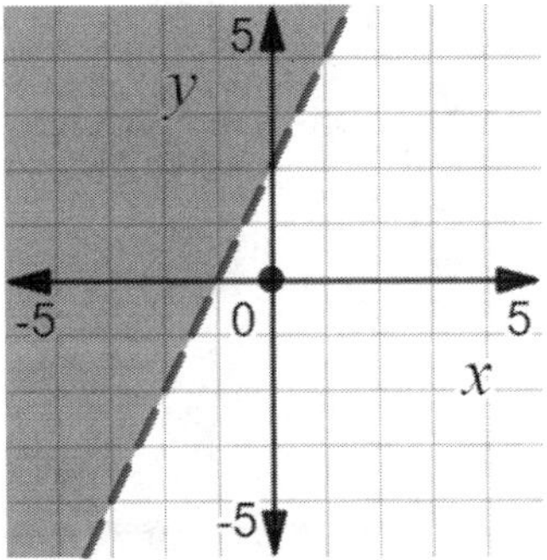

Graphing Compound Inequalities in Two Variables

One way to graph a compound inequality in two variables is to first graph each of the component inequalities. For an *and* inequality, we then shade in only the parts where the two graphs overlap; for an *or* inequality, we shade in any region that pertains to either of the individual inequalities.

Consider the graph of "$y \geq x - 1$ *and* $y \leq -x$":

We first shade in the individual inequalities:

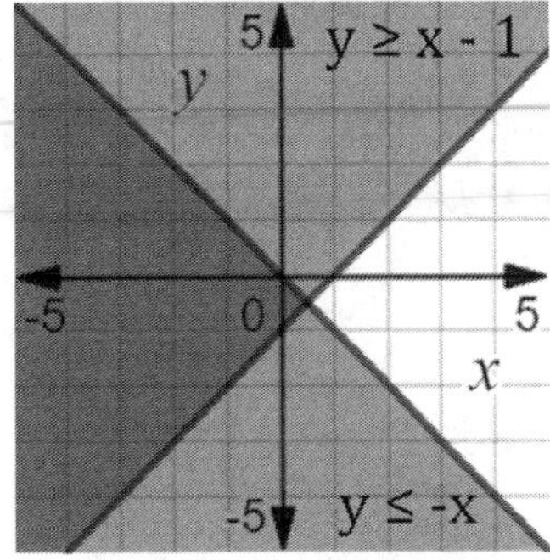

Now, since the compound inequality has an *and*, we only leave shaded the overlap—the part that pertains to *both* inequalities:

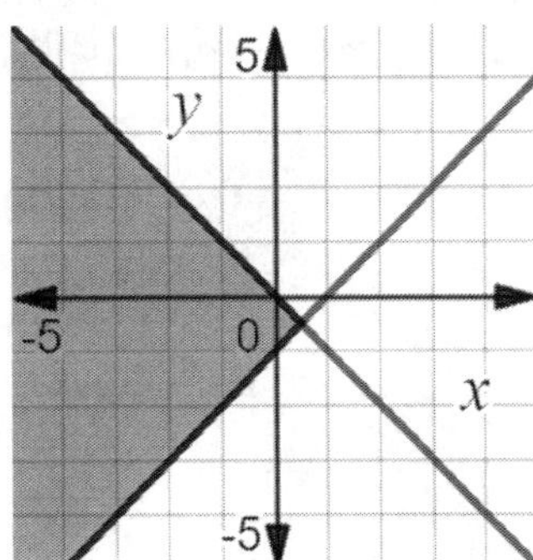

If instead the inequality had been "$y \geq x - 1$ *or* $y \leq -x$," our final graph would involve the *total* shaded area:

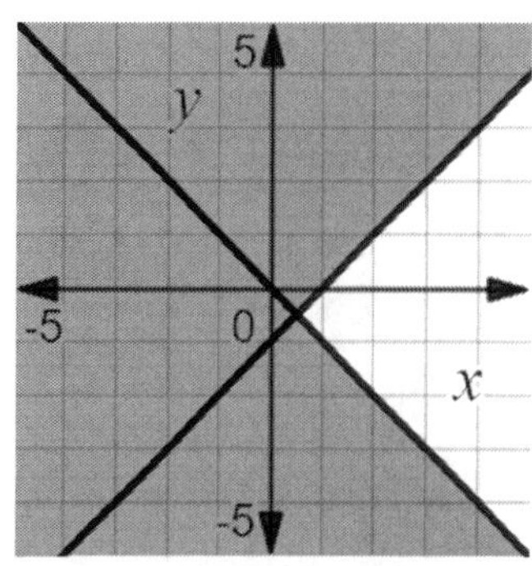

Review Video: Graphing Solutions to Inequalities
Visit mometrix.com/academy and enter code: 391281

PRACTICE

P1. Analyze the following inequalities:

(a) $2 - |x + 1| < 3$
(b) $2(x - 1)^2 + 7 \leq 1$

P2. Graph the following on a number line:

(a) $x \geq 3$
(b) $-2 \leq x \leq 6$
(c) $|x| < 2$

PRACTICE SOLUTIONS

P1. (a) Subtracting 2 from both sides yields $-|x + 1| < 1$; multiplying by -1 and flipping the inequality, since we're multiplying by a negative number, yields $|x + 1| > -1$. But since the absolute value cannot be negative, it's *always* greater than –1, so this inequality is true for all values of x.

(b) Subtracting 7 from both sides yields $2(x - 1)^2 \leq -6$; dividing by 2 yields $(x - 1)^2 \leq -3$. But $(x - 1)^2$ must be nonnegative, and hence cannot be less than or equal to –3; this inequality has no solution.

P2. (a) We would graph the inequality $x \geq 3$ by putting a solid circle at 3 and filling in the part of the line to the right:

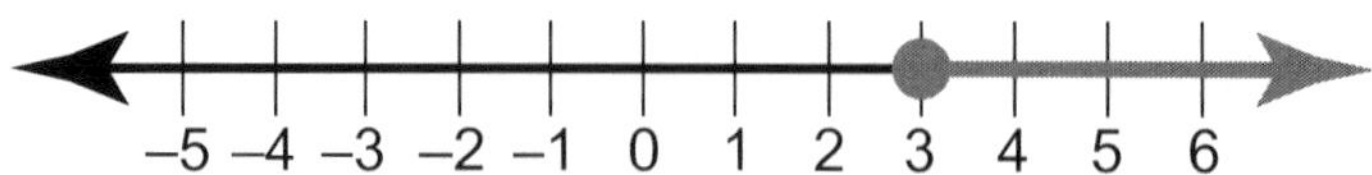

(b) The inequality $-2 \leq x \leq 6$ is equivalent to "$x \geq -2$ and $x \leq 6$." To plot this compound inequality, we first put solid circles at –2 and 6, and then fill in the part of the line *between* these circles:

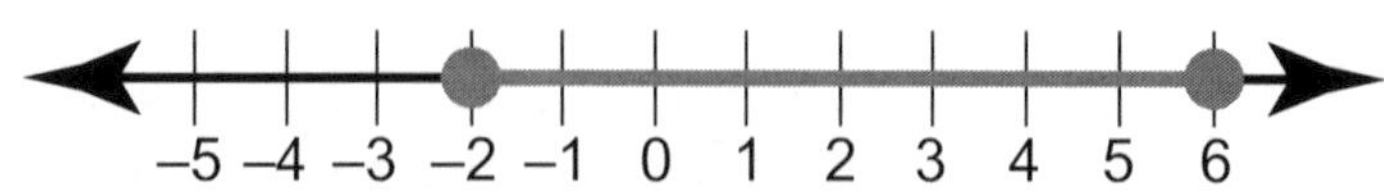

(c) The inequality $|x| < 2$ can be rewritten as "$x > -2$ and $x < 2$." We place hollow circles at the points –2 and 2 and fill in the part of the line between them:

Algebraic Reasoning

Systems of Equations

A **system of equations** is a set of simultaneous equations that all use the same variables. A solution to a system of equations must be true for each equation in the system. **Consistent systems** are those with at least one solution. **Inconsistent systems** are systems of equations that have no solution.

> **Review Video: Substitution and Elimination for Solving Linear Systems**
> Visit mometrix.com/academy and enter code: 958611

Substitution

To solve a system of linear equations by **substitution**, start with the easier equation and solve for one of the variables. Express this variable in terms of the other variable. Substitute this expression in the other equation and solve for the other variable. The solution should be expressed in the form (x, y). Substitute the values into both of the original equations to check your answer. Consider the following system of equations:

$$\begin{aligned} x + 6y &= 15 \\ 3x - 12y &= 18 \end{aligned}$$

Solving the first equation for x: $x = 15 - 6y$

Substitute this value in place of x in the second equation, and solve for y:

$$\begin{aligned} 3(15 - 6y) - 12y &= 18 \\ 45 - 18y - 12y &= 18 \\ 30y &= 27 \\ y &= \frac{27}{30} = \frac{9}{10} = 0.9 \end{aligned}$$

Plug this value for y back into the first equation to solve for x:

$$x = 15 - 6(0.9) = 15 - 5.4 = 9.6$$

Check both equations if you have time:

$$\begin{aligned} 9.6 + 6(0.9) &= 15 \\ 9.6 + 5.4 &= 15 \\ 15 &= 15 \end{aligned} \qquad \begin{aligned} 3(9.6) - 12(0.9) &= 18 \\ 28.8 - 10.8 &= 18 \\ 18 &= 18 \end{aligned}$$

Therefore, the solution is $(9.6, 0.9)$.

> **Review Video: The Substitution Method**
> Visit mometrix.com/academy and enter code: 565151

ELIMINATION

To solve a system of equations using **elimination**, begin by rewriting both equations in standard form $Ax + By = C$. Check to see if the coefficients of one pair of like variables add to zero. If not, multiply one or both of the equations by a non-zero number to make one set of like variables add to zero. Add the two equations to solve for one of the variables. Substitute this value into one of the original equations to solve for the other variable. Check your work by substituting into the other equation. Now, let's look at solving the following system using the elimination method:

$$5x + 6y = 4$$
$$x + 2y = 4$$

If we multiply the second equation by -3, we can eliminate the y terms:

$$5x + 6y = 4$$
$$-3x - 6y = -12$$

Add the equations together and solve for x:

$$2x = -8$$
$$x = \frac{-8}{2} = -4$$

Plug the value for x back in to either of the original equations and solve for y:

$$-4 + 2y = 4$$
$$y = \frac{4+4}{2} = 4$$

Check both equations if you have time:

$$5(-4) + 6(4) = 4 \qquad -4 + 2(4) = 4$$
$$-20 + 24 = 4 \qquad -4 + 8 = 4$$
$$4 = 4 \qquad 4 = 4$$

Therefore, the solution is (-4,4).

Review Video: The Elimination Method
Visit mometrix.com/academy and enter code: 449121

GRAPHICALLY

To solve a system of linear equations **graphically**, plot both equations on the same graph. The solution of the equations is the point where both lines cross. If the lines do not cross (are parallel), then there is **no solution**.

For example, consider the following system of equations:

$$y = 2x + 7$$
$$y = -x + 1$$

Since these equations are given in slope-intercept form, they are easy to graph; the *y* intercepts of the lines are (0,7) and (0,1). The respective slopes are 2 and –1, thus the graphs look like this:

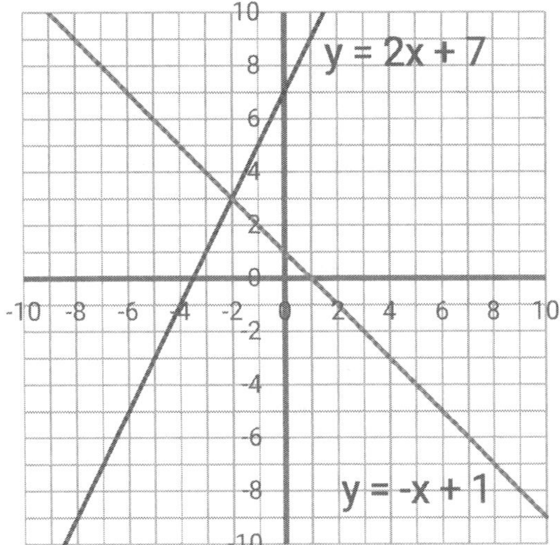

The two lines intersect at the point $(-2,3)$, thus this is the solution to the system of equations.

Solving a system graphically is generally only practical if both coordinates of the solution are integers; otherwise the intersection will lie between gridlines on the graph and the coordinates will be difficult or impossible to determine exactly. It also helps if, as in this example, the equations are in slope-intercept form or some other form that makes them easy to graph. Otherwise, another method of solution (by substitution or elimination) is likely to be more useful.

Solving Systems of Equations Using the Trace Feature

Using the trace feature on a calculator requires that you rewrite each equation, isolating the y-variable on one side of the equal sign. Enter both equations in the graphing calculator and plot the graphs simultaneously. Use the trace cursor to find where the two lines cross. Use the zoom feature if necessary to obtain more accurate results. Always check your answer by substituting into the original equations. The trace method is likely to be less accurate than other methods due to the resolution of graphing calculators but is a useful tool to provide an approximate answer.

Calculations Using Points

Sometimes you need to perform calculations using only points on a graph as input data. Using points, you can determine what the **midpoint** and **distance** are. If you know the equation for a line, you can calculate the distance between the line and the point.

To find the **midpoint** of two points (x_1, y_1) and (x_2, y_2), average the *x*-coordinates to get the *x*-coordinate of the midpoint, and average the *y*-coordinates to get the *y*-coordinate of the midpoint. The formula is: $\left(\frac{x_1+x_2}{2}, \frac{y_1+y_2}{2}\right)$.

The **distance** between two points is the same as the length of the hypotenuse of a right triangle with the two given points as endpoints, and the two sides of the right triangle parallel to the *x*-axis and *y*-axis, respectively. The length of the segment parallel to the *x*-axis is the difference between the *x*-coordinates of the two points. The length of the segment parallel to the *y*-axis is the difference between the *y*-coordinates of the two points. Use the Pythagorean theorem $a^2 + b^2 = c^2$ or $c = \sqrt{a^2 + b^2}$ to find the distance. The formula is $\mathrm{d} = \sqrt{(x_2 - x_1)^2 + (y_2 - y_1)^2}$.

When a line is in the format $Ax + By + C = 0$, where A, B, and C are coefficients, you can use a point (x_1, y_1) not on the line and apply the formula $d = \frac{|Ax_1+By_1+C|}{\sqrt{A^2+B^2}}$ to find the distance between the line and the point (x_1, y_1).

Review Video: Calculations Using Points on a Graph
Visit mometrix.com/academy and enter code: 883228

Practice

P1. Solve the following systems of equations:

(a)
$$\begin{aligned} 3x + 4y &= 9 \\ -12x + 7y &= 10 \end{aligned}$$

(b)
$$\begin{aligned} -3x + 2y &= -1 \\ 4x - 5y &= 6 \end{aligned}$$

P2. Find the distance and midpoint between points (2,4) and (8,6).

Practice Solutions

P1. (a) If we multiply the first equation by 4, we can eliminate the x terms:

$$\begin{aligned} 12x + 16y &= 36 \\ -12x + 7y &= 10 \end{aligned}$$

Add the equations together and solve for y:

$$\begin{aligned} 23y &= 46 \\ y &= 2 \end{aligned}$$

Plug the value for y back in to either of the original equations and solve for x:

$$\begin{aligned} 3x + 4(2) &= 9 \\ x &= \frac{9-8}{3} = \frac{1}{3} \end{aligned}$$

The solution is $\left(\frac{1}{3}, 2\right)$

(b) Solving the first equation for y:

$$\begin{aligned} -3x + 2y &= -1 \\ 2y &= 3x - 1 \\ y &= \frac{3x-1}{2} \end{aligned}$$

Substitute this expression in place of y in the second equation, and solve for x:

$$\begin{aligned} 4x - 5\left(\frac{3x-1}{2}\right) &= 6 \\ 4x - \frac{15x}{2} + \frac{5}{2} &= 6 \\ 8x - 15x + 5 &= 12 \\ -7x &= 7 \\ x &= -1 \end{aligned}$$

Plug the value for x back in to either of the original equations and solve for y:

$$\begin{aligned} -3(-1) + 2y &= -1 \\ 3 + 2y &= -1 \\ 2y &= -4 \\ y &= -2 \end{aligned}$$

The solution is $(-1, -2)$

P2. Use the formulas for distance and midpoint:

$$\begin{aligned} \text{Distance} &= \sqrt{(x_2 - x_1)^2 + (y_2 - y_1)^2} \\ &= \sqrt{(8-2)^2 + (6-4)^2} \\ &= \sqrt{(6)^2 + (2)^2} \\ &= \sqrt{36+4} \\ &= \sqrt{40} \text{ or } 2\sqrt{10} \end{aligned}$$

$$\begin{aligned} \text{Midpoint} &= \left(\frac{x_1 + x_2}{2}, \frac{y_1 + y_2}{2}\right) \\ &= \left(\frac{2+8}{2}, \frac{4+6}{2}\right) \\ &= \left(\frac{10}{2}, \frac{10}{2}\right) \\ &= (5,5) \end{aligned}$$

Polynomial Algebra

Monomials and Polynomials

A **monomial** is a single constant, variable, or product of constants and variables, such as 7, x, $2x$, or x^3y. There will never be addition or subtraction symbols in a monomial. Like monomials have like variables, but they may have different coefficients. **Polynomials** are algebraic expressions that use addition and subtraction to combine two or more monomials. Two terms make a **binomial**, three terms make a **trinomial**, etc. The **degree of a monomial** is the sum of the exponents of the variables. The **degree of a polynomial** is the highest degree of any individual term.

Review Video: Polynomials
Visit mometrix.com/academy and enter code: 305005

Simplifying Polynomials

Simplifying polynomials requires combining like terms. The like terms in a polynomial expression are those that have the same variable raised to the same power. It is often helpful to connect the like terms with arrows or lines in order to separate them from the other monomials. Once you have determined the like terms, you can rearrange the polynomial by placing them together. Remember to include the sign that is in front of each term. Once the like terms are placed together, you can apply each operation and simplify. When adding and subtracting polynomials, only add and subtract the **coefficient**, or the number part; the variable and exponent stay the same.

Review Video: Adding and Subtracting Polynomials
Visit mometrix.com/academy and enter code: 124088

THE FOIL METHOD

In general, multiplying polynomials is done by multiplying each term in one polynomial by each term in the other and adding the results. In the specific case for multiplying binomials, there is a useful acronym, FOIL, that can help you make sure to cover each combination of terms. The **FOIL method** for $(Ax + By)(Cx + Dy)$ would be:

F	Multiply the *first* terms of each binomial	$(\overbrace{Ax}^{first} + By)(\overbrace{Cx}^{first} + Dy)$	ACx^2
O	Multiply the *outer* terms	$(\overbrace{Ax}^{outer} + By)(Cx + \overbrace{Dy}^{outer})$	$ADxy$
I	Multiply the *inner* terms	$(Ax + \overbrace{By}^{inner})(\overbrace{Cx}^{inner} + Dy)$	$BCxy$
L	Multiply the *last* terms of each binomial	$(Ax + \overbrace{By}^{last})(Cx + \overbrace{Dy}^{last})$	BDy^2

Then, add up the result of each and combine like terms: $ACx^2 + (AD + BC)xy + BDy^2$.

For example, using the FOIL method on binomials $(x + 2)$ and $(x - 3)$:

$$\begin{aligned} &\text{First:} && (\boxed{x} + 2)(\boxed{x} + (-3)) && \rightarrow && (x)(x) &&= x^2 \\ &\text{Outer:} && (\boxed{x} + 2)(x + \boxed{(-3)}) && \rightarrow && (x)(-3) &&= -3x \\ &\text{Inner:} && (x + \boxed{2})(\boxed{x} + (-3)) && \rightarrow && (2)(x) &&= 2x \\ &\text{Last:} && (x + \boxed{2})(x + \boxed{(-3)}) && \rightarrow && (2)(-3) &&= -6 \end{aligned}$$

This results in: $(x^2) + (-3x) + (2x) + (-6)$

Combine like terms: $x^2 + (-3 + 2)x + (-6) = x^2 - x - 6$

Review Video: Multiplying Terms Using the FOIL Method
Visit mometrix.com/academy and enter code: 854792

DIVIDING POLYNOMIALS

Use long division to divide a polynomial by either a monomial or another polynomial of equal or lesser degree.

When **dividing by a monomial**, divide each term of the polynomial by the monomial.

When **dividing by a polynomial**, begin by arranging the terms of each polynomial in order of one variable. You may arrange in ascending or descending order, but be consistent with both polynomials. To get the first term of the quotient, divide the first term of the dividend by the first term of the divisor. Multiply the first term of the quotient by the entire divisor and subtract that product from the dividend. Repeat for the second and successive terms until you either get a remainder of zero or a remainder whose degree is less than the degree of the divisor. If the quotient has a remainder, write the answer as a mixed expression in the form:

$$\text{quotient} + \frac{\text{remainder}}{\text{divisor}}$$

For example, we can evaluate the following expression in the same way as long division:

$$\frac{x^3 - 3x^2 - 2x + 5}{x - 5}$$

$$\begin{array}{r}
x^2 \;\; + 2x \;\; + 8 \\
x - 5 \overline{\big) \; x^3 - 3x^2 \;\; - 2x \;\; + 5} \\
-\underline{(x^3 - 5x^2)} \qquad\qquad \\
2x^2 - 2x \qquad \\
-\underline{(2x^2 - 10x)} \qquad \\
8x + 5 \\
-\underline{(8x - 40)} \\
45
\end{array}$$

$$\frac{x^3 - 3x^2 - 2x + 5}{x - 5} = x^2 + 2x + 8 + \frac{45}{x - 5}$$

When **factoring** a polynomial, first check for a common monomial factor, that is, look to see if each coefficient has a common factor or if each term has an x in it. If the factor is a trinomial but not a perfect trinomial square, look for a factorable form, such as one of these:

$$x^2 + (a + b)x + ab = (x + a)(x + b)$$
$$(ac)x^2 + (ad + bc)x + bd = (ax + b)(cx + d)$$

For factors with four terms, look for groups to factor. Once you have found the factors, write the original polynomial as the product of all the factors. Make sure all of the polynomial factors are prime. Monomial factors may be *prime* or *composite*. Check your work by multiplying the factors to make sure you get the original polynomial.

Below are patterns of some special products to remember to help make factoring easier:

- Perfect trinomial squares: $x^2 + 2xy + y^2 = (x + y)^2$ or $x^2 - 2xy + y^2 = (x - y)^2$
- Difference between two squares: $x^2 - y^2 = (x + y)(x - y)$
- Sum of two cubes: $x^3 + y^3 = (x + y)(x^2 - xy + y^2)$
  - Note: the second factor is *not* the same as a perfect trinomial square, so do not try to factor it further.
- Difference between two cubes: $x^3 - y^3 = (x - y)(x^2 + xy + y^2)$
  - Again, the second factor is *not* the same as a perfect trinomial square.
- Perfect cubes: $x^3 + 3x^2y + 3xy^2 + y^3 = (x + y)^3$ and $x^3 - 3x^2y + 3xy^2 - y^3 = (x - y)^3$

Rational Expressions

Rational expressions are fractions with polynomials in both the numerator and the denominator; the value of the polynomial in the denominator cannot be equal to zero. Be sure to keep track of values that make the denominator of the original expression zero as the final result inherits the same restrictions. For example, a denominator of $x - 3$ indicates that the expression is not defined when $x = 3$ and, as such, regardless of any operations done to the expression, it remains undefined there.

To **add or subtract** rational expressions, first find the common denominator, then rewrite each fraction as an equivalent fraction with the common denominator. Finally, add or subtract the numerators to get the numerator of the answer, and keep the common denominator as the denominator of the answer.

When **multiplying** rational expressions, factor each polynomial and cancel like factors (a factor which appears in both the numerator and the denominator). Then, multiply all remaining factors in the numerator to get the numerator of the product, and multiply the remaining factors in the denominator to get the denominator of the product. Remember: cancel entire factors, not individual terms.

To **divide** rational expressions, take the reciprocal of the divisor (the rational expression you are dividing by) and multiply by the dividend.

Review Video: Rational Expressions
Visit mometrix.com/academy and enter code: 415183

Simplifying Rational Expressions

To simplify a rational expression, factor the numerator and denominator completely. Factors that are the same and appear in the numerator and denominator have a ratio of 1. For example, look at the following expression:

$$\frac{x-1}{1-x^2}$$

The denominator, $(1 - x^2)$, is a difference of squares. It can be factored as $(1 - x)(1 + x)$. The factor $1 - x$ and the numerator $x - 1$ are opposites and have a ratio of –1. Rewrite the numerator as $-1(1 - x)$. So, the rational expression can be simplified as follows:

$$\frac{x-1}{1-x^2} = \frac{-1(1-x)}{(1-x)(1+x)} = \frac{-1}{1+x}$$

Note that since the original expression is only defined for $x \neq \{-1, 1\}$, the simplified expression has the same restrictions.

Review Video: Reducing Rational Expressions
Visit mometrix.com/academy and enter code: 788868

Practice

P1. Expand the following polynomials:

(a) $(x + 3)(x - 7)(2x)$

(b) $(x + 2)^2(x - 2)^2$

(c) $(x^2 + 5x + 5)(3x - 1)$

P2. Evaluate the following rational expressions:

(a) $\frac{x^3-2x^2-5x+6}{3x+6}$

(b) $\frac{x^2+4x+4}{4-x^2}$

PRACTICE SOLUTIONS

P1. (a) Apply the FOIL method and the distributive property of multiplication:

$$\begin{aligned}(x+3)(x-7)(2x) &= (x^2-7x+3x-21)(2x)\\ &= (x^2-4x-21)(2x)\\ &= 2x^3-8x^2-42x\end{aligned}$$

(b) Note the difference of squares form:

$$\begin{aligned}(x+2)^2(x-2)^2 &= (x+2)(x+2)(x-2)(x-2)\\ &= [(x+2)(x-2)][(x+2)(x-2)]\\ &= (x^2-4)(x^2-4)\\ &= x^4-8x^2+16\end{aligned}$$

(c) Multiply each pair of monomials and combine like terms:

$$\begin{aligned}(x^2+5x+5)(3x-1) &= 3x^3+15x^2+15x-x^2-5x-5\\ &= 3x^3+14x^2+10x-5\end{aligned}$$

P2. (a) Rather than trying to factor the fourth-degree polynomial, we can use long division:

$$\frac{x^3-2x^2-5x+6}{3x+6} = \frac{x^3-2x^2-5x+6}{3(x+2)}$$

$$\begin{array}{r l}
 & x^2 \;-4x\;+3 \\
x+2\,\big) & x^3-2x^2-5x+6 \\
 & \underline{x^3+2x^2} \\
 & \quad -4x^2-5x \\
 & \quad \underline{-4x^2-8x} \\
 & \qquad\qquad 3x+6 \\
 & \qquad\qquad \underline{3x+6} \\
 & \qquad\qquad\quad 0
\end{array}$$

$$\frac{x^3-2x^2-5x+6}{3(x+2)} = \frac{x^2-4x+3}{3}$$

Note that since the original expression is only defined for $x \neq \{-2\}$, the simplified expression has the same restrictions.

(b) The denominator, $(4 - x^2)$, is a difference of squares. It can be factored as $(2 - x)(2 + x)$. The numerator, $(x^2 + 4x + 4)$, is a perfect square. It can be factored as $(x + 2)(x + 2)$. So, the rational expression can be simplified as follows:

$$\frac{x^2 + 4x + 4}{4 - x^2} = \frac{(x + 2)(x + 2)}{(2 - x)(2 + x)} = \frac{(x + 2)}{(2 - x)}$$

Note that since the original expression is only defined for $x \neq \{-2, 2\}$, the simplified expression has the same restrictions.

Quadratics

Solving Quadratic Equations

Quadratic equations are a special set of trinomials of the form $y = ax^2 + bx + c$ that occur commonly in math and real-world applications. The **roots** of a quadratic equation are the solutions that satisfy the equation when $y = 0$; in other words, where the graph touches the x-axis. There are several ways to determine these solutions including using the quadratic formula, factoring, completing the square, and graphing the function.

Review Video: Quadratic Equations
Visit mometrix.com/academy and enter code: 476276

Quadratic Formula

The **quadratic formula** is used to solve quadratic equations when other methods are more difficult. To use the quadratic formula to solve a quadratic equation, begin by rewriting the equation in standard form $ax^2 + bx + c = 0$, where a, b, and c are coefficients. Once you have identified the values of the coefficients, substitute those values into the quadratic formula

$$x = \frac{-b \pm \sqrt{b^2 - 4ac}}{2a}$$

Evaluate the equation and simplify the expression. Again, check each root by substituting into the original equation. In the quadratic formula, the portion of the formula under the radical $(b^2 - 4ac)$ is called the **discriminant**. If the discriminant is zero, there is only one root: $-\frac{b}{2a}$. If the discriminant is positive, there are two different real roots. If the discriminant is negative, there are no real roots; you will instead find complex roots. Often these solutions don't make sense in context and are ignored.

Review Video: Using the Quadratic Formula
Visit mometrix.com/academy and enter code: 163102

Factoring

To solve a quadratic equation by factoring, begin by rewriting the equation in standard form, $x^2 + bx + c = 0$. Remember that the goal of factoring is to find numbers f and g such that $(x + f)(x + g) = x^2 + (f + g)x + fg$, in other words $(f + g) = b$ and $fg = c$. This can be a really useful method when b and c are integers. Determine the factors of c and look for pairs that could sum to b.

For example, consider finding the roots of $x^2 + 6x - 16 = 0$. The factors of -16 include, -4 and 4, -8 and 2, -2 and 8, -1 and 16, and 1 and -16. The factors that sum to 6 are -2 and 8. Write these factors as the product of two binomials, $0 = (x - 2)(x + 8)$. Finally, since these binomials multiply together to equal zero, set them each equal to zero and solve each for x. This results in $x - 2 = 0$, which simplifies to $x = 2$ and $x + 8 = 0$, which simplifies to $x = -8$. Therefore, the roots of the equation are 2 and -8.

Review Video: Factoring Quadratic Equations
Visit mometrix.com/academy and enter code: 336566

COMPLETING THE SQUARE

One way to find the roots of a quadratic equation is to find a way to manipulate it such that it follows the form of a perfect square $(x^2 + 2px + p^2)$ by adding and subtracting a constant. This process is called **completing the square**. In other words, if you are given a quadratic that is not a perfect square, $x^2 + bx + c = 0$, you can find a constant d that could be added in to make it a perfect square:

$$x^2 + bx + c + (d - d) = 0;\ \{\text{Let } b = 2p \text{ and } c + d = p^2\}$$
$$\text{then: } x^2 + 2px + p^2 - d = 0 \text{ and } d = \frac{b^2}{4} - c$$

Once you have completed the square you can find the roots of the resulting equation:

$$\begin{aligned} x^2 + 2px + p^2 - d &= 0 \\ (x + p)^2 &= d \\ x + p &= \pm\sqrt{d} \\ x &= -p \pm \sqrt{d} \end{aligned}$$

It is worth noting that substituting the original expressions into this solution gives the same result as the quadratic formula where $a = 1$:

$$x = -p \pm \sqrt{d} = -\frac{b}{2} \pm \sqrt{\frac{b^2}{4} - c} = -\frac{b}{2} \pm \frac{\sqrt{b^2 - 4c}}{2} = \frac{-b \pm \sqrt{b^2 - 4c}}{2}$$

Completing the square can be seen as arranging block representations of each of the terms to be as close to a square as possible and then filling in the gaps. For example, consider the quadratic expression $x^2 + 6x + 2$:

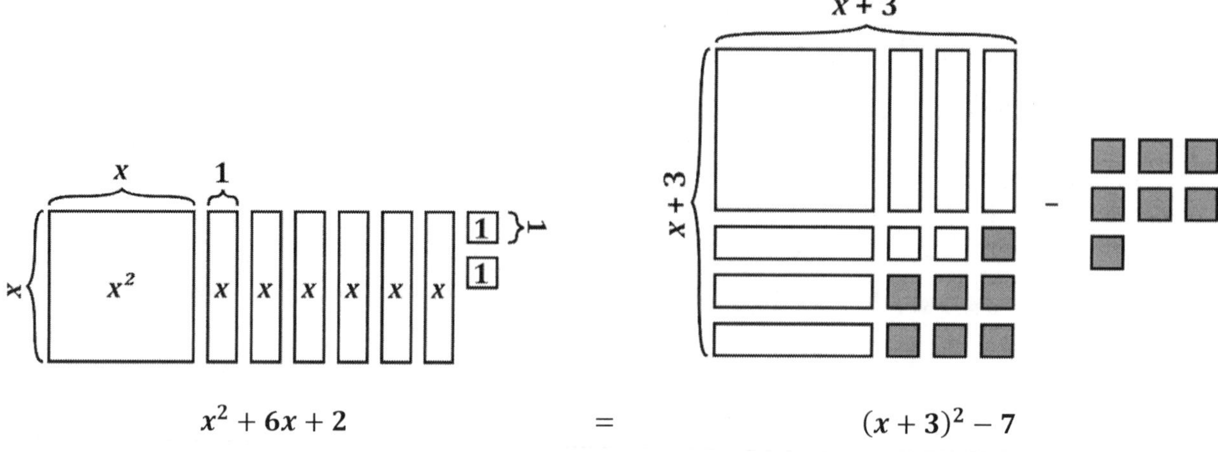

Review Video: Completing the Square
Visit mometrix.com/academy and enter code: 982479

Using Given Roots to Find Quadratic Equation

One way to find the roots of a quadratic equation is to factor the equation and use the **zero product property**, setting each factor of the equation equal to zero to find the corresponding root. We can use this technique in reverse to find an equation given its roots. Each root corresponds to a linear equation which in turn corresponds to a factor of the quadratic equation.

For example, we can find a quadratic equation whose roots are $x = 2$ and $x = -1$. The root $x = 2$ corresponds to the equation $x - 2 = 0$, and the root $x = -1$ corresponds to the equation $x + 1 = 0$.

These two equations correspond to the factors $(x - 2)$ and $(x + 1)$, from which we can derive the equation $(x - 2)(x + 1) = 0$, or $x^2 - x - 2 = 0$.

Any integer multiple of this entire equation will also yield the same roots, as the integer will simply cancel out when the equation is factored. For example, $2x^2 - 2x - 4 = 0$ factors as $2(x - 2)(x + 1) = 0$.

Solving a System of Equations Consisting of a Linear Equation and a Quadratic Equation

Algebraically

Generally, the simplest way to solve a system of equations consisting of a linear equation and a quadratic equation algebraically is through the method of substitution. One possible strategy is to solve the linear equation for y and then substitute that expression into the quadratic equation. After expansion and combining like terms, this will result in a new quadratic equation for x, which, like all quadratic equations, may have zero, one, or two solutions. Plugging each solution for x back into one of the original equations will then produce the corresponding value of y.

For example, consider the following system of equations:

$$x + y = 1$$
$$y = (x + 3)^2 - 2$$

We can solve the linear equation for y to yield $y = -x + 1$. Substituting this expression into the quadratic equation produces $-x + 1 = (x + 3)^2 - 2$. We can simplify this equation:

$$\begin{aligned} -x + 1 &= (x + 3)^2 - 2 \\ -x + 1 &= x^2 + 6x + 9 - 2 \\ -x + 1 &= x^2 + 6x + 7 \\ 0 &= x^2 + 7x + 6 \end{aligned}$$

This quadratic equation can be factored as $(x + 1)(x + 6) = 0$. It therefore has two solutions: $x_1 = -1$ and $x_2 = -6$. Plugging each of these back into the original linear equation yields $y_1 = -x_1 + 1 = -(-1) + 1 = 2$ and $y_2 = -x_2 + 1 = -(-6) + 1 = 7$. Thus, this system of equations has two solutions, $(-1,2)$ and $(-6,7)$.

It may help to check your work by putting each x and y value back into the original equations and verifying that they do provide a solution.

GRAPHICALLY

To solve a system of equations consisting of a linear equation and a quadratic equation graphically, plot both equations on the same graph. The linear equation will, of course, produce a straight line, while the quadratic equation will produce a parabola. These two graphs will intersect at zero, one, or two points; each point of intersection is a solution of the system.

For example, consider the following system of equations:

$$y = -2x + 2$$
$$y = -2x^2 + 4x + 2$$

The linear equation describes a line with a y-intercept of $(0,2)$ and a slope of -2.

To graph the quadratic equation, we can first find the vertex of the parabola: the x-coordinate of the vertex is $h = -\frac{b}{2a} = -\frac{4}{2(-2)} = 1$, and the y coordinate is $k = -2(1)^2 + 4(1) + 2 = 4$. Thus, the vertex lies at $(1,4)$. To get a feel for the rest of the parabola, we can plug in a few more values of x to find more points; by putting in $x = 2$ and $x = 3$ in the quadratic equation, we find that the points

(2,2) and $(3, -4)$ lie on the parabola; by symmetry, so must $(0, 2)$ and $(-1, -4)$. We can now plot both equations:

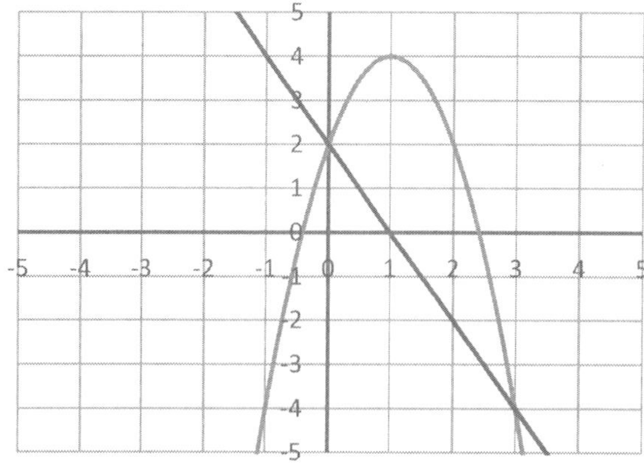

These two curves intersect at the points (0,2) and $(3, -4)$, thus these are the solutions of the equation.

Practice

P1. Find the roots of $y = 2x^2 + 8x + 4$.

P2. Find a quadratic equation with roots $x = 4$ and $x = -6$.

Practice Solutions

P1. First, substitute 0 in for y in the quadratic equation: $0 = 2x^2 + 8x + 4$

Next, try to factor the quadratic equation. Since $a \neq 1$, list the factors of ac, or 8:

$$(1,8), (-1, -8), (2,4), (-2, -4)$$

Look for the factors of ac that add up to b, or 8. Since none do, the equation cannot be factored with whole numbers. Substitute the values of a, b, and c into the quadratic formula, $x = \frac{-b \pm \sqrt{b^2 - 4ac}}{2a}$:

$$x = \frac{-8 \pm \sqrt{8^2 - 4(2)(4)}}{2(2)}$$

Use the order of operations to simplify:

$$x = \frac{-8 \pm \sqrt{64 - 32}}{4}$$

$$x = \frac{-8 \pm \sqrt{32}}{4}$$

Reduce and simplify:

$$x = \frac{-8 \pm \sqrt{(16)(2)}}{4}$$
$$x = \frac{-8 \pm 4\sqrt{2}}{4}$$
$$x = -2 \pm \sqrt{2}$$
$$x = \left(-2 + \sqrt{2}\right) \text{ and } \left(-2 - \sqrt{2}\right)$$

P2. The root $x = 4$ corresponds to the equation $x - 4 = 0$, and the root $x = -6$ corresponds to the equation $x + 6 = 0$. These two equations correspond to the factors $(x - 4)$ and $(x + 6)$, from which we can derive the equation $(x - 4)(x + 6) = 0$, or $x^2 + 2x - 24 = 0$.

Functions

Function and Relation

When expressing functional relationships, the **variables** *x* and *y* are typically used. These values are often written as the **coordinates** (x, y). The *x*-value is the independent variable and the *y*-value is the dependent variable. A **relation** is a set of data in which there is not a unique *y*-value for each *x*-value in the dataset. This means that there can be two of the same *x*-values assigned to different *y*-values. A relation is simply a relationship between the *x*- and *y*-values in each coordinate but does not apply to the relationship between the values of *x* and *y* in the data set. A **function** is a relation where one quantity depends on the other. For example, the amount of money that you make depends on the number of hours that you work. In a function, each *x*-value in the data set has one unique *y*-value because the *y*-value depends on the *x*-value.

Review Video: Definition of a Function
Visit mometrix.com/academy and enter code: 784611

Functions

A function has exactly one value of **output variable** (dependent variable) for each value of the **input variable** (independent variable). The set of all values for the input variable (here assumed to be x) is the domain of the function, and the set of all corresponding values of the output variable (here assumed to be y) is the range of the function. When looking at a graph of an equation, the easiest way to determine if the equation is a function or not is to conduct the vertical line test. If a vertical line drawn through any value of *x* crosses the graph in more than one place, the equation is not a function.

Finding the Domain and Range of a Function

The **domain** of a function $f(x)$ is the set of all input values for which the function is defined. The **range** of a function $f(x)$ is the set of all possible output values of the function—that is, of every possible value of $f(x)$, for any value of *x* in the function's domain. For a function expressed in a table, every input-output pair is given explicitly. To find the domain, we just list all the *x* values and to find the range, we just list all the values of $f(x)$. Consider the following example:

x	-1	4	2	1	0	3	8	6
$f(x)$	3	0	3	−1	−1	2	4	6

In this case, the domain would be {-1, 4, 2, 1, 0, 3, 8, 6}, or, putting them in ascending order, {-1, 0, 1, 2, 3, 4, 6, 8}. (Putting the values in ascending order isn't strictly necessary, but generally makes the set easier to read.) The range would be {3, 0, 3, −1, −1, 2, 4, 6}. Note that some of these values appear more than once. This is entirely permissible for a function; while each value of x must be matched to a unique value of $f(x)$, the converse is not true. We don't need to list each value more than once, so eliminating duplicates, the range is {3, 0, –1, 2, 4, 6}, or, putting them in ascending order, {–1, 0, 2, 3, 4, 6}.

Note that by definition of a function, no input value can be matched to more than one output value. It is good to double-check to make sure that the data given follows this and is therefore actually a function.

Review Video: Domain and Range
Visit mometrix.com/academy and enter code: 778133

Determining a Function

You can determine whether an equation is a **function** by substituting different values into the equation for x. You can display and organize these numbers in a data table. A **data table** contains the values for x and y, which you can also list as coordinates. In order for a function to exist, the table cannot contain any repeating x-values that correspond with different y-values. If each x-coordinate has a unique y-coordinate, the table contains a function. However, there can be repeating y-values that correspond with different x-values. An example of this is when the function contains an exponent. For example, if $x^2 = y$, $2^2 = 4$, and $(-2)^2 = 4$.

Writing a Function Rule Using a Table

If given a set of data, place the corresponding x- and y-values into a table and analyze the relationship between them. Consider what you can do to each x-value to obtain the corresponding y-value. Try adding or subtracting different numbers to and from x and then try multiplying or dividing different numbers to and from x. If none of these **operations** give you the y-value, try combining the operations. Once you find a rule that works for one pair, make sure to try it with each additional set of ordered pairs in the table. If the same operation or combination of operations satisfies each set of coordinates, then the table contains a function. The rule is then used to write the equation of the function in "$y =$" form.

Direct and Inverse Variations of Variables

Variables that vary directly are those that either both increase at the same rate or both decrease at the same rate. For example, in the functions $y = kx$ or $y = kx^n$, where k and n are positive, the value of y increases as the value of x increases and decreases as the value of x decreases.

Variables that vary inversely are those where one increases while the other decreases. For example, in the functions $y = \frac{k}{x}$ or $y = \frac{k}{x^n}$ where k and n are positive, the value of y increases as the value of x decreases and decreases as the value of x increases.

In both cases, k is the constant of variation.

Properties of Functions

There are many different ways to classify functions based on their structure or behavior. Important features of functions include:

- **End behavior**: the behavior of the function at extreme values ($f(x)$ as $x \to \pm\infty$)
- **y-intercept**: the value of the function at $f(0)$

- **Roots**: the values of x where the function equals zero $(f(x) = 0)$
- **Extrema**: minimum or maximum values of the function or where the function changes direction $(f(x) \geq k$ or $f(x) \leq k)$

Classification of Functions

An **invertible function** is defined as a function, $f(x)$, for which there is another function, $f^{-1}(x)$, such that $f^{-1}(f(x)) = x$. For example, if $f(x) = 3x - 2$ the inverse function, $f^{-1}(x)$, can be found:

$$x = 3(f^{-1}(x)) - 2$$
$$\frac{x+2}{3} = f^{-1}(x)$$

$$f^{-1}(f(x)) = \frac{3x - 2 + 2}{3} = \frac{3x}{3} = x$$

Note that $f^{-1}(x)$ is a valid function over all values of x.

In a **one-to-one function**, each value of x has exactly one value for y on the coordinate plane (this is the definition of a function) and each value of y has exactly one value for x. While the vertical line test will determine if a graph is that of a function, the horizontal line test will determine if a function is a one-to-one function. If a horizontal line drawn at any value of y intersects the graph in more than one place, the graph is not that of a one-to-one function. Do not make the mistake of using the horizontal line test exclusively in determining if a graph is that of a one-to-one function. A one-to-one function must pass both the vertical line test and the horizontal line test. As such, one-to-one functions are invertible functions.

A **many-to-one function** is a function whereby the relation is a function, but the inverse of the function is not a function. In other words, each element in the domain is mapped to one and only one element in the range. However, one or more elements in the range may be mapped to the same element in the domain. A graph of a many-to-one function would pass the vertical line test, but not the horizontal line test. This is why many-to-one functions are not invertible.

A **monotone function** is a function whose graph either constantly increases or constantly decreases. Examples include the functions $f(x) = x$, $f(x) = -x$, or $f(x) = x^3$.

An **even function** has a graph that is symmetric with respect to the y-axis and satisfies the equation $f(x) = f(-x)$. Examples include the functions $f(x) = x^2$ and $f(x) = ax^n$, where a is any real number and n is a positive even integer.

An **odd function** has a graph that is symmetric with respect to the origin and satisfies the equation $f(x) = -f(-x)$. Examples include the functions $f(x) = x^3$ and $f(x) = ax^n$, where a is any real number and n is a positive odd integer.

Constant functions are given by the equation $f(x) = b$, where b is a real number. There is no independent variable present in the equation, so the function has a constant value for all x. The graph of a constant function is a horizontal line of slope 0 that is positioned b units from the x-axis. If b is positive, the line is above the x-axis; if b is negative, the line is below the x-axis.

Identity functions are identified by the equation $f(x) = x$, where every value of the function is equal to its corresponding value of x. The only zero is the point (0, 0). The graph is a line with a slope of 1.

In **linear functions**, the value of the function changes in direct proportion to x. The rate of change, represented by the slope on its graph, is constant throughout. The standard form of a linear equation is $ax + cy = d$, where a, c, and d are real numbers. As a function, this equation is commonly in the form $y = mx + b$ or $f(x) = mx + b$ where $m = -\frac{a}{c}$ and $b = \frac{d}{c}$. This is known as the slope-intercept form, because the coefficients give the slope of the graphed function (m) and its y-intercept (b). Solve the equation $mx + b = 0$ for x to get $x = -\frac{b}{m}$, which is the only zero of the function. The domain and range are both the set of all real numbers.

Algebraic functions are those that exclusively use polynomials and roots. These would include polynomial functions, rational functions, square root functions, and all combinations of these functions, such as polynomials as the radicand. These combinations may be joined by addition, subtraction, multiplication, or division, but may not include variables as exponents.

Review Video: Common Functions
Visit mometrix.com/academy and enter code: 629798

Review Video: Even and Odd Functions
Visit mometrix.com/academy and enter code: 278985

Absolute Value Functions

An **absolute value function** is in the format $f(x) = |ax + b|$. Like other functions, the domain is the set of all real numbers. However, because absolute value indicates positive numbers, the range is limited to positive real numbers. To find the zero of an absolute value function, set the portion inside the absolute value sign equal to zero and solve for x. An absolute value function is also known as a piecewise function because it must be solved in pieces—one for if the value inside the absolute value sign is positive, and one for if the value is negative. The function can be expressed as

$$f(x) = \begin{cases} ax + b \text{ if } ax + b \geq 0 \\ -(ax + b) \text{ if } ax + b < 0 \end{cases}$$

This will allow for an accurate statement of the range. The graph of an example absolute value function, $f(x) = |2x - 1|$, is below:

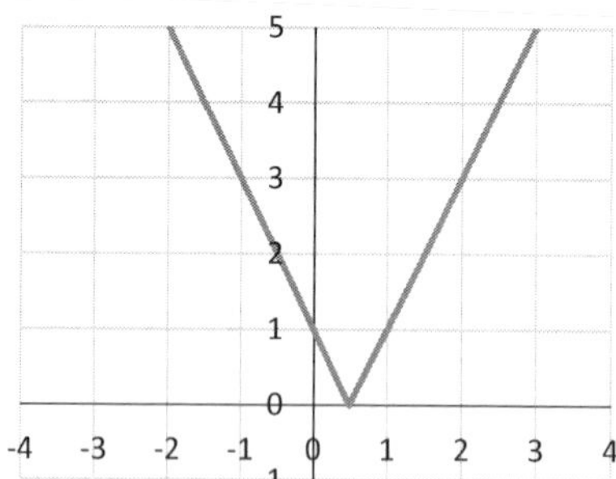

Piecewise Functions

A **piecewise function** is a function that has different definitions on two or more different intervals. The following, for instance, is one example of a piecewise-defined function:

$$f(x) = \begin{cases} x^2, & x < 0 \\ x, & 0 \leq x \leq 2 \\ (x-2)^2, & x > 2 \end{cases}$$

To graph this function, you would simply graph each part separately in the appropriate domain. The final graph would look like this:

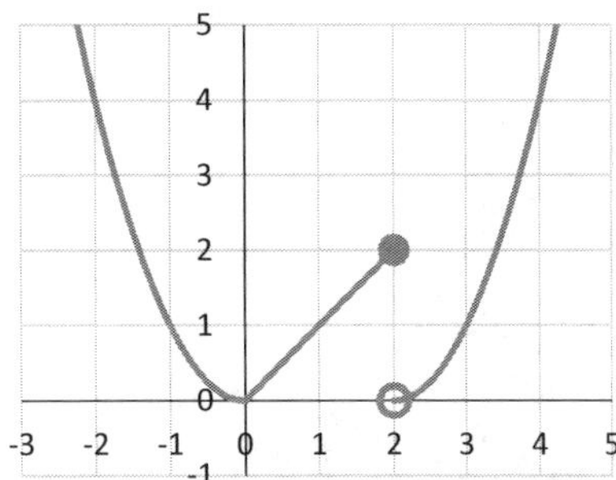

Note the filled and hollow dots at the discontinuity at $x = 2$. This is important to show which side of the graph that point corresponds to. Because $f(x) = x$ on the closed interval $0 \leq x \leq 2$, $f(2) = 2$. The point $(2, 2)$ is therefore marked with a filled circle, and the point (2,0), which is the endpoint of the rightmost $(x - 2)^2$ part of the graph but *not actually part of the function*, is marked with a hollow dot to indicate this.

Review Video: Piecewise Functions
Visit mometrix.com/academy and enter code: 707921

Quadratic Functions

A **quadratic function** is a function in the form $y = ax^2 + bx + c$, where a does not equal 0. While a linear function forms a line, a quadratic function forms a **parabola**, which is a u-shaped figure that either opens upward or downward. A parabola that opens upward is said to be a **positive quadratic function,** and a parabola that opens downward is said to be a **negative quadratic function**. The shape of a parabola can differ, depending on the values of *a*, *b,* and *c*. All parabolas contain a **vertex**, which is the highest possible point, the **maximum**, or the lowest possible point, the **minimum**. This is the point where the graph begins moving in the opposite direction. A quadratic function can have zero, one, or two solutions, and therefore zero, one, or two x-intercepts. Recall that the x-intercepts are referred to as the zeros, or roots, of a function. A quadratic function will have only one y-intercept. Understanding the basic components of a quadratic function can give you an idea of the shape of its graph.

Review Video: Solutions of a Quadratic Equation on a Graph
Visit mometrix.com/academy and enter code: 328231

Example graph of a positive quadratic function, $x^2 + 2x - 3$:

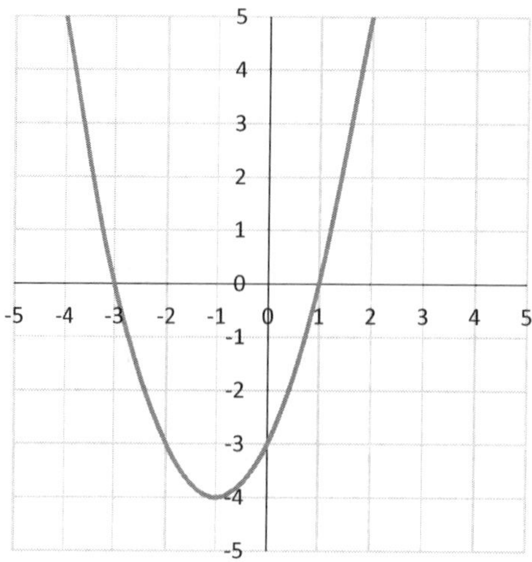

Polynomial Functions

A **polynomial function** is a function with multiple terms and multiple powers of *x*, such as:

$$f(x) = a_n x^n + a_{n-1}x^{n-1} + a_{n-2}x^{n-2} + \cdots + a_1 x + a_0$$

where *n* is a non-negative integer that is the highest exponent in the polynomial and $a_n \neq 0$. The domain of a polynomial function is the set of all real numbers. If the greatest exponent in the polynomial is even, the polynomial is said to be of even degree and the range is the set of real numbers that satisfy the function. If the greatest exponent in the polynomial is odd, the polynomial is said to be odd and the range, like the domain, is the set of all real numbers.

Review Video: Simplifying Rational Polynomial Functions
Visit mometrix.com/academy and enter code: 351038

Rational Functions

A **rational function** is a function that can be constructed as a ratio of two polynomial expressions: $f(x) = \frac{p(x)}{q(x)}$, where $p(x)$ and $q(x)$ are both polynomial expressions and $q(x) \neq 0$. The domain is the set of all real numbers, except any values for which $q(x) = 0$. The range is the set of real numbers that satisfies the function when the domain is applied. When you graph a rational function, you will have vertical asymptotes wherever $q(x) = 0$. If the polynomial in the numerator is of lesser degree than the polynomial in the denominator, the *x*-axis will also be a horizontal asymptote. If the numerator and denominator have equal degrees, there will be a horizontal asymptote not on the *x*-axis. If the degree of the numerator is exactly one greater than the degree of the denominator, the graph will have an oblique, or diagonal, asymptote. The asymptote will be along the line $y = \frac{p_n}{q_{n-1}}x + \frac{p_{n-1}}{q_{n-1}}$, where p_n and q_{n-1} are the coefficients of the highest degree terms in their respective polynomials.

Square Root Functions

A **square root function** is a function that contains a radical and is in the format $f(x) = \sqrt{ax + b}$. The domain is the set of all real numbers that yields a positive radicand or a radicand equal to zero. Because square root values are assumed to be positive unless otherwise identified, the range is all real numbers from zero to infinity. To find the zero of a square root function, set the radicand equal to zero and solve for x. The graph of a square root function is always to the right of the zero and always above the x-axis.

Example graph of a square root function, $f(x) = \sqrt{2x+1}$:

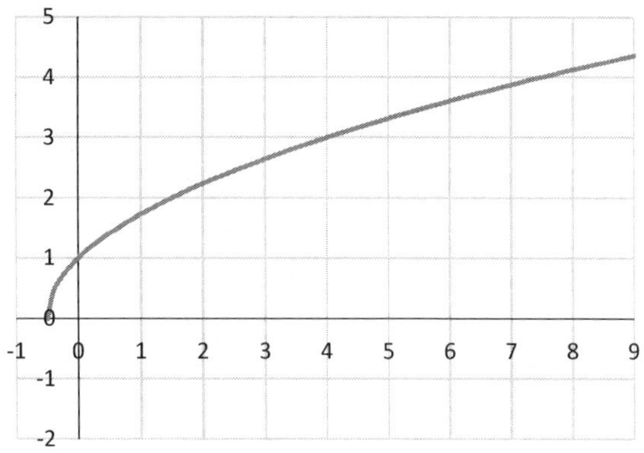

Practice

P1. Martin needs a 20% medicine solution. The pharmacy has a 5% solution and a 30% solution. He needs 50 mL of the solution. If the pharmacist must mix the two solutions, how many milliliters of 5% solution and 30% solution should be used?

P2. Describe two different strategies for solving the following problem:

> Kevin can mow the yard in 4 hours. Mandy can mow the same yard in 5 hours. If they work together, how long will it take them to mow the yard?

P3. A car, traveling at 65 miles per hour, leaves Flagstaff and heads east on I-40. Another car, traveling at 75 miles per hour, leaves Flagstaff 2 hours later, from the same starting point and also heads east on I-40. Determine how many hours it will take the second car to catch the first car by:

(a) Using a table.

(b) Using algebra.

Practice Solutions

P1. To solve this problem, a table may be created to represent the variables, percentages, and total amount of solution. Such a table is shown below:

	mL solution	% medicine	Total mL medicine
5% solution	x	0.05	$0.05x$
30% solution	y	0.30	$0.30y$
Mixture	$x + y = 50$	0.20	$(0.20)(50) = 10$

The variable x may be rewritten as $50 - y$, so the equation $0.05(50 - y) + 0.30y = 10$ may be written and solved for y. Doing so gives $y = 30$. So, 30 mL of 30% solution are needed. Evaluating the expression, $50 - y$ for an x-value of 20, shows that 20 mL of 5% solution are needed.

P2. Two possible strategies both involve the use of rational equations to solve. The first strategy involves representing the fractional part of the yard mowed by each person in one hour and setting this sum equal to the ratio of 1 to the total time needed. The appropriate equation is $1/4 + 1/5 =$

$1/t$, which simplifies as $9/20 = 1/t$, and finally as $t = 20/9$. So the time it will take them to mow the yard, when working together, is a little more than 2.2 hours.

A second strategy involves representing the time needed for each person as two fractions and setting the sum equal to 1 (representing 1 yard). The appropriate equation is $t/4 + t/5 = 1$, which simplifies as $9t/20 = 1$, and finally as $t = 20/9$. This strategy also shows the total time to be a little more than 2.2 hours.

P3. (a) One strategy might involve creating a table of values for the number of hours and distances for each car. The table may be examined to find the same distance traveled and the corresponding number of hours taken. Such a table is shown below:

Car A		Car B	
x (hours)	**y (distance)**	**x (hours)**	**y (distance)**
0	0	0	
1	65	1	
2	130	2	0
3	195	3	75
4	260	4	150
5	325	5	225
6	390	6	300
7	455	7	375
8	520	8	450
9	585	9	525
10	650	10	600
11	715	11	675
12	780	12	750
13	845	13	825
14	910	14	900
15	975	15	975

The table shows that after 15 hours, the distance traveled is the same. Thus, the second car catches up with the first car after a distance of 975 miles and 15 hours.

(b) A second strategy might involve setting up and solving an algebraic equation. This situation may be modeled as $65x = 75(x - 2)$. This equation sets the distances traveled by each car equal to one another. Solving for *x* gives $x = 15$. Thus, once again, the second car will catch up with the first car after 15 hours.

Geometric and Spatial Reasoning

Units of Measurement

Metric Measurement Prefixes

Giga-: one billion (1 *giga*watt is one billion watts)
Mega-: one million (1 *mega*hertz is one million hertz)
Kilo-: one thousand (1 *kilo*gram is one thousand grams)
Deci-: one-tenth (1 *deci*meter is one-tenth of a meter)
Centi-: one-hundredth (1 *centi*meter is one-hundredth of a meter)
Milli-: one-thousandth (1 *milli*liter is one-thousandth of a liter)
Micro-: one-millionth (1 *micro*gram is one-millionth of a gram)

Measurement Conversion

When converting between units, the goal is to maintain the same meaning but change the way it is displayed. In order to go from a larger unit to a smaller unit, multiply the number of the known amount by the equivalent amount. When going from a smaller unit to a larger unit, divide the number of the known amount by the equivalent amount.

Review Video: Metric System Conversions
Visit mometrix.com/academy and enter code: 163709

For complicated conversions, it may be helpful to set up conversion fractions. In these fractions, one fraction is the **conversion factor**. The other fraction has the unknown amount in the numerator. So, the known value is placed in the denominator. Sometimes, the second fraction has the known value from the problem in the numerator and the unknown in the denominator. Multiply the two fractions to get the converted measurement. Note that since the numerator and the denominator of the factor are equivalent, the value of the fraction is 1. That is why we can say that the result in the new units is equal to the result in the old units even though they have different numbers.

It can often be necessary to chain known conversion factors together. As an example, consider converting 512 square inches to square meters. We know that there are 2.54 centimeters in an inch and 100 centimeters in a meter, and we know we will need to square each of these factors to achieve the conversion we are looking for.

$$\frac{512\text{ in}^2}{1}\times\left(\frac{2.54\text{ cm}}{1\text{ in}}\right)^2\times\left(\frac{1\text{ m}}{100\text{ cm}}\right)^2=\frac{512\,\cancel{\text{in}^2}}{1}\times\left(\frac{6.4516\,\cancel{\text{cm}^2}}{1\,\cancel{\text{in}^2}}\right)\times\left(\frac{1\text{ m}^2}{10000\,\cancel{\text{cm}^2}}\right)=0.330\text{ m}^2$$

Review Video: Measurement Conversion
Visit mometrix.com/academy and enter code: 316703

Common Units and Equivalents

Metric Equivalents

1000 μg (microgram)	1 mg
1000 mg (milligram)	1 g
1000 g (gram)	1 kg
1000 kg (kilogram)	1 metric ton
1000 mL (milliliter)	1 L
1000 μm (micrometer)	1 mm
1000 mm (millimeter)	1 m
100 cm (centimeter)	1 m
1000 m (meter)	1 km

Distance and Area Measurement

Unit	Abbreviation	US equivalent	Metric equivalent
Inch	in	1 inch	2.54 centimeters
Foot	ft	12 inches	0.305 meters
Yard	yd	3 feet	0.914 meters
Mile	mi	5280 feet	1.609 kilometers
Acre	ac	4840 square yards	0.405 hectares
Square Mile	sq. mi. or mi.^2	640 acres	2.590 square kilometers

Capacity Measurements

Unit	Abbreviation	US equivalent	Metric equivalent
Fluid Ounce	fl oz	8 fluid drams	29.573 milliliters
Cup	c	8 fluid ounces	0.237 liter
Pint	pt.	16 fluid ounces	0.473 liter
Quart	qt.	2 pints	0.946 liter
Gallon	gal.	4 quarts	3.785 liters
Teaspoon	t or tsp.	1 fluid dram	5 milliliters
Tablespoon	T or tbsp.	4 fluid drams	15 or 16 milliliters
Cubic Centimeter	cc or cm.^{3}	0.271 drams	1 milliliter

Weight Measurements

Unit	Abbreviation	US equivalent	Metric equivalent
Ounce	oz	16 drams	28.35 grams
Pound	lb	16 ounces	453.6 grams
Ton	tn.	2,000 pounds	907.2 kilograms

Volume and Weight Measurement Clarifications

Always be careful when using ounces and fluid ounces. They are not equivalent.

$$1 \text{ pint} = 16 \text{ fluid ounces} \qquad 1 \text{ fluid ounce} \neq 1 \text{ ounce}$$
$$1 \text{ pound} = 16 \text{ ounces} \qquad 1 \text{ pint} \neq 1 \text{ pound}$$

Having one pint of something does not mean you have one pound of it. In the same way, just because something weighs one pound does not mean that its volume is one pint.

In the United States, the word "ton" by itself refers to a short ton or a net ton. Do not confuse this with a long ton (also called a gross ton) or a metric ton (also spelled *tonne*), which have different measurement equivalents.

$$1 \text{ US ton} = 2000 \text{ pounds} \quad \neq \quad 1 \text{ metric ton} = 1000 \text{ kilograms}$$

PRACTICE

P1. Perform the following conversions:

(a) 1.4 meters to centimeters

(b) 218 centimeters to meters

(c) 42 inches to feet

(d) 15 kilograms to pounds

(e) 80 ounces to pounds

(f) 2 miles to kilometers

(g) 5 feet to centimeters

(h) 15.14 liters to gallons

(i) 8 quarts to liters

(j) 13.2 pounds to grams

PRACTICE SOLUTIONS

P1. (a) $\frac{100 \text{ cm}}{1 \text{ m}} = \frac{x \text{ cm}}{1.4 \text{ m}}$ Cross multiply to get $x = 140$

(b) $\frac{100 \text{ cm}}{1 \text{ m}} = \frac{218 \text{ cm}}{x \text{ m}}$ Cross multiply to get $100x = 218$, or $x = 2.18$

(c) $\frac{12 \text{ in}}{1 \text{ ft}} = \frac{42 \text{ in}}{x \text{ ft}}$ Cross multiply to get $12x = 42$, or $x = 3.5$

(d) $15 \text{ kilograms} \times \frac{2.2 \text{ pounds}}{1 \text{ kilogram}} = 33 \text{ pounds}$

(e) $80 \text{ ounces} \times \frac{1 \text{ pound}}{16 \text{ ounces}} = 5 \text{ pounds}$

(f) $2 \text{ miles} \times \frac{1.609 \text{ kilometers}}{1 \text{ mile}} = 3.218 \text{ kilometers}$

(g) $5 \text{ feet} \times \frac{12 \text{ inches}}{1 \text{ foot}} \times \frac{2.54 \text{ centimeters}}{1 \text{ inch}} = 152.4 \text{ centimeters}$

(h) $15.14 \text{ liters} \times \frac{1 \text{ gallon}}{3.785 \text{ liters}} = 4 \text{ gallons}$

(i) $8 \text{ quarts} \times \frac{1 \text{ gallon}}{4 \text{ quarts}} \times \frac{3.785 \text{ liters}}{1 \text{ gallon}} = 7.57 \text{ liters}$

(j) $13.2 \text{ pounds} \times \frac{1 \text{ kilogram}}{2.2 \text{ pounds}} \times \frac{1000 \text{ grams}}{1 \text{ kilogram}} = 6000 \text{ grams}$

LINES AND PLANES

A **point** is a fixed location in space, has no size or dimensions, and is commonly represented by a dot. A **line** is a set of points that extends infinitely in two opposite directions. It has length, but no width or depth. A line can be defined by any two distinct points that it contains. A **line segment** is a portion of a line that has definite endpoints. A **ray** is a portion of a line that extends from a single point on that line in one direction along the line. It has a definite beginning, but no ending.

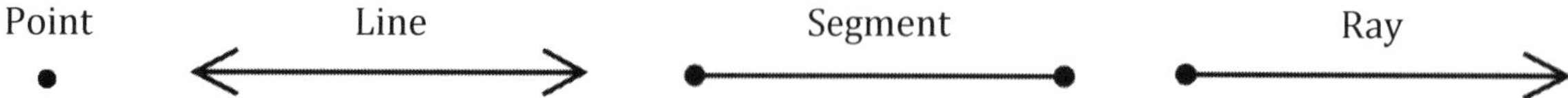

INTERACTIONS BETWEEN LINES

Intersecting lines are lines that have exactly one point in common. **Concurrent lines** are multiple lines that intersect at a single point. **Perpendicular lines** are lines that intersect at right angles. They are represented by the symbol ⊥. The shortest distance from a line to a point not on the line is a perpendicular segment from the point to the line. **Parallel lines** are lines in the same plane that have no points in common and never meet. It is possible for lines to be in different planes, have no points in common, and never meet, but they are not parallel because they are in different planes.

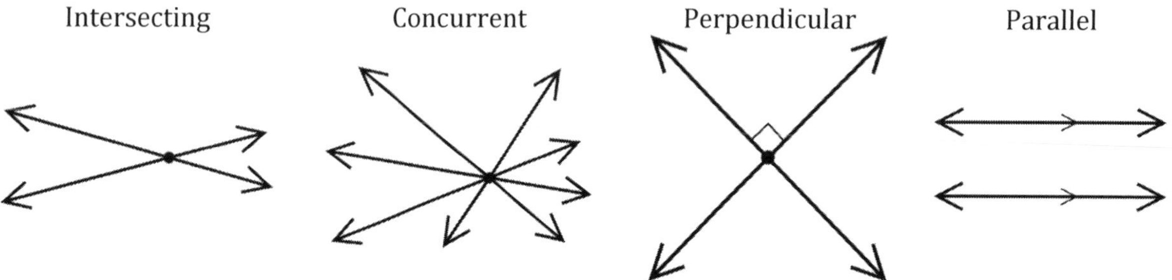

A **transversal** is a line that intersects at least two other lines, which may or may not be parallel to one another. A transversal that intersects parallel lines is a common occurrence in geometry. A **bisector** is a line or line segment that divides another line segment into two equal lengths. A **perpendicular bisector** of a line segment is composed of points that are equidistant from the endpoints of the segment it is dividing.

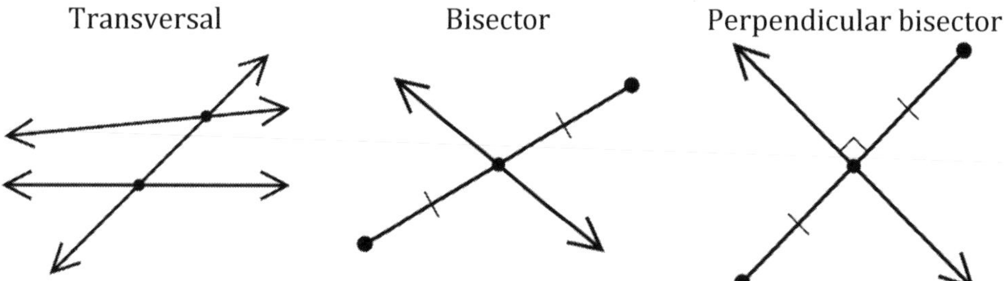

The **projection of a point on a line** is the point at which a perpendicular line drawn from the given point to the given line intersects the line. This is also the shortest distance from the given point to the line. The **projection of a segment on a line** is a segment whose endpoints are the points formed when perpendicular lines are drawn from the endpoints of the given segment to the given line. This is similar to the length a diagonal line appears to be when viewed from above.

Projection of a point on a line

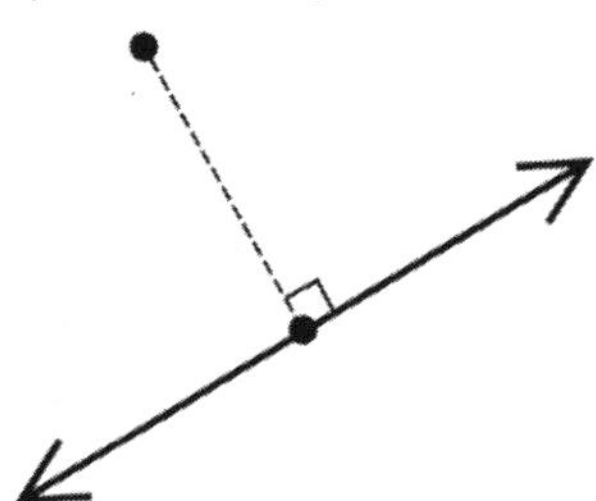

Projection of a segment on a line

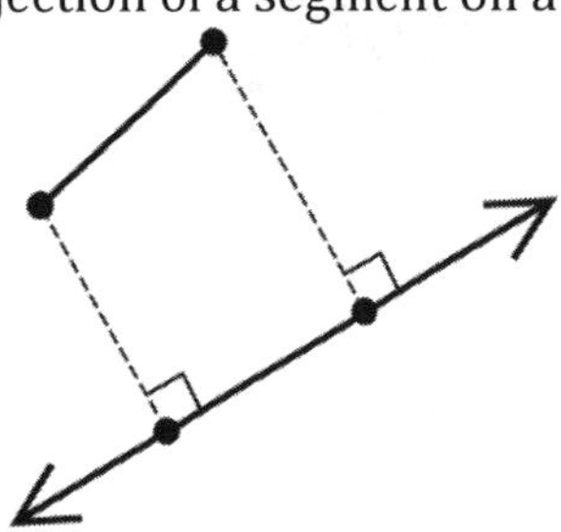

PLANES

A **plane** is a two-dimensional flat surface defined by three non-collinear points. A plane extends an infinite distance in all directions in those two dimensions. It contains an infinite number of points, parallel lines and segments, intersecting lines and segments, as well as parallel or intersecting rays. A plane will never contain a three-dimensional figure or skew lines, which are lines that don't intersect and are not parallel. Two given planes are either parallel or they intersect at a line. A plane may intersect a circular conic surface to form **conic sections**, such as a parabola, hyperbola, circle or ellipse.

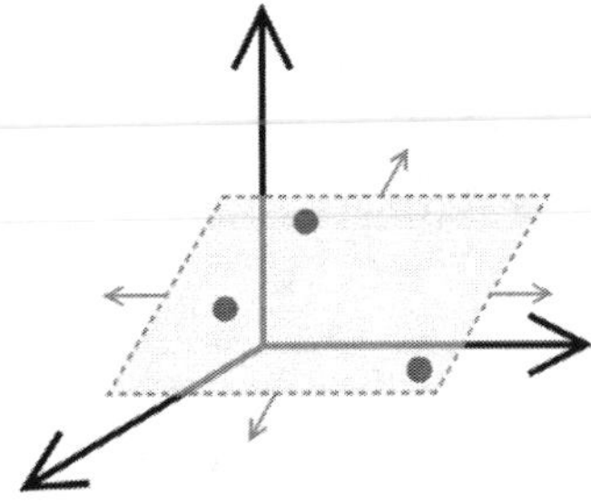

Review Video: Lines and Planes
Visit mometrix.com/academy and enter code: 554267

ANGLES

ANGLES AND VERTICES

An **angle** is formed when two lines or line segments meet at a common point. It may be a common starting point for a pair of segments or rays, or it may be the intersection of lines. Angles are represented by the symbol ∠.

The **vertex** is the point at which two segments or rays meet to form an angle. If the angle is formed by intersecting rays, lines, and/or line segments, the vertex is the point at which four angles are formed. The pairs of angles opposite one another are called vertical angles, and their measures are equal.

- An **acute** angle is an angle with a degree measure less than 90°.
- A **right** angle is an angle with a degree measure of exactly 90°.
- An **obtuse** angle is an angle with a degree measure greater than 90° but less than 180°.
- A **straight angle** is an angle with a degree measure of exactly 180°. This is also a semicircle.

- A **reflex angle** is an angle with a degree measure greater than 180° but less than 360°.

A **full angle** is an angle with a degree measure of exactly 360°. This is also a circle.

Relationships between Angles

Two angles whose sum is exactly 90° are said to be **complementary**. The two angles may or may not be adjacent. In a right triangle, the two acute angles are complementary.

Two angles whose sum is exactly 180° are said to be **supplementary**. The two angles may or may not be adjacent. Two intersecting lines always form two pairs of supplementary angles. Adjacent supplementary angles will always form a straight line.

Two angles that have the same vertex and share a side are said to be **adjacent**. Vertical angles are not adjacent because they share a vertex but no common side.

When two parallel lines are cut by a transversal, the angles that are between the two parallel lines are **interior angles**. In the diagram below, angles 3, 4, 5, and 6 are interior angles.

When two parallel lines are cut by a transversal, the angles that are outside the parallel lines are **exterior angles**. In the diagram below, angles 1, 2, 7, and 8 are exterior angles.

When two parallel lines are cut by a transversal, the angles that are in the same position relative to the transversal and a parallel line are **corresponding angles**. The diagram below has four pairs of corresponding angles: angles 1 and 5, angles 2 and 6, angles 3 and 7, and angles 4 and 8. Corresponding angles formed by parallel lines are congruent.

When two parallel lines are cut by a transversal, the two interior angles that are on opposite sides of the transversal are called **alternate interior angles**. In the diagram below, there are two pairs of alternate interior angles: angles 3 and 6, and angles 4 and 5. Alternate interior angles formed by parallel lines are congruent.

When two parallel lines are cut by a transversal, the two exterior angles that are on opposite sides of the transversal are called **alternate exterior angles**.

Review Video: Angles
Visit mometrix.com/academy and enter code: 264624

In the diagram below, there are two pairs of alternate exterior angles: angles 1 and 8, and angles 2 and 7. Alternate exterior angles formed by parallel lines are congruent.

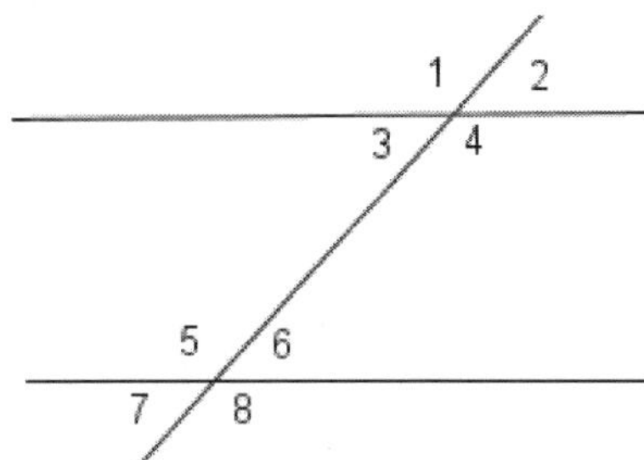

When two lines intersect, four angles are formed. The non-adjacent angles at this vertex are called vertical angles. Vertical angles are congruent. In the diagram, $\angle ABD \cong \angle CBE$ and $\angle ABC \cong \angle DBE$.

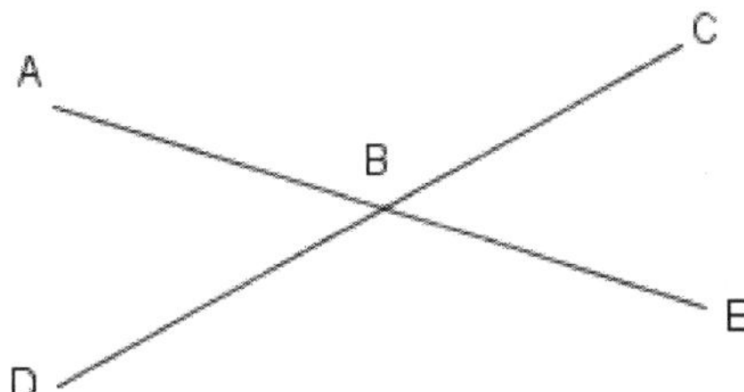

Practice

P1. Find the measure of angles **(a)**, **(b)**, and **(c)** based on the figure with two parallel lines, two perpendicular lines and one transversal:

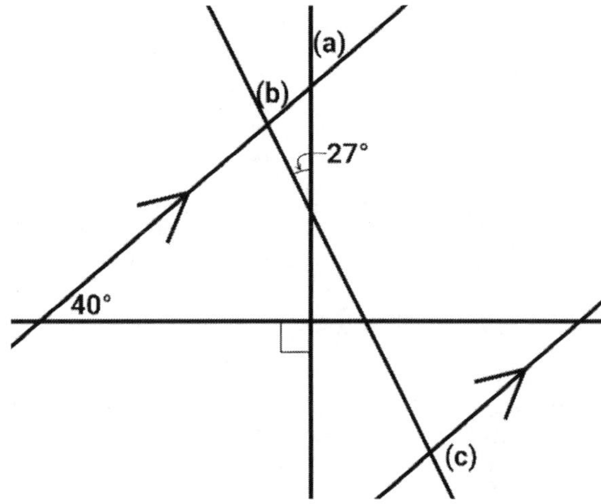

Practice Solutions

P1. (a) The vertical angle paired with (a) is part of a right triangle with the 40° angle. Thus the measure can be found:

$$90° = 40° + a$$
$$a = 50°$$

(b) The triangle formed by the supplementary angle to (b) is part of a triangle with the vertical angle paired with (a) and the given angle of 27°. Since $a = 50°$:

$$\begin{aligned} 180° &= (180° - b) + 50° + 27° \\ 103° &= 180° - b \\ -77° &= -b \\ 77° &= b \end{aligned}$$

(c) As they are part of a transversal crossing parallel lines, angles (b) and (c) are supplementary. Thus $c = 103°$

$$V = \frac{1}{3}\pi r^2 h = \frac{1}{3}\pi(5\text{ yd})^2(7\text{ yd}) = \frac{35\pi}{3}\text{ yd}^3 \cong 36.65\text{ yd}^3$$

Two-Dimensional Shapes

Polygons

A **polygon** is a closed, two-dimensional figure with three or more straight line segments called **sides**. The point at which two sides of a polygon intersect is called the **vertex**. In a polygon, the number of sides is always equal to the number of vertices. A polygon with all sides congruent and all angles equal is called a **regular polygon**. Common polygons are:

$$\begin{aligned} \text{Triangle} &= 3\text{ sides} \\ \text{Quadrilateral} &= 4\text{ sides} \\ \text{Pentagon} &= 5\text{ sides} \\ \text{Hexagon} &= 6\text{ sides} \\ \text{Heptagon} &= 7\text{ sides} \\ \text{Octagon} &= 8\text{ sides} \\ \text{Nonagon} &= 9\text{ sides} \\ \text{Decagon} &= 10\text{ sides} \\ \text{Dodecagon} &= 12\text{ sides} \end{aligned}$$

More generally, an n-gon is a polygon that has n angles and n sides.

The sum of the interior angles of an n-sided polygon is $(n - 2) \times 180°$. For example, in a triangle $n = 3$. So the sum of the interior angles is $(3 - 2) \times 180° = 180°$. In a quadrilateral, $n = 4$, and the sum of the angles is $(4 - 2) \times 180° = 360°$.

Apothem and Radius

A line segment from the center of a polygon that is perpendicular to a side of the polygon is called the **apothem**. A line segment from the center of a polygon to a vertex of the polygon is called a

radius. In a regular polygon, the apothem can be used to find the area of the polygon using the formula $A = \frac{1}{2}ap$, where a is the apothem, and p is the perimeter.

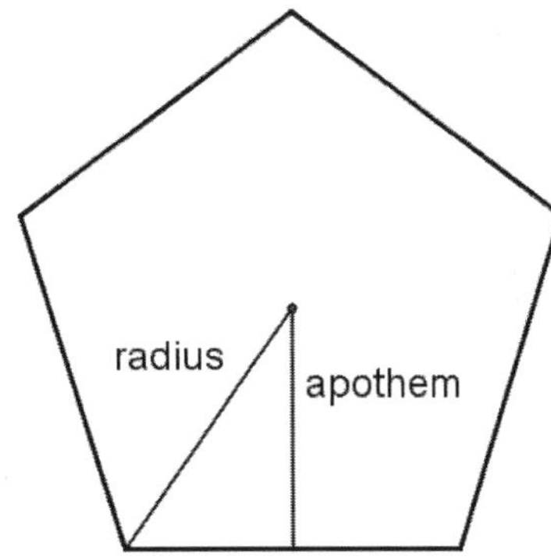

A **diagonal** is a line segment that joins two non-adjacent vertices of a polygon. The number of diagonals a polygon has can be found by using the formula:

$$\text{number of diagonals} = \frac{n(n-3)}{2}$$

Note that n is the number of sides in the polygon. This formula works for all polygons, not just regular polygons.

Review Video: Diagonals of Parallelograms, Rectangles, and Rhombi
Visit mometrix.com/academy and enter code: 320040

Convex and Concave Polygons

A **convex polygon** is a polygon whose diagonals all lie within the interior of the polygon. A **concave polygon** is a polygon with a least one diagonal that is outside the polygon. In the diagram below, quadrilateral $ABCD$ is concave because diagonal $\overline{AC}$ lies outside the polygon and quadrilateral $EFGH$ is convex because both diagonals lie inside the polygon

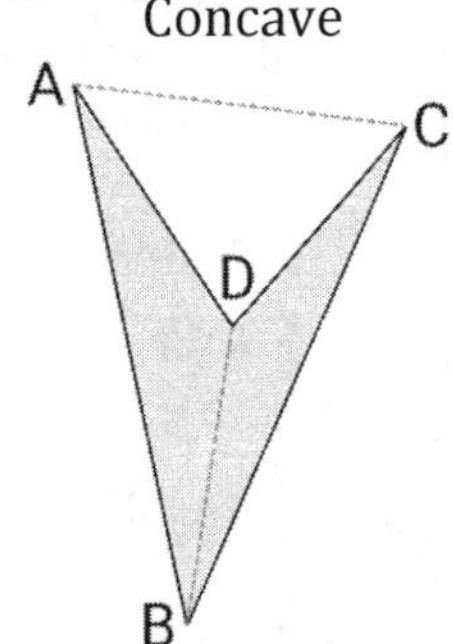

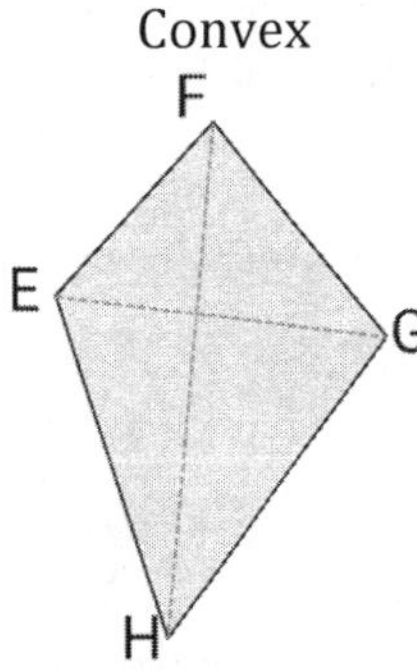

Congruence and Similarity

Congruent figures are geometric figures that have the same size and shape. All corresponding angles are equal, and all corresponding sides are equal. Congruence is indicated by the symbol $\cong$.

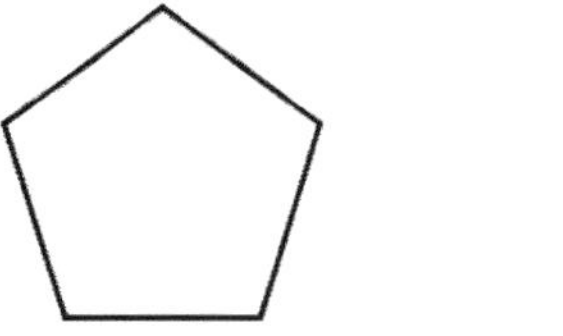
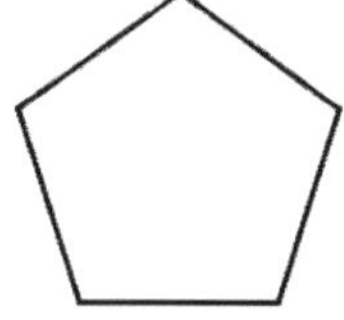

Congruent polygons

Similar figures are geometric figures that have the same shape, but do not necessarily have the same size. All corresponding angles are equal, and all corresponding sides are proportional, but they do not have to be equal. It is indicated by the symbol $\sim$.

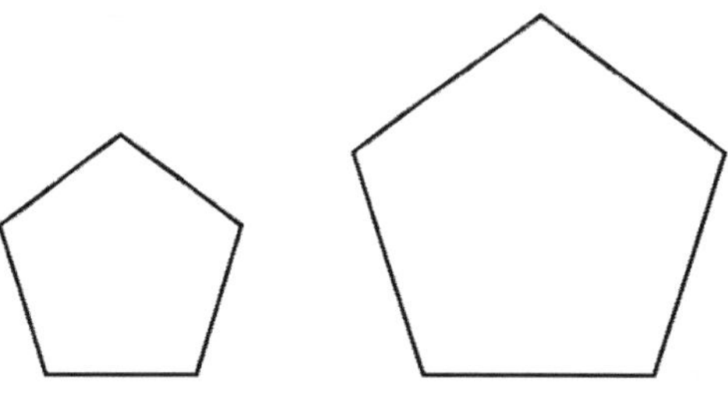

Similar polygons

Note that all congruent figures are also similar, but not all similar figures are congruent.

Review Video: Intro to Polygons
Visit mometrix.com/academy and enter code: 271869

Line of Symmetry

A line that divides a figure or object into congruent parts is called a **line of symmetry**. An object may have no lines of symmetry, one line of symmetry, or multiple (i.e., more than one) lines of symmetry.

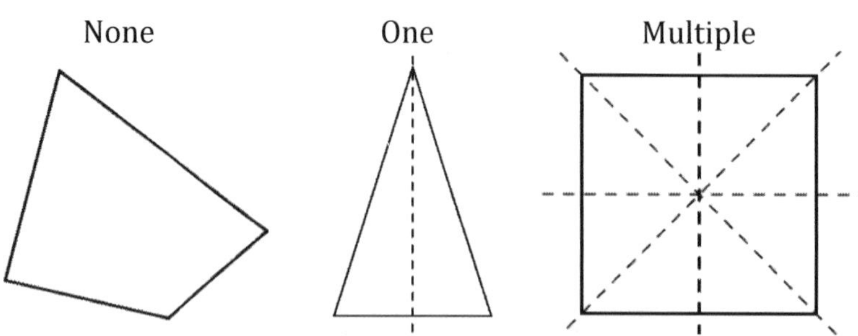

Review Video: Symmetry
Visit mometrix.com/academy and enter code: 528106

TRIANGLES

A triangle is a three-sided figure with the sum of its interior angles being 180°. The **perimeter of any triangle** is found by summing the three side lengths; $P = a + b + c$. For an equilateral triangle, this is the same as $P = 3a$, where a is any side length, since all three sides are the same length.

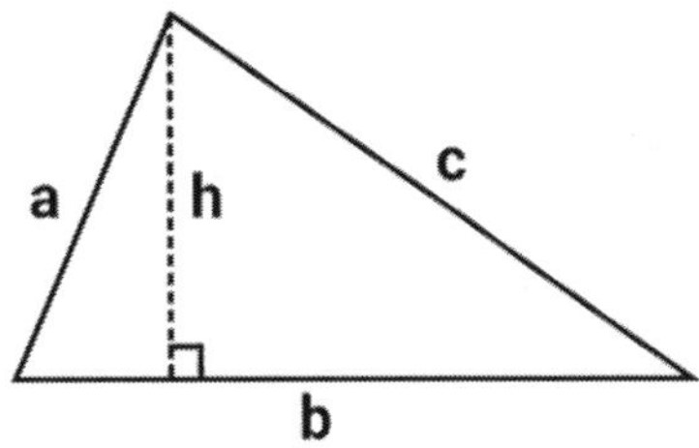

The **area of any triangle** can be found by taking half the product of one side length, referred to as the base and often given the variable b, and the perpendicular distance from that side to the opposite vertex, called the altitude or height and given the variable h. In equation form that is $A = \frac{1}{2}bh$. Another formula that works for any triangle is $A = \sqrt{s(s-a)(s-b)(s-c)}$, where s is the semiperimeter: $\frac{a+b+c}{2}$, and a, b, and c are the lengths of the three sides. Special cases include isosceles triangles, $A = \frac{1}{2}b\sqrt{a^2 - \frac{b^2}{4}}$, where b is the unique side and a is the length of one of the two congruent sides, and equilateral triangles, $A = \frac{\sqrt{3}}{4}a^2$, where a is the length of a side.

Review Video: Area and Perimeter of a Triangle
Visit mometrix.com/academy and enter code: 853779

PARTS OF A TRIANGLE

An **altitude** of a triangle is a line segment drawn from one vertex perpendicular to the opposite side. In the diagram that follows, $\overline{BE}$, $\overline{AD}$, and $\overline{CF}$ are altitudes. The length of an altitude is also called the height of the triangle. The three altitudes in a triangle are always concurrent. The point of concurrency of the altitudes of a triangle, O, is called the **orthocenter**. Note that in an obtuse triangle, the orthocenter will be outside the triangle, and in a right triangle, the orthocenter is the vertex of the right angle.

A **median** of a triangle is a line segment drawn from one vertex to the midpoint of the opposite side. In the diagram that follows, $\overline{BH}$, $\overline{AG}$, and $\overline{CI}$ are medians. This is not the same as the altitude, except the altitude to the base of an isosceles triangle and all three altitudes of an equilateral triangle. The point of concurrency of the medians of a triangle, T, is called the **centroid**. This is the same point as the orthocenter only in an equilateral triangle. Unlike the orthocenter, the centroid is always inside the triangle. The centroid can also be considered the exact center of the triangle. Any shape triangle can be perfectly balanced on a tip placed at the centroid. The centroid is also the point that is two-thirds the distance from the vertex to the opposite side.

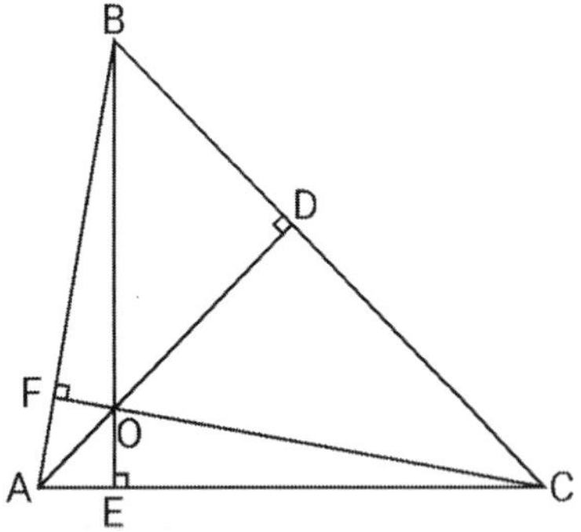

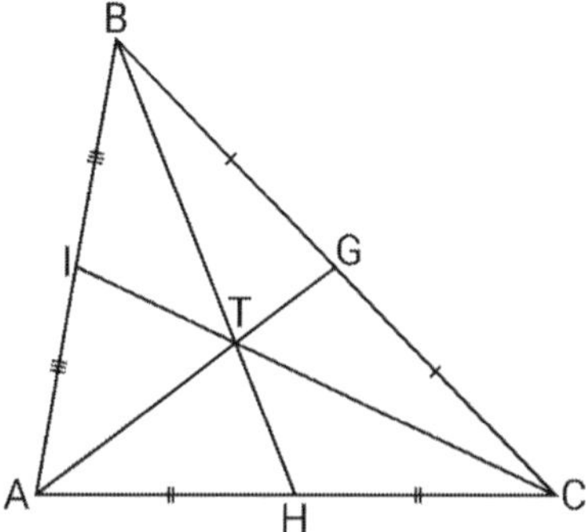

Review Video: Incenter, Circumcenter, Orthocenter, and Centroid
Visit mometrix.com/academy and enter code: 598260

QUADRILATERALS

A **quadrilateral** is a closed two-dimensional geometric figure that has four straight sides. The sum of the interior angles of any quadrilateral is 360°.

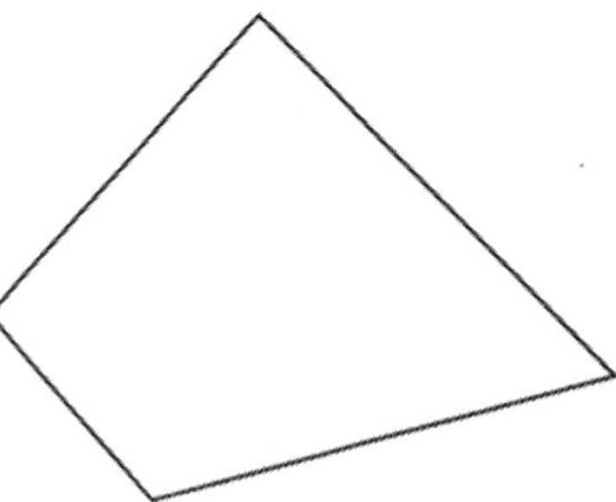

KITE

A **kite** is a quadrilateral with two pairs of adjacent sides that are congruent. A result of this is perpendicular diagonals. A kite can be concave or convex and has one line of symmetry.

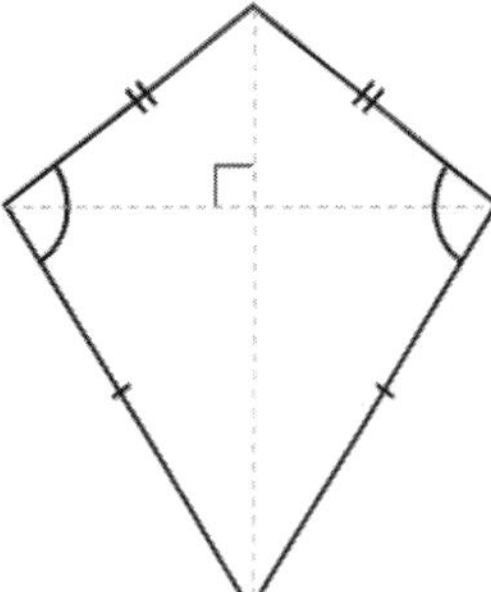

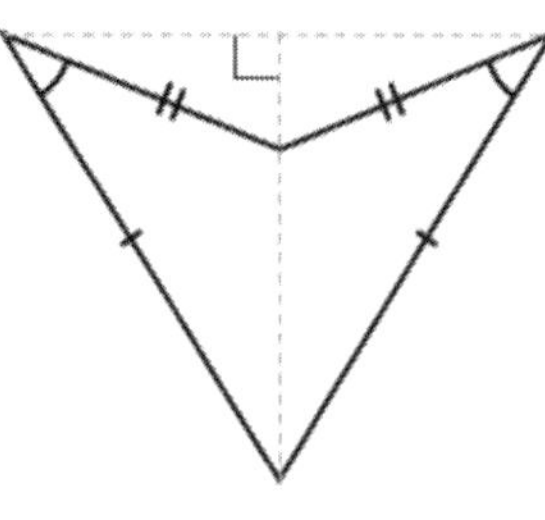

TRAPEZOID

Trapezoid: A trapezoid is defined as a quadrilateral that has at least one pair of parallel sides. There are no rules for the second pair of sides. So there are no rules for the diagonals and no lines of symmetry for a trapezoid.

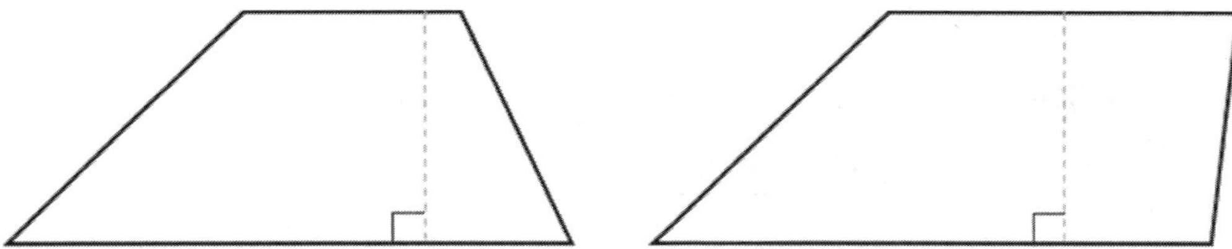

The **area of a trapezoid** is found by the formula $A = \frac{1}{2}h(b_1 + b_2)$, where h is the height (segment joining and perpendicular to the parallel bases), and b_1 and b_2 are the two parallel sides (bases). Do not use one of the other two sides as the height unless that side is also perpendicular to the parallel bases.

The **perimeter of a trapezoid** is found by the formula $P = a + b_1 + c + b_2$, where a, b_1, c, and b_2 are the four sides of the trapezoid.

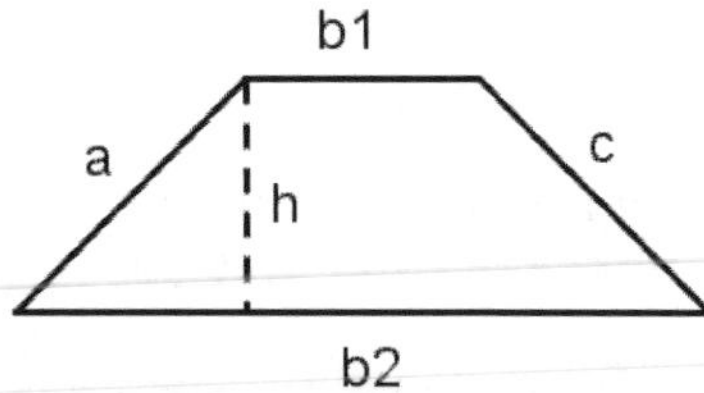

Review Video: Area and Perimeter of a Trapezoid
Visit mometrix.com/academy and enter code: 587523

Isosceles trapezoid: A trapezoid with equal base angles. This gives rise to other properties including: the two nonparallel sides have the same length, the two non-base angles are also equal, and there is one line of symmetry through the midpoints of the parallel sides.

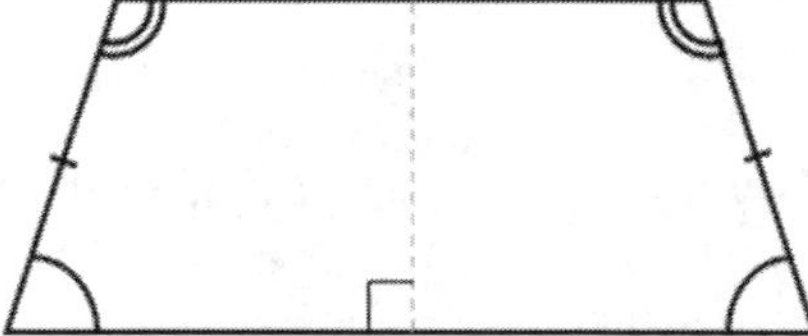

PARALLELOGRAM

A **parallelogram** is a quadrilateral that has two pairs of opposite parallel sides. As such it is a special type of trapezoid. The sides that are parallel are also congruent. The opposite interior angles are always congruent, and the consecutive interior angles are supplementary. The diagonals of a parallelogram divide each other. Each diagonal divides the parallelogram into two congruent triangles. A parallelogram has no line of symmetry, but does have 180-degree rotational symmetry about the midpoint.

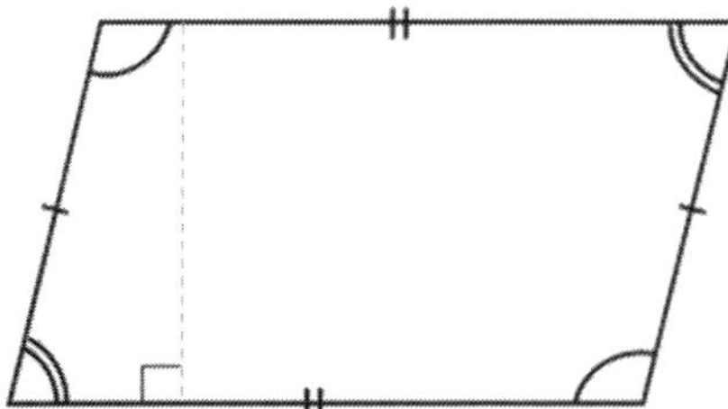

The **area of a parallelogram** is found by the formula $A = bh$, where b is the length of the base, and h is the height. Note that the base and height correspond to the length and width in a rectangle, so this formula would apply to rectangles as well. Do not confuse the height of a parallelogram with the length of the second side. The two are only the same measure in the case of a rectangle.

The **perimeter of a parallelogram** is found by the formula $P = 2a + 2b$ or $P = 2(a + b)$, where a and b are the lengths of the two sides.

Review Video: Area and Perimeter of a Parallelogram
Visit mometrix.com/academy and enter code: 718313

Rectangle

A **rectangle** is a quadrilateral with four right angles. All rectangles are parallelograms and trapezoids, but not all parallelograms or trapezoids are rectangles. The diagonals of a rectangle are congruent. Rectangles have two lines of symmetry (through each pair of opposing midpoints) and 180-degree rotational symmetry about the midpoint.

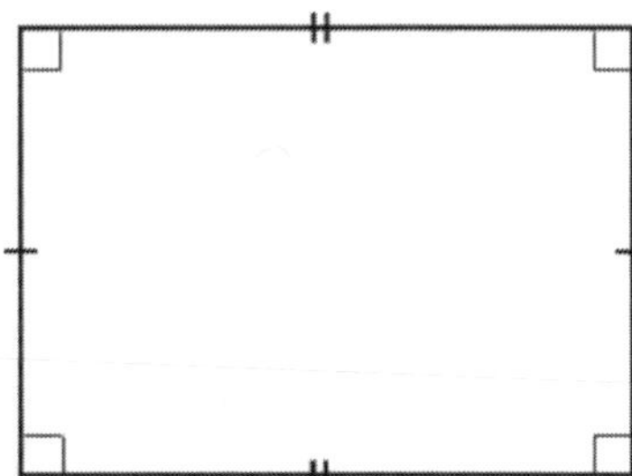

The **area of a rectangle** is found by the formula $A = lw$, where A is the area of the rectangle, l is the length (usually considered to be the longer side) and w is the width (usually considered to be the shorter side). The numbers for l and w are interchangeable.

The **perimeter of a rectangle** is found by the formula $P = 2l + 2w$ or $P = 2(l + w)$, where l is the length, and w is the width. It may be easier to add the length and width first and then double the result, as in the second formula.

Rhombus

A **rhombus** is a quadrilateral with four congruent sides. All rhombuses are parallelograms and kites; thus, they inherit all the properties of both types of quadrilaterals. The diagonals of a rhombus are perpendicular to each other. Rhombi have two lines of symmetry (along each of the diagonals) and 180° rotational symmetry. The **area of a rhombus** is half the product of the diagonals: $A = \frac{d_1 d_2}{2}$ and the perimeter of a rhombus is: $P = 2\sqrt{(d_1)^2 + (d_2)^2}$

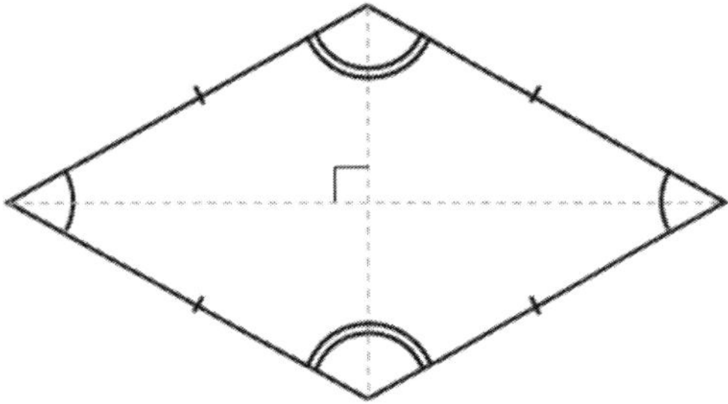

SQUARE

A **square** is a quadrilateral with four right angles and four congruent sides. Squares satisfy the criteria of all other types of quadrilaterals. The diagonals of a square are congruent and perpendicular to each other. Squares have four lines of symmetry (through each pair of opposing midpoints and along each of the diagonals) as well as 90° rotational symmetry about the midpoint.

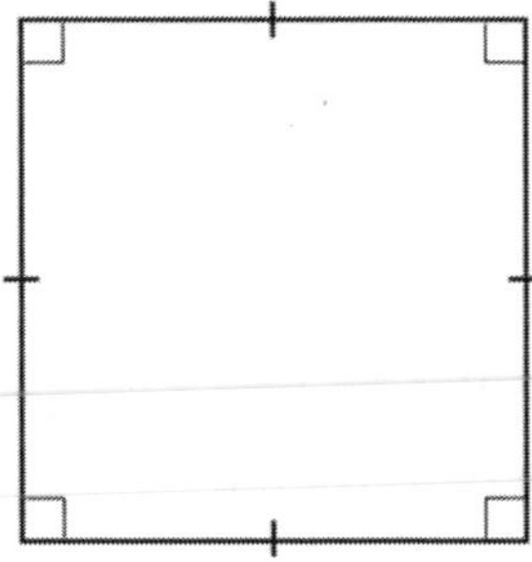

The **area of a square** is found by using the formula $A = s^2$, where s is the length of one side. The **perimeter of a square** is found by using the formula $P = 4s$, where s is the length of one side. Because all four sides are equal in a square, it is faster to multiply the length of one side by 4 than to add the same number four times. You could use the formulas for rectangles and get the same answer.

CIRCLES

The **center** of a circle is the single point from which every point on the circle is **equidistant**. The **radius** is a line segment that joins the center of the circle and any one point on the circle. All radii of a circle are equal. Circles that have the same center but not the same length of radii are **concentric**. The **diameter** is a line segment that passes through the center of the circle and has both endpoints on the circle. The length of the diameter is exactly twice the length of the radius. Point O in the diagram below is the center of the circle, segments $\overline{OX}$, $\overline{OY}$, and $\overline{OZ}$ are radii; and segment $\overline{XZ}$ is a diameter.

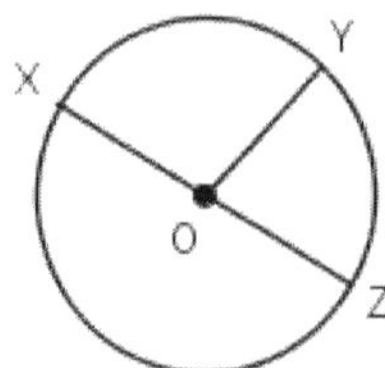

Review Video: Points of a Circle
Visit mometrix.com/academy and enter code: 420746

Review Video: The Diameter, Radius, and Circumference of Circles
Visit mometrix.com/academy and enter code: 448988

The **area of a circle** is found by the formula $A = \pi r^2$, where r is the length of the radius. If the diameter of the circle is given, remember to divide it in half to get the length of the radius before proceeding.

The **circumference** of a circle is found by the formula $C = 2\pi r$, where r is the radius. Again, remember to convert the diameter if you are given that measure rather than the radius.

Review Video: Area and Circumference of a Circle
Visit mometrix.com/academy and enter code: 243015

PRACTICE

P1. Find the area and perimeter of the following quadrilaterals:

(a) A square with side length 2.5 cm.

(b) A parallelogram with height 3 m, base 4 m, and other side 6 m.

(c) A rhombus with diagonals 15 in and 20 in.

P2. Calculate the area of a triangle with side lengths of 7 ft, 8 ft, and 9 ft.

PRACTICE SOLUTIONS

P1. (a) $A = s^2 = (2.5 \text{ cm})^2 = 6.25 \text{ cm}^2$; $P = 4s = 4 \times 2.5 \text{ cm} = 10 \text{ cm}$

(b) $A = bh = (3 \text{ m})(4 \text{ m}) = 12 \text{ m}^2$; $P = 2a + 2b = 2 \times 6 \text{ m} + 2 \times 4 \text{ m} = 20 \text{ m}$

(c) $A = \frac{d_1 d_2}{2} = \frac{(15 \text{ in})(20 \text{ in})}{2} = 150 \text{ in}^2$;
$P = 2\sqrt{(d_1)^2 + (d_2)^2} = 2\sqrt{(15 \text{ in})^2 + (20 \text{ in})^2} = 2\sqrt{625 \text{ in}^2} = 50 \text{ in}$

P2. Given only side lengths, we can use the semi perimeter to the find the area based on the formula, $A = \sqrt{s(s-a)(s-b)(s-c)}$, where s is the semiperimeter, $\frac{a+b+c}{2} = \frac{7+8+9}{2} = 12$ ft:

$$\begin{aligned} A &= \sqrt{12(12-7)(12-8)(12-9)} \\ &= \sqrt{(12)(5)(4)(3)} \\ &= 12\sqrt{5}\text{ ft}^2 \end{aligned}$$

Three-Dimensional Shapes

Solids

The **surface area of a solid object** is the area of all sides or exterior surfaces. For objects such as prisms and pyramids, a further distinction is made between base surface area (B) and lateral surface area (LA). For a prism, the total surface area (SA) is $SA = LA + 2B$. For a pyramid or cone, the total surface area is $SA = LA + B$.

Review Video: How to Calculate the Volume of 3D Objects
Visit mometrix.com/academy and enter code: 163343

The **surface area of a sphere** can be found by the formula $A = 4\pi r^2$, where r is the radius. The volume is given by the formula $V = \frac{4}{3}\pi r^3$, where r is the radius. Both quantities are generally given in terms of π.

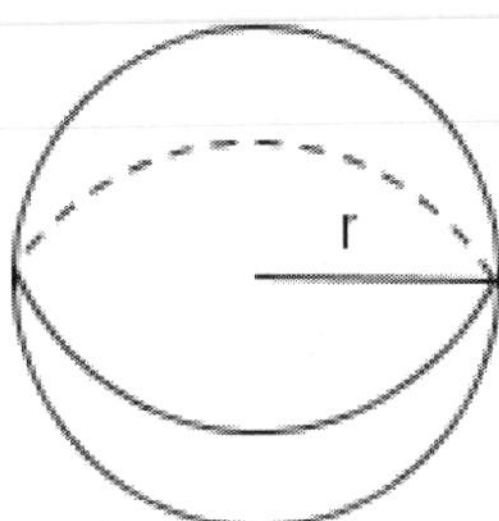

The **volume of any prism** is found by the formula $V = Bh$, where B is the area of the base, and h is the height (perpendicular distance between the bases). The surface area of any prism is the sum of the areas of both bases and all sides. It can be calculated as $SA = 2B + Ph$, where P is the perimeter of the base.

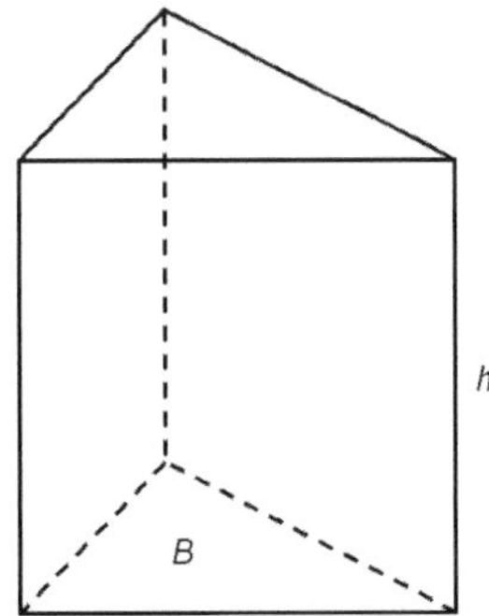

Review Video: Volume and Surface Area of a Prism
Visit mometrix.com/academy and enter code: 420158

For a **rectangular prism**, the volume can be found by the formula $V = lwh$, where V is the volume, l is the length, w is the width, and h is the height. The surface area can be calculated as $SA = 2lw + 2hl + 2wh$ or $SA = 2(lw + hl + wh)$.

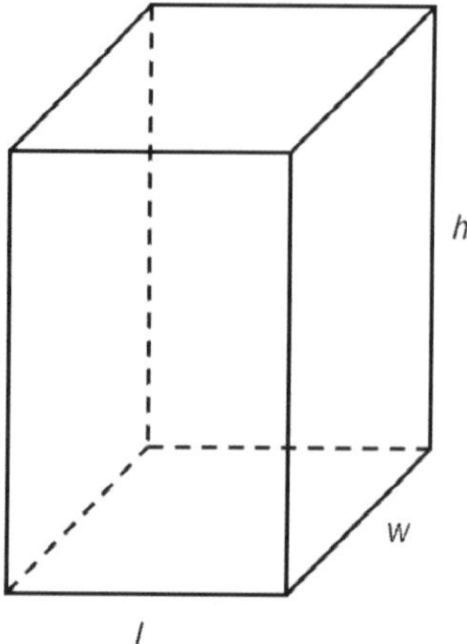

Review Video: Volume and Surface Area of a Rectangular Prism
Visit mometrix.com/academy and enter code: 282814

The **volume of a cube** can be found by the formula $V = s^3$, where s is the length of a side. The surface area of a cube is calculated as $SA = 6s^2$, where SA is the total surface area and s is the length of a side. These formulas are the same as the ones used for the volume and surface area of a rectangular prism, but simplified since all three quantities (length, width, and height) are the same.

Review Video: Volume and Surface Area of a Cube
Visit mometrix.com/academy and enter code: 664455

The **volume of a cylinder** can be calculated by the formula $V = \pi r^2 h$, where r is the radius, and h is the height. The surface area of a cylinder can be found by the formula $SA = 2\pi r^2 + 2\pi rh$. The first term is the base area multiplied by two, and the second term is the perimeter of the base multiplied by the height.

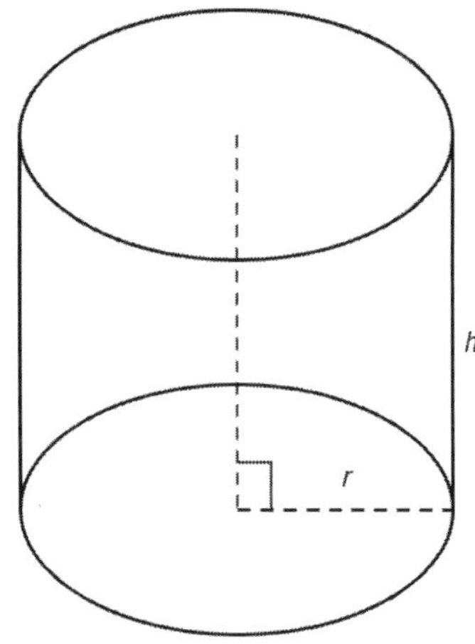

Review Video: Finding the Volume and Surface Area of a Right Circular Cylinder
Visit mometrix.com/academy and enter code: 226463

The **volume of a pyramid** is found by the formula $V = \frac{1}{3}Bh$, where B is the area of the base, and h is the height (perpendicular distance from the vertex to the base). Notice this formula is the same as $\frac{1}{3}$ times the volume of a prism. Like a prism, the base of a pyramid can be any shape.

Finding the **surface area of a pyramid** is not as simple as the other shapes we've looked at thus far. If the pyramid is a right pyramid, meaning the base is a regular polygon and the vertex is directly over the center of that polygon, the surface area can be calculated as $SA = B + \frac{1}{2}Ph_s$, where P is the perimeter of the base, and h_s is the slant height (distance from the vertex to the midpoint of one side of the base). If the pyramid is irregular, the area of each triangle side must be calculated individually and then summed, along with the base.

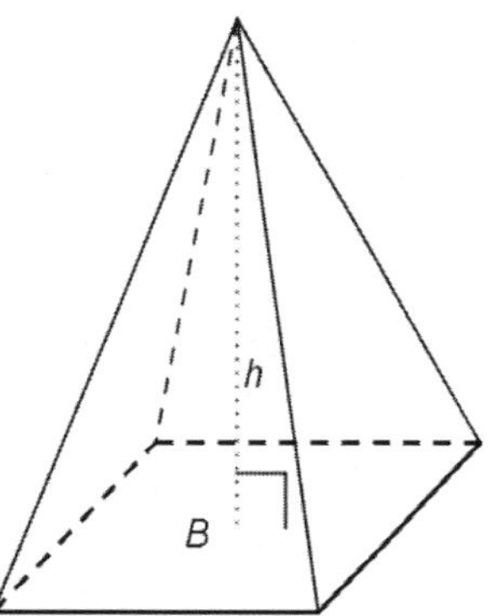

Review Video: Finding the Volume and Surface Area of a Pyramid
Visit mometrix.com/academy and enter code: 621932

The **volume of a cone** is found by the formula $V = \frac{1}{3}\pi r^2 h$, where r is the radius, and h is the height. Notice this is the same as $\frac{1}{3}$ times the volume of a cylinder. The surface area can be calculated as $SA = \pi r^2 + \pi rs$, where s is the slant height. The slant height can be calculated using the Pythagorean theorem to be $\sqrt{r^2 + h^2}$, so the surface area formula can also be written as $SA = \pi r^2 + \pi r\sqrt{r^2 + h^2}$.

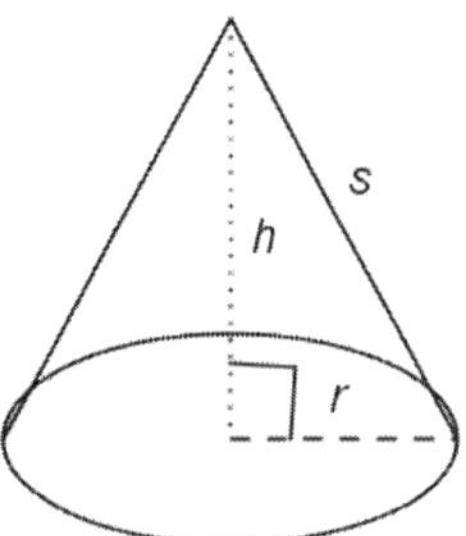

Review Video: Volume and Surface Area of a Right Circular Cone
Visit mometrix.com/academy and enter code: 573574

Practice

P1. Find the surface area and volume of the following solids:

(a) A cylinder with radius 5 m and height 0.5 m.

(b) A trapezoidal prism with base area of 254 mm^2, base perimeter 74 mm, and height 10 mm.

(c) A half sphere (radius 5 yds) on the base of an inverted cone with the same radius and a height of 7 yds.

Practice Solutions

P1. (a) $SA = 2\pi r^2 + 2\pi rh = 2\pi(5\text{ m})^2 + 2\pi(5\text{ m})(0.5\text{ m}) = 55\pi\text{ m}^2 \cong 172.79\text{ m}^2$;
$V = \pi r^2 h = \pi(5\text{ m})^2(0.5\text{ m}) = 12.5\pi\text{ m}^3 \cong 39.27\text{ m}^3$

(b) $SA = 2B + Ph = 2(254\text{ mm}^2) + (74\text{ mm})(10\text{ mm}) = 1248\text{ mm}^2$;
$V = Bh = (254\text{ mm}^2)(10\text{ mm}) = 2540\text{ mm}^3$

(c) We can find s, the slant height using the Pythagorean theorem, and since this solid is made of parts of simple solids, we can combine the formulas to find surface area and volume:

$$s = \sqrt{r^2 + h^2} = \sqrt{(5\text{ yd})^2 + (7\text{ yd})^2} = \sqrt{74}\text{ yd}$$

$$\begin{aligned} SA_{Total} &= (SA_{sphere})/2 + SA_{cone} - SA_{base} \\ &= \frac{4\pi r^2}{2} + (\pi rs + \pi r^2) - \pi r^2 \\ &= 2\pi(5\text{ yd})^2 + \pi(5\text{ yd})(\sqrt{74}\text{ yd}) \\ &= 5\pi(10 + \sqrt{74})\text{ yd}^2 \\ &\cong 292.20\text{ yd}^2 \end{aligned}$$

$$\begin{aligned} V_{Total} &= (V_{sphere})/2 + V_{cone} \\ &= \frac{\frac{4}{3}\pi r^3}{2} + \frac{1}{3}\pi r^2 h \\ &= \frac{2}{3}\pi(5\text{ yd})^3 + \frac{1}{3}\pi(5\text{ yd})^2(7\text{ yd}) \\ &= \frac{5^2 \times \pi}{3}(10 + 7)\text{ yd}^3 \\ &\cong 445.06\text{ yd}^3 \end{aligned}$$

Transformations

Rotation

A **rotation** is a transformation that turns a figure around a point called the **center of rotation**, which can lie anywhere in the plane. If a line is drawn from a point on a figure to the center of rotation, and another line is drawn from the center to the rotated image of that point, the angle between the two lines is the **angle of rotation**. The vertex of the angle of rotation is the center of rotation.

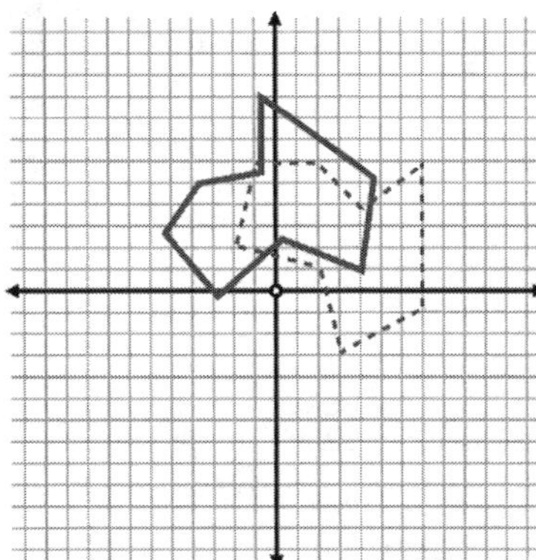

Translation and Dilation

A **translation** is a transformation which slides a figure from one position in the plane to another position in the plane. The original figure and the translated figure have the same size, shape, and orientation. A **dilation** is a transformation which proportionally stretches or shrinks a figure by a **scale factor**. The dilated image is the same shape and orientation as the original image but a different size. A polygon and its dilated image are similar.

Translation

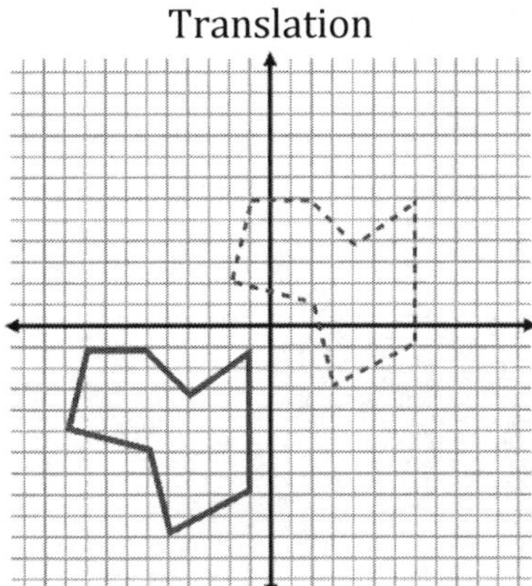

Dilation

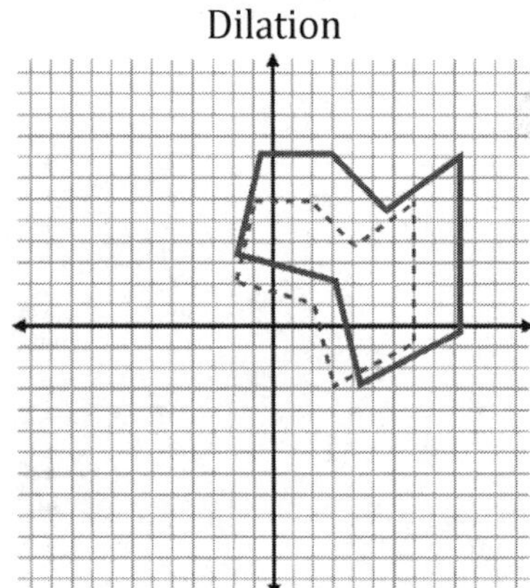

Reflection

A **reflection of a figure over a line** (a "flip") creates a congruent image that is the same distance from the line as the original figure but on the opposite side. The **line of reflection** is the perpendicular bisector of any line segment drawn from a point on the original figure to its reflected image (unless the point and its reflected image happen to be the same point, which happens when a figure is reflected over one of its own sides). A **reflection of a figure over a point** (an inversion) in two dimensions is the same as the rotation of the figure 180° about that point. The image of the figure is congruent to the original figure. The **point of reflection** is the midpoint of a line segment which connects a point in the figure to its image (unless the point and its reflected image happen to be the same point, which happens when a figure is reflected in one of its own points).

Reflection of a figure over a line

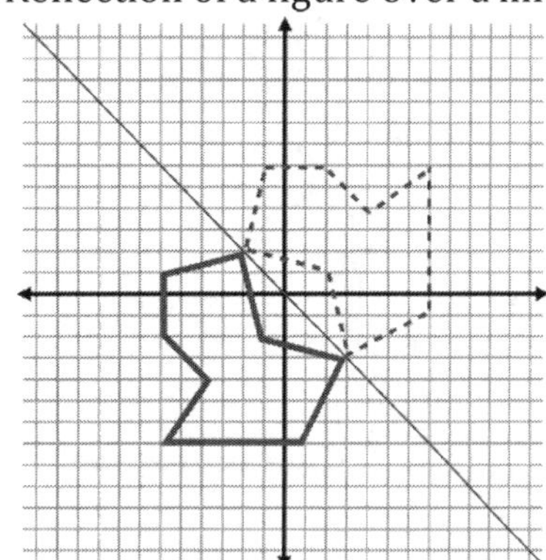

Reflection of a figure over a point

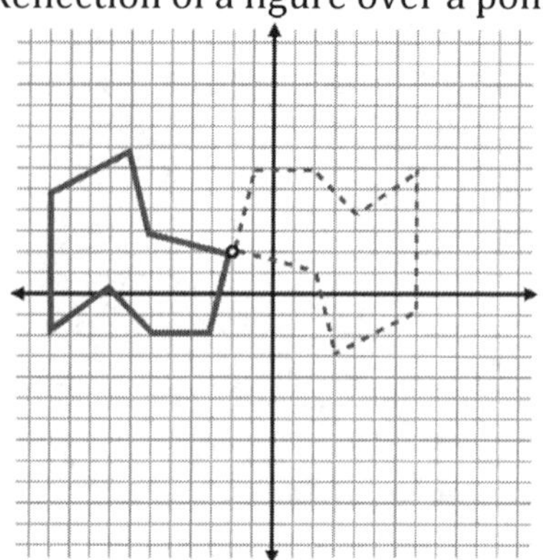

Review Video: Rotation
Visit mometrix.com/academy and enter code: 602600
Review Video: Translation
Visit mometrix.com/academy and enter code: 718628
Review Video: Dilation
Visit mometrix.com/academy and enter code: 471630
Review Video: Reflection
Visit mometrix.com/academy and enter code: 955068

PRACTICE

P1. Use the coordinate plane to reflect the figure below across the y-axis.

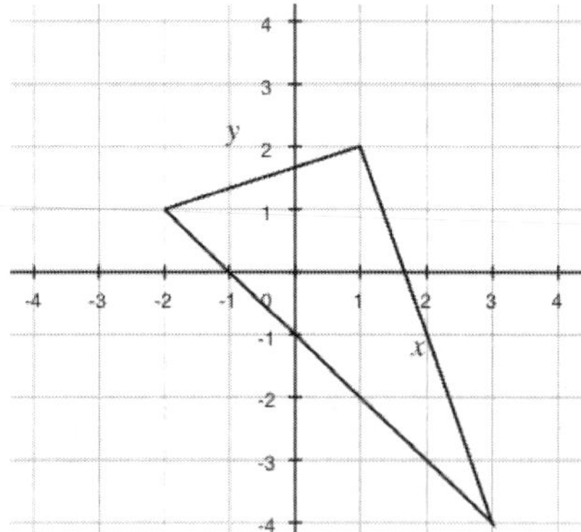

P2. Use the coordinate plane to enlarge the figure below by a factor of 2.

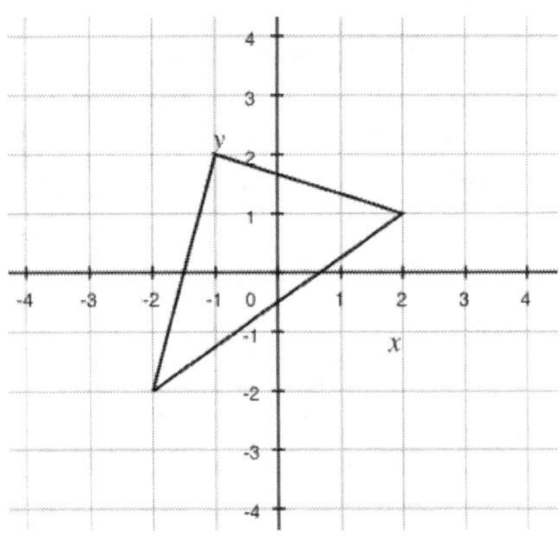

PRACTICE SOLUTIONS

P1. To reflect the image across the y-axis, replace each x-coordinate of the points that are the vertex of the triangle, x, with its negative, $-x$.

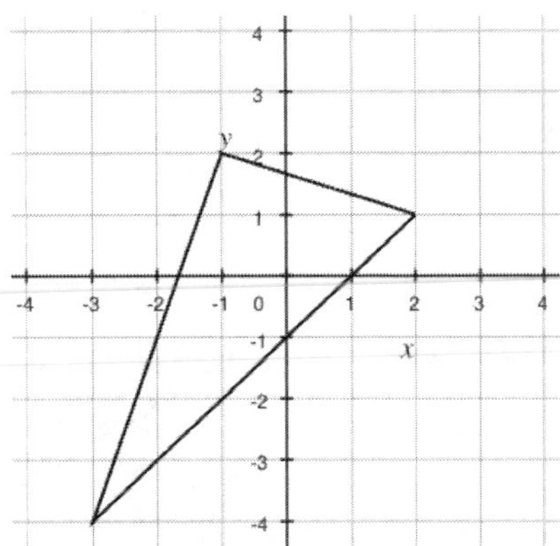

P2. An enlargement can be found by multiplying each coordinate of the coordinate pairs located at the triangle's vertices by 2. The original coordinates were $(-1, 2), (2, 1), (-2, -2)$, so the new coordinates are $(-2, 4), (4, 2), (-4, -4)$:

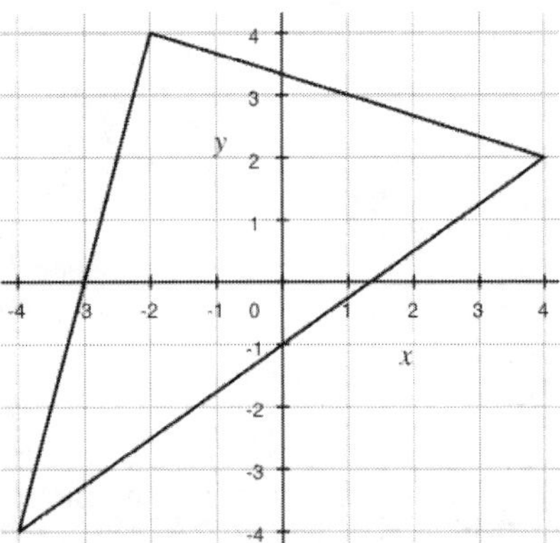

TRIANGLE CLASSIFICATION AND PROPERTIES

CLASSIFICATIONS OF TRIANGLES

A **scalene triangle** is a triangle with no congruent sides. A scalene triangle will also have three angles of different measures. The angle with the largest measure is opposite the longest side, and the angle with the smallest measure is opposite the shortest side. An **acute triangle** is a triangle whose three angles are all less than 90°. If two of the angles are equal, the acute triangle is also an **isosceles triangle**. An isosceles triangle will also have two congruent angles opposite the two congruent sides. If the three angles are all equal, the acute triangle is also an **equilateral triangle**. An equilateral triangle will also have three congruent angles, each 60°. All equilateral triangles are also acute triangles. An **obtuse triangle** is a triangle with exactly one angle greater than 90°. The other two angles may or may not be equal. If the two remaining angles are equal, the obtuse triangle is also an isosceles triangle. A **right triangle** is a triangle with exactly one angle equal to 90°. All right triangles follow the Pythagorean theorem. A right triangle can never be acute or obtuse.

The table below illustrates how each descriptor places a different restriction on the triangle:

Angles / Sides	**Acute: All angles < 90°**	**Obtuse: One angle > 90°**	**Right: One angle = 90°**
Scalene: No equal side lengths	$90° > \angle a > \angle b > \angle c$ $x > y > z$	$\angle a > 90° > \angle b > \angle c$ $x > y > z$	$90° = \angle a > \angle b > \angle c$ $x > y > z$
Isosceles: Two equal side lengths	$90° > \angle a, \angle b, or\ \angle c$ $\angle b = \angle c, \quad y = z$	$\angle a > 90° > \angle b = \angle c$ $x > y = z$	$\angle a = 90°, \angle b = \angle c = 45°$ $x > y = z$
Equilateral: Three equal side lengths	$60° = \angle a = \angle b = \angle c$ $x = y = z$		

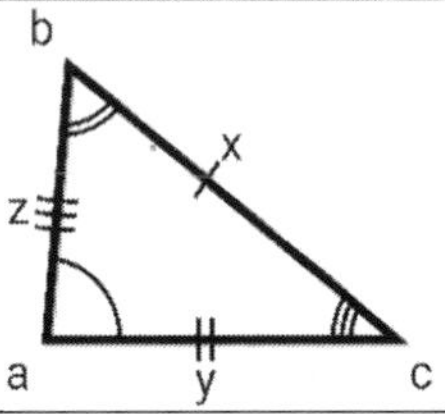

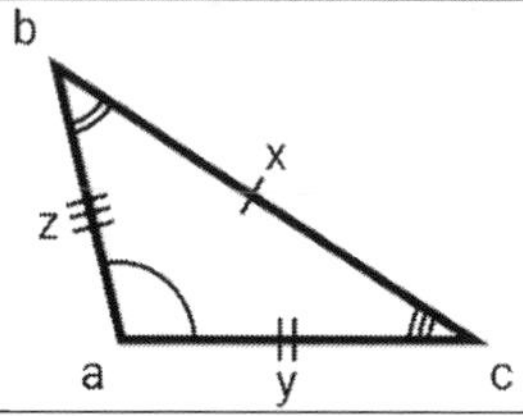

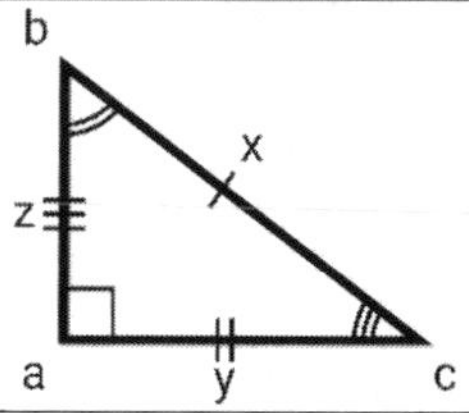

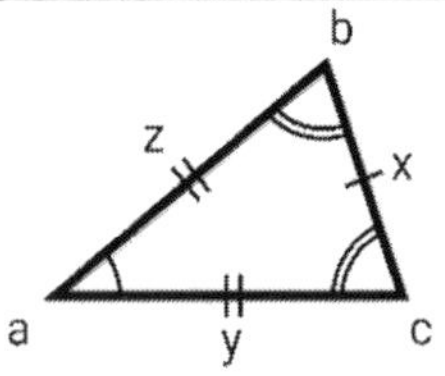

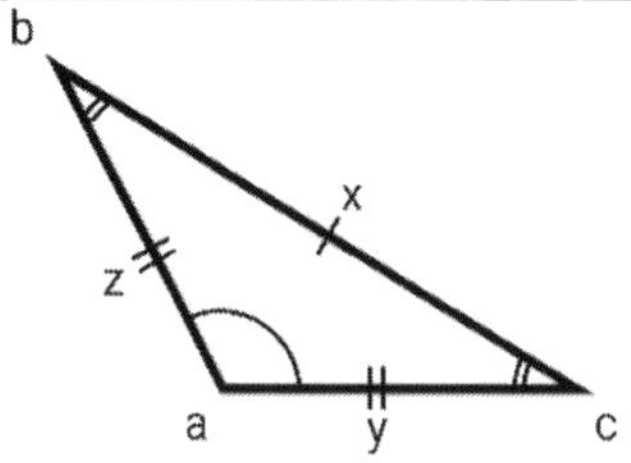

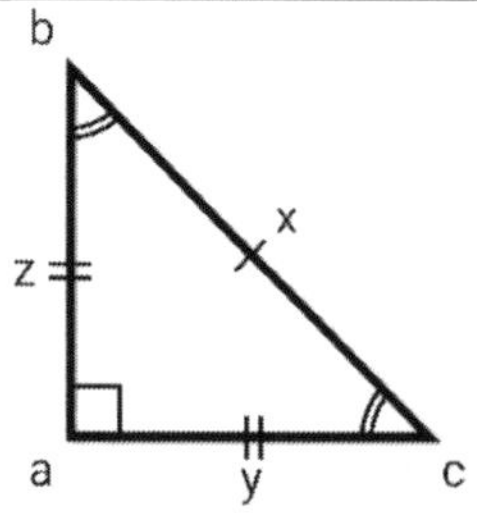

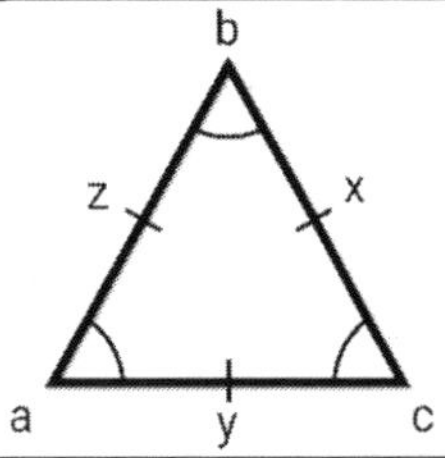

Review Video: Introduction to Types of Triangles
Visit mometrix.com/academy and enter code: 511711

SIMILARITY AND CONGRUENCE RULES

Similar triangles are triangles whose corresponding angles are equal and whose corresponding sides are proportional. Represented by AAA. Similar triangles whose corresponding sides are congruent are also congruent triangles.

Triangles can be shown to be **congruent** in 5 ways:

- **SSS**: Three sides of one triangle are congruent to the three corresponding sides of the second triangle.
- **SAS**: Two sides and the included angle (the angle formed by those two sides) of one triangle are congruent to the corresponding two sides and included angle of the second triangle.
- **ASA**: Two angles and the included side (the side that joins the two angles) of one triangle are congruent to the corresponding two angles and included side of the second triangle.
- **AAS**: Two angles and a non-included side of one triangle are congruent to the corresponding two angles and non-included side of the second triangle.
- **HL**: The hypotenuse and leg of one right triangle are congruent to the corresponding hypotenuse and leg of the second right triangle.

Review Video: Similar Triangles
Visit mometrix.com/academy and enter code: 398538

GENERAL RULES FOR TRIANGLES

The **triangle inequality theorem** states that the sum of the measures of any two sides of a triangle is always greater than the measure of the third side. If the sum of the measures of two sides were equal to the third side, a triangle would be impossible because the two sides would lie flat across the third side and there would be no vertex. If the sum of the measures of two of the sides was less than the third side, a closed figure would be impossible because the two shortest sides would never meet. In other words, for a triangle with sides lengths A, B, and C: $A + B > C$, $B + C > A$, and $A + C > B$.

The sum of the measures of the interior angles of a triangle is always 180°. Therefore, a triangle can never have more than one angle greater than or equal to 90°.

In any triangle, the angles opposite congruent sides are congruent, and the sides opposite congruent angles are congruent. The largest angle is always opposite the longest side, and the smallest angle is always opposite the shortest side.

The line segment that joins the midpoints of any two sides of a triangle is always parallel to the third side and exactly half the length of the third side.

Review Video: General Rules (Triangle Inequality Theorem)
Visit mometrix.com/academy and enter code: 166488

PRACTICE

P1. Given the following pairs of triangles, determine whether they are similar, congruent, or neither (note that the figures are not drawn to scale):

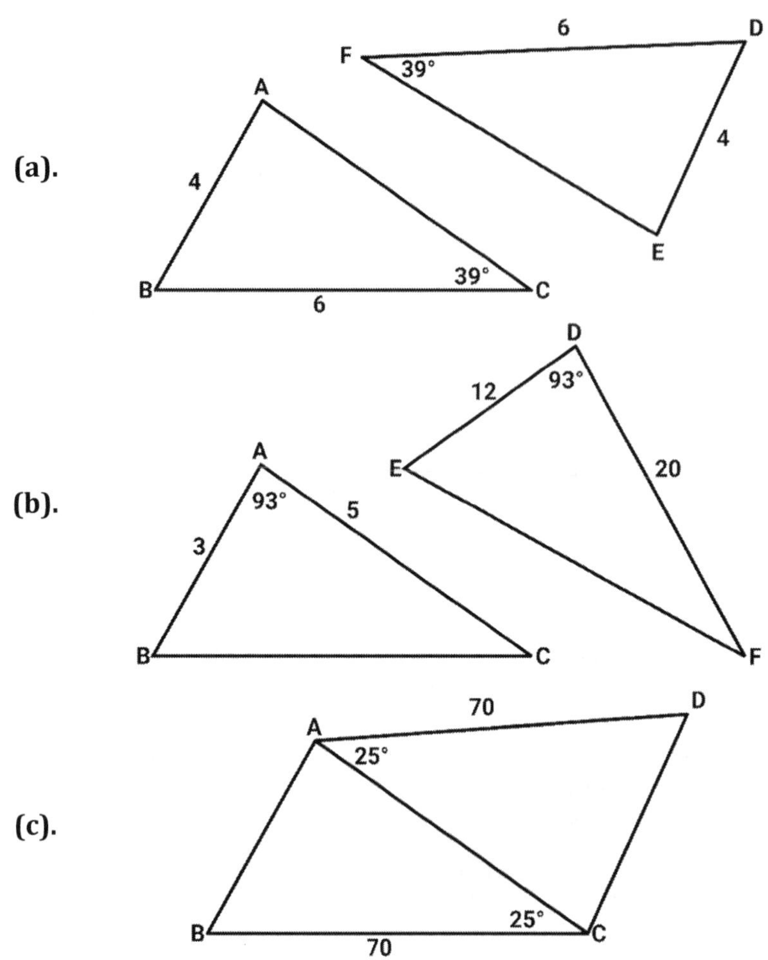

PRACTICE SOLUTIONS

P1. (a). Neither: We are given that two sides lengths and an angle are equal, however, the angle given is not between the given side lengths. That means there are two possible triangles that could satisfy the given measurements. Thus, we cannot be certain of congruence:

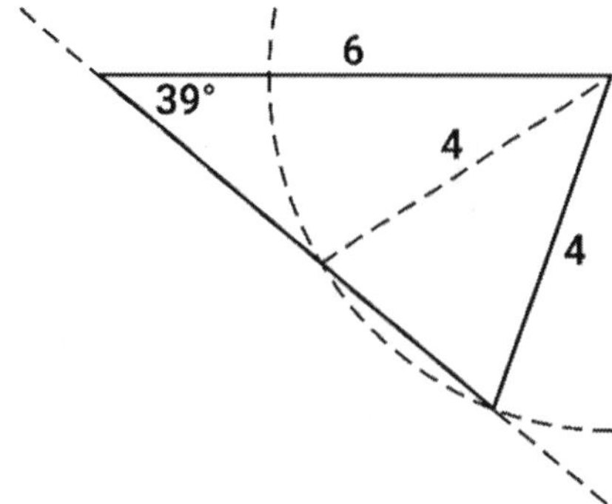

(b) Similar: Since we are given a side-angle-side of each triangle and the side lengths given are scaled evenly $\left(\frac{3}{5} \times \frac{4}{4} = \frac{12}{20}\right)$ and the angles are equal. Thus, $\Delta ABC \sim \Delta DEF$. If the side lengths were equal, then they would be congruent.

(c) Congruent: Even though we aren't given a measurement for the shared side of the figure, since it is shared it is equal. So, this is a case of SAS. Thus, $\Delta ABC \cong \Delta CDA$

Introductory Trigonometry

Pythagorean Theorem

The side of a triangle opposite the right angle is called the **hypotenuse**. The other two sides are called the legs. The Pythagorean theorem states a relationship among the legs and hypotenuse of a right triangle: $(a^2 + b^2 = c^2)$, where a and b are the lengths of the legs of a right triangle, and c is the length of the hypotenuse. Note that this formula will only work with right triangles.

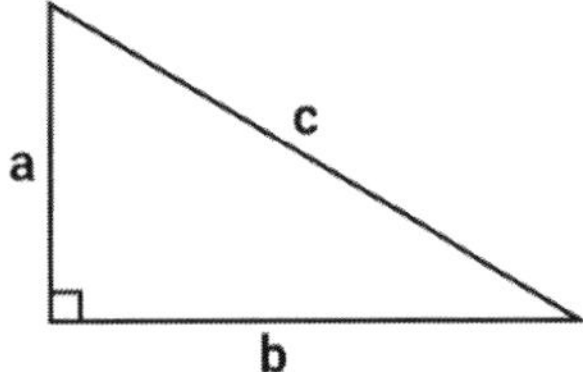

Review Video: Pythagorean Theorem
Visit mometrix.com/academy and enter code: 906576

Trigonometric Formulas

In the diagram below, angle C is the right angle, and side c is the hypotenuse. Side a is the side opposite to angle A and side b is the side opposite to angle B. Using ratios of side lengths as a means to calculate the sine, cosine, and tangent of an acute angle only works for right triangles.

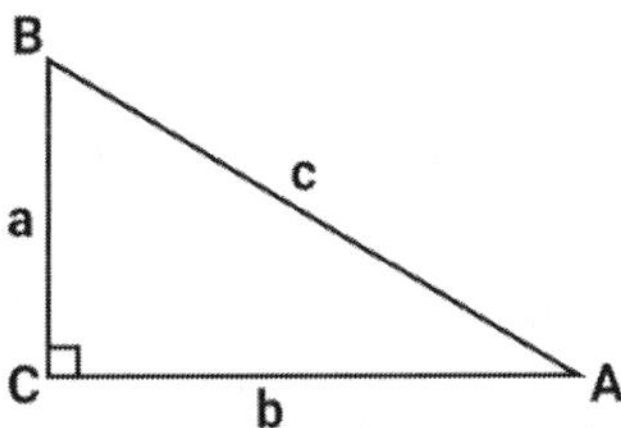

$$\sin A = \frac{\text{opposite side}}{\text{hypotenuse}} = \frac{a}{c} \qquad \csc A = \frac{1}{\sin A} = \frac{\text{hypotenuse}}{\text{opposite side}} = \frac{c}{a}$$

$$\cos A = \frac{\text{adjacent side}}{\text{hypotenuse}} = \frac{b}{c} \qquad \sec A = \frac{1}{\cos A} = \frac{\text{hypotenuse}}{\text{adjacent side}} = \frac{c}{b}$$

$$\tan A = \frac{\text{opposite side}}{\text{adjacent side}} = \frac{a}{b} \qquad \cot A = \frac{1}{\tan A} = \frac{\text{adjacent side}}{\text{opposite side}} = \frac{b}{a}$$

Laws of Sines and Cosines

The **law of sines** states that $\frac{\sin A}{a} = \frac{\sin B}{b} = \frac{\sin C}{c}$, where A, B, and C are the angles of a triangle, and a, b, and c are the sides opposite their respective angles. This formula will work with all triangles, not just right triangles.

The **law of cosines** is given by the formula $c^2 = a^2 + b^2 - 2ab(\cos C)$, where a, b, and c are the sides of a triangle, and C is the angle opposite side c. This is a generalized form of the Pythagorean theorem that can be used on any triangle.

> **Review Video: Law of Sines**
> Visit mometrix.com/academy and enter code: 206844
>
> **Review Video: Law of Cosines**
> Visit mometrix.com/academy and enter code: 158911

PRACTICE

P1. Calculate the following values based on triangle MNO:

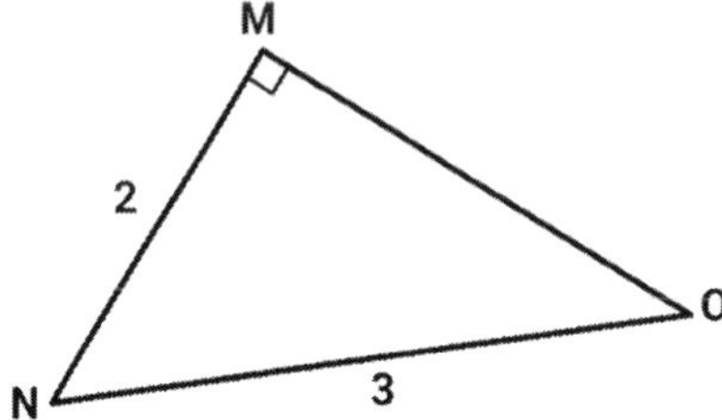

(a) length of $\overline{MO}$

(b) $\sin(\angle NOM)$

(c) area of the triangle, if the units of the measurements are in miles

PRACTICE SOLUTIONS

P1. (a) Since triangle MNO is a right triangle, we can use the simple form of Pythagoras theorem to find the missing side length:

$$\begin{aligned}\left(\overline{MO}\right)^2 + 2^2 &= 3^2 \\ \left(\overline{MO}\right)^2 &= 9 - 4 \\ \overline{MO} &= \sqrt{5}\end{aligned}$$

(b) Recall that sine of an angle in a right triangle is the ratio of the opposite side to the hypotenuse. So, $\sin(\angle NOM) = 2/3$

(c) Since triangle MNO is a right triangle, we can use either of the legs as the height and the other as the base in the simple formula for the area of a triangle:

$$\begin{aligned}A &= \frac{bh}{2} \\ &= \frac{(2\text{ mi})(\sqrt{5}\text{ mi})}{2} \\ &= \sqrt{5}\text{ mi}^2\end{aligned}$$

Probabilistic and Statistical Reasoning

DISPLAYING INFORMATION

FREQUENCY TABLES

Frequency tables show how frequently each unique value appears in a set. A **relative frequency table** is one that shows the proportions of each unique value compared to the entire set. Relative frequencies are given as percentages; however, the total percent for a relative frequency table will not necessarily equal 100 percent due to rounding. An example of a frequency table with relative frequencies is below.

Favorite Color	Frequency	Relative Frequency
Blue	4	13%
Red	7	22%
Green	3	9%
Purple	6	19%
Cyan	12	38%

Review Video: Data Interpretation of Graphs
Visit mometrix.com/academy and enter code: 200439

CIRCLE GRAPHS

Circle graphs, also known as *pie charts*, provide a visual depiction of the relationship of each type of data compared to the whole set of data. The circle graph is divided into sections by drawing radii to create central angles whose percentage of the circle is equal to the individual data's percentage of the whole set. Each 1% of data is equal to 3.6° in the circle graph. Therefore, data represented by a 90° section of the circle graph makes up 25% of the whole. When complete, a circle graph often looks like a pie cut into uneven wedges. The pie chart below shows the data from the frequency table referenced earlier where people were asked their favorite color.

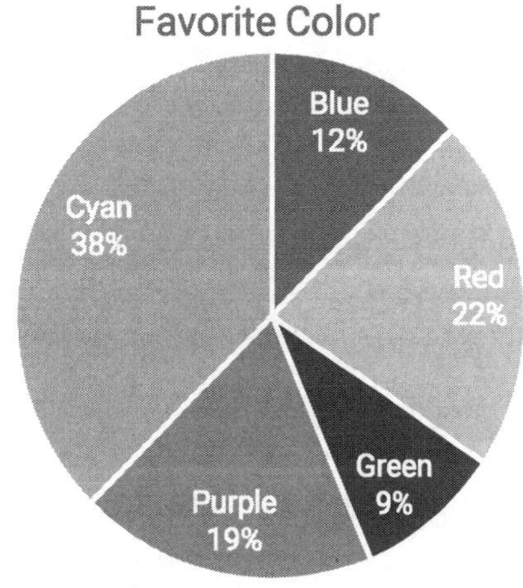

PICTOGRAPHS

A **pictograph** is a graph, generally in the horizontal orientation, that uses pictures or symbols to represent the data. Each pictograph must have a key that defines the picture or symbol and gives the quantity each picture or symbol represents. Pictures or symbols on a pictograph are not always shown as whole elements. In this case, the fraction of the picture or symbol shown represents the same fraction of the quantity a whole picture or symbol stands for. For example, a row with $3\frac{1}{2}$ ears of corn, where each ear of corn represents 100 stalks of corn in a field, would equal $3\frac{1}{2} \times 100 = 350$ stalks of corn in the field.

LINE GRAPHS

Line graphs have one or more lines of varying styles (solid or broken) to show the different values for a set of data. The individual data are represented as ordered pairs, much like on a Cartesian plane. In this case, the *x*- and *y*-axes are defined in terms of their units, such as dollars or time. The individual plotted points are joined by line segments to show whether the value of the data is increasing (line sloping upward), decreasing (line sloping downward), or staying the same (horizontal line). Multiple sets of data can be graphed on the same line graph to give an easy visual comparison. An example of this would be graphing achievement test scores for different groups of students over the same time period to see which group had the greatest increase or decrease in performance from year to year (as shown below).

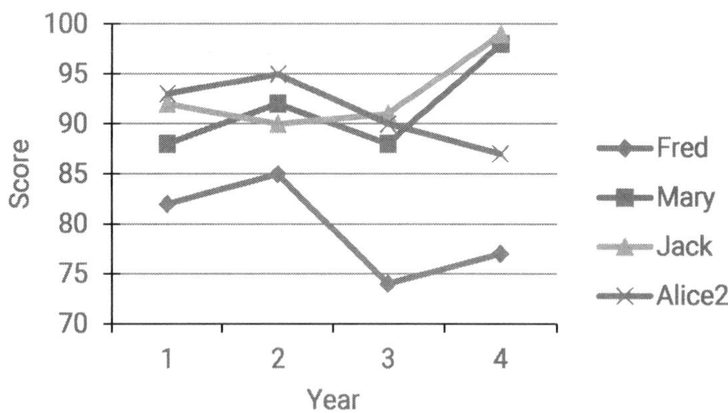

Review Video: How to Create a Line Graph
Visit mometrix.com/academy and enter code: 480147

LINE PLOTS

A **line plot**, also known as a *dot plot*, has plotted points that are not connected by line segments. In this graph, the horizontal axis lists the different possible values for the data, and the vertical axis lists the number of times the individual value occurs. A single dot is graphed for each value to show the number of times it occurs. This graph is more closely related to a bar graph than a line graph. Do not connect the dots in a line plot or it will misrepresent the data.

Review Video: Line Plot
Visit mometrix.com/academy and enter code: 754610

STEM AND LEAF PLOTS

A **stem and leaf plot** is useful for depicting groups of data that fall into a range of values. Each piece of data is separated into two parts: the first, or left, part is called the stem; the second, or right, part is called the leaf. Each stem is listed in a column from smallest to largest. Each leaf that has the common stem is listed in that stem's row from smallest to largest. For example, in a set of two-digit numbers, the digit in the tens place is the stem, and the digit in the ones place is the leaf. With a stem and leaf plot, you can easily see which subset of numbers (10s, 20s, 30s, etc.) is the largest.

This information is also readily available by looking at a histogram, but a stem and leaf plot also allows you to look closer and see exactly which values fall in that range. Using all of the test scores from above, we can assemble a stem and leaf plot like the one below.

Test Scores

Stem	Leaves
7	4 8
8	2 5 7 8 8
9	0 0 1 2 2 3 5 8 9

Review Video: Stem-and-Leaf Plots
Visit mometrix.com/academy and enter code: 302339

Bar Graphs

A **bar graph** is one of the few graphs that can be drawn correctly in two different configurations – both horizontally and vertically. A bar graph is similar to a line plot in the way the data is organized on the graph. Both axes must have their categories defined for the graph to be useful. Rather than placing a single dot to mark the point of the data's value, a bar, or thick line, is drawn from zero to the exact value of the data, whether it is a number, percentage, or other numerical value. Longer bar lengths correspond to greater data values. To read a bar graph, read the labels for the axes to find the units being reported. Then, look where the bars end in relation to the scale given on the corresponding axis and determine the associated value.

The bar chart below represents the responses from our favorite-color survey.

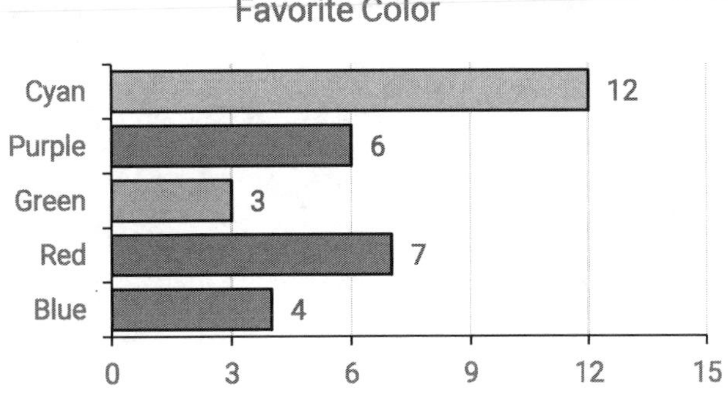

Histograms

At first glance, a **histogram** looks like a vertical bar graph. The difference is that a bar graph has a separate bar for each piece of data and a histogram has one continuous bar for each *range* of data. For example, a histogram may have one bar for the range 0–9, one bar for 10–19, etc. While a bar graph has numerical values on one axis, a histogram has numerical values on both axes. Each range is of equal size, and they are ordered left to right from lowest to highest. The height of each column on a histogram represents the number of data values within that range. Like a stem and leaf plot, a histogram makes it easy to glance at the graph and quickly determine which range has the greatest quantity of values. A simple example of a histogram is below.

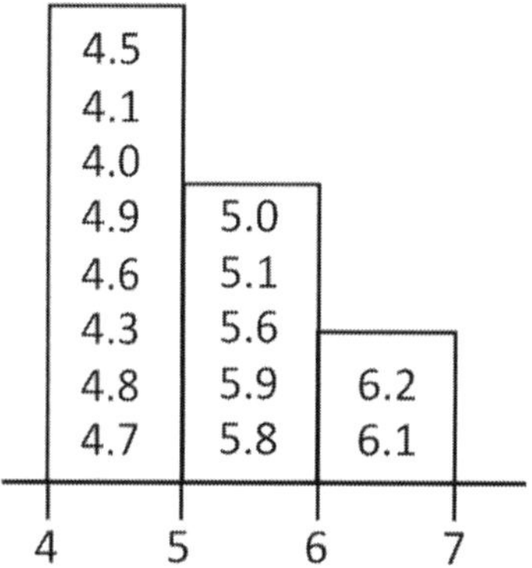

Bivariate Data

Bivariate data is simply data from two different variables. (The prefix *bi-* means *two.*) In a *scatter plot*, each value in the set of data is plotted on a grid similar to a Cartesian plane, where each axis represents one of the two variables. By looking at the pattern formed by the points on the grid, you can often determine whether or not there is a relationship between the two variables, and what that relationship is, if it exists. The variables may be directly proportionate, inversely proportionate, or show no proportion at all. It may also be possible to determine if the data is linear, and if so, to find an equation to relate the two variables. The following scatter plot shows the relationship between preference for brand "A" and the age of the consumers surveyed.

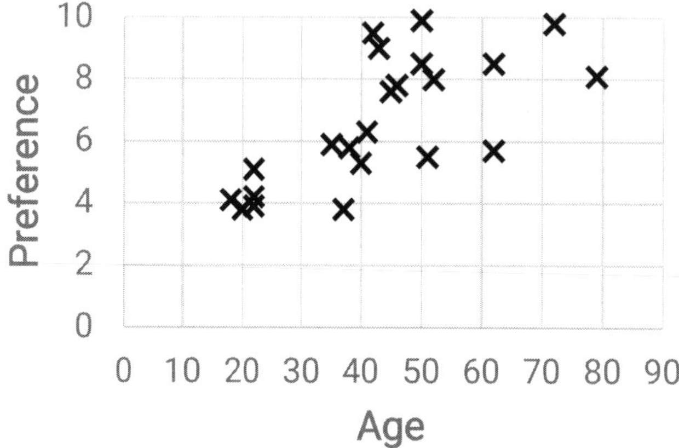

SCATTER PLOTS

Scatter plots are also useful in determining the type of function represented by the data and finding the simple regression. Linear scatter plots may be positive or negative. Nonlinear scatter plots are generally exponential or quadratic. Below are some common types of scatter plots:

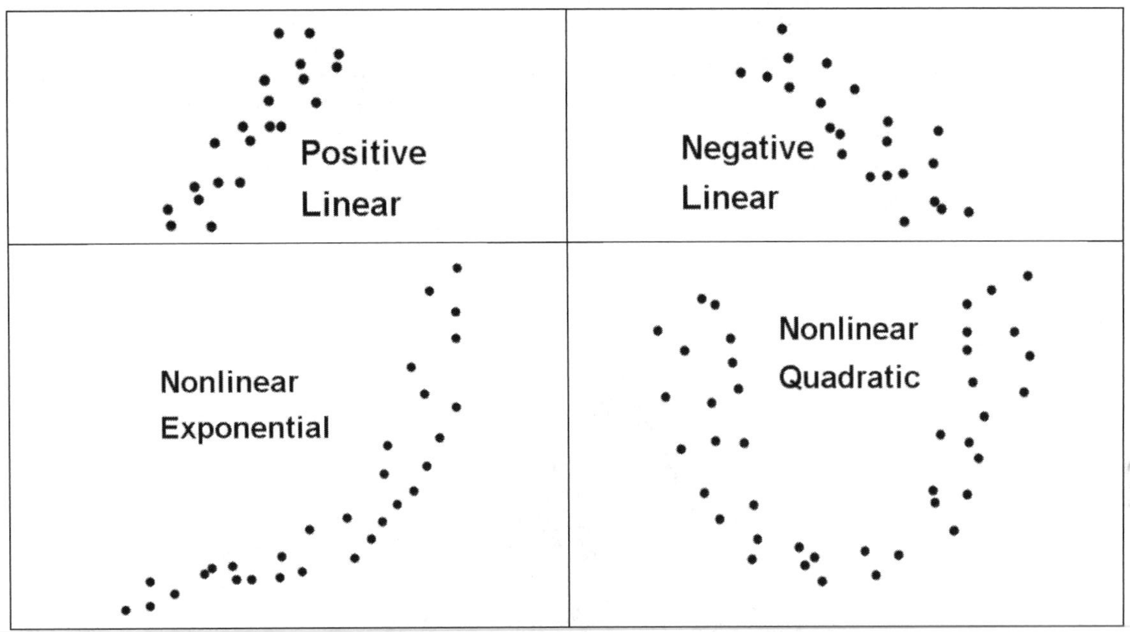

Review Video: What is a Scatter Plot?
Visit mometrix.com/academy and enter code: 596526

5-NUMBER SUMMARY

The **5-number summary** of a set of data gives a very informative picture of the set. The five numbers in the summary include the minimum value, maximum value, and the three quartiles. This information gives the reader the range and median of the set, as well as an indication of how the data is spread about the median.

BOX AND WHISKER PLOTS

A **box-and-whisker plot** is a graphical representation of the 5-number summary. To draw a box-and-whisker plot, plot the points of the 5-number summary on a number line. Draw a box whose ends are through the points for the first and third quartiles. Draw a vertical line in the box through the median to divide the box in half. Draw a line segment from the first quartile point to the minimum value and from the third quartile point to the maximum value.

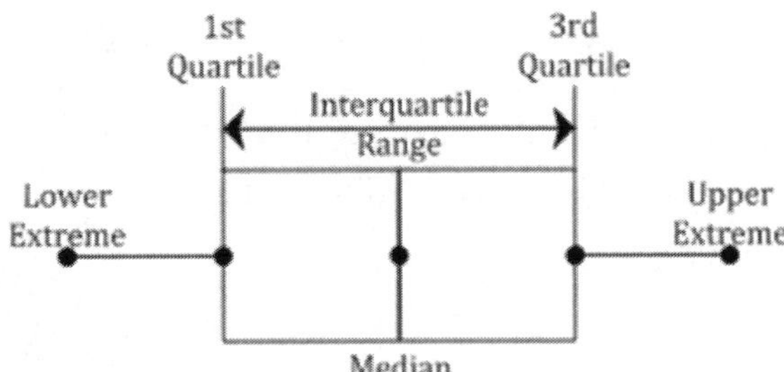

68-95-99.7 Rule

The **68–95–99.7 rule** describes how a normal distribution of data should appear when compared to the mean. This is also a description of a normal bell curve. According to this rule, 68 percent of the data values in a normally distributed set should fall within one standard deviation of the mean (34 percent above and 34 percent below the mean), 95 percent of the data values should fall within two standard deviations of the mean (47.5 percent above and 47.5 percent below the mean), and 99.7 percent of the data values should fall within three standard deviations of the mean, again, equally distributed on either side of the mean. This means that only 0.3 percent of all data values should fall more than three standard deviations from the mean. On the graph below, the normal curve is centered on the y-axis. The x-axis labels are how many standard deviations away from the center you are. Therefore, it is easy to see how the 68-95-99.7 rule can apply.

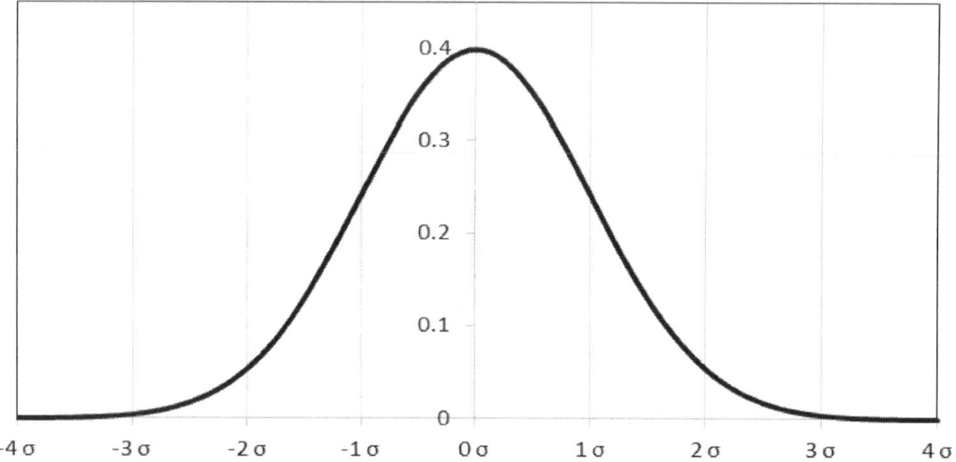

Probability

Probability is the likelihood of a certain outcome occurring for a given event. An **event** is any situation that produces a result. It could be something as simple as flipping a coin or as complex as launching a rocket. Determining the probability of an outcome for an event can be equally simple or complex. As such, there are specific terms used in the study of probability that need to be understood:

- **Compound event**—an event that involves two or more independent events (rolling a pair of dice and taking the sum)
- **Desired outcome** (or success)—an outcome that meets a particular set of criteria (a roll of 1 or 2 if we are looking for numbers less than 3)
- **Independent events**—two or more events whose outcomes do not affect one another (two coins tossed at the same time)
- **Dependent events**—two or more events whose outcomes affect one another (two cards drawn consecutively from the same deck)
- **Certain outcome**—probability of outcome is 100% or 1
- **Impossible outcome**—probability of outcome is 0% or 0

- **Mutually exclusive outcomes**—two or more outcomes whose criteria cannot all be satisfied in a single event (a coin coming up heads and tails on the same toss)
- **Random variable**—refers to all possible outcomes of a single event which may be discrete or continuous.

Review Video: Intro to Probability
Visit mometrix.com/academy and enter code: 212374

THEORETICAL AND EXPERIMENTAL PROBABILITY

Theoretical probability can usually be determined without actually performing the event. The likelihood of an outcome occurring, or the probability of an outcome occurring, is given by the formula:

$$P(A) = \frac{\text{Number of acceptable outcomes}}{\text{Number of possible outcomes}}$$

Note that $P(A)$ is the probability of an outcome A occurring, and each outcome is just as likely to occur as any other outcome. If each outcome has the same probability of occurring as every other possible outcome, the outcomes are said to be equally likely to occur. The total number of acceptable outcomes must be less than or equal to the total number of possible outcomes. If the two are equal, then the outcome is certain to occur and the probability is 1. If the number of acceptable outcomes is zero, then the outcome is impossible and the probability is 0. For example, if there are 20 marbles in a bag and 5 are red, then the theoretical probability of randomly selecting a red marble is 5 out of 20, ($\frac{5}{20} = \frac{1}{4}$, 0.25, or 25%).

If the theoretical probability is unknown or too complicated to calculate, it can be estimated by an experimental probability. **Experimental probability**, also called empirical probability, is an estimate of the likelihood of a certain outcome based on repeated experiments or collected data. In other words, while theoretical probability is based on what *should* happen, experimental probability is based on what *has* happened. Experimental probability is calculated in the same way as theoretical probability, except that actual outcomes are used instead of possible outcomes. The more experiments performed or datapoints gathered, the better the estimate should be.

Theoretical and experimental probability do not always line up with one another. Theoretical probability says that out of 20 coin-tosses, 10 should be heads. However, if we were actually to toss 20 coins, we might record just 5 heads. This doesn't mean that our theoretical probability is incorrect; it just means that this particular experiment had results that were different from what was predicted. A practical application of empirical probability is the insurance industry. There are no set functions that define lifespan, health, or safety. Insurance companies look at factors from hundreds of thousands of individuals to find patterns that they then use to set the formulas for insurance premiums.

Review Video: Empirical Probability
Visit mometrix.com/academy and enter code: 513468

COMPLEMENT OF AN EVENT

Sometimes it may be easier to calculate the possibility of something not happening, or the **complement of an event**. Represented by the symbol $\bar{A}$, the complement of A is the probability that event A does not happen. When you know the probability of event A occurring, you can use the formula $P(\bar{A}) = 1 - P(A)$, where $P(\bar{A})$ is the probability of event A not occurring, and $P(A)$ is the probability of event A occurring.

Addition Rule

The **addition rule** for probability is used for finding the probability of a compound event. Use the formula $P(A \text{ or } B) = P(A) + P(B) - P(A \text{ and } B)$, where $P(A \text{ and } B)$ is the probability of both events occurring to find the probability of a compound event. The probability of both events occurring at the same time must be subtracted to eliminate any overlap in the first two probabilities.

Conditional Probability

Given two events A and B, the **conditional probability** $P(A|B)$ is the probability that event A will occur, given that event B has occurred. The conditional probability cannot be calculated simply from $P(A)$ and $P(B)$; these probabilities alone do not give sufficient information to determine the conditional probability. It can, however, be determined if you are also given the probability of the intersection of events A and B, $P(A \cap B)$, the probability that events A and B both occur. Specifically, $P(A|B) = \frac{P(A \cap B)}{P(B)}$. For instance, suppose you have a jar containing two red marbles and two blue marbles, and you draw two marbles at random. Consider event A being the event that the first marble drawn is red, and event B being the event that the second marble drawn is blue. $P(A)$ is $\frac{1}{2}$, and $P(A \cap B)$ is $\frac{1}{3}$. (The latter may not be obvious, but may be determined by finding the product of $\frac{1}{2}$ and $\frac{2}{3}$). Therefore $P(A|B) = \frac{1/3}{1/2} = \frac{2}{3}$.

Conditional Probability in Everyday Situations

Conditional probability often arises in everyday situations in, for example, estimating the risk or benefit of certain activities. The conditional probability of having a heart attack given that you exercise daily may be smaller than the overall probability of having a heart attack. The conditional probability of having lung cancer given that you are a smoker is larger than the overall probability of having lung cancer. Note that changing the order of the conditional probability changes the meaning: the conditional probability of having lung cancer given that you are a smoker is a very different thing from the probability of being a smoker given that you have lung cancer. In an extreme case, suppose that a certain rare disease is caused only by eating a certain food, but even then, it is unlikely. Then the conditional probability of having that disease given that you eat the dangerous food is nonzero but low, but the conditional probability of having eaten that food given that you have the disease is 100%!

Review Video: Conditional Probability
Visit mometrix.com/academy and enter code: 397924

Multiplication Rule

The **multiplication rule** can be used to find the probability of two independent events occurring using the formula $P(A \text{ and } B) = P(A) \times P(B)$, where $P(A \text{ and } B)$ is the probability of two independent events occurring, $P(A)$ is the probability of the first event occurring, and $P(B)$ is the probability of the second event occurring.

The multiplication rule can also be used to find the probability of two dependent events occurring using the formula $P(A \text{ and } B) = P(A) \times P(B|A)$, where $P(A \text{ and } B)$ is the probability of two dependent events occurring and $P(B|A)$ is the probability of the second event occurring after the first event has already occurred. Before using the multiplication rule, you MUST first determine whether the two events are *dependent* or *independent*.

Use a **combination of the multiplication** rule and the rule of complements to find the probability that at least one outcome of the element will occur. This is given by the general formula $P(\text{at least one event occurring}) = 1 - P(\text{no outcomes occurring})$. For example, to find the probability that at least one even number will show when a pair of dice is rolled, find the probability that two odd numbers will be rolled (no even numbers) and subtract from one. You can always use a tree diagram or make a chart to list the possible outcomes when the sample space is small, such as in the dice-rolling example, but in most cases it will be much faster to use the multiplication and complement formulas.

Review Video: Multiplication Rule
Visit mometrix.com/academy and enter code: 782598

PRACTICE

P1. Determine the theoretical probability of the following events:

(a) Rolling an even number on a regular 6-sided die.

(b) Not getting a red ball when selecting one from a bag of 3 red balls, 4 black balls, and 2 green balls.

(c) Rolling a standard die and then selecting a card from a standard deck that is less than the value rolled.

PRACTICE SOLUTIONS

P1. (a). The values on the faces of a regular die are 1, 2, 3, 4, 5, and 6. Since three of these are even numbers (2, 4, 6), The probability of rolling an even number is $\frac{3}{6} = \frac{1}{2} = 0.5 = 50\%$.

(b) The bag contains a total of 9 balls, 6 of which are not red, so the probability of selecting one non-red ball would be $\frac{6}{9} = \frac{2}{3} \cong 0.667 \cong 66.7\%$.

(c) In this scenario, we need to determine how many cards could satisfy the condition for each possible value of the die roll. If a one is rolled, there is no way to achieve the desired outcome, since no cards in a standard deck are less than 1. If a two is rolled, then any of the four aces would achieve the desired result. If a three is rolled, then either an ace or a two would satisfy the condition, and so on. Note that any value on the die is equally likely to occur, meaning that the probability of each roll is $\frac{1}{6}$. Putting all this in a table can help:

Roll	Cards < Roll	Probability of Card	Probability of Event
1	-	$\frac{0}{52} = 0$	$\frac{1}{6} \times 0 = 0$
2	1	$\frac{4}{52} = \frac{1}{13}$	$\frac{1}{6} \times \frac{1}{13} = \frac{1}{78}$
3	1,2	$\frac{8}{52} = \frac{2}{13}$	$\frac{1}{6} \times \frac{2}{13} = \frac{2}{78}$

Roll	Cards < Roll	Probability of Card	Probability of Event
4	1,2,3	$\frac{12}{52} = \frac{3}{13}$	$\frac{1}{6} \times \frac{3}{13} = \frac{3}{78}$
5	1,2,3,4	$\frac{16}{52} = \frac{4}{13}$	$\frac{1}{6} \times \frac{4}{13} = \frac{4}{78}$
6	1,2,3,4,5	$\frac{20}{52} = \frac{5}{13}$	$\frac{1}{6} \times \frac{5}{13} = \frac{5}{78}$

Assuming that each value of the die is equally likely, then the probability of selecting a card less than the value of the die is the sum of the probabilities of each way to achieve the desired outcome: $\frac{0+1+2+3+4+5}{78} = \frac{15}{78} = \frac{5}{26} \cong 0.192 \cong 19.2\%$.

Statistical Analysis

Measures of Central Tendency

A **measure of central tendency** is a statistical value that gives a reasonable estimate for the center of a group of data. There are several different ways of describing the measure of central tendency. Each one has a unique way it is calculated, and each one gives a slightly different perspective on the data set. Whenever you give a measure of central tendency, always make sure the units are the same. If the data has different units, such as hours, minutes, and seconds, convert all the data to the same unit, and use the same unit in the measure of central tendency. If no units are given in the data, do not give units for the measure of central tendency.

Mean

The **statistical mean** of a group of data is the same as the arithmetic average of that group. To find the mean of a set of data, first convert each value to the same units, if necessary. Then find the sum of all the values, and count the total number of data values, making sure you take into consideration each individual value. If a value appears more than once, count it more than once. Divide the sum of the values by the total number of values and apply the units, if any. Note that the mean does not have to be one of the data values in the set, and may not divide evenly.

$$\text{mean} = \frac{\text{sum of the data values}}{\text{quantity of data values}}$$

For instance, the mean of the data set {88, 72, 61, 90, 97, 68, 88, 79, 86, 93, 97, 71, 80, 84, 89} would be the sum of the fifteen numbers divided by 15:

$$\frac{88 + 72 + 61 + 90 + 97 + 68 + 88 + 79 + 86 + 93 + 97 + 71 + 80 + 84 + 88}{15} = \frac{1242}{15} = 82.8$$

While the mean is relatively easy to calculate and averages are understood by most people, the mean can be very misleading if it is used as the sole measure of central tendency. If the data set has outliers (data values that are unusually high or unusually low compared to the rest of the data values), the mean can be very distorted, especially if the data set has a small number of values. If unusually high values are countered with unusually low values, the mean is not affected as much. For example, if five of twenty students in a class get a 100 on a test, but the other 15 students have an average of 60 on the same test, the class average would appear as 70. Whenever the mean is skewed by outliers, it is always a good idea to include the median as an alternate measure of central tendency.

A **weighted mean**, or weighted average, is a mean that uses "weighted" values. The formula is weighted mean $= \frac{w_1x_1+w_2x_2+w_3x_3...+w_nx_n}{w_1+w_2+w_3+\cdots+w_n}$. Weighted values, such as $w_1, w_2, w_3, ... w_n$ are assigned to each member of the set $x_1, x_2, x_3, ... x_n$. When calculating the weighted mean, make sure a weight value for each member of the set is used.

MEDIAN

The **statistical median** is the value in the middle of the set of data. To find the median, list all data values in order from smallest to largest or from largest to smallest. Any value that is repeated in the set must be listed the number of times it appears. If there are an odd number of data values, the median is the value in the middle of the list. If there is an even number of data values, the median is the arithmetic mean of the two middle values.

For example, the median of the data set {88, 72, 61, 90, 97, 68, 88, 79, 86, 93, 97, 71, 80, 84, 88} is 86 since the ordered set is {61, 68, 71, 72, 79, 80, 84, **86**, 88, 88, 88, 90, 93, 97, 97}.

The big disadvantage of using the median as a measure of central tendency is that is relies solely on a value's relative size as compared to the other values in the set. When the individual values in a set of data are evenly dispersed, the median can be an accurate tool. However, if there is a group of rather large values or a group of rather small values that are not offset by a different group of values, the information that can be inferred from the median may not be accurate because the distribution of values is skewed.

MODE

The **statistical mode** is the data value that occurs the greatest number of times in the data set. It is possible to have exactly one mode, more than one mode, or no mode. To find the mode of a set of data, arrange the data like you do to find the median (all values in order, listing all multiples of data values). Count the number of times each value appears in the data set. If all values appear an equal number of times, there is no mode. If one value appears more than any other value, that value is the mode. If two or more values appear the same number of times, but there are other values that appear fewer times and no values that appear more times, all of those values are the modes.

For example, the mode of the data set {**88**, 72, 61, 90, 97, 68, **88**, 79, 86, 93, 97, 71, 80, 84, **88**} is 88.

The main disadvantage of the mode is that the values of the other data in the set have no bearing on the mode. The mode may be the largest value, the smallest value, or a value anywhere in between in the set. The mode only tells which value or values, if any, occurred the greatest number of times. It does not give any suggestions about the remaining values in the set.

Review Video: Mean, Median, and Mode
Visit mometrix.com/academy and enter code: 286207

DISPERSION

A **measure of dispersion** is a single value that helps to "interpret" the measure of central tendency by providing more information about how the data values in the set are distributed about the measure of central tendency. The measure of dispersion helps to eliminate or reduce the disadvantages of using the mean, median, or mode as a single measure of central tendency, and give a more accurate picture of the dataset as a whole. To have a measure of dispersion, you must know or calculate the range, standard deviation, or variance of the data set.

RANGE

The **range** of a set of data is the difference between the greatest and lowest values of the data in the set. To calculate the range, you must first make sure the units for all data values are the same, and then identify the greatest and lowest values. If there are multiple data values that are equal for the highest or lowest, just use one of the values in the formula. Write the answer with the same units as the data values you used to do the calculations.

Review Video: Statistical Range
Visit mometrix.com/academy and enter code: 778541

STANDARD DEVIATION

Standard deviation is a measure of dispersion that compares all the data values in the set to the mean of the set to give a more accurate picture. To find the standard deviation of a sample, use the formula

$$s = \sqrt{\frac{\sum_{i=1}^{n}(x_i - \bar{x})^2}{n-1}}$$

Note that s is the standard deviation of a sample, x represents the individual values in the data set, $\bar{x}$ is the mean of the data values in the set, and n is the number of data values in the set. The higher the value of the standard deviation is, the greater the variance of the data values from the mean. The units associated with the standard deviation are the same as the units of the data values.

Review Video: Standard Deviation
Visit mometrix.com/academy and enter code: 419469

VARIANCE

The **variance** of a sample, or just variance, is the square of the standard deviation of that sample. While the mean of a set of data gives the average of the set and gives information about where a specific data value lies in relation to the average, the variance of the sample gives information about the degree to which the data values are spread out and tells you how close an individual value is to the average compared to the other values. The units associated with variance are the same as the units of the data values squared.

PERCENTILE

Percentiles and quartiles are other methods of describing data within a set. **Percentiles** tell what percentage of the data in the set fall below a specific point. For example, achievement test scores are often given in percentiles. A score at the 80th percentile is one which is equal to or higher than 80 percent of the scores in the set. In other words, 80 percent of the scores were lower than that score.

Quartiles are percentile groups that make up quarter sections of the data set. The first quartile is the 25th percentile. The second quartile is the 50th percentile; this is also the median of the dataset. The third quartile is the 75th percentile.

OUTLIER

An outlier is an extremely high or extremely low value in the data set. It may be the result of measurement error, in which case, the outlier is not a valid member of the data set. However, it may also be a valid member of the distribution. Unless a measurement error is identified, the experimenter cannot know for certain if an outlier is or is not a member of the distribution. There are arbitrary methods that can be employed to designate an extreme value as an outlier. One method designates an outlier (or possible outlier) to be any value less than $Q_1 - 1.5(IQR)$ or any value greater than $Q_3 + 1.5(IQR)$.

DATA ANALYSIS

SIMPLE REGRESSION

In statistics, **simple regression** is using an equation to represent a relation between independent and dependent variables. The independent variable is also referred to as the explanatory variable or the predictor and is generally represented by the variable x in the equation. The dependent variable, usually represented by the variable y, is also referred to as the response variable. The equation may be any type of function – linear, quadratic, exponential, etc. The best way to handle this task is to use the regression feature of your graphing calculator. This will easily give you the curve of best fit and provide you with the coefficients and other information you need to derive an equation.

LINE OF BEST FIT

In a scatter plot, the **line of best fit** is the line that best shows the trends of the data. The line of best fit is given by the equation $\hat{y} = ax + b$, where a and b are the regression coefficients. The regression coefficient a is also the slope of the line of best fit, and b is also the y-coordinate of the point at which the line of best fit crosses the y-axis. Not every point on the scatter plot will be on the line of best fit. The differences between the y-values of the points in the scatter plot and the corresponding y-values according to the equation of the line of best fit are the residuals. The line of best fit is also called the least-squares regression line because it is also the line that has the lowest sum of the squares of the residuals.

CORRELATION COEFFICIENT

The **correlation coefficient** is the numerical value that indicates how strong the relationship is between the two variables of a linear regression equation. A correlation coefficient of –1 is a perfect negative correlation. A correlation coefficient of +1 is a perfect positive correlation. Correlation coefficients close to –1 or +1 are very strong correlations. A correlation coefficient equal to zero indicates there is no correlation between the two variables. This test is a good indicator of whether or not the equation for the line of best fit is accurate. The formula for the correlation coefficient is

$$r = \frac{\sum_{i=1}^{n}(x_i - \bar{x})(y_i - \bar{y})}{\sqrt{\sum_{i=1}^{n}(x_i - \bar{x})^2}\sqrt{\sum_{i=1}^{n}(y_i - \bar{y})^2}}$$

where r is the correlation coefficient, n is the number of data values in the set, (x_i, y_i) is a point in the set, and $\bar{x}$ and $\bar{y}$ are the means.

Practice

P1. Given the following graph, determine the range of patient ages:

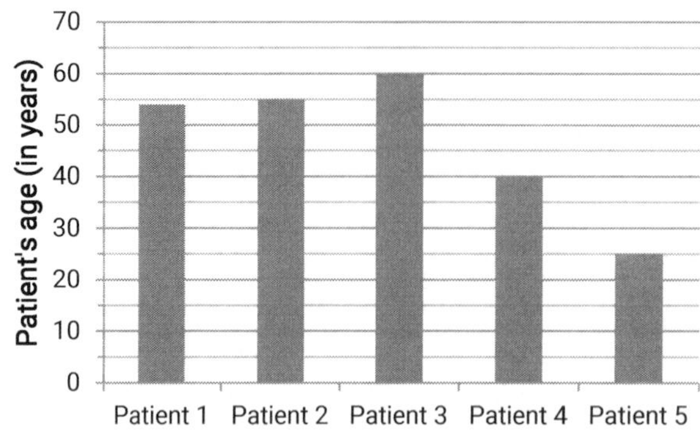

P2. Calculate the sample variance for the dataset $\{10, 13, 12, 5, 8, 18\}$

Practice Solutions

P1. Patient 1 is 54 years old; Patient 2 is 55 years old; Patient 3 is 60 years old; Patient 4 is 40 years old; and Patient 5 is 25 years old. The range of patient ages is the age of the oldest patient minus the age of the youngest patient. In other words, $60 - 25 = 35$. The range of ages is 35 years.

P2. To find the variance, first find the mean:

$$\frac{10 + 13 + 12 + 5 + 8 + 18}{6} = \frac{66}{6} = 11$$

Now, apply the formula for sample variance:

$$\begin{aligned} s^2 &= \frac{\sum_{i=1}^{n}(x_i - \bar{x})^2}{n-1} = \frac{\sum_{i=1}^{6}(x_i - 11)^2}{6-1} \\ &= \frac{(10-11)^2 + (13-11)^2 + (12-11)^2 + (5-11)^2 + (8-11)^2 + (18-11)^2}{5} \\ &= \frac{(-1)^2 + 2^2 + 1^2 + (-6)^2 + (-3)^2 + 7^2}{5} \\ &= \frac{1 + 4 + 1 + 36 + 9 + 49}{5} \\ &= \frac{100}{5} = 20 \end{aligned}$$

Reading

Literary Text Analysis

Setting and Time Frame

A literary text has both a setting and time frame. A **setting** is the place in which the story as a whole is set. The **time frame** is the period in which the story is set. This may refer to the historical period the story takes place in or if the story takes place over a single day. Both setting and time frame are relevant to a text's meaning because they help the reader place the story in time and space. An author uses setting and time frame to anchor a text, create a mood, and enhance its meaning; helping a reader understand why a character acts the way he does, or why certain events in the story are important. The setting impacts the **plot** and character **motivations**, while the time frame helps place the story in **chronological context**.

Example

Read the following excerpt from The Adventures of Huckleberry Finn by Mark Twain and analyze the relevance of setting to the text's meaning:

> We said there warn't no home like a raft, after all. Other places do seem so cramped up and smothery, but a raft don't. You feel mighty free and easy and comfortable on a raft.

This excerpt from *The Adventures of Huckleberry Finn* by Mark Twain reveals information about the **setting** of the book. By understanding that the main character, Huckleberry Finn, lives on a raft, the reader can place the story on a river, in this case, the Mississippi River in the South before the Civil War. The information about the setting also gives the reader clues about the **character** of Huck Finn: he clearly values independence and freedom and he likes the outdoors. The information about the setting in the quote helps the reader to better understand the rest of the text.

Theme

The theme of a passage is what the reader learns from the text or the passage. It is the lesson or **moral** contained in the passage. It also is a unifying idea that is used throughout the text; it can take the form of a common setting, idea, symbol, design, or recurring event. A passage can have two or more themes that convey its overall idea. The theme or themes of a passage are often based on **universal themes**. They can frequently be expressed using well-known sayings about life, society, or human nature, such as "Hard work pays off" or "Good triumphs over evil." Themes are not usually stated **explicitly**. The reader must figure them out by carefully reading the passage. Themes are often the reason why passages are written; they give a passage unity and meaning. Themes are created through **plot development**. The events of a story help shape the themes of a passage.

Review Video: Themes in Literature
Visit mometrix.com/academy and enter code: 732074

Example

Explain why "Take care of what you care about" accurately describes the theme of the following excerpt.

> Luca collected baseball cards, but he wasn't very careful with them. He left them around the house. His dog liked to chew. Luca and his friend Bart were looking at his collection. Then they went outside. When Luca got home, he saw his dog chewing on his cards. They were ruined.

This excerpt tells the story of a boy who is careless with his baseball cards and leaves them lying around. His dog ends up chewing them and ruining them. The lesson is that if you care about something, you need to take care of it. This is the point of the story. The **theme** is the lesson that a story teaches. Some stories have more than one theme, but this is not really true of this excerpt. The reader needs to figure out the theme based on what happens in the story. Sometimes, as in the case of fables, the theme is stated directly in the text. However, this is not usually the case.

Similar Themes across Cultures

A brief study of world literature suggests that writers from vastly different cultures address **similar themes**. For instance, works like the *Odyssey* and *Hamlet* both consider the individual's battle for self-control and independence. In most cultures, authors address themes of *personal growth and the struggle for maturity*. Another universal theme is the *conflict between the individual and society*. Works that are as culturally disparate as *Native Son*, the *Aeneid*, and *1984* dramatize how people struggle to maintain their personalities and dignity in large (sometimes) oppressive groups. Finally, many cultures have versions of the *hero's or heroine's journey* in which an adventurous person must overcome many obstacles in order to gain greater knowledge, power, and perspective. Some famous works that treat this theme are the *Epic of Gilgamesh*, Dante's *Divine Comedy*, and Cervantes' *Don Quixote.*

Differences in Addressing Themes in Various Cultures and Genres

Authors from different **genres** and **cultures** may address similar themes, but they do so in different ways. For instance, poets are likely to address subject matter indirectly through the use of *images and allusions*. In a play, the author is more likely to dramatize themes by using characters to express opposing viewpoints; this disparity is known as a *dialectical approach*. In a passage, the author does not need to express themes directly; indeed, they can be expressed through *events and actions*. In some regional literatures, such as Greece or England, authors tend to use more irony. In the 1950s, Latin American authors popularized the use of unusual and surreal events to show themes about real life in the genre of magical realism. Japanese authors use the well-established poetic form of the haiku to organize their treatment of common themes.

Conflict

Read the following paragraph and discuss the type of conflict present:

> Timothy was shocked out of sleep by the appearance of a bear just outside his tent. After panicking for a moment, he remembered some advice he had read in preparation for this trip: he should make noise so the bear would not be startled. As Timothy started to hum and sing, the bear wandered away.

There are three main types of conflict in literature: **man versus man**, man versus nature, and **man versus self**. This paragraph is an example of man versus nature. Timothy is in conflict with the bear. Even though no physical conflict like an attack exists, Timothy is pitted against the bear.

Timothy uses his knowledge to "defeat" the bear and keep himself safe. The solution to the conflict is that Timothy makes noise, the bear wanders away, and Timothy is safe.

> **Review Video: Conflict**
> Visit mometrix.com/academy and enter code: 559550

Conflict Resolution

The way the conflict is **resolved** depends on the type of conflict. The plot of any book starts with the lead up to the conflict, then the conflict itself, and finally the solution, or **resolution**, to the conflict. In *man versus man* conflicts, the conflict is often resolved by two parties coming to some sort of agreement or by one party triumphing over the party. In *man versus nature* conflicts, the conflict is often resolved by man coming to some realization about some aspect of nature. In *man versus self* conflicts, the conflict is often resolved by the character growing or coming to an understanding about part of himself.

Syntax and Word Choice

Authors use words and **syntax**, or sentence structure, to make their texts unique, convey their own writing style, and sometimes to make a point or emphasis. They know that word choice and syntax contribute to the reader's understanding of the text as well as to the tone and mood of a text.

> **Review Video: Syntax**
> Visit mometrix.com/academy and enter code: 242280

Figurative Language

There are many types of language devices that authors use to convey their meaning in a descriptive way. Understanding these concepts will help you understand what you read. These types of devices are called **figurative language** – language that goes beyond the literal meaning of a word or phrase. **Descriptive language** that evokes imagery in the reader's mind is one type of figurative language. **Exaggeration** is another type of figurative language. Also, when you compare two things, you are using figurative language. **Similes** and **metaphors** are ways of comparing things, and both are types of figurative language commonly found in poetry. An example of figurative language (a simile in this case): *The child howled like a coyote when her mother told her to pick up the toys.* In this example, the child's howling is compared to that of a coyote and helps the reader understand the sound being made by the child.

> **Review Video: Figurative Language**
> Visit mometrix.com/academy and enter code: 584902

Metaphor

A **metaphor** is a type of figurative language in which the writer equates one thing with a different thing. For instance: *The bird was an arrow arcing through the sky.* In this sentence, the arrow is serving as a metaphor for the bird. The point of a metaphor is to encourage the reader to consider the item being described in a *different way.* Let's continue with this metaphor for a bird: you are asked to envision the bird's flight as being similar to the arc of an arrow. So, you imagine the flight to be swift and bending. Metaphors are a way for the author to describe an item *without being direct and obvious.* This literary device is a lyrical and suggestive way of providing information. Note that the reference for a metaphor will not always be mentioned explicitly by the author. Consider the following description of a forest in winter: *Swaying skeletons reached for the sky and groaned as the* *wind blew through them.* In this example, the author is using *skeletons* as a metaphor for leafless trees. This metaphor creates a spooky tone while inspiring the reader's imagination.

Review Video: Metaphors in Writing
Visit mometrix.com/academy and enter code: 133295

Simile

A **simile** is a figurative expression that is similar to a metaphor, yet the expression requires the use of the distancing words *like* or *as*. Some examples: *The sun was like an orange*, *eager as a beaver*, and *nimble as a mountain goat.* Because a simile includes *like* or *as*, the device creates a space between the description and the thing being described. If an author says that *a house was like a shoebox*, then the tone is different than the author saying that the house *was* a shoebox. In a simile, authors explicitly indicate that the description is **not** the same thing as the thing being described. In a metaphor, there is no such distinction. The decision of which device to use will be made based on the authors' intended **tone**.

Review Video: Similes
Visit mometrix.com/academy and enter code: 642949

Personification

Another type of figurative language is **personification**. This is the description of a nonhuman thing as if the item were **human**. Literally, the word means the process of making something into a person. The general intent of personification is to describe things in a manner that will be comprehensible to readers. When an author states that a tree *groans* in the wind, he or she does not mean that the tree is emitting a low, pained sound from a mouth. Instead, the author means that the tree is making a noise similar to a human groan. Of course, this personification establishes a tone of sadness or suffering. A different tone would be established if the author said that the tree was *swaying* or *dancing*.

Review Video: Personification
Visit mometrix.com/academy and enter code: 260066

Allusion

An allusion is an uncited but recognizable reference to something else. Authors use language to make allusions to places, events, artwork, and other books in order to make their own text richer. For example, an author may allude to a very important text in order to make his own text seem more important. Martin Luther King, Jr. started his "I Have a Dream" speech by saying "Five score years ago…" This is a clear allusion to President Abraham Lincoln's "Gettysburg Address" and served to remind people of the significance of the event. An author may allude to a place to ground his text or make a cultural reference to make readers feel included. There are many reasons that authors make allusions.

Review Video: Allusions
Visit mometrix.com/academy and enter code: 294065

Comic Relief

Comic relief is the use of comedy by an author to break up a dramatic or tragic scene and infuse it with a bit of **lightheartedness**. In William Shakespeare's *Hamlet*, two gravediggers digging the grave for Ophelia share a joke while they work. The death and burial of Ophelia are tragic moments that directly follow each other. Shakespeare uses an instance of comedy to break up the tragedy and give his audience a bit of a break from the tragic drama. Authors sometimes use comic relief so that their work will be less depressing; other times they use it to create irony or contrast between the darkness of the situation and the lightness of the joke. Often, authors will use comedy to parallel what is happening in the tragic scenes.

Review Video: Comic Relief
Visit mometrix.com/academy and enter code: 779604

Literary Text Analysis Chapter Quiz

1. The period in which the story is set is known as what?

a. Time frame
b. Setting
c. Plot
d. Moral

2. In which of the following is the theme stated directly in the text?

a. Fable
b. Novel
c. Biography
d. Folktale

3. Which of the following is NOT one of the three main types of conflict?

a. Man versus man
b. Man versus machine
c. Man versus nature
d. Man versus self

4. An author can break up a dramatic or tragic scene and infuse it with a bit of lightheartedness by using what?

a. Comic relief
b. Allusion
c. Figurative language
d. Personification

5. *The ship groaned against every wave that beat upon its bow* is an example of what?

a. Personification
b. Metaphor
c. Simile
d. Allusion

Informational Text Analysis

Understanding a Passage

One of the most important skills in reading comprehension is the identification of **topics** and **main ideas.** There is a subtle difference between these two features. The topic is the subject of a text (i.e., what the text is all about). The main idea, on the other hand, is the most important point being made by the author. The topic is usually expressed in a few words at the most while the main idea often needs a full sentence to be completely defined. As an example, a short passage might have the topic of penguins and the main idea could be written as *Penguins are different from other birds in many ways*. In most nonfiction writing, the topic and the main idea will be **stated directly** and often appear in a sentence at the very beginning or end of the text. When being tested on an understanding of the author's topic, you may be able to skim the passage for the general idea, by reading only the first sentence of each paragraph. A body paragraph's first sentence is often—but not always—the main **topic sentence** which gives you a summary of the content in the paragraph.

However, there are cases in which the reader must figure out an **unstated** topic or main idea. In these instances, you must read every sentence of the text and try to come up with an overarching idea that is supported by each of those sentences.

Note: The main idea should not be confused with the thesis statement. While the main idea gives a brief, general summary of a text, the thesis statement provides a specific perspective on an issue that the author supports with evidence.

Review Video: Topics and Main Ideas
Visit mometrix.com/academy and enter code: 407801

Supporting details provide evidence and backing for the main point. In order to show that a main idea is correct, or valid, authors add details that prove their point. All texts contain details, but they are only classified as supporting details when they serve to reinforce some larger point. Supporting details are most commonly found in informative and persuasive texts. In some cases, they will be clearly indicated with terms like *for example* or *for instance*, or they will be enumerated with terms like *first*, *second*, and *last*. However, you need to be prepared for texts that do not contain those indicators. As a reader, you should consider whether the author's supporting details really back up his or her main point. Supporting details can be factual and correct, yet they may not be **relevant** to the author's point. Conversely, supporting details can seem pertinent, but they can be ineffective because they are based on opinion or assertions that cannot be proven.

Review Video: Supporting Details
Visit mometrix.com/academy and enter code: 396297

An example of a main idea is: *Giraffes live in the Serengeti of Africa*. A supporting detail about giraffes could be: *A giraffe in this region benefits from a long neck by reaching twigs and leaves on tall trees.* The main idea gives the general idea that the text is about giraffes. The supporting detail gives a specific fact about how the giraffes eat.

Topic and Summary Sentences

Topic and summary sentences are a convenient way to encapsulate the **main idea** of a text. In some textbooks and academic articles, the author will place a **topic** or **summary sentence** at the beginning of each section as a means of preparing the reader for what is to come. Research suggests that the brain is more receptive to new information when it has been prepared by the presentation of the main idea or some key words. The phenomenon is somewhat akin to the primer coat of paint that allows subsequent coats of paint to absorb more easily. A good topic sentence will be **clear** and not contain any **jargon**. When topic or summary sentences are not provided, good readers can jot down their own so that they can find their place in a text and refresh their memory.

EVALUATING A PASSAGE

When reading informational texts, there is importance in understanding the logical conclusion of the author's ideas. **Identifying a logical conclusion** can help you determine whether you agree with the writer or not. Coming to this conclusion is much like making an inference: the approach requires you to combine the information given by the text with what you already know in order to make a logical conclusion. If the author intended the reader to draw a certain conclusion, then you can expect the author's argumentation and detail to be leading in that direction.

One way to approach the task of drawing conclusions is to make brief **notes** of all the points made by the author. When the notes are arranged on paper, they may clarify the logical conclusion. Another way to approach conclusions is to consider whether the reasoning of the author raises any pertinent questions. Sometimes you will be able to draw several conclusions from a passage. On occasion these will be conclusions that were never imagined by the author. Therefore, be aware that these conclusions must be **supported directly by the text**.

Review Video: Identifying Logical Conclusions
Visit mometrix.com/academy and enter code: 281653

A reader should always be drawing conclusions from the text. Sometimes conclusions are **implied** from written information, and other times the information is **stated directly** within the passage. One should always aim to draw conclusions from information stated within a passage, rather than to draw them from mere implications. At times an author may provide some information and then describe a counterargument. Readers should be alert for direct statements that are subsequently rejected or weakened by the author. Furthermore, you should always read through the entire passage before drawing conclusions. Many readers are trained to expect the author's conclusions at either the beginning or the end of the passage, but many texts do not adhere to this format.

Drawing conclusions from information implied within a passage requires confidence on the part of the reader. **Implications** are things that the author does not state directly, but readers can assume based on what the author does say. Consider the following passage: *I stepped outside and opened my umbrella. By the time I got to work, the cuffs of my pants were soaked*. The author never states that it is raining, but this fact is clearly implied. Conclusions based on implication must be well supported by the text. In order to draw a solid conclusion, readers should have **multiple pieces of evidence**. If readers have only one piece, they must be assured that there is no other possible explanation than their conclusion. A good reader will be able to draw many conclusions from information implied by the text, which will be a great help on the exam.

As an aid to drawing conclusions, **outlining** the information contained in the passage should be a familiar skill to readers. An effective outline will reveal the structure of the passage and will lead to solid conclusions. An effective outline will have a title that refers to the basic subject of the text though the title does not need to restate the main idea. In most outlines, the main idea will be the first major section. Each major idea of the passage will be established as the head of a category. For instance, the most common outline format calls for the main ideas of the passage to be indicated with Roman numerals. In an effective outline of this kind, each of the main ideas will be represented by a Roman numeral and none of the Roman numerals will designate minor details or secondary ideas. Moreover, all supporting ideas and details should be placed in the appropriate place on the outline. An outline does not need to include every detail listed in the text, but the outline should feature all of those that are central to the argument or message. Each of these details should be listed under the appropriate main idea.

Review Video: Outlining
Visit mometrix.com/academy and enter code: 584445

Ideas from a text can also be organized using **graphic organizers**. A graphic organizer is a way to simplify information and take key points from the text. A graphic organizer such as a timeline may have an event listed for a corresponding date on the timeline while an outline may have an event listed under a key point that occurs in the text. Each reader needs to create the type of graphic organizer that works the best for him or her in terms of being able to recall information from a story. Examples include a *spider-map,* which takes a main idea from the story and places it in a bubble with supporting points branching off the main idea. An *outline* is useful for diagramming the main and supporting points of the entire story, and a *Venn diagram* classifies information as separate or overlapping.

Review Video: Graphic Organizers
Visit mometrix.com/academy and enter code: 665513

A helpful tool is the ability to **summarize** the information that you have read in a paragraph or passage format. This process is similar to creating an effective outline. First, a summary should accurately define the main idea of the passage though the summary does not need to explain this main idea in exhaustive detail. The summary should continue by laying out the most important supporting details or arguments from the passage. All of the significant supporting details should be included, and none of the details included should be irrelevant or insignificant. Also, the summary should accurately report all of these details. Too often, the desire for brevity in a summary leads to the sacrifice of clarity or accuracy. Summaries are often difficult to read because they omit all of the graceful language, digressions, and asides that distinguish great writing. However, an effective summary should contain much the same message as the original text.

Review Video: Summarizing Text
Visit mometrix.com/academy and enter code: 172903

Paraphrasing is another method that the reader can use to aid in comprehension. When paraphrasing, one puts what they have read into their words by rephrasing what the author has written, or one "translates" all of what the author shared into their words by including as many details as they can.

Informational Text Analysis Chapter Quiz

1. All of the following are examples of terms often used to indicate supporting details EXCEPT?

a. For instance
b. First
c. Last
d. Conversely

2. Which of the following provides a specific perspective on an issue that the author supports with evidence?

a. Topic sentence
b. Main idea
c. Jargon
d. Thesis statement

3. All of the following are graphic organizers EXCEPT

a. Timeline
b. Venn diagram
c. Outline
d. Fly map

4. *Space travel* is an example of what?

a. Topic
b. Main idea
c. Thesis statement
d. Summary sentence

5. *Space travel is costly but worth it* is an example of what?

a. Topic
b. Supporting detail
c. Main idea
d. Jargon

Inferences

Making Inferences

An inference is a conclusion that a reader can make based on the facts and other information in a passage or a story. An inference is based both on what is *found in a passage or a story* and what is *known from personal experience*. For instance, a story may say that a character is frightened and that he can hear the sounds of howling in the distance. Based on both what is in the text and personal knowledge, it might be a logical conclusion that the character is frightened because he hears the sound of wolves. A good inference is supported by the information in a passage. Inferences are different from **explicit information**, which is clearly stated in a passage. Inferences are not stated in a passage. A reader must put the information together to come up with a logical conclusion.

Read the excerpt and decide why Jana finally relaxed.

> Jana loved her job, but the work was very demanding. She had trouble relaxing. She called a friend, but she still thought about work. She ordered a pizza, but eating it did not help. Then her kitten jumped on her lap and began to purr. Jana leaned back and began to hum a little tune. She felt better.

You can draw the conclusion that Jana relaxes because her kitten jumped on her lap. The kitten purred, and Jana leaned back and hummed a tune. Then, she felt better. The excerpt does not explicitly say that this is the reason why she was able to relax. The text leaves the matter unclear, but the reader can infer or make a "best guess" that this is the reason she is relaxing. This is a logical conclusion based on the information in the passage. It is the best conclusion a reader can make based on the information he or she has read. Inferences are based on the information in a passage, but they are not directly stated in the passage.

Review Video: Inference
Visit mometrix.com/academy and enter code: 379203

Test-taking tip: While being tested on your ability to make correct inferences, you must look for **contextual clues**. An answer can be *true* but not *correct*. The contextual clues will help you find the answer that is the **best answer** out of the given choices. Be careful in your reading to understand the context in which a phrase is stated. When asked for the implied meaning of a statement made in the passage, you should immediately locate the statement and read the **context** in which the statement was made. Also, look for an answer choice that has a similar phrase to the statement in question.

Making Predictions

When reading a good passage, readers are moved to engage actively in the text. One part of being an active reader involves making predictions. A **prediction** is a guess about what will happen next. Readers constantly make predictions based on what they have read and what they already know. Consider the following sentence: *Staring at the computer screen in shock, Kim blindly reached over for the brimming glass of water on the shelf to her side.* The sentence suggests that Kim is agitated, and that she is not looking at the glass that she is going to pick up. So, a reader might predict that Kim is going to knock over the glass. Of course, not every prediction will be accurate: perhaps Kim will pick the glass up cleanly. Nevertheless, the author has certainly created the expectation that the water might be spilled. Predictions are always subject to revision as the reader acquires more information.

Review Video: Predictive Reading
Visit mometrix.com/academy and enter code: 437248

Test-taking tip: To respond to questions requiring future predictions, your answers should be based on evidence of past or present behavior.

Drawing Conclusions

A common type of inference that a reader has to make is **drawing a conclusion**. The reader makes this conclusion based on the information provided within a text. Certain facts are included to help a reader come to a specific conclusion. For example, a story may open with a man trudging through the snow on a cold winter day, dragging a sled behind him. The reader can logically **infer** from the setting of the story that the man is wearing heavy winter clothes in order to stay warm. Information is implied based on the setting of a story, which is why **setting** is an important element of the text. If the same man in the example was trudging down a beach on a hot summer day, dragging a surf board behind him, the reader would assume that the man is not wearing heavy clothes. The reader makes inferences based on their own experiences and the information presented to them in the story.

Test-taking tip: When asked for a *conclusion* that may be drawn, look for critical "hedge" phrases, such as *likely*, *may*, *can*, *will often*, among many others. When you are being tested on this knowledge, remember the question that writers insert into these hedge phrases to cover every possibility. Often an answer will be wrong simply because there is no room for exception. Extreme positive or negative answers (such as always or never) are usually not correct. The reader **should not** use any outside knowledge that is not gathered directly or reasonably inferred from the passage. Correct answers can be derived straight from the passage.

Example

Read the following sentence and draw a conclusion based upon the information presented:

> "You know the reason Mother proposed not having any presents this Christmas was because it is going to be a hard winter for everyone; and she thinks we ought not to spend money for pleasure, when our men are suffering so in the army." (from *Little Women* by Louisa May Alcott)

Based on the information in the sentence, the reader can conclude, or **infer**, that the men are away at war while the women are still at home. The pronoun *our* gives a clue to the reader that the character is speaking about men she knows. In addition, the reader can assume that the character is speaking to a brother or sister, since the term Mother is used by the character while speaking to another person. The reader can also come to the conclusion that the characters celebrate Christmas, since it is mentioned in the **context** of the sentence. In the sentence, the Mother is presented as an unselfish character who is opinionated and thinks about the wellbeing of other people.

Comparing Two Stories

When presented with two different stories, there will be **similarities** and **differences** between the two. A reader needs to make a list or other graphic organizer of the points presented in each story. Once the reader has written down the main point and supporting points for each story, the two sets of ideas can be compared. The reader can then present each idea and show how it is the same or different in the other story. This is called **comparing and contrasting ideas**.

The reader can compare ideas by stating, for example: "In Story 1, the author believes that humankind will one day land on Mars, whereas in Story 2, the author believes that Mars is too far away for humans to ever step foot on." Note that the two viewpoints are different in each story that the reader is comparing. A reader may state that: "Both stories discussed the likelihood of humankind landing on Mars." This statement shows how the viewpoint presented in both stories is based on the same topic, rather than how each viewpoint is different. The reader will complete a comparison of two stories with a conclusion.

Review Video: Comparison of Two Stories
Visit mometrix.com/academy and enter code: 833765

Inferences Chapter Quiz

1. Which of the following statements is TRUE concerning an inference and a prediction?

a. An inference is directly stated in the passage.
b. A prediction is never subject to revision as the reader acquires more information.
c. Inferences are not stated in a passage.
d. One part of being a passive reader involves making predictions.

2. Phrases that are especially helpful when drawing conclusions are known as what?

a. Root
b. Shrub
c. Bush
d. Hedge

3. What prediction can be reasonably made about the following paragraph?

Peter darted over the underbrush with a confidence established only by endless repetition. The air pricked his lungs with each icy inhale as the dew softened the thud of his strides as he bounded through the trees. The time change had left the path significantly darker than he remembered as he approached the thickest tangle of roots along the path.

a. Peter is unlikely to travel this path again.
b. Peter plans to turn around and come back later.
c. Peter is going to trip and fall.
d. Peter is going to encounter a wild animal.

Author's Craft

Organization of the Text

The way a text is organized can help readers to understand the author's intent and his or her conclusions. There are various ways to organize a text, and each one has a purpose and use. Usually, authors will organize information logically in a passage so the reader can follow and locate the information within the text. However, since not all passages are written with the same logical structure, you need to be familiar with several different types of passage structure.

Chronological

When using **chronological** order, the author presents information in the order that it happened. For example, biographies are typically written in chronological order. The subject's birth and childhood are presented first, followed by their adult life, and lastly the events leading up to the person's death.

Review Video: Chronology
Visit mometrix.com/academy and enter code: 804598

Cause and Effect

One of the most common text structures is **cause and effect**. A cause is an act or event that makes something happen, and an effect is the thing that happens as a result of the cause. A cause-and-effect relationship is not always explicit, but there are some terms in English that signal causes, such as *since*, *because*, and *due to*. Furthermore, terms that signal effects include *consequently, therefore, this lead(s) to*. As an example, consider the sentence *Because the sky was clear, Ron did not bring an umbrella*. The cause is the clear sky, and the effect is that Ron did not bring an umbrella. However, readers may find that sometimes the cause-and-effect relationship will not be clearly noted. For instance, the sentence *He was late and missed the meeting* does not contain any signaling words, but the sentence still contains a cause (he was late) and an effect (he missed the meeting).

Review Video: Rhetorical Strategy of Cause-and-Effect Analysis
Visit mometrix.com/academy and enter code: 725944

Be aware of the possibility for a single cause to have multiple effects (e.g., *Single cause*: Because you left your homework on the table, your dog engulfs the assignment. *Multiple effects*: As a result, you receive a failing grade; your parents do not allow you to visit your friends; you miss out on the new movie and meeting a potential significant other).

Also, there is a chance of a single effect to have many causes. (e.g., *Single effect*: Alan has a fever. *Many causes*: (1) An unexpected cold front came through the area, and (2) Alan forgot to take his multi-vitamin.)

Now, an effect can become the cause of another effect. This is known as a cause and effect chain. (e.g., As a result of her hatred for not doing work, Lynn got ready for her exam. This led to her passing her test with high marks. Hence, her resume was accepted, and her application was accepted.)

Persuasive essays, in which an author tries to make a convincing argument and change the minds of readers, usually include cause-and-effect relationships. However, these relationships should not always be taken at face value. Frequently, an author will assume a cause or take an effect for granted. To read a persuasive essay effectively, readers need to judge the cause-and-effect relationships that the author is presenting. For instance, imagine an author wrote the following: *The parking deck has been unprofitable because people would prefer to ride their bikes.* The relationship is clear: the cause is that people prefer to ride their bikes, and the effect is that the parking deck has been unprofitable. However, readers should consider whether this argument is conclusive. Perhaps there are other reasons for the failure of the parking deck: a down economy, excessive fees, etc. Too often, authors present causal relationships as if they are fact rather than opinion. Readers should be on the alert for these dubious claims.

Descriptive Text

In a sense, almost all writing is descriptive, insofar as an author seeks to describe events, ideas, or people to the reader. Some texts, however, are primarily concerned with **description**. A descriptive text focuses on a particular subject and attempts to depict the subject in a way that will be clear to readers. Descriptive texts contain many adjectives and adverbs (i.e., words that give shades of meaning and create a more detailed mental picture for the reader). A descriptive text fails when it is unclear to the reader. A descriptive text will certainly be informative and may be persuasive and entertaining as well.

Problem-Solution

Some nonfiction texts are organized to **present a problem** followed by a solution. For this type of text, the problem is often explained before the solution is offered. In some cases, as when the problem is well known, the solution may be introduced briefly at the beginning. Other passages may focus on the solution, and the problem will be referenced only occasionally. Some texts will outline multiple solutions to a problem, leaving readers to choose among them. If the author has an interest or an allegiance to one solution, he or she may fail to mention or describe accurately some of the other solutions. Readers should be careful of the author's agenda when reading a problem-solution text. Only by understanding the author's perspective and interests can one develop a proper judgment of the proposed solution.

Compare and Contrast

Many texts follow the **compare-and-contrast** model in which the similarities and differences between two ideas or things are explored. Analysis of the similarities between ideas is called comparison. In an ideal comparison, the author places ideas or things in an equivalent structure (i.e., the author presents the ideas in the same way). If an author wants to show the similarities between cricket and baseball, then he or she may do so by summarizing the equipment and rules for each game. Be mindful of the similarities as they appear in the passage and take note of any differences that are mentioned. Often, these small differences will only reinforce the more general similarity.

Review Video: Compare and Contrast Essays
Visit mometrix.com/academy and enter code: 798319

Thinking critically about ideas and conclusions can seem like a daunting task. One way to ease this task is to understand the basic elements of ideas and writing techniques. Looking at the way different ideas relate to each other can be a good way for readers to begin their analysis. For instance, sometimes authors will write about two ideas that are in opposition to each other. Or one author will provide his or her ideas on a topic, and another author may respond in opposition. The analysis of these opposing ideas is known as **contrast**. Contrast is often marred by the author's obvious partiality to one of the ideas. A discerning reader will be put off by an author who does not engage in a fair fight. In an analysis of opposing ideas, both ideas should be presented in clear and reasonable terms. If the author does prefer a side, you need to read carefully to determine the areas where the author shows or avoids this preference. In an analysis of opposing ideas, you should proceed through the passage by marking the major differences point by point with an eye that is looking for an explanation of each side's view. For instance, in an analysis of capitalism and communism, there is an importance in outlining each side's view on labor, markets, prices, personal responsibility, etc. Additionally, as you read through the passages, you should note whether the opposing views present each side in a similar manner.

SEQUENCE

Readers must be able to identify a text's **sequence**, or the order in which things happen. Often, when the sequence is very important to the author, the text is indicated with signal words like *first*, *then*, *next*, and *last*. However, a sequence can be merely implied and must be noted by the reader. Consider the sentence *He walked through the garden and gave water and fertilizer to the plants*. Clearly, the man did not walk through the garden before he collected water and fertilizer for the plants. So, the implied sequence is that he first collected water, then he collected fertilizer, next he walked through the garden, and last he gave water or fertilizer as necessary to the plants. Texts do not always proceed in an orderly sequence from first to last. Sometimes they begin at the end and start over at the beginning. As a reader, you can enhance your understanding of the passage by taking brief notes to clarify the sequence.

Review Video: Sequence
Visit mometrix.com/academy and enter code: 489027

TRANSITIONS

Transitional words and phrases are devices that guide readers through a text. You are no doubt familiar with the common transitions, though you may never have considered how they operate. Some transitional phrases (*after*, *before*, *during*, *in the middle of*) give information about time. Some indicate that an example is about to be given (*for example*, *in fact*, *for instance*). Writers use them to compare (*also*, *likewise*) and contrast (*however*, *but*, *yet*). Transitional words and phrases can suggest addition (*and*, *also*, *furthermore*, *moreover*) and logical relationships (*if*, *then*, *therefore*, *as a result*, *since*). Finally, transitional words and phrases can separate the steps in a process (*first*, *second*, *last*).

Review Video: What are Transition Words?
Visit mometrix.com/academy and enter code: 707563

POINT OF VIEW

Another element that impacts a text is the author's point of view. The **point of view** of a text is the perspective from which a passage is told. An author will always have a point of view about a story before he or she draws up a plot line. The author will know what events they want to take place, how they want the characters to interact, and how they want the story to resolve. An author will also have an opinion on the topic or series of events which is presented in the story that is based on their prior experience and beliefs.

The two main points of view that authors use, especially in a work of fiction, are first person and third person. If the narrator of the story is also the main character, or *protagonist*, the text is written in first-person point of view. In first person, the author writes from the perspective of *I*. Third-person point of view is probably the most common that authors use in their passages. Using third person, authors refer to each character by using *he* or *she*. In third-person omniscient, the narrator is not a character in the story and tells the story of all of the characters at the same time.

Review Video: Point of View
Visit mometrix.com/academy and enter code: 383336

PURPOSES FOR WRITING

In order to be an effective reader, one must pay attention to the author's **position** and purpose. Even those texts that seem objective and impartial, like textbooks, have a position and bias. Readers need to take these positions into account when considering the author's message. When an author uses emotional language or clearly favors one side of an argument, his or her position is clear. However, the author's position may be evident not only in what he or she writes, but also in what he or she doesn't write. In a normal setting, a reader would want to review some other texts on the same topic in order to develop a view of the author's position. If this was not possible, then you would want to acquire some background about the author. However, since you are in the middle of an exam and the only source of information is the text, you should look for language and argumentation that seems to indicate a particular stance on the subject.

Review Video: Author's Position
Visit mometrix.com/academy and enter code: 827954

Usually, identifying the **purpose** of an author is easier than identifying his or her position. In most cases, the author has no interest in hiding his or her purpose. A text that is meant to entertain, for instance, should be written to please the reader. Most narratives, or stories, are written to entertain, though they may also inform or persuade. Informative texts are easy to identify, while the most difficult purpose of a text to identify is persuasion because the author has an interest in making this purpose hard to detect. When a reader discovers that the author is trying to persuade, he or she should be skeptical of the argument. For this reason, persuasive texts often try to establish an entertaining tone and hope to amuse the reader into agreement. On the other hand, an informative tone may be implemented to create an appearance of authority and objectivity.

An author's purpose is evident often in the organization of the text (e.g., section headings in bold font points to an informative text). However, you may not have such organization available to you in your exam. Instead, if the author makes his or her main idea clear from the beginning, then the likely purpose of the text is to inform. If the author begins by making a claim and provides various arguments to support that claim, then the purpose is probably to persuade. If the author tells a story or seems to want the attention of the reader more than to push a particular point or deliver information, then his or her purpose is most likely to entertain. As a reader, you must judge authors on how well they accomplish their purpose. In other words, you need to consider the type of passage (e.g., technical, persuasive, etc.) that the author has written and if the author has followed the requirements of the passage type.

Review Video: Understanding the Author's Intent
Visit mometrix.com/academy and enter code: 511819

PERSUASIVE WRITING

In a persuasive essay, the author is attempting to change the reader's mind or **convince** him or her of something that he or she did not believe previously. There are several identifying characteristics of **persuasive writing**. One is **opinion presented as fact**. When authors attempt to persuade readers, they often present their opinions as if they were fact. Readers must be on guard for statements that sound factual but which cannot be subjected to research, observation, or experiment. Another characteristic of persuasive writing is **emotional language**. An author will often try to play on the emotions of readers by appealing to their sympathy or sense of morality. When an author uses colorful or evocative language with the intent of arousing the reader's passions, then the author may be attempting to persuade. Finally, in many cases, a persuasive text will give an **unfair explanation of opposing positions**, if these positions are mentioned at all.

Informative Texts

An **informative text** is written to educate and enlighten readers. Informative texts are almost always nonfiction and are rarely structured as a story. The intention of an informative text is to deliver information in the most comprehensible way. So, look for the structure of the text to be very clear. In an informative text, the thesis statement is one or two sentences that normally appears at the end of the first paragraph. The author may use some colorful language, but he or she is likely to put more emphasis on clarity and precision. Informative essays do not typically appeal to the emotions. They often contain facts and figures and rarely include the opinion of the author; however, readers should remain aware of the possibility for a bias as those facts are presented. Sometimes a persuasive essay can resemble an informative essay, especially if the author maintains an even tone and presents his or her views as if they were established fact.

Review Video: Informative Text
Visit mometrix.com/academy and enter code: 924964

Entertaining Texts

The success or failure of an author's intent to **entertain** is determined by those who read the author's work. Entertaining texts may be either fiction or nonfiction, and they may describe real or imagined people, places, and events. Entertaining texts are often narratives or poems. A text that is written to entertain is likely to contain **colorful language** that engages the imagination and the emotions. Such writing often features a great deal of figurative language, which typically enlivens the subject matter with images and analogies.

Though an entertaining text is not usually written to persuade or inform, authors may accomplish both of these tasks in their work. An entertaining text may *appeal to the reader's emotions* and cause him or her to think differently about a particular subject. In any case, entertaining texts tend to showcase the personality of the author more than other types of writing.

Expression of Feelings

When an author intends to **express feelings,** he or she may use **expressive and bold language**. An author may write with emotion for any number of reasons. Sometimes, authors will express feelings because they are describing a personal situation of great pain or happiness. In other situations, authors will attempt to persuade the reader and will use emotion to stir up the passions. This kind of expression is easy to identify when the writer uses phrases like *I felt* and *I sense*. However, readers may find that the author will simply describe feelings without introducing them. As a reader, you must know the importance of recognizing when an author is expressing emotion and not to become overwhelmed by sympathy or passion. Readers should maintain some **detachment** so that they can still evaluate the strength of the author's argument or the quality of the writing.

Review Video: Emotional Language in Literature
Visit mometrix.com/academy and enter code: 759390

Types of Passages

Narrative Passage

A **narrative** passage is a story that can be fiction or nonfiction. However, there are a few elements that a text must have in order to be classified as a narrative. First, the text must have a **plot** (i.e., a series of events). Narratives often proceed in a clear sequence, but this is not a requirement. If the narrative is good, then these events will be interesting to readers. Second, a narrative has **characters**. These characters could be people, animals, or even inanimate objects—so long as they participate in the plot. Third, a narrative passage often contains **figurative language** which is meant to stimulate the imagination of readers by making comparisons and observations. For instance, a *metaphor*, a common piece of figurative language, is a description of one thing in terms of another. *The moon was a frosty snowball* is an example of a metaphor. In the literal sense this is obviously untrue, but the comparison suggests a certain mood for the reader.

Expository Passage

An **expository** passage aims to **inform** and enlighten readers. The passage is nonfiction and usually centers around a simple, easily defined topic. Since the goal of exposition is to teach, such a passage should be as clear as possible. Often, an expository passage contains helpful organizing words, like *first*, *next*, *for example*, and *therefore*. These words keep the reader **oriented** in the text. Although expository passages do not need to feature colorful language and artful writing, they are often more effective with these features. For a reader, the challenge of expository passages is to maintain steady attention. Expository passages are not always about subjects that will naturally interest a reader, so the writer is often more concerned with **clarity** and **comprehensibility** than with engaging the reader. By reading actively, you will ensure a good habit of focus when reading an expository passage.

Review Video: Expository Passages
Visit mometrix.com/academy and enter code: 256515

Technical Passage

A **technical** passage is written to *describe* a complex object or process. Technical writing is common in medical and technological fields, in which complex ideas of mathematics, science, and engineering need to be explained *simply* and *clearly*. To ease comprehension, a technical passage usually proceeds in a very logical order. Technical passages often have clear headings and subheadings, which are used to keep the reader oriented in the text. Additionally, you will find that these passages divide sections up with numbers or letters. Many technical passages look more like an outline than a piece of prose. The amount of **jargon** or difficult vocabulary will vary in a technical passage depending on the intended audience. As much as possible, technical passages try to avoid language that the reader will have to research in order to understand the message, yet readers will find that jargon cannot always be avoided.

Review Video: Technical Passages
Visit mometrix.com/academy and enter code: 478923

Persuasive Passage

A **persuasive** passage is meant to change the mind of readers and lead them into **agreement** with the author. The persuasive intent may be very obvious or quite difficult to discern. In some cases, a persuasive passage will be indistinguishable from one that is informative. Both passages make an assertion and offer supporting details. However, a persuasive passage is more likely to appeal to the reader's **emotions** and to make claims based on **opinion**. Persuasive passages may not describe alternate positions, but when they do, they often display significant **bias**. Readers may find that a persuasive passage is giving the author's viewpoint, or the passage may adopt a seemingly objective tone. A persuasive passage is successful if it can make a convincing argument and win the trust of the reader.

Review Video: Persuasive Essay
Visit mometrix.com/academy and enter code: 621428

Author's Craft Chapter Quiz

1. ***Since today is the last day of school, I don't have to wake up early tomorrow*** **is an example of which type of text organization?**

a. Cause and effect
b. Chronological
c. Problem and solution
d. Compare and contrast

2. Which of the following is typically written in chronological order?

a. Biography
b. Science fiction novel
c. Persuasive essay
d. Descriptive text

3. An effect that becomes the cause of another effect is known as what?

a. Cause and effect sandwich
b. Cause and effect train
c. Cause and effect web
d. Cause and effect chain

4. Which of the following is TRUE about first-person or third-person point of view?

a. First-person point of view is the most common.
b. The author refers to each character as *he* or *she* in first-person point of view.
c. Third-person omniscient occurs when the narrator is not a character in the story.
d. Only first-person point of view contains a protagonist.

5. All of the following are necessary elements of a narrative passage EXCEPT?

a. The text must have a plot.
b. The text must proceed in a clear sequence.
c. There must be characters.
d. The text should contain figurative language.

Argumentation

EVALUATING AN ARGUMENT

Argumentative and persuasive passages take a stand on a debatable issue, seek to explore all sides of the issue, and find the best possible solution. Argumentative and persuasive passages should not be combative or abusive. The word *argument* may remind you of two or more people shouting at each other and walking away in anger. However, an argumentative or persuasive passage should be a calm and reasonable presentation of an author's ideas for others to consider. When an author writes reasonable arguments, his or her goal is not to win or have the last word. Instead, authors want to reveal current understanding of the question at hand and suggest a solution to a problem. The purpose of argument and persuasion in a free society is to reach the best solution.

EVIDENCE

The term **text evidence** refers to information that supports a main point or minor points and can help lead the reader to a conclusion. Information used as text evidence is precise, descriptive, and factual. A main point is often followed by supporting details that provide evidence to back up a claim. For example, a passage may include the claim that winter occurs during opposite months in the Northern and Southern hemispheres. Text evidence based on this claim may include countries where winter occurs in opposite months along with reasons that winter occurs at different times of the year in separate hemispheres (due to the tilt of the Earth as it rotates around the sun).

Review Video: Textual Evidence
Visit mometrix.com/academy and enter code: 486236

Evidence needs to be provided that supports the thesis and additional arguments. Most arguments must be supported by facts or statistics. Facts are something that is known with certainty and have been verified by several independent individuals. Examples and illustrations add an emotional component to arguments. With this component, you persuade readers in ways that facts and statistics cannot. The emotional component is effective when used with objective information that can be confirmed.

CREDIBILITY

The text used to support an argument can be the argument's downfall if the text is not credible. A text is **credible**, or believable, when the author is knowledgeable and objective, or unbiased. The author's motivations for writing the text play a critical role in determining the credibility of the text and must be evaluated when assessing that credibility. Reports written about the ozone layer by an environmental scientist and a hairdresser will have a different level of credibility.

Review Video: Author Credibility
Visit mometrix.com/academy and enter code: 827257

APPEAL TO EMOTION

Sometimes, authors will appeal to the reader's emotion in an attempt to persuade or to distract the reader from the weakness of the argument. For instance, the author may try to inspire the pity of the reader by delivering a heart-rending story. An author also might use the bandwagon approach, in which he suggests that his opinion is correct because it is held by the majority. Some authors resort to name-calling, in which insults and harsh words are delivered to the opponent in an attempt to distract. In advertising, a common appeal is the celebrity testimonial, in which a famous person endorses a product. Of course, the fact that a famous person likes something should not really mean anything to the reader. These and other emotional appeals are usually evidence of poor reasoning and a weak argument.

Review Video: Reading Logical Fallacies
Visit mometrix.com/academy and enter code: 644845

Counter Arguments

When authors give both sides to the argument, they build trust with their readers. As a reader, you should start with an undecided or neutral position. If an author presents only his or her side to the argument, then you will need to be concerned at best.

Building common ground with neutral or opposed readers can be appealing to skeptical readers. Sharing values with undecided readers can allow people to switch positions without giving up what they feel is important. For people who may oppose a position, they need to feel that they can change their minds without betraying who they are as a person. This appeal to having an open mind can be a powerful tool in arguing a position without antagonizing other views. Objections can be countered on a point-by-point basis or in a summary paragraph. Be mindful of how an author points out flaws in counter arguments. If they are unfair to the other side of the argument, then you should lose trust with the author.

Opinions, Facts, and Fallacies

Critical thinking skills are mastered through understanding various types of writing and the different purposes of authors in writing their passages. Every author writes for a purpose. When you understand their purpose and how they accomplish their goal, you will be able to analyze their writing and determine whether or not you agree with their conclusions.

Readers must always be conscious of the distinction between fact and opinion. A **fact** can be subjected to analysis and can be either proved or disproved. An **opinion**, on the other hand, is the author's personal thoughts or feelings which may not be alterable by research or evidence. If the author writes that the distance from New York City to Boston is about two hundred miles, then he or she is stating a fact. If the author writes that New York City is too crowded, then he or she is giving an opinion because there is no objective standard for "too crowded." Opinions are often supported by facts. For instance, the author might cite the population density of New York City as compared to that of other major American cities as evidence of an overcrowded population. An opinion supported by fact tends to be more convincing. On the other hand, when authors support their opinions with other opinions, readers should not be persuaded by the argument to any degree.

When you have an argumentative passage, you need to be sure that facts are presented to the reader from reliable sources. An opinion is what the author thinks about a given topic. An opinion is not common knowledge or proven by expert sources, instead the information is the personal beliefs and thoughts of the author. To distinguish between fact and opinion, a reader needs to consider the type of source that is presenting information, the information that backs-up a claim, and the author's motivation to have a certain point-of-view on a given topic. For example, if a panel of scientists has conducted multiple studies on the effectiveness of taking a certain vitamin, then the results are more likely to be factual than a company that is selling a vitamin and claims that taking the vitamin can produce positive effects. The company is motivated to sell their product, and the scientists are using the scientific method to prove a theory. Remember: if you find sentences that contain phrases such as "I think...", then the statement is an opinion.

Review Video: Fact or Opinion
Visit mometrix.com/academy and enter code: 870899

In their attempts to persuade, writers often make mistakes in their thinking patterns and writing choices. These patterns and choices are important to understand so you can make an informed decision. Every author has a point-of-view, but authors demonstrate a bias when they ignore reasonable counterarguments or distort opposing viewpoints. A bias is evident whenever the author is unfair or inaccurate in his or her presentation. Bias may be intentional or unintentional, and readers should be skeptical of the author's argument. Remember that a biased author may still be correct; however, the author will be correct in spite of his or her bias, not because of the bias.

A **stereotype** is a bias applied specifically to a group or place. Stereotyping is considered to be particularly abhorrent because the practice promotes negative generalizations about people. Readers should be very cautious of authors who stereotype in their writing. These faulty assumptions typically reveal the author's ignorance and lack of curiosity.

Review Video: Bias and Stereotype
Visit mometrix.com/academy and enter code: 644829

Argumentation Chapter Quiz

1. What is the purpose of argument and persuasion in a free society?

a. To reach the best solution for a given issue
b. To dismantle the arguments of opponents
c. To silence all dissention
d. To win the argument without having to be combative

2. The bandwagon approach refers to the idea that

a. An author's opinion is correct because they are the first to suggest it.
b. An author's opinion is correct because it is held by the majority.
c. An author's opinion is incorrect because there are many others who suggested it before them.
d. An author's opinion is correct because a celebrity agrees with it.

3. Which of the following is NOT an opinion?

a. Dogs are better than cats in every conceivable way.
b. Broccoli is not very tasty.
c. Texas is the second largest state in the US.
d. Rock music from the 80s is better than modern rock.

Vocabulary

Denotative vs. Connotative Meaning

The **denotative** meaning of a word is the literal meaning. The **connotative** meaning goes beyond the denotative meaning to include the emotional reaction that a word may invoke. The connotative meaning often takes the denotative meaning a step further due to associations which the reader makes with the denotative meaning. Readers can differentiate between the denotative and connotative meanings by first recognizing how authors use each meaning. Most non-fiction, for example, is fact-based and authors do not use flowery, figurative language. The reader can assume that the writer is using the denotative meaning of words. In fiction, the author may use the connotative meaning. Readers can determine whether the author is using the denotative or connotative meaning of a word by implementing context clues.

Review Video: Connotation and Denotation
Visit mometrix.com/academy and enter code: 310092

Context Clues

Readers of all levels will encounter words that they have either never seen or encountered on a limited basis. The best way to define a word in **context** is to look for nearby words that can assist in learning the meaning of the word. For instance, unfamiliar nouns are often accompanied by examples that provide a definition. Consider the following sentence: *Dave arrived at the party in hilarious garb: a leopard-print shirt, buckskin trousers, and high heels.* If a reader was unfamiliar with the meaning of garb, he or she could read the examples (i.e., a leopard-print shirt, buckskin trousers, and high heels) and quickly determine that the word means *clothing*. Examples will not always be this obvious. Consider this sentence: *Parsley, lemon, and flowers were just a few of items he used as garnishes.* Here, the word *garnishes* is exemplified by parsley, lemon, and flowers. Readers who have eaten in a few restaurants will probably be able to identify a garnish as something used to decorate a plate.

Review Video: Context
Visit mometrix.com/academy and enter code: 613660

In addition to looking at the context of a passage, readers can use contrasts to define an unfamiliar word in context. In many sentences, the author will not describe the unfamiliar word directly; instead, he or she will describe the opposite of the unfamiliar word. Thus, you are provided with some information that will bring you closer to defining the word. Consider the following example: *Despite his intelligence, Hector's low brow and bad posture made him look obtuse.* The author writes that Hector's appearance does not convey intelligence. Therefore, *obtuse* must mean unintelligent. Here is another example: *Despite the horrible weather, we were beatific about our trip to Alaska*. The word *despite* indicates that the speaker's feelings were at odds with the weather. Since the weather is described as *horrible*, then *beatific* must mean something positive.

In some cases, there will be very few contextual clues to help a reader define the meaning of an unfamiliar word. When this happens, one strategy that readers may employ is **substitution**. A good reader will brainstorm some possible synonyms for the given word, and he or she will substitute these words into the sentence. If the sentence and the surrounding passage continue to make sense, then the substitution has revealed at least some information about the unfamiliar word. Consider the sentence: *Frank's admonition rang in her ears as she climbed the mountain.* A reader unfamiliar with *admonition* might come up with some substitutions like *vow, promise, advice, complaint*, or *compliment*. All of these words make general sense of the sentence though their meanings are diverse. The process has suggested; however, that an admonition is some sort of message. The substitution strategy is rarely able to pinpoint a precise definition, but this process can be effective as a last resort.

Occasionally, you will be able to define an unfamiliar word by looking at the descriptive words in the context. Consider the following sentence: *Fred dragged the recalcitrant boy kicking and screaming up the stairs.* The words *dragged*, *kicking*, and *screaming* all suggest that the boy does not want to go up the stairs. The reader may assume that *recalcitrant* means something like unwilling or protesting. In this example, an unfamiliar adjective was identified.

Additionally, using description to define an unfamiliar noun is a common practice compared to unfamiliar adjectives, as in this sentence: *Don's wrinkled frown and constantly shaking fist identified him as a curmudgeon of the first order.* Don is described as having a *wrinkled frown and constantly shaking fist* suggesting that a *curmudgeon* must be a grumpy man. Contrasts do not always provide detailed information about the unfamiliar word, but they at least give the reader some clues.

When a word has more than one meaning, readers can have difficulty with determining how the word is being used in a given sentence. For instance, the verb *cleave*, can mean either *join* or *separate*. When readers come upon this word, they will have to select the definition that makes the most sense. Consider the following sentence: *Hermione's knife cleaved the bread cleanly*. Since, a knife cannot join bread together, the word must indicate separation. A slightly more difficult example would be the sentence: *The birds cleaved to one another as they flew from the oak tree.* Immediately, the presence of the words *to one another* should suggest that in this sentence *cleave* is being used to mean *join*. Discovering the intent of a word with multiple meanings requires the same tricks as defining an unknown word: look for contextual clues and evaluate the substituted words.

Synonyms and Antonyms

When you understand how words relate to each other, you will discover more in a passage. This is explained by understanding **synonyms** (e.g., words that mean the same thing) and **antonyms** (e.g., words that mean the opposite of one another). As an example, *dry* and *arid* are synonyms, and *dry* and *wet* are antonyms.

There are many pairs of words in English that can be considered synonyms, despite having slightly different definitions. For instance, the words *friendly* and *collegial* can both be used to describe a warm interpersonal relationship, and one would be correct to call them synonyms. However, *collegial* (kin to *colleague*) is often used in reference to professional or academic relationships, and *friendly* has no such connotation.

If the difference between the two words is too great, then they should not be called synonyms. *Hot* and *warm* are not synonyms because their meanings are too distinct. A good way to determine whether two words are synonyms is to substitute one word for the other word and verify that the meaning of the sentence has not changed. Substituting *warm* for *hot* in a sentence would convey a different meaning. Although warm and hot may seem close in meaning, warm generally means that the temperature is moderate, and hot generally means that the temperature is excessively high.

Antonyms are words with opposite meanings. *Light* and *dark*, *up* and *down*, *right* and *left*, *good* and *bad*: these are all sets of antonyms. Be careful to distinguish between antonyms and pairs of words that are simply different. *Black* and *gray*, for instance, are not antonyms because gray is not the opposite of black. *Black* and *white*, on the other hand, are antonyms.

Not every word has an antonym. For instance, many nouns do not: What would be the antonym of *chair*? During your exam, the questions related to antonyms are more likely to concern adjectives. You will recall that adjectives are words that describe a noun. Some common adjectives include *purple*, *fast*, *skinny*, and *sweet*. From those four adjectives, *purple* is the item that lacks a group of obvious antonyms.

Review Video: What are Synonyms and Antonyms?
Visit mometrix.com/academy and enter code: 105612

Vocabulary Chapter Quiz

1. What method can a reader use to determine which meaning of a word an author intends?

a. Paraphrasing
b. Substituting
c. Summarizing
d. Deconstructing

2. Which of the following pairs are synonyms?

a. Warm and hot
b. Sharp and dull
c. Drinks and beverages
d. Black and gray

3. Which of the following pairs are antonyms?

a. Generous and frugal
b. Cat and dog
c. Witch and wizard
d. Black and gray

Writing

Conventions of Grammar and Usage

The Eight Parts of Speech

Nouns

When you talk about a person, place, thing, or idea, you are talking about **nouns**. The two main types of nouns are **common** and **proper** nouns. Also, nouns can be abstract (i.e., general) or concrete (i.e., specific).

Common nouns are the class or group of people, places, and things (Note: Do not capitalize common nouns). Examples of common nouns:

> *People*: boy, girl, worker, manager
>
> *Places*: school, bank, library, home
>
> *Things*: dog, cat, truck, car

Proper nouns are the names of a specific person, place, or thing (Note: Capitalize all proper nouns). Examples of proper nouns:

> *People*: Abraham Lincoln, George Washington, Martin Luther King, Jr.
>
> *Places*: Los Angeles, California / New York / Asia
>
> *Things*: Statue of Liberty, Earth*, Lincoln Memorial
>
> *Note: When you talk about the planet that we live on, you capitalize *Earth*. When you mean the dirt, rocks, or land, you lowercase *earth*.

General nouns are the names of conditions or ideas. **Specific nouns** name people, places, and things that are understood by using your senses.

General nouns:

> *Condition*: beauty, strength
>
> *Idea*: truth, peace

Specific nouns:

> *People*: baby, friend, father
>
> *Places*: town, park, city hall
>
> *Things*: rainbow, cough, apple, silk, gasoline

Collective nouns are the names for a person, place, or thing that may act as a whole. The following are examples of collective nouns: *class, company, dozen, group, herd, team,* and *public*.

Pronouns

Pronouns are words that are used to stand in for a noun. A pronoun may be classified as personal, intensive, relative, interrogative, demonstrative, indefinite, and reciprocal.

Personal: *Nominative* is the case for nouns and pronouns that are the subject of a sentence. *Objective* is the case for nouns and pronouns that are an object in a sentence. *Possessive* is the case for nouns and pronouns that show possession or ownership.

Singular

	Nominative	Objective	Possessive
First Person	I	me	my, mine
Second Person	you	you	your, yours
Third Person	he, she, it	him, her, it	his, her, hers, its

Plural

	Nominative	Objective	Possessive
First Person	we	us	our, ours
Second Person	you	you	your, yours
Third Person	they	them	their, theirs

Intensive: I myself, you yourself, he himself, she herself, the (thing) itself, we ourselves, you yourselves, they themselves

Relative: which, who, whom, whose

Interrogative: what, which, who, whom, whose

Demonstrative: this, that, these, those

Indefinite: all, any, each, everyone, either/neither, one, some, several

Reciprocal: each other, one another

Review Video: Nouns and Pronouns
Visit mometrix.com/academy and enter code: 312073

Verbs

If you want to write a sentence, then you need a verb in your sentence. Without a verb, you have no sentence. The verb of a sentence explains action or being. In other words, the verb shows the subject's movement or the movement that has been done to the subject.

Transitive and Intransitive Verbs

A transitive verb is a verb whose action (e.g., drive, run, jump) points to a receiver (e.g., car, dog, kangaroo). Intransitive verbs do not point to a receiver of an action. In other words, the action of the verb does not point to a subject or object.

Transitive: He plays the piano. | The piano was played by him.

Intransitive: He plays. | John writes well.

A dictionary will let you know whether a verb is transitive or intransitive. Some verbs can be transitive and intransitive.

Action Verbs and Linking Verbs

An action verb is a verb that shows what the subject is doing in a sentence. In other words, an action verb shows action. A sentence can be complete with one word: an action verb. Linking verbs are intransitive verbs that show a condition (i.e., the subject is described but does no action).

Linking verbs link the subject of a sentence to a noun or pronoun, or they link a subject with an adjective. You always need a verb if you want a complete sentence. However, linking verbs are not able to complete a sentence.

Common linking verbs include *appear, be, become, feel, grow, look, seem, smell, sound,* and *taste.* However, any verb that shows a condition and has a noun, pronoun, or adjective that describes the subject of a sentence is a linking verb.

Action: He sings. | Run! | Go! | I talk with him every day. | She reads.

Linking:

Incorrect: I am.

Correct: I am John. | I smell roses. | I feel tired.

Note: Some verbs are followed by words that look like prepositions, but they are a part of the verb and a part of the verb's meaning. These are known as phrasal verbs and examples include *call off, look up*, and *drop off.*

Review Video: Action Verbs and Linking Verbs
Visit mometrix.com/academy and enter code: 743142

Voice

Transitive verbs come in active or passive voice. If the subject does an action or receives the action of the verb, then you will know whether a verb is active or passive. When the subject of the sentence is doing the action, the verb is **active voice**. When the subject receives the action, the verb is **passive voice**.

Active: Jon drew the picture. (The subject *Jon* is doing the action of *drawing a picture.*)

Passive: The picture is drawn by Jon. (The subject *picture* is receiving the action from Jon.)

Verb Tenses

A verb tense shows the different form of a verb to point to the time of an action. The present and past tense are shown by changing the verb's form. An action in the present *I talk* can change form for the past: *I talked*. However, for the other tenses, an auxiliary (i.e., helping) verb is needed to show the change in form. These helping verbs include *am, are, is* | *have, has, had* | *was, were, will* (or *shall*).

Present: I talk	Present perfect: I have talked
Past: I talked	Past perfect: I had talked
Future: I will talk	Future perfect: I will have talked

Present: The action happens at the current time.

Example: He *walks* to the store every morning.

To show that something is happening right now, use the progressive present tense: I *am walking*.

Past: The action happened in the past.

Example: He *walked* to the store an hour ago.

Future: The action is going to happen later.

Example: I *will walk* to the store tomorrow.

Present perfect: The action started in the past and continues into the present.

Example: I *have walked* to the store three times today.

Past perfect: The second action happened in the past. The first action came before the second.

Example: Before I walked to the store (Action 2), I *had walked* to the library (Action 1).

Future perfect: An action that uses the past and the future. In other words, the action is complete before a future moment.

Example: When she comes for the supplies (future moment), I *will have walked* to the store (action completed in the past).

Review Video: Present Perfect, Past Perfect, and Future Perfect Verb Tenses
Visit mometrix.com/academy and enter code: 269472

CONJUGATING VERBS

When you need to change the form of a verb, you are **conjugating** a verb. The key parts of a verb are first person singular, present tense (dream); first person singular, past tense (dreamed); and the past participle (dreamed). Note: the past participle needs a helping verb to make a verb tense. For example, I *have dreamed* of this day. | I *am dreaming* of this day.

Present Tense: Active Voice

	Singular	**Plural**
First Person	I dream	We dream
Second Person	You dream	You dream
Third Person	He, she, it dreams	They dream

Mood

There are three moods in English: the indicative, the imperative, and the subjunctive.

The **indicative mood** is used for facts, opinions, and questions.

Fact: You can do this.

Opinion: I think that you can do this.

Question: Do you know that you can do this?

The **imperative** is used for orders or requests.

Order: You are going to do this!

Request: Will you do this for me?

The **subjunctive mood** is for wishes and statements that go against fact.

Wish: I wish that I were going to do this.

Statement against fact: If I were you, I would do this. (This goes against fact because I am not you. You have the chance to do this, and I do not have the chance.)

The mood that causes trouble for most people is the subjunctive mood. If you have trouble with any of the moods, then be sure to practice.

Adjectives

An adjective is a word that is used to modify a noun or pronoun. An adjective answers a question: *Which one? What kind of?* or *How many?* Usually, adjectives come before the words that they modify, but they may also come after a linking verb.

Which one? The *third* suit is my favorite.

What kind? This suit is *navy blue*.

How many? Can I look over the *four* neckties for the suit?

Articles

Articles are adjectives that are used to mark nouns. There are only three: the **definite** (i.e., limited or fixed amount) article *the*, and the **indefinite** (i.e., no limit or fixed amount) articles *a* and *an*. Note: *An* comes before words that start with a vowel sound (i.e., vowels include *a*, *e*, *i*, *o*, *u*, and *y*). For example, "Are you going to get an **u**mbrella?"

Definite: I lost *the* bottle that belongs to me.

Indefinite: Does anyone have *a* bottle to share?

Comparison with Adjectives

Some adjectives are relative and other adjectives are absolute. Adjectives that are **relative** can show the comparison between things. Adjectives that are **absolute** can show comparison. However, they show comparison in a different way. Let's say that you are reading two books. You think that one book is perfect, and the other book is not exactly perfect. It is not possible for the book to be more perfect than the other. Either you think that the book is perfect, or you think that the book is not perfect.

The adjectives that are relative will show the different **degrees** of something or someone to something else or someone else. The three degrees of adjectives include positive, comparative, and superlative.

The **positive** degree is the normal form of an adjective.

Example: This work is *difficult.* | She is *smart.*

The **comparative** degree compares one person or thing to another person or thing.

Example: This work is *more difficult* than your work. | She is *smarter* than me.

The **superlative** degree compares more than two people or things.

Example: This is the *most difficult* work of my life. | She is the *smartest* lady in school.

Review Video: What is an Adjective?
Visit mometrix.com/academy and enter code: 470154

Adverbs

An adverb is a word that is used to **modify** a verb, adjective, or another adverb. Usually, adverbs answer one of these questions: *When?*, *Where?*, *How?*, and *Why?* . The negatives *not* and *never* are known as adverbs. Adverbs that modify adjectives or other adverbs **strengthen** or **weaken** the words that they modify.

Examples:

He walks quickly through the crowd.

The water flows smoothly on the rocks.

Note: While many adverbs end in *-ly*, you need to remember that not all adverbs end in *-ly*. Also, some words that end in *-ly* are adjectives, not adverbs. Some examples include: *early, friendly, holy, lonely, silly*, and *ugly*. To know if a word that ends in *-ly* is an adjective or adverb, you need to check your dictionary.

Examples:

He is *never* angry.

You talk *too* loudly.

Comparison with Adverbs

The rules for comparing adverbs are the same as the rules for adjectives.

The **positive** degree is the standard form of an adverb.

Example: He arrives soon. | She speaks softly to her friends.

The **comparative** degree compares one person or thing to another person or thing.

Example: He arrives sooner than Sarah. | She speaks more softly than him.

The **superlative** degree compares more than two people or things.

Example: He arrives soonest of the group. | She speaks most softly of any of her friends.

Review Video: What is an Adverb?
Visit mometrix.com/academy and enter code: 713951

Prepositions

A preposition is a word placed before a noun or pronoun that shows the relationship between an object and another word in the sentence.

Common prepositions:

about	before	during	on	under
after	beneath	for	over	until
against	between	from	past	up
among	beyond	in	through	with
around	by	of	to	within
at	down	off	toward	without

Examples:

The napkin is *in* the drawer.

The Earth rotates *around* the Sun.

The needle is *beneath* the haystack.

Can you find me *among* the words?

Review Video: What is a Preposition?
Visit mometrix.com/academy and enter code: 946763

Conjunctions

Conjunctions join words, phrases, or clauses, and they show the connection between the joined pieces. **Coordinating** conjunctions connect equal parts of sentences. **Correlative** conjunctions show the connection between pairs. **Subordinating** conjunctions join subordinate (i.e., dependent) clauses with independent clauses.

Coordinating Conjunctions

The coordinating conjunctions include: *and, but, yet, or, nor, for,* and *so*

Examples:

The rock was small, but it was heavy.

She drove in the night, and he drove in the day.

Correlative Conjunctions

The correlative conjunctions are: *either...or* | *neither...nor* | *not only...but also*

Examples:

Either you are coming *or* you are staying.

He ran *not only* three miles *but also* swam 200 yards.

Review Video: Coordinating and Correlative Conjunctions
Visit mometrix.com/academy and enter code: 390329

Subordinating Conjunctions

Common subordinating conjunctions include:

after	since	whenever
although	so that	where
because	unless	wherever
before	until	whether
in order that	when	while

Examples:

I am hungry *because* I did not eat breakfast.

He went home *when* everyone left.

Review Video: Subordinating Conjunctions
Visit mometrix.com/academy and enter code: 958913

Interjections

An interjection is a word for **exclamation** (i.e., great amount of feeling) that is used alone or as a piece to a sentence. Often, they are used at the beginning of a sentence for an **introduction**. Sometimes, they can be used in the middle of a sentence to show a **change** in thought or attitude.

Common Interjections: Hey! | Oh, | Ouch! | Please! | Wow!

Subjects and Predicates

Subjects

Every sentence has two things: a subject and a verb. The **subject** of a sentence names who or what the sentence is all about. The subject may be directly stated in a sentence, or the subject may be the implied *you*.

The **complete subject** includes the simple subject and all of its modifiers. To find the complete subject, ask *Who* or *What* and insert the verb to complete the question. The answer is the complete subject. To find the **simple subject**, remove all of the modifiers (adjectives, prepositional phrases, etc.) in the complete subject. Being able to locate the subject of a sentence helps with many problems, such as those involving sentence fragments and subject-verb agreement.

Examples:

The small red car is the one that he wants for Christmas.

(The complete subject is *the small red car.*)

The young artist is coming over for dinner.

(The complete subject is *the young artist.*)

Review Video: Subjects
Visit mometrix.com/academy and enter code: 444771

In **imperative** sentences, the verb's subject is understood (e.g., [You] Run to the store) but not actually present in the sentence. Normally, the subject comes before the verb. However, the subject comes after the verb in sentences that begin with *There are* or *There was.*

Direct:

John knows the way to the park.

(Who knows the way to the park? Answer: John)

The cookies need ten more minutes.

(What needs ten minutes? Answer: The cookies)

By five o' clock, Bill will need to leave.

(Who needs to leave? Answer: Bill)

Remember: The subject can come after the verb.

There are five letters on the table for him.

(What is on the table? Answer: Five letters)

There were coffee and doughnuts in the house.

(What was in the house? Answer: Coffee and doughnuts)

Implied:

Go to the post office for me.

(Who is going to the post office? Answer: You are.)

Come and sit with me, please?

(Who needs to come and sit? Answer: You do.)

PREDICATES

In a sentence, you always have a predicate and a subject. The subject tells what the sentence is about, and the **predicate** explains or describes the subject.

Think about the sentence: *He sings.* In this sentence, we have a subject (He) and a predicate (sings). This is all that is needed for a sentence to be complete. Would we like more information? Of course, we would like to know more. However, if this is all the information that you are given, you have a complete sentence.

Now, let's look at another sentence:

John and Jane sing on Tuesday nights at the dance hall.

What is the subject of this sentence?

Answer: John and Jane.

What is the predicate of this sentence?

Answer: Everything else in the sentence (sing on Tuesday nights at the dance hall).

Review Video: What is a Predicate?
Visit mometrix.com/academy and enter code: 511780

Subject-Verb Agreement

Verbs **agree** with their subjects in number. In other words, *singular* subjects need *singular* verbs. *Plural* subjects need *plural* verbs. Singular is for one person, place, or thing. Plural is for more than one person, place, or thing. Subjects and verbs must also agree in person: first, second, or third. The present tense ending *-s* is used on a verb if its subject is third person singular; otherwise, the verb takes no ending.

Review Video: Subject-Verb Agreement
Visit mometrix.com/academy and enter code: 479190

Number Agreement Examples:

Single Subject and Verb: *Dan calls home.*

(Dan is one person. So, the singular verb *calls* is needed.)

Plural Subject and Verb: *Dan and Bob call home.*

(More than one person needs the plural verb *call.*)

Person Agreement Examples:

First Person: I *am* walking.

Second Person: You *are* walking.

Third Person: He *is* walking.

Complications with Subject-Verb Agreement

Words Between Subject and Verb

Words that come between the simple subject and the verb may serve as an effective distraction, but they have no bearing on subject-verb agreement.

Examples:

The joy of my life returns home tonight.

(**Singular Subject**: joy. **Singular Verb**: returns)

The phrase *of my life* does not influence the verb *returns.*

The question that still remains unanswered is "Who are you?"

(**Singular Subject**: question. **Singular Verb**: is)

Don't let the phrase "*that still remains*..." trouble you. The subject *question* goes with *is.*

Compound Subjects

A compound subject is formed when two or more nouns joined by *and*, *or*, or *nor* jointly act as the subject of the sentence.

Joined by And

When a compound subject is joined by *and*, it is treated as a plural subject and requires a plural verb.

Examples:

You and Jon are invited to come to my house.

(**Plural Subject**: You and Jon. **Plural Verb**: are)

The pencil and paper belong to me.

(**Plural Subject**: pencil and paper. **Plural Verb**: belong)

Joined by Or/Nor

For a compound subject joined by *or* or *nor*, the verb must agree in number with the part of the subject that is closest to the verb (italicized in the examples below).

Examples:

Today or *tomorrow is* the day.

(**Subject**: Today / tomorrow. **Verb**: is)

Stan or *Phil wants* to read the book.

(**Subject**: Stan / Phil. **Verb**: wants)

Neither the books nor the *pen is* on the desk.

(**Subject**: Books / Pen. **Verb**: is)

Either the blanket or *pillows arrive* this afternoon.

(**Subject**: Blanket / Pillows. **Verb**: arrive)

Indefinite Pronouns as Subject

An indefinite pronoun is a pronoun that does not refer to a specific noun. Indefinite pronouns may be only singular, be only plural, or change depending on how they are used.

Always Singular

Pronouns such as *each*, *either*, *everybody*, *anybody*, *somebody*, and *nobody* are always singular.

Examples:

Each of the runners *has* a different bib number.

(**Singular Subject**: Each. **Singular Verb**: has)

Is either of you ready for the game?

(**Singular Subject**: Either. **Singular Verb**: is)

Note: The words *each* and *either* can also be used as adjectives (e.g., *each* person is unique). When one of these adjectives modifies the subject of a sentence, it is always a singular subject.

Everybody grows a day older every day.

(**Singular Subject**: Everybody. **Singular Verb**: grows)

Anybody is welcome to bring a tent.

(**Singular Subject**: Anybody. **Singular Verb**: is)

Always Plural

Pronouns such as *both*, *several*, and *many* are always plural.

Examples:

Both of the siblings *were* too tired to argue.

(**Plural Subject**: Both. **Plural Verb**: were)

Many have tried, but none have succeeded.

(**Plural Subject**: Many. **Plural Verb**: have tried)

Depend on Context

Pronouns such as *some*, *any*, *all*, *none*, *more*, and *most* can be either singular or plural depending on what they are representing in the context of the sentence.

Examples:

All of my dog's food *was* still there in his bowl

(**Singular Subject**: All. **Singular Verb**: was)

By the end of the night, *all* of my guests *were* already excited about coming to my next party.

(**Plural Subject**: All. **Plural Verb**: were)

Other Cases Involving Plural or Irregular Form

Some nouns are **singular in meaning but plural in form**: news, mathematics, physics, and economics.

The *news is* coming on now.

Mathematics is my favorite class.

Some nouns are plural in form and meaning, and have **no singular equivalent**: scissors and pants.

Do these *pants come* with a shirt?

The *scissors are* for my project.

Mathematical operations are **irregular** in their construction, but are normally considered to be **singular in meaning**.

One plus one is two.

Three times three is nine.

Note: Look to your **dictionary** for help when you aren't sure whether a noun with a plural form has a singular or plural meaning.

Complements

A complement is a noun, pronoun, or adjective that is used to give more information about the subject or verb in the sentence.

Direct Objects

A direct object is a noun or pronoun that takes or receives the **action** of a verb. (Remember: a complete sentence does not need a direct object, so not all sentences will have them. A sentence needs only a subject and a verb.) When you are looking for a direct object, find the verb and ask *who* or *what.*

Examples:

I took the blanket. (Who or what did I take? *The blanket*)

Jane read books. (Who or what does Jane read? *Books*)

Indirect Objects

An indirect object is a word or group of words that show how an action had an **influence** on someone or something. If there is an indirect object in a sentence, then you always have a direct object in the sentence. When you are looking for the indirect object, find the verb and ask *to/for whom or what.*

Examples:

> We taught the old dog a new trick.
>
> (To/For Whom or What was taught? *The old dog*)
>
> I gave them a math lesson.
>
> (To/For Whom or What was given? *Them*)

Review Video: Direct and Indirect Objects
Visit mometrix.com/academy and enter code: 817385

Predicate Nominatives and Predicate Adjectives

As we looked at previously, verbs may be classified as either action verbs or linking verbs. A linking verb is so named because it links the subject to words in the predicate that describe or define the subject. These words are called predicate nominatives (if nouns or pronouns) or predicate adjectives (if adjectives).

Examples:

> My father is a *lawyer.*
>
> (Father is the **subject**. Lawyer is the **predicate nominative**.)
>
> Your mother is *patient.*
>
> (Mother is the **subject**. Patient is the **predicate adjective**.)

Pronoun Usage

The **antecedent** is the noun that has been replaced by a pronoun. A pronoun and its antecedent **agree** when they have the same number (singular or plural) and gender (male, female, or neuter).

Examples:

> **Singular agreement**: *John* came into town, and *he* played for us.
>
> (The word *he* replaces *John.*)
>
> **Plural agreement**: *John and Rick* came into town, and *they* played for us.
>
> (The word *they* replaces *John and Rick.*)

To determine which is the correct pronoun to use in a compound subject or object, try each pronoun **alone** in place of the compound in the sentence. Your knowledge of pronouns will tell you which one is correct.

Example:

Bob and (I, me) will be going.

Test: (1) *I will be going* or (2) *Me will be going*. The second choice cannot be correct because *me* cannot be used as the subject of a sentence. Instead, *me* is used as an object.

Answer: Bob and I will be going.

When a pronoun is used with a noun immediately following (as in "we boys"), try the sentence **without the added noun**.

Example:

(We/Us) boys played football last year.

Test: (1) *We played football last ye*ar or (2) *Us played football last year*. Again, the second choice cannot be correct because *us* cannot be used as a subject of a sentence. Instead, *us* is used as an object.

Answer: We boys played football last year.

Review Video: Pronoun Antecedent Agreement
Visit mometrix.com/academy and enter code: 919704

A pronoun should point clearly to the **antecedent**. Here is how a pronoun reference can be unhelpful if it is not directly stated or puzzling.

Unhelpful: Ron and Jim went to the store, and *he* bought soda.

(Who bought soda? Ron or Jim?)

Helpful: Jim went to the store, and *he* bought soda.

(The sentence is clear. Jim bought the soda.)

Some pronouns change their form by their placement in a sentence. A pronoun that is a subject in a sentence comes in the **subjective case**. Pronouns that serve as objects appear in the **objective case**. Finally, the pronouns that are used as possessives appear in the **possessive case**.

Examples:

Subjective case: *He* is coming to the show.

(The pronoun *He* is the subject of the sentence.)

Objective case: Josh drove *him* to the airport.

(The pronoun *him* is the object of the sentence.)

Possessive case: The flowers are *mine*.

(The pronoun *mine* shows ownership of the flowers.)

The word *who* is a subjective-case pronoun that can be used as a **subject**. The word *whom* is an objective-case pronoun that can be used as an **object**. The words *who* and *whom* are common in subordinate clauses or in questions.

Examples:

Subject: He knows who wants to come.

(*Who* is the subject of the verb *wants*.)

Object: He knows the man whom we want at the party.

(*Whom* is the object of *we want*.)

Clauses

A clause is a group of words that contains both a subject and a predicate (verb). There are two types of clauses: independent and dependent. An **independent clause** contains a complete thought, while a **dependent (or subordinate) clause** does not. A dependent clause includes a subject and a verb, and may also contain objects or complements, but it cannot stand as a complete thought without being joined to an independent clause. Dependent clauses function within sentences as adjectives, adverbs, or nouns.

Example:

Independent Clause: I am running

Dependent Clause: because I want to stay in shape

The clause *I am running* is an independent clause: it has a subject and a verb, and it gives a complete thought. The clause *because I want to stay in shape* is a dependent clause: it has a subject and a verb, but it does not express a complete thought. It adds detail to the independent clause to which it is attached.

Combined: I am running because I want to stay in shape.

Review Video: Clauses
Visit mometrix.com/academy and enter code: 940170

Types of Dependent Clauses

Adjective Clauses

An **adjective clause** is a dependent clause that modifies a noun or a pronoun. Adjective clauses begin with a relative pronoun (*who, whose, whom, which,* and *that*) or a relative adverb (*where, when,* and *why*).

Also, adjective clauses come after the noun that the clause needs to explain or rename. This is done to have a clear connection to the independent clause.

Examples:

I learned the reason *why I won the award.*

This is the place *where I started my first job.*

An adjective clause can be an essential or nonessential clause. An essential clause is very important to the sentence. **Essential clauses** explain or define a person or thing. **Nonessential clauses** give more information about a person or thing but are not necessary to define them. Nonessential clauses are set off with commas while essential clauses are not.

Examples:

Essential: A person *who works hard at first* can often rest later in life.

Nonessential: Neil Armstrong, *who walked on the moon*, is my hero.

Review Video: Adjective Clauses and Phrases
Visit mometrix.com/academy and enter code: 520888

Adverb Clauses

An **adverb clause** is a dependent clause that modifies a verb, adjective, or adverb. In sentences with multiple dependent clauses, adverb clauses are usually placed immediately before or after the independent clause. An adverb clause is introduced with words such as *after, although, as, before, because, if, since, so, unless, when, where*, and *while*.

Examples:

When you walked outside, I called the manager.

I will go with you *unless you want to stay*.

Noun Clauses

A **noun clause** is a dependent clause that can be used as a subject, object, or complement. Noun clauses begin with words such as *how, that, what, whether, which, who*, and *why*. These words can also come with an adjective clause. Unless the noun clause is being used as the subject of the sentence, it should come after the verb of the independent clause.

Examples:

The real mystery is *how you avoided serious injury*.

What you learn from each other depends on your honesty with others.

Subordination

When two related ideas are not of equal importance, the ideal way to combine them is to make the more important idea an independent clause, and the less important idea a dependent or subordinate clause. This is called **subordination**.

Example:

Separate ideas: The team had a perfect regular season. The team lost the championship.

Subordinated: Despite having a perfect regular season, *the team lost the championship*.

Phrases

A phrase is a group of words that functions as a single part of speech, usually a noun, adjective, or adverb. A phrase is not a complete thought, but it adds **detail** or **explanation** to a sentence, or **renames** something within the sentence.

Prepositional Phrases

One of the most common types of phrases is the prepositional phrase. A **prepositional phrase** begins with a preposition and ends with a noun or pronoun that is the object of the preposition. Normally, the prepositional phrase functions as an **adjective** or an **adverb** within the sentence.

Examples:

The picnic is *on the blanket.*

I am sick *with a fever* today.

Among the many flowers, John found a four-leaf clover.

Verbal Phrases

A verbal is a word or phrase that is formed from a verb but does not function as a verb. Depending on its particular form, it may be used as a noun, adjective, or adverb. A verbal does **not** replace a verb in a sentence.

Examples:

Correct: *Walk* a mile daily.

(*Walk* is the verb of this sentence. The subject is the implied *you.*)

Incorrect: *To walk* a mile.

(*To walk* is a type of verbal. This is not a sentence since there is no functional verb)

There are three types of verbals: **participles**, **gerunds**, and **infinitives**. Each type of verbal has a corresponding **phrase** that consists of the verbal itself along with any complements or modifiers.

Participles

A **participle** is a type of verbal that always functions as an adjective. The present participle always ends with *-ing*. Past participles end with *-d, -ed, -n,* or *-t.*

Examples: Verb: *dance* | Present Participle: *dancing* | Past Participle: *danced*

Participial phrases most often come right before or right after the noun or pronoun that they modify.

Examples:

Shipwrecked on an island, the boys started to fish for food.

Having been seated for five hours, we got out of the car to stretch our legs.

Praised for their work, the group accepted the first-place trophy.

Gerunds

A **gerund** is a type of verbal that always functions as a noun. Like present participles, gerunds always end with *-ing*, but they can be easily distinguished from one another by the part of speech they represent (participles always function as adjectives). Since a gerund or gerund phrase always functions as a noun, it can be used as the subject of a sentence, the predicate nominative, or the object of a verb or preposition.

Examples:

We want to be known for *teaching the poor*. (Object of preposition)

Coaching this team is the best job of my life. (Subject)

We like *practicing our songs* in the basement. (Object of verb)

INFINITIVES

An **infinitive** is a type of verbal that can function as a noun, an adjective, or an adverb. An infinitive is made of the word *to* + the basic form of the verb. As with all other types of verbal phrases, an infinitive phrase includes the verbal itself and all of its complements or modifiers.

Examples:

To join the team is my goal in life. (Noun)

The animals have enough food *to eat for the night*. (Adjective)

People lift weights *to exercise their muscles*. (Adverb)

Review Video: Gerunds, Participles, and Infinitives
Visit mometrix.com/academy and enter code: 634263

APPOSITIVE PHRASES

An **appositive** is a word or phrase that is used to explain or rename nouns or pronouns. Noun phrases, gerund phrases, and infinitive phrases can all be used as appositives.

Examples:

Terriers, *hunters at heart*, have been dressed up to look like lap dogs.

(The noun phrase *hunters at heart* renames the noun *terriers*.)

His plan, *to save and invest his money*, was proven as a safe approach.

(The infinitive phrase explains what the plan is.)

Appositive phrases can be **essential** or **nonessential**. An appositive phrase is essential if the person, place, or thing being described or renamed is too general for its meaning to be understood without the appositive.

Examples:

Essential: Two Founding Fathers George Washington and Thomas Jefferson served as presidents.

Nonessential: George Washington and Thomas Jefferson, two Founding Fathers, served as presidents.

ABSOLUTE PHRASES

An absolute phrase is a phrase that consists of **a noun followed by a participle**. An absolute phrase provides **context** to what is being described in the sentence, but it does not modify or explain any particular word; it is essentially independent.

Examples:

> *The alarm ringing*, he pushed the snooze button.
>
> *The music paused*, she continued to dance through the crowd.

Note: Absolute phrases can be confusing, so don't be discouraged if you have a difficult time with them.

PARALLELISM

When multiple items or ideas are presented in a sentence in series, such as in a list, the items or ideas must be stated in grammatically equivalent ways. In other words, if one idea is stated in gerund form, the second cannot be stated in infinitive form. For example, to write, *I enjoy reading and to study* would be incorrect. An infinitive and a gerund are not equivalent. Instead, you should write *I enjoy reading and studying*. In lists of more than two, it can be harder to keep everything straight, but all items in a list must be parallel.

Example:

> **Incorrect**: He stopped at the office, grocery store, and the pharmacy before heading home.
>
> The first and third items in the list of places include the article *the*, so the second item needs it as well.
>
> **Correct**: He stopped at the office, *the* grocery store, and the pharmacy before heading home.

Example:

> **Incorrect**: While vacationing in Europe, she went biking, skiing, and climbed mountains.
>
> The first and second items in the list are gerunds, so the third item must be as well.
>
> **Correct**: While vacationing in Europe, she went biking, skiing, and *mountain climbing*.

Review Video: Parallel Construction
Visit mometrix.com/academy and enter code: 831988

SENTENCE PURPOSE

There are four types of sentences: declarative, imperative, interrogative, and exclamatory.

A **declarative** sentence states a fact and ends with a period.

> Example: *The football game starts at seven o'clock.*

An **imperative** sentence tells someone to do something and generally ends with a period. (An urgent command might end with an exclamation point instead.)

> Example: *Don't forget to buy your ticket.*

An **interrogative** sentence asks a question and ends with a question mark.

Example: *Are you going to the game on Friday?*

An **exclamatory** sentence shows strong emotion and ends with an exclamation point.

Example: *I can't believe we won the game!*

Review Video: Functions of a Sentence
Visit mometrix.com/academy and enter code: 475974

Sentence Structure

Sentences are classified by structure based on the type and number of clauses present. The four classifications of sentence structure are the following:

Simple: A simple sentence has one independent clause with no dependent clauses. A simple sentence may have **compound elements** (i.e., compound subject or verb).

Examples:

Judy *watered* the lawn. (single subject, single *verb*)

Judy and Alan *watered* the lawn. (compound subject, single *verb*)

Judy *watered* the lawn and *pulled* weeds. (single subject, compound *verb*)

Judy and Alan *watered* the lawn and *pulled* weeds. (compound subject, compound *verb*)

Compound: A compound sentence has two or more independent clauses with no dependent clauses. Usually, the independent clauses are joined with a comma and a coordinating conjunction or with a semicolon.

Examples:

The time has come, and we are ready.

I woke up at dawn; the sun was just coming up.

Complex: A complex sentence has one independent clause and at least one *dependent clause*.

Examples:

Although he had the flu, Harry went to work.

Marcia got married *after she finished college*.

Compound-Complex: A compound-complex sentence has at least two independent clauses and at least one *dependent clause*.

Examples:

John is my friend *who went to India*, and he brought back souvenirs.

You may not realize this, but we heard the music *that you played last night.*

Review Video: Sentence Structure
Visit mometrix.com/academy and enter code: 700478

SENTENCE FRAGMENTS

Usually when the term *sentence fragment* comes up, it is because you have to decide whether or not a group of words is a complete sentence, and if it's not a complete sentence, you're about to have to fix it. Recall that a group of words must contain at least one **independent clause** in order to be considered a sentence. If it doesn't contain even one independent clause, it would be called a **sentence fragment**. (If it contains two or more independent clauses that are not joined correctly, it would be called a run-on sentence.)

The process to use for **repairing** a sentence fragment depends on what type of fragment it is. If the fragment is a dependent clause, it can sometimes be as simple as removing a subordinating word (e.g., when, because, if) from the beginning of the fragment. Alternatively, a dependent clause can be incorporated into a closely related neighboring sentence. If the fragment is missing some required part, like a subject or a verb, the fix might be as simple as adding it in.

Examples:

Fragment: Because he wanted to sail the Mediterranean.

Removed subordinating word: He wanted to sail the Mediterranean.

Combined with another sentence: Because he wanted to sail the Mediterranean, he booked a Greek island cruise.

RUN-ON SENTENCES

Run-on sentences consist of multiple independent clauses that have not been joined together properly. Run-on sentences can be corrected in several different ways:

Join clauses properly: This can be done with a comma and coordinating conjunction, with a semicolon, or with a colon or dash if the second clause is explaining something in the first.

Example:

Incorrect: I went on the trip, we visited lots of castles.

Corrected: I went on the trip, and we visited lots of castles.

Split into separate sentences: This correction is most effective when the independent clauses are very long or when they are not closely related.

Example:

Incorrect: The drive to New York takes ten hours, my uncle lives in Boston.

Corrected: The drive to New York takes ten hours. My uncle lives in Boston.

Make one clause dependent: This is the easiest way to make the sentence correct and more interesting at the same time. It's often as simple as adding a subordinating word between the two clauses

Example:

Incorrect: I finally made it to the store and I bought some eggs.

Corrected: When I finally made it to the store, I bought some eggs.

Reduce to one clause with a compound verb: If both clauses have the same subject, remove the subject from the second clause, and you now have just one clause with a compound verb.

Example:

Incorrect: The drive to New York takes ten hours, it makes me very tired.

Corrected: The drive to New York takes ten hours and makes me very tired.

Note: While these are the simplest ways to correct a run-on sentence, often the best way is to completely reorganize the thoughts in the sentence and rewrite it.

Review Video: Fragments and Run-on Sentences
Visit mometrix.com/academy and enter code: 541989

Dangling and Misplaced Modifiers

Dangling Modifiers

A dangling modifier is a dependent clause or verbal phrase that does not have a **clear logical connection** to a word in the sentence.

Example:

Dangling: *Reading each magazine article*, the stories caught my attention.

The word *stories* cannot be modified by *Reading each magazine article*. People can read, but stories cannot read. Therefore, the subject of the sentence must be a person.

Corrected: Reading each magazine article, *I* was entertained by the stories.

Example:

Dangling: Ever since childhood, my grandparents have visited me for Christmas.

The speaker in this sentence can't have been visited by her grandparents when *they* were children, since she wouldn't have been born yet. Either the modifier should be **clarified** or the sentence should be **rearranged** to specify whose childhood is being referenced.

Clarified: Ever since I was a child, my grandparents have visited for Christmas.

Rearranged: Ever since childhood, I have enjoyed my grandparents visiting for Christmas.

Misplaced Modifiers

Because modifiers are grammatically versatile, they can be put in many different places within the structure of a sentence. The danger of this versatility is that a modifier can accidentally be placed where it is modifying the wrong word or where it is not clear which word it is modifying.

Example:

Misplaced: She read the book to a crowd *that was filled with beautiful pictures.*

The book was filled with beautiful pictures, not the crowd.

Corrected: She read the book *that was filled with beautiful pictures* to a crowd.

Example:

Ambiguous: Derek saw a bus nearly hit a man *on his way to work.*

Was Derek on his way to work? Or was the other man?

Derek: *On his way to work*, Derek saw a bus nearly hit a man.

The other man: Derek saw a bus nearly hit a man *who was on his way to work.*

Split Infinitives

A split infinitive occurs when a modifying word comes between the word *to* and the verb that pairs with *to*.

Example: To *clearly* explain vs. *To explain* clearly | To *softly* sing vs. *To sing* softly

Though considered improper by some, split infinitives may provide better clarity and simplicity in some cases than the alternatives. As such, avoiding them should not be considered a universal rule.

Double Negatives

Standard English allows **two negatives** only when a **positive** meaning is intended. For example, *The team was not displeased with their performance.* Double negatives to emphasize negation are not used in standard English.

Negative modifiers (e.g., never, no, and not) should not be paired with other negative modifiers or negative words (e.g., none, nobody, nothing, or neither). The modifiers *hardly, barely*, and *scarcely* are considered negatives in standard English, so they should not be used with other negatives.

Conventions of Grammar and Usage Chapter Quiz

1. How many parts of speech are there?

a. Five
b. Six
c. Seven
d. Eight

2. Adjectives that are used to mark nouns are known as what?

a. Complementary
b. Relative
c. Absolute
d. Articles

3. Which of the following sentences uses an example of a superlative adjective?

a. She is the most brilliant woman I've ever encountered.
b. Work was exhausting today.
c. I had much more fun than the last time we went.
d. That dress looks stunning on you.

4. Which of the following is NOT a verbal?

a. Gerund
b. Participle
c. Preposition
d. Infinitive

5. Which of the following is an example of a split infinitive?

a. Sitting quietly in the back, the cat rested.
b. I have to carefully listen when the radio comes on if I want to win the prize they're offering.
c. Me and Jim swam down at the creek every day last summer.
d. I used the key on the door that was red.

Conventions of Punctuation

End Punctuation

Periods

Use a period to end all sentences except direct questions, exclamations.

Declarative Sentence

A declarative sentence gives information or makes a statement.

Examples: I can fly a kite. | The plane left two hours ago.

Imperative Sentence

An imperative sentence gives an order or command.

Examples: You are coming with me. | Bring me that note.

Periods for Abbreviations

Examples: 3 P.M. | 2 A.M. | Mr. Jones | Mrs. Stevens | Dr. Smith | Bill Jr. | Pennsylvania Ave.

Note: an abbreviation is a shortened form of a word or phrase.

Question Marks

Question marks should be used following a direct question. A polite request can be followed by a period instead of a question mark.

Direct Question: What is for lunch today? | How are you? | Why is that the answer?

Polite Requests: Can you please send me the item tomorrow. | Will you please walk with me on the track.

Review Video: Question Marks
Visit mometrix.com/academy and enter code: 118471

Exclamation Marks

Exclamation marks are used after a word group or sentence that shows much feeling or has special importance. Exclamation marks should not be overused. They are saved for proper **exclamatory interjections**.

Example: We're going to the finals! | You have a beautiful car! | That's crazy!

Review Video: Exclamation Points
Visit mometrix.com/academy and enter code: 199367

Commas

The comma is a punctuation mark that can help you understand connections in a sentence. Not every sentence needs a comma. However, if a sentence needs a comma, you need to put it in the right place. A comma in the wrong place (or an absent comma) will make a sentence's meaning unclear. These are some of the rules for commas:

1. Use a comma **before a coordinating conjunction** joining independent clauses
   Example: Bob caught three fish, and I caught two fish.

2. Use a comma after an introductory phrase or an adverbial clause

   Examples:

   After the final out, we went to a restaurant to celebrate.
   Studying the stars, I was surprised at the beauty of the sky.

3. Use a comma between items in a series.

   Example: I will bring the turkey, the pie, and the coffee.

4. Use a comma **between coordinate adjectives** not joined with *and*

   Incorrect: The kind, brown dog followed me home.
   Correct: The *kind, loyal* dog followed me home.
   Not all adjectives are **coordinate** (i.e., equal or parallel). There are two simple ways to know if your adjectives are coordinate. One, you can join the adjectives with *and*: *The kind and loyal dog*. Two, you can change the order of the adjectives: *The loyal, kind dog.*

5. Use commas for **interjections** and **after *yes* and *no*** responses

   Examples:

   Interjection: Oh, I had no idea. | Wow, you know how to play this game.
   Yes and No: *Yes,* I heard you. | *No,* I cannot come tomorrow.

6. Use commas to separate nonessential modifiers and nonessential appositives

   Examples:

   Nonessential Modifier: John Frank, who is coaching the team, was promoted today.
   Nonessential Appositive: Thomas Edison, an American inventor, was born in Ohio.

7. Use commas to set off nouns of direct address, interrogative tags, and contrast

   Examples:

   Direct Address: You, *John,* are my only hope in this moment.
   Interrogative Tag: This is the last time, *correct*?
   Contrast: You are my friend, *not my enemy.*

8. Use commas with dates, addresses, geographical names, and titles

   Examples:

   Date: *July 4, 1776,* is an important date to remember.
   Address: He is meeting me at *456 Delaware Avenue, Washington, D.C.,* tomorrow morning.
   Geographical Name: *Paris, France,* is my favorite city.
   Title: John Smith, *Ph. D.,* will be visiting your class today.

9. Use commas to **separate expressions like *he said* and *she said*** if they come between a sentence of a quote

   Examples:

   "I want you to know," he began, "that I always wanted the best for you."
   "You can start," Jane said, "with an apology."

Review Video: Commas
Visit mometrix.com/academy and enter code: 786797

SEMICOLONS

The semicolon is used to connect major sentence pieces of equal value. Some rules for semicolons include:

1. Use a semicolon **between closely connected independent clauses** that are not connected with a coordinating conjunction.

   Examples:

   She is outside; we are inside.
   You are right; we should go with your plan.

2. Use a semicolon **between independent clauses linked with a transitional word.**

   Examples:

   I think that we can agree on this*; however,* I am not sure about my friends.
   You are looking in the wrong places*; therefore,* you will not find what you need.

3. Use a semicolon **between items in a series that has internal punctuation.**

   Example: I have visited New York, New York; Augusta, Maine; and Baltimore, Maryland.

Review Video: Semicolon Usage
Visit mometrix.com/academy and enter code: 370605

COLONS

The colon is used to call attention to the words that follow it. A colon must come after a **complete independent clause**. The rules for colons are as follows:

1. Use a colon after an independent clause to **make a list**

   Example: I want to learn many languages: Spanish, German, and Italian.

2. Use a colon for **explanations** or to **give a quote**

   Examples:

   Quote: He started with an idea: "We are able to do more than we imagine."
   Explanation: There is one thing that stands out on your resume: responsibility.

3. Use a colon **after the greeting in a formal letter**, to **show hours and minutes**, and to **separate a title and subtitle**

   Examples:

   Greeting in a formal letter: Dear Sir: | To Whom It May Concern:
   Time: It is 3:14 P.M.
   Title: The essay is titled "America: A Short Introduction to a Modern Country"

Review Video: Colons
Visit mometrix.com/academy and enter code: 868673

Parentheses

Parentheses are used for additional information. Also, they can be used to put labels for letters or numbers in a series. Parentheses should be not be used very often. If they are overused, parentheses can be a distraction instead of a help.

Examples:

> **Extra Information**: The rattlesnake (see Image 2) is a dangerous snake of North and South America.
>
> **Series**: Include in the email (1) your name, (2) your address, and (3) your question for the author.

Review Video: Parentheses
Visit mometrix.com/academy and enter code: 947743

Quotation Marks

Use quotation marks to close off **direct quotations** of a person's spoken or written words. Do not use quotation marks around indirect quotations. An indirect quotation gives someone's message without using the person's exact words. Use **single quotation marks** to close off a quotation inside a quotation.

> **Direct Quote**: Nancy said, "I am waiting for Henry to arrive."
>
> **Indirect Quote**: Henry said that he is going to be late to the meeting.
>
> **Quote inside a Quote**: The teacher asked, "Has everyone read 'The Gift of the Magi'?"

Quotation marks should be used around the titles of **short works**: newspaper and magazine articles, poems, short stories, songs, television episodes, radio programs, and subdivisions of books or web sites.

Examples:

> "Rip van Winkle" (short story by Washington Irving)
>
> "O Captain! My Captain!" (poem by Walt Whitman)

Although it is not standard usage, quotation marks are sometimes used to highlight **irony**, or the use of words to mean something other than their dictionary definition. This type of usage should be employed sparingly, if at all.

Examples:

The boss warned Frank that he was walking on "thin ice."

(Frank is not walking on real ice. Instead, Frank is being warned to avoid mistakes.)

The teacher thanked the young man for his "honesty."

(In this example, the quotation marks around *honesty* show that the teacher does not believe the young man's explanation.)

Review Video: Quotation Marks
Visit mometrix.com/academy and enter code: 884918

Periods and commas are put **inside** quotation marks. Colons and semicolons are put **outside** the quotation marks. Question marks and exclamation points are placed inside quotation marks when they are part of a quote. When the question or exclamation mark goes with the whole sentence, the mark is left outside of the quotation marks.

Examples:

Period and comma: We read "The Gift of the Magi," "The Skylight Room," and "The Cactus."

Semicolon: They watched "The Nutcracker"; then, they went home.

Exclamation mark that is a part of a quote: The crowd cheered, "Victory!"

Question mark that goes with the whole sentence: Is your favorite short story "The Tell-Tale Heart"?

APOSTROPHES

An apostrophe is used to show **possession** or the **deletion of letters in contractions**. An apostrophe is not needed with the possessive pronouns *his, hers, its, ours, theirs, whose*, and *yours*.

Singular Nouns: David's car | a book's theme | my brother's board game

Plural Nouns with -*s*: the scissors' handle | boys' basketball

Plural Nouns without -*s*: Men's department | the people's adventure

Review Video: When to Use an Apostrophe
Visit mometrix.com/academy and enter code: 213068

Review Video: Punctuation Errors in Possessive Pronouns
Visit mometrix.com/academy and enter code: 221438

HYPHENS

Hyphens are used to **separate compound words**. Use hyphens in the following cases:

1. **Compound numbers** between 21 and 99 when written out in words
   Example: This team needs *twenty-five* points to win the game.

2. **Written-out fractions** that are used as **adjectives**

   Correct: The recipe says that we need a *three-fourths* cup of butter.
   Incorrect: *One-fourth* of the road is under construction.

3. Compound words used as **adjectives that come before a noun**

   Correct: The *well-fed* dog took a nap.
   Incorrect: The dog was *well-fed* for his nap.

4. Compound words that would be **hard to read** or **easily confused with other words**

   Examples: Semi-irresponsible | Anti-itch | Re-sort

Note: This is not a complete set of the rules for hyphens. A dictionary is the best tool for knowing if a compound word needs a hyphen.

Review Video: Hyphens
Visit mometrix.com/academy and enter code: 981632

Dashes

Dashes are used to show a **break** or a **change in thought** in a sentence or to act as parentheses in a sentence. When typing, use two hyphens to make a dash. Do not put a space before or after the dash. The following are the rules for dashes:

1. To set off **parenthetical statements** or an **appositive with internal punctuation**

   Example: The three trees—oak, pine, and magnolia—are coming on a truck tomorrow.

2. To show a **break or change in tone or thought**

   Example: The first question—how silly of me—does not have a correct answer.

Ellipsis Marks

The ellipsis mark has three periods (...) to show when **words have been removed** from a quotation. If a full sentence or more is removed from a quoted passage, you need to use four periods to show the removed text and the end punctuation mark. The ellipsis mark should not be used at the beginning of a quotation. The ellipsis mark should also not be used at the end of a quotation unless some words have been deleted from the end of the final sentence.

Example:

> "Then he picked up the groceries...paid for them...later he went home."

BRACKETS

There are two main reasons to use brackets:

1. When **placing parentheses inside of parentheses**
   Example: The hero of this story, Paul Revere (a silversmith and industrialist [see Ch. 4]), rode through towns of Massachusetts to warn of advancing British troops.
2. When adding **clarification or detail** to a quotation that is **not part of the quotation**
   Example:
   > The father explained, "My children are planning to attend my alma mater [State University]."

Review Video: Brackets
Visit mometrix.com/academy and enter code: 727546

Conventions of Punctuation Chapter Quiz

1. Which of the following conventions of punctuation best represents the sentence below?

Eli Whitney, who invented the cotton gin, was born today.

a. Interjection
b. Direct address
c. Interrogative tag
d. Nonessential modifier

2. Which of the following is the correct punctuation for the example below?

I cannot think of a way out of this____ however, we have to keep going.

a. :
b. ;
c. ,
d. .

3. Which punctuation should you expect to use when creating a list?

a. :
b. ;
c. ,
d. .

4. How many periods should be included in an ellipsis if a full sentence or more is removed from a quoted passage?

a. Two
b. Three
c. Four
d. Five

5. Which punctuation should you use to highlight irony?

a. Hyphens
b. Dashes
c. Quotation marks
d. Exclamation points

Conventions of Spelling

General Spelling Rules

Words Ending with a Consonant

Usually, the final consonant is **doubled** on a word before adding a suffix. This is the rule for single syllable words, words ending with one consonant, and multi-syllable words with the last syllable accented. The following are examples:

- *beg* becomes *begging* (single syllable)
- *shop* becomes *shopped* (single syllable)
- *add* becomes *adding* (already ends in double consonant, do not add another *d*)
- *deter* becomes *deterring* (multi-syllable, accent on last syllable)
- *regret* becomes *regrettable* (multi-syllable, accent on last syllable)
- *compost* becomes *composting* (do not add another *t* because the accent is on the first syllable)

Words Ending with Y or C

The general rule for words ending in *y* is to keep the *y* when adding a suffix if the **y is preceded by a vowel**. If the word **ends in a consonant and y** the *y* is changed to an *i* before the suffix is added (unless the suffix itself begins with *i*). The following are examples:

- *pay* becomes *paying* (keep the *y*)
- *bully* becomes *bullied* (change to *i*)
- *bully* becomes *bullying* (keep the *y* because the suffix is *–ing*)

If a word ends with *c* and the suffix begins with an *e, i,* or *y*, the letter *k* is usually added to the end of the word. The following are examples:

- panic becomes panicky
- mimic becomes mimicking

Words Containing IE or EI, and/or Ending with E

Most words are spelled with an *i* before *e*, except when they follow the letter *c*, **or** sound like *a*. For example, the following words are spelled correctly according to these rules:

- piece, friend, believe (*i* before *e*)
- receive, ceiling, conceited (except after *c*)
- weight, neighborhood, veil (sounds like *a*)

To add a suffix to words ending with the letter *e*, first determine if the *e* is silent. If it is, the *e* will be kept if the added suffix begins with a consonant. If the suffix begins with a vowel, the *e* is dropped. The following are examples:

- *age* becomes *ageless* (keep the *e*)
- *age* becomes *aging* (drop the *e*)

An exception to this rule occurs when the word ends in *ce* or *ge* and the suffix *able* or *ous* is added; these words will retain the letter *e*. The following are examples:

- courage becomes courageous
- notice becomes noticeable

Words Ending with ISE or IZE

A small number of words end with *ise*. Most of the words in the English language with the same sound end in *ize*. The following are examples:

- advertise, advise, arise, chastise, circumcise, and comprise
- compromise, demise, despise, devise, disguise, enterprise, excise, and exercise
- franchise, improvise, incise, merchandise, premise, reprise, and revise
- supervise, surmise, surprise, and televise

Words that end with *ize* include the following:

- accessorize, agonize, authorize, and brutalize
- capitalize, caramelize, categorize, civilize, and demonize
- downsize, empathize, euthanize, idolize, and immunize
- legalize, metabolize, mobilize, organize, and ostracize
- plagiarize, privatize, utilize, and visualize

(Note that some words may technically be spelled with *ise*, especially in British English, but it is more common to use *ize*. Examples include *symbolize/symbolise* and *baptize/baptise*.)

Words Ending with CEED, SEDE, or CEDE

There are only three words in the English language that end with *ceed*: *exceed, proceed,* and *succeed*. There is only one word in the English language that ends with *sede*: *supersede*. Most other words that sound like *sede* or *ceed* end with *cede*. The following are examples:

- concede, recede, and precede

Words Ending in ABLE or IBLE

For words ending in *able* or *ible*, there are no hard and fast rules. The following are examples:

- adjustable, unbeatable, collectable, deliverable, and likeable
- edible, compatible, feasible, sensible, and credible

There are more words ending in *able* than *ible*; this is useful to know if guessing is necessary.

Words Ending in ANCE or ENCE

The suffixes *ence, ency,* and *ent* are used in the following cases:

- the suffix is preceded by the letter *c* but sounds like *s* – *innocence*
- the suffix is preceded by the letter *g* but sounds like *j* – *intelligence, negligence*

The suffixes *ance, ancy,* and *ant* are used in the following cases:

- the suffix is preceded by the letter *c* but sounds like *k* – *significant, vacant*
- the suffix is preceded by the letter *g* with a hard sound – *elegant, extravagance*

If the suffix is preceded by other letters, there are no clear rules. For example: *finance, abundance,* and *assistance* use the letter *a,* while *decadence, competence,* and *excellence* use the letter *e*.

Words Ending in tion, sion, or cian

Words ending in *tion, sion,* or *cian* all sound like *shun* or *zhun*. There are no rules for which ending is used for words. The following are examples:

- action, agitation, caution, fiction, nation, and motion
- admission, expression, mansion, permission, and television
- electrician, magician, musician, optician, and physician (note that these words tend to describe occupations)

Words with the ai or ia Combination

When deciding if *ai* or *ia* is correct, the combination of *ai* usually sounds like one vowel sound, as in *Britain*, while the vowels in *ia* are pronounced separately, as in *guardian*. The following are examples:

- captain, certain, faint, hair, malaise, and praise (*ai* makes one sound)
- bacteria, beneficiary, diamond, humiliation, and nuptial (*ia* makes two sounds)

Rules for Plurals

Nouns Ending in ch, sh, s, x, or z

When a noun ends in the letters *ch, sh, s, x,* or *z*, an *es* instead of a singular *s* is added to the end of the word to make it plural. The following are examples:

- church becomes churches
- bush becomes bushes
- bass becomes basses
- mix becomes mixes
- buzz becomes buzzes

This is the rule with proper names as well; the Ross family would become the Rosses.

Nouns Ending in y or ay/ey/iy/oy/uy

If a noun ends with a **consonant and y**, the plural is formed by replacing the *y* with *ies*. For example, *fly* becomes *flies* and *puppy* becomes *puppies*. If a noun ends with a **vowel and *y***, the plural is formed by adding an *s*. For example, *alley* becomes *alleys* and *boy* becomes *boys*.

Nouns Ending in f or fe

Most nouns ending in *f* or *fe* are pluralized by replacing the *f* with *v* and adding *es*. The following are examples:

- knife becomes knives; self becomes selves; wolf becomes wolves.

An exception to this rule is the word *roof; roof* becomes *roofs*.

Nouns Ending in o

Most nouns ending with a **consonant and *o*** are pluralized by adding *es*. The following are examples:

- hero becomes heroes; tornado becomes tornadoes; potato becomes potatoes

Most nouns ending with a **vowel and *o*** are pluralized by adding *s*. The following are examples:

- portfolio becomes portfolios; radio becomes radios; cameo becomes cameos.

An exception to these rules is seen with musical terms ending in *o*. These words are pluralized by adding *s* even if they end in a consonant and *o*. The following are examples: *soprano* becomes *sopranos; banjo* becomes *banjos; piano* becomes *pianos.*

Letters, Numbers, and Symbols

Letters and numbers become plural by adding an apostrophe and *s*. The following are examples:

- The *L's* are the people whose names begin with the letter *L*.
- They broke the teams down into groups of *3's*.
- The sorority girls were all *KD's*.

Compound Nouns

A **compound noun** is a noun that is made up of two or more words; they can be written with hyphens. For example, *mother-in-law* or *court-martial* are compound nouns. To make them plural, an *s* or *es* is added to the noun portion of the word. The following are examples: *mother-in-law* becomes *mothers-in-law; court-martial* becomes *courts-martial.*

Exceptions

Some words do not fall into any specific category for making the singular form plural. They are **irregular**. Certain words become plural by changing the vowels within the word. The following are examples:

- woman becomes women; goose becomes geese; foot becomes feet

Some words change in unusual ways in the plural form. The following are examples:

- mouse becomes mice; ox becomes oxen; person becomes people

Some words are the same in both the singular and plural forms. The following are examples:

- *Salmon*, *deer*, and *moose* are the same whether singular or plural.

Commonly Misspelled Words

accidentally	accommodate	accompanied	accompany
achieved	acknowledgment	across	address
aggravate	aisle	ancient	anxiety
apparently	appearance	arctic	argument
arrangement	attendance	auxiliary	awkward
bachelor	barbarian	beggar	beneficiary
biscuit	brilliant	business	cafeteria
calendar	campaign	candidate	ceiling
cemetery	changeable	changing	characteristic
chauffeur	colonel	column	commit
committee	comparative	compel	competent
competition	conceive	congratulations	conqueror
conscious	coolly	correspondent	courtesy
curiosity	cylinder	deceive	deference

deferred	definite	describe	desirable
desperate	develop	diphtheria	disappear
disappoint	disastrous	discipline	discussion
disease	dissatisfied	dissipate	drudgery
ecstasy	efficient	eighth	eligible
embarrass	emphasize	especially	exaggerate
exceed	exhaust	exhilaration	existence
explanation	extraordinary	familiar	fascinate
February	fiery	finally	forehead
foreign	foreigner	foremost	forfeit
ghost	glamorous	government	grammar
grateful	grief	grievous	handkerchief
harass	height	hoping	hurriedly
hygiene	hypocrisy	imminent	incidentally
incredible	independent	indigestible	inevitable
innocence	intelligible	intentionally	intercede
interest	irresistible	judgment	legitimate
liable	library	likelihood	literature
maintenance	maneuver	manual	mathematics
mattress	miniature	mischievous	misspell
momentous	mortgage	neither	nickel
niece	ninety	noticeable	notoriety
obedience	obstacle	occasion	occurrence
omitted	operate	optimistic	organization
outrageous	pageant	pamphlet	parallel
parliament	permissible	perseverance	persuade
physically	physician	possess	possibly
practically	prairie	preceding	prejudice
prevalent	professor	pronunciation	pronouncement
propeller	protein	psychiatrist	psychology
quantity	questionnaire	rally	recede
receive	recognize	recommend	referral
referred	relieve	religious	resistance
restaurant	rhetoric	rhythm	ridiculous
sacrilegious	salary	scarcely	schedule
secretary	sentinel	separate	severely
sheriff	shriek	similar	soliloquy
sophomore	species	strenuous	studying
suffrage	supersede	suppress	surprise
symmetry	temperament	temperature	tendency
tournament	tragedy	transferred	truly
twelfth	tyranny	unanimous	unpleasant
usage	vacuum	valuable	vein
vengeance	vigilance	villain	Wednesday
weird	wholly		

Commonly Confused Words

Which, That, and Who

The words *which*, *that*, and *who* can act as **relative pronouns** to help clarify or describe a noun.

Which is used for things only.

Example: Andrew's car, *which is old and rusty,* broke down last week.

That is used for people or things. *That* is usually informal when used to describe people.

Example: Is this the only book *that Louis L'Amour wrote?*

Example: Is Louis L'Amour the author *that wrote Western novels?*

Who is used for people or for animals that have a name.

Example: Mozart was the composer *who wrote those operas.*

Example: John's dog, *who is called Max,* is large and fierce.

Homophones

Homophones are words that sound alike (or similar), but they have different **spellings** and **definitions**.

To, Too, and Two

To can be an adverb or a preposition for showing direction, purpose, and relationship. See your dictionary for the many other ways use *to* in a sentence.

Examples: I went to the store. | I want to go with you.

Too is an adverb that means *also, as well, very, or more than enough.*

Examples: I can walk a mile too. | You have eaten too much.

Two is the second number in the series of numbers (e.g., one (1), two, (2), three (3)...)

Example: You have two minutes left.

There, Their, and They're

There can be an adjective, adverb, or pronoun. Often, *there* is used to show a place or to start a sentence.

Examples: I went there yesterday. | There is something in his pocket.

Their is a pronoun that is used to show ownership.

Examples: He is their father. | This is their fourth apology this week.

They're is a contraction of *they are.*

Example: Did you know that they're in town?

Knew and New

Knew is the past tense of *know.*

Example: I knew the answer.

New is an adjective that means something is current, has not been used, or modern.

Example: This is my new phone.

Then and Than

Then is an adverb that indicates sequence or order:

Example: I'm going to run to the library and then come home.

Than is special-purpose word used only for comparisons:

Example: Susie likes chips better than candy.

Its and It's

Its is a pronoun that shows ownership.

Example: The guitar is in its case.

It's is a contraction of *it is.*

Example: It's an honor and a privilege to meet you.

Note: The *h* in honor is silent, so the sound of the vowel *o* must have the article *an.*

Your and You're

Your is a pronoun that shows ownership.

Example: This is your moment to shine.

You're is a contraction of *you are.*

Example: Yes, you're correct.

Affect and Effect

There are two main reasons that **affect** and **effect** are so often confused: 1) both words can be used as either a noun or a verb, and 2) unlike most homophones, their usage and meanings are closely related to each other. Here is a quick rundown of the four usage options:

Affect (n): feeling, emotion, or mood that is displayed

Example: The patient had a flat *affect.* (i.e., his face showed little or no emotion)

Affect (v): to alter, to change, to influence

Example: The sunshine *affects* the plant's growth.

Effect (n): a result, a consequence

Example: What *effect* will this weather have on our schedule?

Effect (v): to bring about, to cause to be

Example: These new rules will *effect* order in the office.

The noun form of *affect* is rarely used outside of technical medical descriptions, so if a noun form is needed on the test, you can safely select *effect.* The verb form of *effect* is not as rare as the noun form of *affect*, but it's still not all that likely to show up on your test. If you need a verb and you can't decide which to use based on the definitions, choosing *affect* is your best bet.

Homographs

Homographs are words that share the same spelling, and they have multiple meanings. To figure out which meaning is being used, you should be looking for context clues. The context clues give hints to the meaning of the word. For example, the word *spot* has many meanings. It can mean "a place" or "a stain or blot." In the sentence "After my lunch, I saw a spot on my shirt," the word *spot* means "a stain or blot." The context clues of "After my lunch…" and "on my shirt" guide you to this decision.

Bank

(noun): an establishment where money is held for savings or lending

(verb): to collect or pile up

Content

(noun): the topics that will be addressed within a book

(adjective): pleased or satisfied

Fine

(noun): an amount of money that acts a penalty for an offense

(adjective): very small or thin

Incense

(noun): a material that is burned in religious settings and makes a pleasant aroma

(verb): to frustrate or anger

LEAD

(noun): the first or highest position

(verb): to direct a person or group of followers

OBJECT

(noun): a lifeless item that can be held and observed

(verb): to disagree

PRODUCE

(noun): fruits and vegetables

(verb): to make or create something

REFUSE

(noun): garbage or debris that has been thrown away

(verb): to not allow

SUBJECT

(noun): an area of study

(verb): to force or subdue

TEAR

(noun): a fluid secreted by the eyes

(verb): to separate or pull apart

Conventions of Spelling Chapter Quiz

1. What is usually done to the last consonant of a word that a suffix is being added to?

a. It is doubled.
b. It is tripled.
c. It is removed.
d. It is left as is.

2. Which of the following is the correct spelling?

a. Acessorize
b. Accessorise
c. Accessorize
d. Accesorize

3. Which of the following is NOT a correctly hyphenated compound noun?

a. City-state
b. Runner-up
c. Father-in-law
d. Rain-forest

Essay Revision and Editing

Rhetorical Devices

There are many types of language devices that authors use to convey their meaning in a descriptive way. Understanding these concepts will help you understand what you read. These types of devices are called **figurative language**—language that goes beyond the literal meaning of a word or phrase. **Descriptive language** specifically evokes imagery in the reader's mind to make a story come alive. **Exaggeration** is a type of figurative language in which an author carries an idea beyond the truth in order to emphasize something. A **simile** is a type of figurative language that compares two things that are not actually alike, using words such as *like* and *as*. A **metaphor** takes the comparison one step further by fully equating the two things rather than just saying they are similar.

A **figure-of-speech** is a word or phrase that departs from straightforward, literal language. Figures-of-speech are often used and crafted for emphasis, freshness of expression, or clarity. However, clarity of a passage may suffer from use of these devices. As an example of the figurative use of a word, consider the sentence: *I am going to crown you.* The author may mean:

- I am going to place a literal crown on your head.
- I am going to symbolically exalt you to the place of kingship.
- I am going to punch you in the head with my clenched fist.
- I am going to put a second checker piece on top of your checker piece to signify that it has become a king.

Review Video: Figures of Speech
Visit mometrix.com/academy and enter code: 111295

A **metaphor** is a type of figurative language in which the writer equates something with another thing that is not particularly similar. For instance, *the bird was an arrow arcing through the sky*. In this sentence, the arrow is serving as a metaphor for the bird. The point of a metaphor is to encourage the reader to consider the item being described in a *different way*. Let's continue with this metaphor for a bird: you are asked to envision the bird's flight as being similar to the arc of an arrow. So, you imagine the flight to be swift and bending. Metaphors are a way for the author to describe an item *without being direct and obvious*. This literary device is a lyrical and suggestive way of providing information. Note that the reference for a metaphor will not always be mentioned explicitly by the author. Consider the following description of a forest in winter: *Swaying skeletons reached for the sky and groaned as the wind blew through them.* In this example, the author is using *skeletons* as a metaphor for leafless trees. This metaphor creates a spooky tone while inspiring the reader's imagination.

A **simile** is a figurative expression that is similar to a metaphor, but the expression uses a distancing word: *like* or *as*. Examples include phrases such as *the sun was like an orange*, *eager as a beaver*, and *nimble as a mountain goat*. Because a simile includes *like* or *as*, the device creates more space between the description and the thing being described than does a metaphor. If an author says that *a house was like a shoebox*, then the tone is different than the author saying that the house *was* a shoebox. Authors will choose between a metaphor and a simile depending on their intended tone.

Another type of figurative language is **personification**. This is the description of a nonhuman thing as if the item were **human**. Literally, the word means the process of making something into a person. The general intent of personification is to describe things in a manner that will be comprehensible to readers. When an author states that a tree *groans* in the wind, he or she does not mean that the tree is emitting a low, pained sound from a mouth. Instead, the author means that the tree is making a noise similar to a human groan. Of course, this personification establishes a tone of sadness or suffering. A different tone would be established if the author said that the tree was *swaying* or *dancing*.

Level of Formality

The relationship between writer and reader is important in choosing a **level of formality** as most writing requires some degree of formality. **Formal writing** is for addressing a superior in a school or work environment. Business letters, textbooks, and newspapers use a moderate to high level of formality. **Informal writing** is appropriate for private letters, personal e-mails, and business correspondence between close associates.

For your exam, you will want to be aware of informal and formal writing. One way that this can be accomplished is to watch for shifts in point of view in the essay. For example, unless writers are using a personal example, they will rarely refer to themselves (e.g., "*I* think that *my* point is very clear.") to avoid being informal when they need to be formal.

Also, be mindful of an author who addresses his or her audience **directly** in their writing (e.g., "Readers, *like you*, will understand this argument.") as this can be a sign of informal writing. Good writers understand the need to be consistent with their level of formality. Shifts in levels of formality or point of view can confuse readers and cause them to discount the message.

Clichés

Clichés are phrases that have been **overused** to the point that the phrase has no importance or has lost the original meaning. The phrases have no originality and add very little to a passage. Therefore, most writers will avoid the use of clichés. Another option is to make changes to a cliché so that it is not predictable and empty of meaning.

Examples:

> When life gives you lemons, make lemonade.
>
> Every cloud has a silver lining.

Jargon

Jargon is a **specialized vocabulary** that is used among members of a trade or profession. Since jargon is understood by only a small audience, writers will use jargon in passages that will only be read by a specialized audience. For example, medical jargon should be used in a medical journal but not in a New York Times article. Jargon includes exaggerated language that tries to impress rather than inform. Sentences filled with jargon are not precise and difficult to understand.

Examples:

> "He is going to *toenail* these frames for us." (Toenail is construction jargon for nailing at an angle.)
>
> "They brought in a *kip* of material today." (Kip refers to 1000 pounds in architecture and engineering.)

SLANG

Slang is an **informal** and sometimes private language that is understood by some individuals. Slang has some usefulness, but the language can have a small audience. So, most formal writing will not include this kind of language.

Examples:

> "Yes, the event was a blast!" (In this sentence, *blast* means that the event was a great experience.)
>
> "That attempt was an epic fail." (By *epic fail*, the speaker means that his or her attempt was not a success.)

COLLOQUIALISM

A colloquialism is a word or phrase that is found in informal writing. Unlike slang, **colloquial language** will be familiar to a greater range of people. Colloquial language can include some slang, but these are limited to contractions for the most part.

Examples:

> "Can *y'all* come back another time?" (Y'all is a contraction of "you all" which has become a colloquialism.)
>
> "Will you stop him from building this *castle in the air*?" (A "castle in the air" is an improbable or unlikely event.)

TONE

Tone may be defined as the writer's **attitude** toward the topic, and to the audience. This attitude is reflected in the language used in the writing. The tone of a work should be **appropriate to the topic** and to the intended audience. Some texts should not contain slang or jargon, although these may be fine in a different piece. Tone can range from humorous to serious and all levels in between. It may be more or less formal, depending on the purpose of the writing and its intended audience. All these nuances in tone can flavor the entire writing and should be kept in mind as the work evolves.

WORD SELECTION

A writer's choice of words is a **signature** of their style. Careful thought about the use of words can improve a piece of writing. A passage can be an exciting piece to read when attention is given to the use of vivid or specific nouns rather than general ones. When using an active verb, one should be sure that the verb is used in the active voice instead of the passive voice. Verbs are in the active voice when the subject is the one doing the action. A verb is in the passive voice when the subject is the recipient of an action.

Example:

> General: His kindness will never be forgotten.
>
> Specific: His thoughtful gifts and bear hugs will never be forgotten.

Attention should also be given to the kind of verbs that are used in sentences. Active verbs (e.g., run, swim) should be about an action. Whenever possible, an **active verb should replace a linking verb** to provide clear examples for arguments and to strengthen a passage overall.

Example:

Passive: The winners were called to the stage by the judges.

Active: The judges called the winners to the stage.

Review Video: Word Usage
Visit mometrix.com/academy and enter code: 197863

Conciseness

Conciseness is writing what you need to get your message across in the fewest words possible. Planning is important in writing concise messages. If you have in mind what you need to write beforehand, it will be easier to make a message short and to the point. Do not state the obvious.

Revising is also important. After the message is written, make sure you have short sentences. When reviewing the information, imagine a conversation taking place, and concise writing will likely result.

Transitions

Transitions are bridges between what has been read and what is about to be read. Transitions smooth the reader's path between sentences and inform the reader of major connections to new ideas forthcoming in the text. Transitional phrases should be used with care, selecting the appropriate phrase for a transition. Tone is another important consideration in using transitional phrases, varying the tone for different audiences. For example, in a scholarly essay, *in summary* would be preferable to the more informal *in short.*

When working with transitional words and phrases, writers usually find a natural flow that indicates when a transition is needed. In reading a draft of the text, it should become apparent where the flow is uneven or rough. At this point, the writer can add transitional elements during the revision process. Revising can also afford an opportunity to delete transitional devices that seem heavy handed or unnecessary.

Types of Transitions

Appropriate transition words help clarify the relationships between sentences and paragraphs, and they create a much more cohesive essay. Below are listed several categories of transitions that you will need to be familiar with along with some associated transition words:

- **Logical Continuation**: therefore, as such, for this reason, thus, consequently, as a result
- **Extended Argument**: moreover, furthermore, also
- **Example or Illustration**: for instance, for example
- **Comparison**: similarly, likewise, in like manner
- **Contrast**: however, nevertheless, by contrast
- **Restatement or Clarification**: in other words, to put it another way
- **Generalization or General Application**: in broad terms, broadly speaking, in general

Essay Revision and Editing Chapter Quiz

1. Which of the following is frequently used in formal writing?

a. Colloquialism
b. Figurative language
c. Jargon
d. Slang

2. Which of the following is NOT a type of transition?

a. Logical continuation
b. Shortened argument
c. Example
d. Restatement

3. Which of the following is TRUE?

a. Whenever possible, an active verb should replace a linking verb.
b. Planning is not important in writing concise messages.
c. Transitional phrases should be used whenever possible.
d. No texts should contain slang or jargon.

Essay

INTRODUCTION

The purpose of the introduction is to capture the reader's attention and announce the essay's main idea. Normally, the introduction contains 50-80 words, or 3-5 sentences. An introduction can begin with an interesting quote, a question, or a strong opinion—something that will **engage** the reader's interest and prompt them to keep reading. If you are writing your essay to a specific prompt, your introduction should include a **restatement or summarization** of the prompt so that the reader will have some context for your essay. Finally, your introduction should briefly state your **thesis or main idea**: the primary thing you hope to communicate to the reader through your essay. Don't try to include all of the details and nuances of your thesis, or all of your reasons for it, in the introduction. That's what the rest of the essay is for!

THESIS STATEMENT

The thesis is the main idea of the essay. A temporary thesis should be established early in the writing process because it will serve to keep the writer focused as ideas develop. This temporary thesis is subject to change as you continue to write.

The temporary thesis has two parts: a topic (i.e., the focus of your essay based on the prompt) and a comment. The comment makes an important point about the topic. A temporary thesis should be interesting and specific. Also, you need to limit the topic to a manageable scope. These three criteria are useful tools to measure the effectiveness of any temporary thesis:

- Does the focus of my essay have enough interest to hold an audience?
- Is the focus of my essay specific enough to generate interest?
- Is the focus of my essay manageable for the time limit? Too broad? Too narrow?

The thesis should be a generalization rather than a fact because the thesis prepares readers for facts and details that support the thesis. The process of bringing the thesis into sharp focus may help in outlining major sections of the work. Once the thesis and introduction are complete, you can address the body of the work.

Review Video: Thesis Statements
Visit mometrix.com/academy and enter code: 691033

SUPPORTING THE THESIS

Throughout your essay, the thesis should be explained clearly and supported adequately by additional arguments. The thesis sentence needs to contain a clear statement of the purpose of your essay and a comment about the thesis. With the thesis statement, you have an opportunity to state what is noteworthy of this particular treatment of the prompt. Each sentence and paragraph should build on and support the thesis.

When you respond to the prompt, use parts of the passage to support your argument or defend your position. With supporting evidence from the passage, you strengthen your argument because readers can see your attention to the entire passage and your response to the details and facts within the passage. You can use facts, details, statistics, and direct quotations from the passage to uphold your position. Be sure to point out which information comes from the original passage and base your argument around that evidence.

Paragraphs

After the introduction of a passage, a series of body paragraphs will carry a message through to the conclusion. A paragraph should be unified around a main point. Normally, a good topic sentence summarizes the paragraph's main point. A topic sentence is a general sentence that gives an introduction to the paragraph.

The sentences that follow are a support to the topic sentence. However, the topic sentence can come as the final sentence to the paragraph if the earlier sentences give a clear explanation of the topic sentence. Overall, the paragraphs need to stay true to the main point. This means that any unnecessary sentences that do not advance the main point should be removed.

The main point of a paragraph requires adequate development (i.e., a substantial paragraph that covers the main point). A paragraph of two or three sentences does not cover a main point. This is true when the main point of the paragraph gives strong support to the argument of the thesis. An occasional short paragraph is fine as a transitional device. However, a well-developed argument will have paragraphs with more than a few sentences.

Methods of Developing Paragraphs

A common method of development with paragraphs can be done with **examples**. These examples are the supporting details to the main idea of a paragraph or a passage. When authors write about something that their audience may not understand, they can provide an example to show their point. When authors write about something that is not easily accepted, they can give examples to prove their point.

Illustrations are extended examples that require several sentences. Well selected illustrations can be a great way for authors to develop a point that may not be familiar to their audience.

Analogies make comparisons between items that appear to have nothing in common. Analogies are employed by writers to provoke fresh thoughts about a subject. These comparisons may be used to explain the unfamiliar, to clarify an abstract point, or to argue a point. Although analogies are effective literary devices, they should be used carefully in arguments. Two things may be alike in some respects but completely different in others.

Cause and effect is an excellent device used when the cause and effect are accepted as true. One way that authors can use cause and effect is to state the effect in the topic sentence of a paragraph and add the causes in the body of the paragraph. With this method, an author's paragraphs can have structure which always strengthens writing.

Types of Paragraphs

A **paragraph of narration** tells a story or a part of a story. Normally, the sentences are arranged in chronological order (i.e., the order that the events happened). However, flashbacks (i.e., beginning the story at an earlier time) can be included.

A **descriptive paragraph** makes a verbal portrait of a person, place, or thing. When specific details are used that appeal to one or more of the senses (i.e., sight, sound, smell, taste, and touch), authors give readers a sense of being present in the moment.

A **process paragraph** is related to time order (i.e., First, you open the bottle. Second, you pour the liquid, etc.). Usually, this describes a process or teaches readers how to perform a process.

Comparing two things draws attention to their similarities and indicates a number of differences. When authors contrast, they focus only on differences. Both comparisons and contrasts may be used point-by-point or in following paragraphs.

Reasons for starting a new paragraph include:

1. To mark off the introduction and concluding paragraphs
2. To signal a shift to a new idea or topic
3. To indicate an important shift in time or place
4. To explain a point in additional detail
5. To highlight a comparison, contrast, or cause and effect relationship

Paragraph Length

Most readers find that their comfort level for a paragraph is between 100 and 200 words. Shorter paragraphs cause too much starting and stopping, and give a choppy effect. Paragraphs that are too long often test the attention span of readers. Two notable exceptions to this rule exist. In scientific or scholarly papers, longer paragraphs suggest seriousness and depth. In journalistic writing, constraints are placed on paragraph size by the narrow columns in a newspaper format.

The first and last paragraphs of a text will usually be the introduction and conclusion. These special-purpose paragraphs are likely to be shorter than paragraphs in the body of the work. Paragraphs in the body of the essay follow the subject's outline; one paragraph per point in short essays and a group of paragraphs per point in longer works. Some ideas require more development than others, so it is good for a writer to remain flexible. A paragraph of excessive length may be divided, and shorter ones may be combined.

Coherent Paragraphs

A smooth flow of sentences and paragraphs without gaps, shifts, or bumps will lead to paragraph coherence. Ties between old and new information can be smoothed by several methods:

- Linking ideas clearly, from the topic sentence to the body of the paragraph, is essential for a smooth transition. The topic sentence states the main point, and this should be followed by specific details, examples, and illustrations that support the topic sentence. The support may be direct or indirect. In indirect support, the illustrations and examples may support a sentence that in turn supports the topic directly.
- The repetition of key words adds coherence to a paragraph. To avoid dull language, variations of the key words may be used.
- Parallel structures are often used within sentences to emphasize the similarity of ideas and connect sentences giving similar information.
- Maintaining a consistent verb tense throughout the paragraph helps. Shifting tenses affects the smooth flow of words and can disrupt the coherence of the paragraph.

Chapter Quiz Answer Key

Literary Text Analysis

1. A: The time frame is the period in which the story is set. This may refer to the historical period the story takes place in or the time span of the story (e.g., takes place over a single day or over a few weeks).

2. A: The theme is the lesson that a story teaches. Sometimes, as in the case of fables, the theme is stated directly in the text. However, this is not usually the case with other types of texts.

3. B: There are three main types of conflict in literature: man versus man, man versus nature, and man versus self.

4. A: Comic relief is the use of comedy by an author to break up a dramatic or tragic scene and infuse it with a bit of lightheartedness.

5. A: Another type of figurative language is personification. This is the description of a nonhuman thing as if the item were human. Literally, the word means the process of making something into a person. The general intent of personification is to describe things in a manner that will be comprehensible to readers. When an author states that a tree groans in the wind, he or she does not mean that the tree is emitting a low, pained sound from a mouth. Instead, the author means that the tree is making a noise similar to a human groan.

Informational Text Analysis

1. D: Supporting details are most commonly found in informative and persuasive texts. In some cases, they will be clearly indicated with terms like *for example* or *for instance*, or they will be enumerated with terms like *first*, *second*, and *last*.

2. D: The main idea should not be confused with the thesis statement. While the main idea gives a brief, general summary of a text, the thesis statement provides a specific perspective on an issue that the author supports with evidence.

3. D: Readers need to create the type of graphic organizer that best helps them recall information from a story. A timeline will have events listed with their corresponding dates to help keep track of the story's plot. A spider map takes a main idea from the story and places it in a bubble with supporting points branching off the main idea. An outline is useful for diagramming the main and supporting points of the entire story, and a Venn diagram classifies information as separate or overlapping.

4. A: The topic is usually expressed in a few words at the most while the main idea often needs a full sentence to be completely defined. As an example, a short passage might have the topic of penguins and the main idea could be written as: *Penguins are different from other birds in many ways.*

5. C: The topic is usually expressed in a few words at the most while the main idea often needs a full sentence to be completely defined. As an example, a short passage might have the topic of penguins and the main idea could be written as: *Penguins are different from other birds in many ways.*

Inferences

1. C: A good inference is a logical conclusion supported by the information in a passage and is different from explicit information, which is clearly stated in a passage.

2. D: When asked for a conclusion that may be drawn, look for critical hedge phrases, such as *likely, may, can,* and *will often*, among many others. When you are being tested on this knowledge, remember the question that writers insert into these hedge phrases to cover every possibility.

3. C: Peter is likely going to trip and fall because of the roots along the path. The change in lighting will probably cause him to fall, even though he has run this way many times before. It is more likely that his confidence in knowing the path will push him to keep going rather than turn around or begin taking a new path. Encountering a wild animal is the least likely outcome, as nothing in the passage gives any indication that there are any animals in his vicinity.

Author's Craft

1. A: One of the most common text structures is cause and effect. A cause is an act or event that makes something happen, and an effect is the thing that happens as a result of the cause. A cause-and-effect relationship is not always explicit, but there are some terms in English that signal causes, such as *since*, *because*, and *due to*. Furthermore, terms that signal effects include *consequently*, *therefore*, and *this led to*. As an example, consider the sentence: *Because the sky was clear, Ron did not bring an umbrella*. The cause is the clear sky, and the effect is that Ron did not bring an umbrella.

2. A: When using chronological order, the author presents information in the order that it happened. For example, biographies are typically written in chronological order, starting with the subject's birth and childhood, and then proceeding to his or her adult life and death.

3. D: An effect can become the cause of another effect. This is known as a cause-and-effect chain. (e.g., *As a result of her hatred for not doing work, Lynn got ready for her exam. This led to her passing her test with high marks. Hence, she received an A in the course and was named valedictorian of her graduating class.*)

4. C: In first person, the author writes from the perspective of *I*, while in third person, the author usually refers to each character by using *he* or *she*. Third-person point of view is the most commonly used. In third-person omniscient, the narrator is not a character in the story; rather, the narrator tells the story of all of the characters at the same time.

5. B: A narrative passage is a story that can be fiction or nonfiction, and there are a few elements that a text must have in order to be classified as a narrative. First, the text must have a plot (i.e., a series of events). Narratives often proceed in a clear sequence, but this is not a requirement. If the narrative is good, then these events will be interesting to readers. Second, a narrative has characters. These characters could be people, animals, or even inanimate objects—so long as they participate in the plot. Third, a narrative passage often contains figurative language that is meant to stimulate the imagination of readers by making comparisons and observations.

Argumentation

1. A: Argumentative and persuasive passages should not be combative or abusive. When an author writes reasonable arguments, his or her goal is not to win or have the last word. Instead, authors want to reveal current understandings of the question at hand and suggest solutions to a problem. The purpose of argument and persuasion in a free society is to reach the best solution.

2. B: An author also might use the bandwagon approach, which is when he or she suggests that his or her opinion is correct because it is held by the majority.

3. C: A fact can be analyzed and be proven true or false. An opinion, on the other hand, is an author's personal thoughts or feelings, which may not be alterable by research or evidence. If the author writes that the driving distance from New York City to Boston is about 215 miles, then he or she is stating a fact. If the author writes that New York City is too crowded, then he or she is giving an opinion because there is no objective standard for being too crowded.

Vocabulary

1. B: Readers can determine which meaning of a word an author is using by looking at context clues. In some cases, however, there will be very few contextual clues to help a reader define the meaning of an unfamiliar word. When this happens, one strategy that readers may employ is substitution. A good reader will brainstorm some possible synonyms for the given word, and he or she will substitute these words into the sentence. If the sentence and the surrounding passage continue to make sense, then the substitution has revealed at least some information about the unfamiliar word.

2. C: This is explained by understanding synonyms (words that mean the same thing) and antonyms (words that mean the opposite of one another). If the difference between the two words is too great, then they should not be called synonyms. *Hot* and *warm* are not synonyms because their meanings are too distinct. A good way to determine whether two words are synonyms is to substitute one word for the other word and verify that the meaning of the sentence has not changed. Substituting *warm* for *hot* in a sentence would convey a different meaning. Although *warm* and *hot* may seem close in meaning, *warm* generally means that the temperature is moderate, and *hot* generally means that the temperature is excessively high. In this case, *drinks* and *beverages* are essentially equivalent and are therefore synonyms.

3. A: Antonyms are words with opposite meanings. *Light* and *dark*, *up* and *down*, *right* and *left*, *good* and *bad*: these are all sets of antonyms. Being frugal is the opposite of being generous, which makes the terms antonyms. Be careful to distinguish between antonyms and pairs of words that are simply different. *Black* and *gray*, for instance, are not antonyms because gray is not the opposite of black. *Black* and *white*, on the other hand, are antonyms. *Cats* and *dogs* are animal counterparts, but they do not mean opposite things. *Witch* and *wizard* function in a similar way, in that they are not opposites of each other but are instead only male and female counterparts.

Conventions of Grammar and Usage

1. D: There are eight total parts of speech: nouns, pronouns, verbs, adjectives, adverbs, prepositions, conjunctions, and interjections.

2. D: Articles are adjectives that are used to mark nouns. There are only three: the definite (i.e., limited or fixed amount) article *the*, and the indefinite (i.e., no limit or fixed amount) articles *a* and *an*.

3. A: The adjectives that are relative will show the different degrees of something or someone to something else or someone else. The three degrees of adjectives include positive, comparative, and superlative.

The positive degree is the normal form of an adjective.

> Example: This work is *difficult.* | She is *smart.*

The comparative degree compares one person or thing to another person or thing.

> Example: This work is *more difficult* than your work. | She is *smarter* than me.

The superlative degree compares more than two people or things.

> Example: This is the *most difficult* work of my life. | She is the *smartest* lady in school.

4. C: There are three types of verbals: participles, gerunds, and infinitives. Each type of verbal has a corresponding phrase that consists of the verbal itself along with any complements or modifiers.

5. B: A split infinitive occurs when a modifying word comes between the word *to* and the verb that pairs with *to*.

> Example: To *clearly* explain vs. *To explain* clearly | To *softly* sing vs. *To sing* softly

Though considered improper by some, split infinitives may provide better clarity and simplicity in some cases than the alternatives. As such, avoiding them should not be considered a universal rule.

Conventions of Punctuation

1. D: A nonessential modifier is a phrase that further identifies or gives information about something or someone in the sentence but is not necessary (essential) for the sentence to be sufficiently descriptive.

2. B: Use a semicolon between independent clauses linked with a transitional word.

Examples:

I think that we can agree on this*; however,* I am not sure about my friends.

You are looking in the wrong places*; therefore,* you will not find what you need

3. A: The colon is used to call attention to the words that follow it. A colon must come after a complete independent clause. The rules for colons are as follows:

1. Use a colon after an independent clause to make a list
   Example: I want to learn many languages: Spanish, German, and Italian.

2. Use a colon for explanations or to give a quote
   Examples:
   Quote: He started with an idea: "We are able to do more than we imagine."
   Explanation: There is one thing that stands out on your resume: responsibility.

3. Use a colon after the greeting in a formal letter, to show hours and minutes, and to separate a title and subtitle
   Examples:
   Greeting in a formal letter: Dear Sir: | To Whom It May Concern:
   Time: It is 3:14 P.M.
   Title: The essay is titled "America: A Short Introduction to a Modern Country"

4. C: If a full sentence or more is removed from a quoted passage, you need to use four periods to show the removed text and the end punctuation mark.

5. C: Although it is not standard usage, quotation marks are sometimes used to highlight irony, or the use of words to mean something other than their dictionary definition. This type of usage should be employed sparingly, if at all.

Conventions of Spelling

1. A: Usually, the final consonant is doubled on a word before adding a suffix. One-syllable words have the final consonant doubled when the word ends *vowel-consonant*. Multisyllabic words that end *vowel-consonant* are treated the same only when the last syllable is stressed.

2. C: A small number of words end with *ise*. Most of the words in the English language with the same sound end in *ize*. Words that end with *ize* include the following:

- Accessorize, agonize, authorize, and brutalize

3. D: Rainforest is a compound noun, but it is not hyphenated.

Essay Revision and Editing

1. B: There are many types of language devices that authors use to convey their meaning in a descriptive way. These types of devices all fall under the umbrella of figurative language, which is language that goes beyond the literal meaning of a word or phrase. Jargon is specialized vocabulary that is used among members of a trade or profession. Since jargon is understood by only a small audience, writers will use jargon in passages that will only be read by a specialized audience. Slang is an informal and sometimes private language that is understood by some individuals. Slang has some usefulness, but the language can have a small audience. Most formal writing will not include this kind of language. A colloquialism is a word or phrase that is found in informal writing.

2. B: Appropriate transition words help clarify the relationships between sentences and paragraphs, and they create a much more cohesive essay. Listed below are several categories of transitions that you will need to be familiar with, along with some of their associated transition words.

- Logical continuation: therefore, as such, for this reason, thus, consequently, as a result
- Extended argument: moreover, furthermore, also
- Example or illustration: for instance, for example
- Comparison: similarly, likewise, in like manner
- Contrast: however, nevertheless, by contrast
- Restatement or clarification: in other words, to put it another way
- Generalization or general application: in broad terms, broadly speaking, in general

3. A: Attention should also be given to the kind of verbs that are used in sentences. Active verbs (e.g., run, swim) should be used to describe action. Whenever possible, an active verb should replace a linking verb to provide clear examples for arguments and to strengthen a passage overall.

TSI Practice Test #1

Want to take this practice test in an online interactive format?
Check out the bonus page, which includes interactive practice questions and much more: **http://www.mometrix.com/bonus948/tsi**

Math

1. If $x + y > 0$ when $x > y$, which of the following cannot be true?

A. $x = 3$ and $y = 0$
B. $x = -3$ and $y = 0$
C. $x = -4$ and $y = -3$
D. $x = 3$ and $y = -3$

Question 2 is based on the following table.

Hours	1	2	3
Cost	\$3.60	\$7.20	\$10.80

2. The table shows the cost of renting a bicycle for 1, 2, or 3 hours. Which of the following equations best represents the data, if *C* represents the cost and *h* represents the time (in hours) of the rental?

A. $C = 3.60h$
B. $C = h + 3.60$
C. $C = 3.60h + 10.80$
D. $C = \frac{10.80}{h}$

3. Rafael has a business selling computers. He buys computers from the manufacturer for \$450 each and sells them for \$800. Each month he must also pay fixed costs of \$3,000 for rent and utilities at his store. If he sells *n* computers in a month, which of the following equations can be used to calculate his monthly profit?

A. $P = n(800 - 450 - 3{,}000)$
B. $P = 3{,}000 \times n(800 - 450)$
C. $P = n(800 - 450) - 3{,}000$
D. $P = n(800 - 450) + 3{,}000$

4. If $-\frac{1}{3}x + 7 = 4$, what is the value for $\frac{1}{3}x + 3$?

A. 3
B. 6
C. 9
D. 12

5. Jack and Kevin play in a basketball game. If the ratio of points scored by Jack to points scored by Kevin is 4 to 3, which of the following could NOT be the total number of points scored by the two boys?

A. 14
B. 16
C. 28
D. 35

6. How many 3-inch segments can a 4.5-yard line be divided into?

A. 45
B. 54
C. 64
D. 84

7. Which of the following expressions is equivalent to $(a+b)(a-b)$?

A. $a^2 - b^2$
B. $(a+b)^2$
C. $(a-b)^2$
D. $ab(a-b)$

8. If $2^4 = 4^x$, what is the value of x?

A. 2
B. 4
C. 6
D. 8

9. Simplify the following expression: $(2x^2 + 3x + 2) - (x^2 + 2x - 3)$

A. $x^2 + x + 5$
B. $x^2 + x - 1$
C. $x^2 + 5x + 5$
D. $x^2 + 5x - 1$

10. Which of the following is equivalent to $\left(\sqrt[3]{x^4}\right)^5$?

A. $x^{\frac{12}{5}}$
B. $x^{\frac{15}{4}}$
C. $x^{\frac{20}{3}}$
D. x^{60}

Question 11 is based on the following figure (figure may not be to scale):

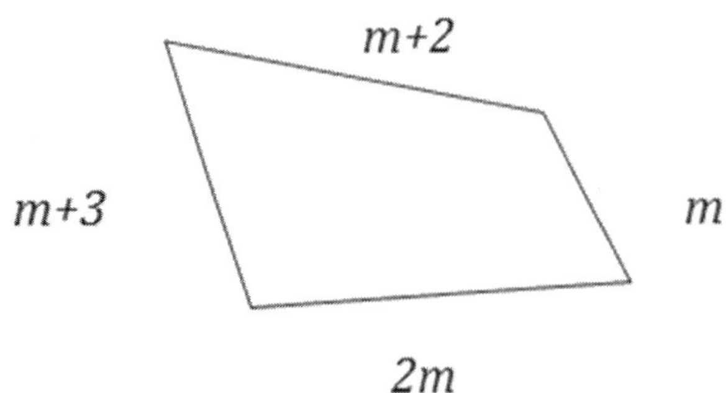

11. The figure shows an irregular quadrilateral and the lengths of its individual sides. Which of the following equations best represents the perimeter of the quadrilateral?

A. $2m^4 + 5$
B. $4m + 5$
C. $5m + 5$
D. $4m^2 + 5$

12. Which of the following could be a graph of the function $y = \frac{1}{x}$?

A. 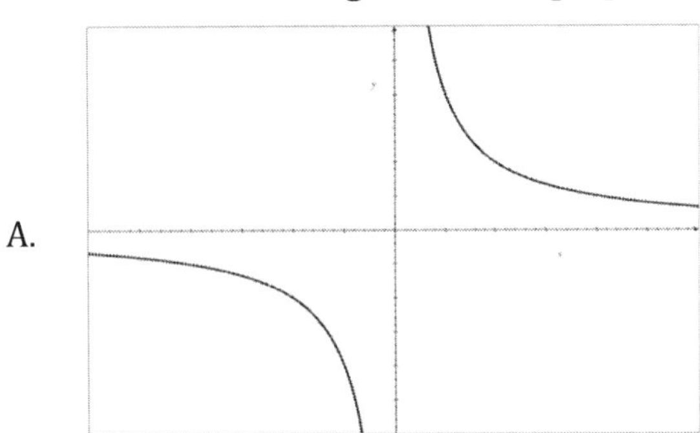

B. 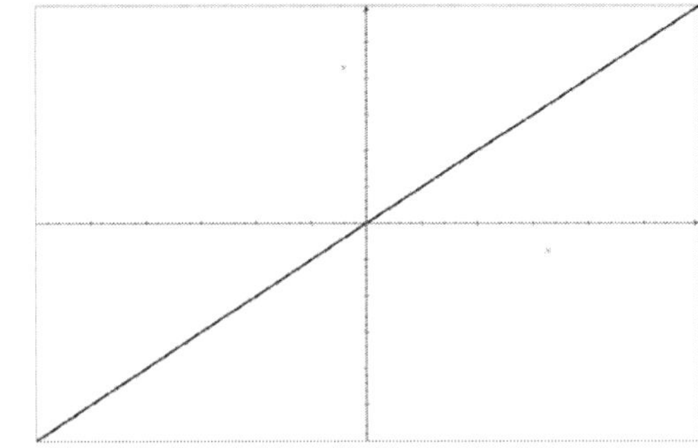

C. 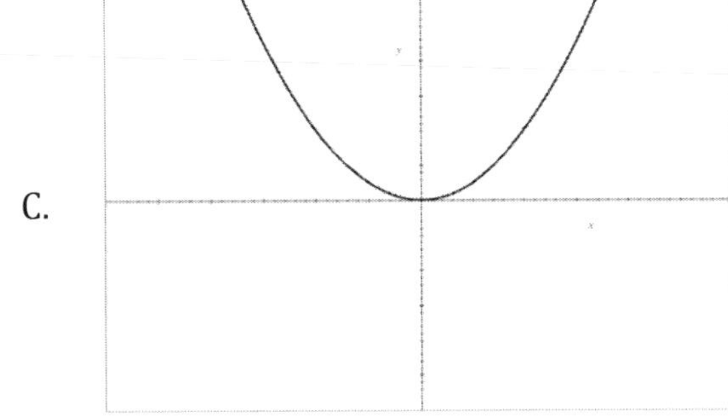

D. 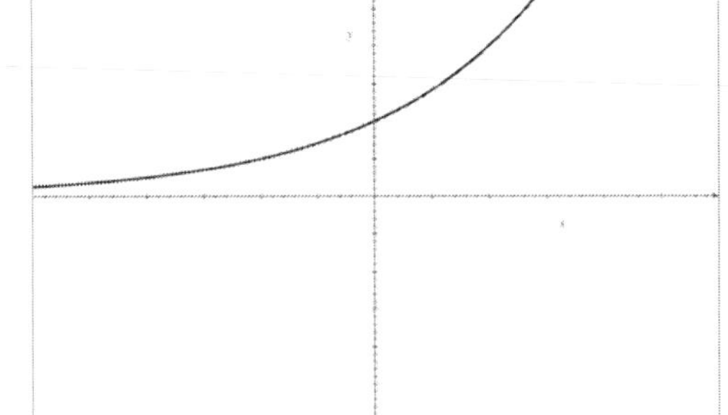

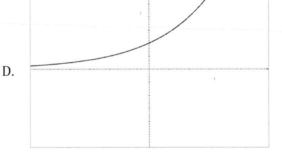

13. The graph below shows the number of miles Jen runs each day, Monday through Friday. What fraction of the time does she run at least four miles?

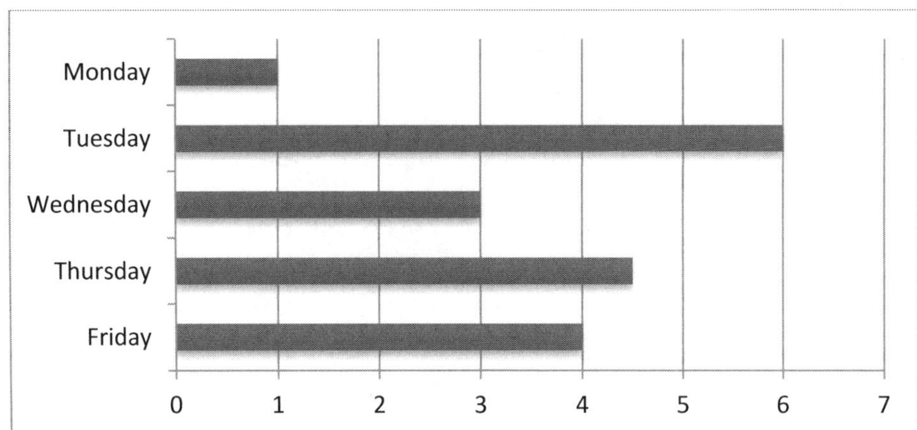

A. $\frac{3}{7}$
B. $\frac{3}{2}$
C. $\frac{2}{5}$
D. $\frac{3}{5}$

Question 14 is based upon the following figure (figure may not be to scale):

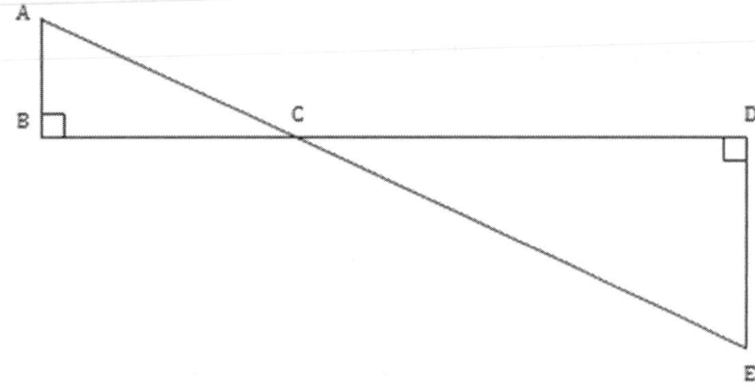

14. In the figure above, segment BC is 4 units long, segment CD is 8 units long, and segment DE is 6 units long. What is the length of segment AC?

A. 4 units
B. 5 units
C. 6 units
D. 8 units

15. Janelle bought 3 movie tickets and an order of popcorn for her family for $32.50. Jon bought 4 tickets and 2 orders of popcorn for his family for $46. How much does a ticket cost?

A. $4.00
B. $6.50
C. $7.75
D. $9.50

16. Which of the following are complementary angles?

A. 71° and 19°
B. 90° and 90°
C. 90° and 45°
D. 15° and 30°

17. Given the double bar graph shown below, which of the following statements is true?

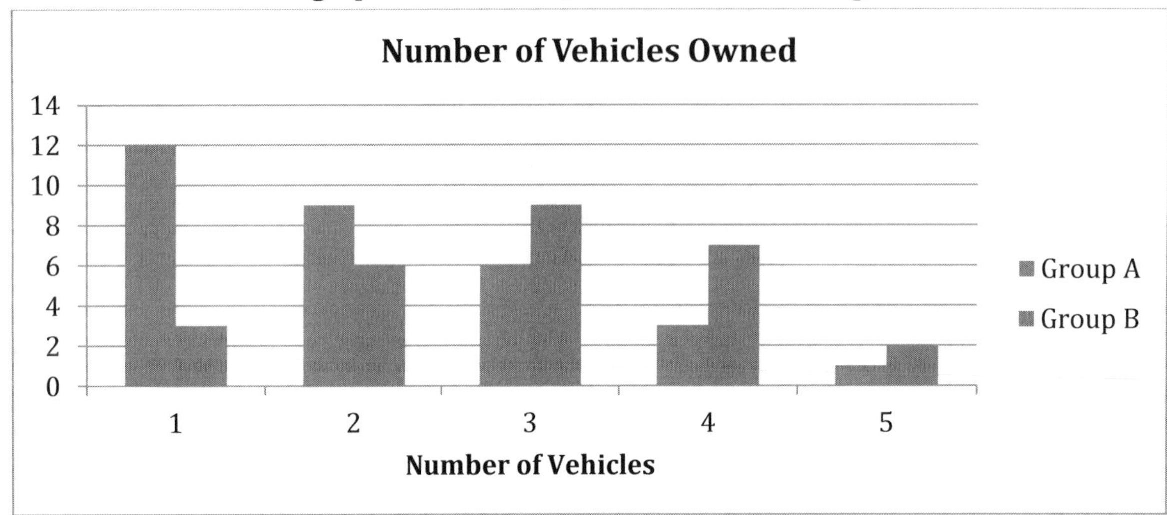

A. Group A is negatively skewed, while Group B is approximately normal.
B. Group A is positively skewed, while Group B is approximately normal.
C. Group A is approximately normal, while Group B is negatively skewed.
D. Group A is approximately normal, while Group B is positively skewed.

18. Which of the following correlation coefficients represents the weakest correlation?

A. 0.3
B. −0.1
C. 0.4
D. −0.9

19. Elizabeth has a standard die that is labeled 1 to 6, and she rolls it 100 times. Which of the following experimental outcomes is NOT likely?

A. 67 rolls will show a number greater than 2.
B. 50 rolls will show an even number.
C. 75 rolls will show a number less than 4.
D. 33 rolls will show a number less than 3.

20. A bag contains 8 red marbles, 3 blue marbles, and 4 green marbles. What is the probability Carlos draws a red marble, does not replace it, and then draws another red marble?

A. $\frac{4}{15}$
B. $\frac{32}{105}$
C. $\frac{64}{225}$
D. $\frac{2}{15}$

English Language Arts and Reading

For questions 1–15, read each passage and then choose the best answer to the accompanying questions. Answer the questions on the basis of what is stated or implied in the passage(s).

The following passage is adapted from Edith Wharton, Ethan Frome, *originally published in 1911. Use this passage to answer questions 1-4.*

(1) It was there that, several years ago, I saw him [Ethan] for the first time; and the sight pulled me up sharp. (2) Even then he was the most striking figure in Starkfield, though he was but the ruin of a man. (3) It was not so much his great height that marked him, for the "natives" were easily singled out by their lank longitude from the stockier foreign breed: it was the careless powerful look he had, in spite of a lameness checking each step like the jerk of a chain. (4) There was something bleak and unapproachable in his face, and he was so stiffened and grizzled that I took him for an old man and was surprised to hear that he was not more than fifty-two. (5) I had this from Harmon Gow, who had driven the stage from Bettsbridge to Starkfield in pre-trolley days and knew the chronicle of all the families on his line.

(6) "He's looked that way ever since he had his smash-up; and that's twenty-four years ago come next February," Harmon threw out between reminiscent pauses.

(7) The "smash-up" it was—I gathered from the same informant—which, besides drawing the red gash across Ethan Frome's forehead, had so shortened and warped his right side that it cost him a visible effort to take the few steps from his buggy to the post-office window. (8) He used to drive in from his farm every day at about noon, and as that was my own hour for fetching my mail I often passed him in the porch or stood beside him while we waited on the motions of the distributing hand behind the grating. (9) I noticed that, though he came so punctually, he seldom received anything but a copy of the *Bettsbridge Eagle*, which he put without a glance into his sagging pocket. (10) At intervals, however, the post-master would hand him an envelope addressed to Mrs. Zenobia—or Mrs. Zeena—Frome, and usually bearing conspicuously in the upper left-hand corner the address of some manufacturer of patent medicine and the name of his specific. (11) These documents my neighbour would also pocket without a glance, as if too much used to them to wonder at their number and variety, and would then turn away with a silent nod to the post-master.

(12) Every one in Starkfield knew him and gave him a greeting tempered to his own grave mien; but his taciturnity was respected and it was only on rare occasions that one of the older men of the place detained him for a word. (13) When this happened he would listen quietly, his blue eyes on the speaker's face, and answer in so low a tone that his words never reached me; then he would climb stiffly into his buggy, gather up the reins in his left hand and drive slowly away in the direction of his farm.

(14) "It was a pretty bad smash-up?" I questioned Harmon, looking after Frome's retreating figure, and thinking how gallantly his lean brown head, with its shock of light hair, must have sat on his strong shoulders before they were bent out of shape.

(15) "Wust kind," my informant assented. (16) "More'n enough to kill most men. (17) But the Fromes are tough. (18) Ethan'll likely touch a hundred."

1. The first paragraph (sentences 1–5) indicates that Ethan Frome is ____________ in appearance.

A. ugly
B. unusual
C. pathetic
D. youthful

2. As used in sentence 12, "tempered" most nearly means

A. Adjusted
B. Angry
C. Calm
D. Gloomy

3. The reader can infer which of the following from the passage?

A. Ethan is depressed due to his physical limitations.
B. Ethan is taller than anyone else in town.
C. Ethan is suffering the effects of an event from decades earlier.
D. Ethan looks forward to picking up the mail daily.

4. In paragraph 3, the author implies that Ethan's wife (Zeena) is ______________.

A. overbearing
B. respectful
C. in poor health
D. concerned for her husband

Use these two passages to answer the question that follows:

Passage 1

While many people join a gym on January 1 to "get in shape," studies show that exercise is much less effective for weight loss than simply eating healthier. Burning off a few hundred extra calories may mean working out strenuously for 45 minutes or more, while giving up a morning donut or sugar-laden latte can do the same, with the additional benefit of ridding the body of the unhealthy ingredients that slow the metabolism and spike the blood sugar. Exercise is good for heart health and muscle growth, but ultimately almost futile in the weight loss department unless it is paired with an improved diet.

Passage 2

A healthy diet is undoubtedly important for anyone trying to lose weight. But how many people are frustrated time and time again by unsuccessful diets? Clearly, eating right isn't always enough. To truly lose and maintain the loss, the metabolism must be improved, and the best way to do this is through regular exercise. If a person consistently works out, this can have the single greatest effect on his or her weight loss of any action. Whether this exercise is swimming, weight lifting, a routine designed by a personal trainer, or simply walking during lunch break every day, exercise is an important way to improve health and slim the waistline.

5. The author of Passage 2 would most likely disagree with the claim of Passage 1's author that

A. Eating healthy is important for weight loss
B. Eating right is not alone sufficient for weight loss
C. Giving up unhealthy eating habits can make a difference in weight loss efforts
D. Exercise makes very little difference in weight loss

Use these two passages to answer the question that follows:

Passage 1

Statistics show that 75 percent of businesses fail to last 15 years or more. One of the biggest struggles of new businesses is making their presence known and reaching their target consumers. With the growth of social media, small businesses have found a new voice, new ways to reach potential customers without as many of the challenges of cost and limited distribution that come with traditional advertising methods. Social media also gives businesses a way to directly interact with customers, giving a more personal avenue for marketing.

Passage 2

One of the casualties of social media has been small businesses. While social media allows them to have a "presence" and build relationships, it is a minefield that can easily destroy fledgling businesses. The anonymity of the internet has given rise to "trolls," who can start arguments, file public complaints, and question a business's ethics without any personal knowledge or experience. Monitoring a company's social media profile and attempting to diplomatically interact online is a constant, difficult job, and a single disgruntled comment (sometimes not even on the correct business's page) can have catastrophic effects on a young business.

6. The authors of both passages would likely agree with which of the following statements?

A. Social media gives companies the opportunity to communicate with potential customers on an individual level.
B. Social media has made advertising easier for small businesses.
C. Social media has proven to be an unprecedented challenge for small businesses.
D. Social media gives small businesses the opportunity to reach customers around the world without cost.

7. Consider the following passage:

The Amazon rainforest is one of the most important ecosystems in the world. However, it is slowly being destroyed. Areas of the rainforest are being cleared for farms and roads, and much of the wood is also being harvested and sold. There are several compelling reasons to protect this area. First, a significant number of pharmaceuticals are made from plants that have been discovered in the rainforest, and it's quite possible there are still important plants that have not yet been discovered. Secondly, the rainforest provides a significant portion of the world's oxygen and also absorbs great amounts of carbon dioxide. Without rainforests, global warming could accelerate.

What is the main purpose of this passage?

A. To present the major reasons why the Amazon rainforest is being destroyed
B. To explain why the Amazon rainforest should be protected
C. To argue that rainforest destruction is a major cause of global warming
D. To discuss how the rainforest has helped in the development of medications

8. Consider the following passage:

Howard Gardner was a psychologist best known for developing the theory of multiple intelligences. Basically, the theory states that the idea of general intelligence or overall intelligence is somewhat inaccurate. The concept is misleading because people often show intelligence in different areas. He argued that there are actually different types of intelligence. One of these types is interpersonal intelligence, which allows people to relate and interact well with others. People with intrapersonal intelligence, on the other hand, are in touch with their own feelings. They enjoy thinking about theories and developing their own thoughts and ideas. People with linguistic intelligence learn best by taking notes and reading textbooks. They often excel in traditional academic environments, as many academic subjects stress these types of activities. The other proposed types of intelligence are kinesthetic, musical, spatial, and logical or mathematical.

What can be concluded from this passage?

A. Gardner believed that linguistic intelligence was the most desirable type to have.
B. Most people who have a high level of intrapersonal intelligence do well in school.
C. People who have a high level of interpersonal intelligence work well in groups.
D. People who have mathematical intelligence would do the best on a standard IQ test.

9. Consider the following passage:

To reduce the amount of plastic and other materials that are discarded, zero waste grocery stores are opening across the nation. These encourage the use of reusable containers to cut down on the amount consumers are throwing away. Customers bring their own containers to fill, purchasing anything from dried fruit to baking mix to honey to liquid soap. By putting the products directly in their own containers, consumers cut down on the copious amounts of foam trays, plastic wrap, clamshells, and even grocery bags that are used once and then trashed. However, zero waste of packaging does not mean zero waste overall. Without the preserving effects of plastic or tin cans, food expires more quickly and must be disposed of if not sold in time. Stores must make judicious decisions in their effort to truly be zero waste.

As used in the last sentence, "judicious" most nearly means

A. Judgmental
B. Wise
C. Slow
D. New

10. Consider the following passage:

One of the earliest known fabrics is cotton. Remnants have been found dating to 6,000 BC in South America, and use of cotton in the Middle East and India also dates back millennia. Cotton reached Europe later but quickly became a popular trade item. The industrial revolutions of the US and Britain, particularly Eli Whitney's invention of the cotton gin, allowed production of cloth to increase enormously. In the southern US, plantations produced mass quantities of cotton, relying heavily on slave labor to grow and harvest the crops. Cotton tended to be "king" in the south, even after the Civil War, until boll weevils were introduced in the late nineteenth century. These insects wreaked havoc on cotton fields for decades until pesticides and other control methods were developed to manage the problem. Cotton continues to be manufactured in huge quantities today, in both genetically modified and organic forms.

Which of the following resulted from the invention of the cotton gin?

A. It slowed the production of cotton.
B. It allowed the US to produce cloth independently.
C. It solved the problem of the boll weevil.
D. It aided increased production of cotton.

11. Consider the following passage:

The US dollar has been in use since before the United States was a sovereign nation. Originally, the Continental Congress issued "Continentals" in 1775, paper money in various denominations of dollars. Skyrocketing inflation just a few years later led to the collapse of this currency, but in 1792 Congress established the United States Mint to create coinage. Both gold and silver dollars and fractions of dollars were minted. Paper money was based on a gold standard, meaning that a bill was worth a specific amount of gold. This gold standard was temporarily dropped during America's participation in World War I, and permanently dropped during the Great Depression.

As used in the first sentence, "sovereign" most nearly means

A. Powerful
B. Independent
C. A British coin
D. Possessing a gold standard

12. Consider the following passage:

Being online comes with very real risks, as hackers can steal personal and financial information. Users can take several precautions to minimize risk, such as purchasing a good anti-virus and anti-spyware program. Passwords themselves are also important, but it is vital that passwords be secure. First, a password should be something easy to remember, but it shouldn't be something others can guess easily. A user's own name, phone number, and street name are all bad choices, as people could easily find this information. Longer passwords are more secure, and those that use a mixture of uppercase and lowercase letters and a combination of letters and numbers are more secure than those that don't. Finally, passwords should be changed often. This can make remembering them more difficult, but the added security is worth the extra effort.

What is the main purpose of this passage?

A. To discuss the major risks associated with internet use
B. To talk about the importance of anti-virus programs
C. To outline important considerations for passwords
D. To discuss why certain types of passwords shouldn't be used

13. Consider the following passage:

When people are conducting research, particularly historical research, they usually rely on primary and secondary sources. Primary sources are the more direct type of information. A primary source is an account of an event that is produced by individuals who were actually present. Some examples of primary sources include a person's diary entry about an event, an interview with an eyewitness, a newspaper article, or a transcribed conversation. Secondary sources are pieces of information that are constructed through the use of other primary sources. Often, the person who creates the secondary source was not actually present at the event. Secondary sources could include books, research papers, and magazine articles.

Which of the following is NOT a secondary source?

A. Research paper
B. Book
C. Eyewitness interview
D. Magazine article

14. Consider the following passage:

Many people fail to realize just how crucial getting a good night's sleep actually is. It is usually suggested that adults should get about seven hours of sleep every night and that younger children should get even more. Sleep is believed to improve memory. This is one reason why it is always preferable to sleep the night before a test rather than stay up for the entire night to review the information. Similarly, sleep also improves concentration and mental alertness. Those who get sufficient sleep are able to concentrate on work tasks better and also react faster when they are driving a car, for example. Finally, people who get enough sleep have better immunity against illness. The reason for this is not fully understood, but researchers believe that an increase in the production of growth hormone and melatonin plays a role.

What is the main purpose of this passage?

A. To talk about the benefits of sleep
B. To discuss how much sleep people should get
C. To identify which hormones can boost immunity
D. To present strategies for improving memory and concentration

15. Consider the following passage:

> Feudalism was a social system that existed in parts of Europe during the Middle Ages. Essentially, there were several different classes within a feudal society. The king controlled all of the land in his jurisdiction and divided it among a few barons. The barons then divided up their portions among knights. It was then split up again and distributed to serfs, the lowest members of feudal society. They were permitted to farm small sections of land, but had to give a portion of their food to the knights in exchange for this privilege. They also had to give free labor to the knights in exchange for using their land. Serfs had very few rights; they couldn't even leave their land without permission from the knight who controlled it. The system of feudalism ended when money began to be used as currency instead of land.

What can be concluded from this passage?

A. Serfs were in a better position when the economy changed to a money-based one.
B. There were more knights in a typical feudal society than barons.
C. The knights did not have to do anything for the barons in exchange for land.
D. Most feudal societies in Europe were ruled by more than one king.

For questions 16–19, read the following early draft of an essay and then choose the best answer to the question or the best completion of the statement.

(1) In the early 1760s, Paul Revere ran a busy metalworking shop. (2) People from all over Boston came to buy the silver and gold cups, medals, and cutlery he made. (3) Everything changed in 1765 when many colonists ran low on money and stopped shopping at Paul's shop.

(4) Things got worse when they passed the Stamp Act. (5) The Stamp Act created a tax to help the British earn money. (6) Colonists like Paul Revere hated the Stamp Act because it made things more expensive.

(7) Under the Stamp Act, colonists needed to pay a tax to England on everything that was printed, such as newspapers, magazines, and business contracts. (8) This allowed the British government to collect more money. (9) The Stamp Act made it very expensive for Paul to run his business.

(10) Paul wasn't just angry about buying stamps. (11) He also felt that the British shouldn't be allowed to tax the colonies, since there were no American colonists in the British parliament. (12) Paul and the other colonists didn't want taxation without representation. (13) So the colonists refused to buy stamps. (14) They were determined to get the Stamp Act repealed.

(15) Paul joined a group called the Sons of Liberty, which staged demonstrations at the Liberty Tree, a huge elm tree that stood in Boston. (16) Paul drew cartoons and wrote poems about liberty and published them in the local newspaper, the *Boston Gazette*.

(17) A year later the Stamp Act was officially repealed, leading to celebration throughout Boston. (18) Some members of the Sons of Liberty constructed a paper obelisk with pictures and verses about the struggle to repeal the Stamp Act and hung it from the Liberty Tree. (19) Paul made a copper engraving showing the pictures and verses on the obelisk's four sides. (20) His engraving records the celebration under the Liberty Tree. (21) Even though Paul Revere may be better known for his silver work and famous ride, his engravings, like the engraving of the obelisk, help us see the American Revolution through his eyes.

16. Which of the following sentences could be removed from the third paragraph, as it is unnecessary?

A. Sentence 7
B. Sentence 8
C. Sentence 9
D. Sentence 10

17. In sentence 4, which of the following should replace "they" to avoid confusion?

A. Paul's customers
B. the colonists
C. the British
D. the metalworkers

18. Which of the following sentences would best support the author's argument if added to the third paragraph?

A. Colonists were forced to purchase stamped paper made in London for printing.
B. The British reminded the colonists that many citizens of England did not own property, so they were also taxed without representation.
C. The Stamp Act fell out of favor among British manufacturers as well, because business slowed among colonists.
D. The Stamp Act was replaced with the Declaratory Act, which had a new set of regulations and taxes.

19. What is the most effective way to combine sentences 13 and 14?

A. Determined to get the Stamp Act repealed, the colonists refused to buy stamps.
B. Refusing to buy stamps, they were determined to get the Stamp Act repealed.
C. The colonists were determined to get the Stamp Act repealed, so refusing to buy stamps.
D. So the colonists refused to buy stamps, were determined to get the Stamp Act repealed.

For questions 20–30, select the best version of the underlined part of the sentence. If you think the original sentence is best, choose the first answer.

20. <u>Likewise</u> his favorite ice cream flavor was chocolate, he enjoyed strawberry as well.

A. Likewise
B. Although
C. Accordingly
D. However

21. Oxygen forms a covalent bond with <u>hydrogen, the</u> atoms share electrons.

A. hydrogen, the
B. hydrogen; the
C. hydrogen, moreover the
D. hydrogen. As the

22. <u>Photography, a hobby</u> that is increasingly available to the general public with the development of inexpensive cameras and online tutorials.

A. Photography, a hobby
B. Photography, a hobby,
C. Photography—a hobby—
D. Photography is a hobby

23. Charles settled on <u>their</u> favorite park bench, ignoring the three hopeful dogs that sniffed at his pockets.

A. their
B. its
C. his
D. theirs

24. Running and leaping joyfully, the <u>leaves were scattered by the playing children</u>.

A. leaves were scattered by the playing children
B. leaves by the playing children were scattered
C. playing children scattered the leaves
D. children, scattering the leaves, playing

25. <u>Stopping long enough to buy a bagel, Mia</u> rushed to the bus stop.

A. Stopping long enough to buy a bagel, Mia
B. Mia stopped long enough to buy a bagel, she
C. Long enough to buy a bagel, Mia stopped and
D. Mia, stopped long enough to buy a bagel,

26. Children who aren't nurtured during infancy are more likely to develop attachment disorders, <u>which can cause persisting and severely problems</u> later in life.

A. which can cause persisting and severely problems
B. that can cause persisting and severe problem
C. they can cause persistent and severe problem
D. which can cause persistent and severe problems

27. While speed is a measure of how fast an object is moving, velocity measures how fast an object is moving <u>and also indicates in what direction</u> it is traveling.

A. and also indicates in what direction
B. and only indicates in which direction
C. and also indicate in which directions
D. and only indicated in what direction

28. Many companies are now using social networking sites like Facebook and MySpace <u>to market there service and product.</u>

A. to market there service and product
B. to market their services and products
C. and market their service and products
D. which market their services and products

29. An autoclave is a tool used mainly in hospitals <u>to sterilizing surgical tools and hypodermic needles</u>.

A. to sterilizing surgical tools and hypodermic needles
B. for sterilize surgical tools and hypodermic needles
C. to sterilize surgical tools and hypodermic needles
D. for sterilizing the surgical tool and hypodermic needle

30. <u>The bizarre creatures known by electric eels</u> are capable of emitting an incredible 600 volts of electricity.

A. The bizarre creatures known by electric eels
B. A bizarre creature known as electric eels
C. The bizarre creatures known to electric eels
D. The bizarre creatures known as electric eels

Essay

Some states have legalized the sale and use of marijuana, bringing attention to the possibility of national legalization and regulation of the drug. Please write a multiple-paragraph persuasive essay (approximately 350–500 words) discussing what you believe the federal government's position should be on this issue.

Answers and Explanations for Test #1

Math

1. D: First, test each expression to see which satisfies the condition $x > y$. This condition is not met in answer choices B and C, so these need not be considered further. Next, test the remaining choices to see which satisfy the inequality $x + y > 0$. It can be seen that this inequality holds for choice A but not for choice D, since $x + y = 3 + (-3) = 3 - 3 = 0$. In this case, the sum $x + y$ is not greater than 0.

2. A: This equation represents a linear relationship that has a slope of 3.60 and passes through the origin. The table indicates that for each hour of renting, the cost increases by $3.60. This corresponds to the slope of the equation. Of course, if the bicycle is not rented at all (0 hours) there will be no charge ($0). If plotted on the Cartesian plane, the line would have a y-intercept of 0. Answer choice A is the only one that shows a relationship satisfying these criteria.

3. C: Rafael's profit on each computer is given by the difference between the price he pays and the price he charges his customer, or $800 – $450. If he sells n computers in a month, his total profit will be n times this difference, or $n(800 - 450)$. However, it is necessary to subtract his fixed costs of $3,000 from this to compute his final profit per month.

4. B: Subtracting 7 from both sides of the equation yields $-\frac{1}{3}x = -3$. In order to get the term x by itself, multiply both sides by –3. This gives $x = 9$. Now we substitute this value into the given equation: $\frac{1}{3}(9) + 3$. This gives us $3 + 3$, which is 6.

5. B: Every possible combination of scores is a multiple of 7, since the two terms of the ratio have a sum of 7. Choice B is not a multiple of 7, so it cannot be a combination of the boys' scores.

6. B: There are 12 inches in a foot and 3 feet in a yard. Therefore, 4.5 yards is equal to 162 inches. To determine the number of 3-inch segments, divide 162 by 3.

7. A: Compute the product using the FOIL method, in which the *F*irst term, then the *O*uter terms, the *I*nner terms, and finally the *L*ast terms are figured in sequence of multiplication. As a result, $(a + b)(a - b) = a^2 + ba - ab - b^2$. Since ab is equal to ba, the middle terms cancel each other, which leaves $a^2 - b^2$.

8. A: $2^4 = 2 \times 2 \times 2 \times 2 = 16$. Therefore, $4^x = 16$, so $x = 2$.

9. A: $(2x^2 + 3x + 2) - (x^2 + 2x - 3) = (2x^2 + 3x + 2) + (-1)(x^2 + 2x - 3)$. First, distribute the -1 to remove the parentheses: $2x^2 + 3x + 2 - x^2 - 2x + 3$. Next, combine like terms: $(2x^2 - x^2) + (3x - 2x) + (2 + 3) = x^2 + x + 5$.

10. C: The nth root of x is equivalent to x to the power of $\frac{1}{n}$, i.e., $\sqrt[n]{x} = x^{\frac{1}{n}}$. This means in particular that $\sqrt[3]{x} = x^{\frac{1}{3}}$, and so $\left(\sqrt[3]{(x^4)}\right)^5 = \left((x^4)^{\frac{1}{3}}\right)^5$. Raising a power to another power is equivalent to multiplying the exponents together, so this equals $x^{4 \times \frac{1}{3} \times 5} = x^{\frac{20}{3}}$.

11. C: The perimeter (P) of the quadrilateral is simply the sum of its sides, or

$$P = m + (m + 2) + (m + 3) + 2m$$

Combine like terms by adding the variables (the terms with m) together and then adding the constants, resulting in $P = 5m + 5$.

12. A: This is a typical plot of an inverse variation, in which the product of the dependent and independent variables, x and y, is always equal to the same value. In this case, the product is always equal to 1, so the plot occupies the first and third quadrants of the coordinate plane. As x increases and approaches infinity, y decreases and approaches zero, maintaining the constant product. In contrast, answer B is a linear plot corresponding to an equation of the form $y = x$. Answer C is a quadratic plot corresponding to $y = x^2$. Answer D is an exponential plot corresponding to $y = 2^x$.

13. D: The graph shows five days that Jen runs. On three of the days (Tuesday, Thursday, and Friday), she runs four or more miles. So three out of five days, or $\frac{3}{5}$ of the time, she runs at least four miles.

14. B: The two right triangles are similar because they share a pair of vertical angles (angle ACB and angle ECD). Vertical angles are always congruent. Obviously both right angles (angle B and angle D) are congruent. Thus, angles A and E are congruent because of the triangular sum theorem.

With similar triangles, corresponding sides will be proportional. Segment $\overline{BC}$ is half the length of $\overline{CD}$, therefore $\overline{AC}$ will be half the length of $\overline{CE}$. The length of $\overline{CE}$ can be computed from the Pythagorean theorem, since it is the hypotenuse of a right triangle for which the lengths of the other two sides are known: $\overline{CE} = \sqrt{6^2 + 8^2} = \sqrt{100} = 10$.

The length of $\overline{AC}$ will be half of this value, or 5 units.

15. D: We can create a system of equations to solve for the cost of tickets and popcorn. If Janelle purchased 3 tickets and 1 order of popcorn for $32.50, we can write the equation: $3t + p = 32.5$, where t is tickets and p is popcorn. If Jon purchased 4 tickets and 2 orders of popcorn for $46, this can be written as: $4t + 2p = 46$. We can multiply the first equation by 2 and the second equation by -1 to eliminate a variable:

$$6t + 2p = 65$$
$$-4t - 2p = -46$$

We add these two equations together to obtain $2t = 19$. Dividing both sides by 2 yields $t = 9.5$. So each ticket costs $9.50.

16. A: Complementary angles are two angles that add to 90°. Of the given answer choices, only choice A contains angles that add up to 90° (71° and 19°).

17. B: Data is said to be positively skewed when it contains a high number of relatively low values. In this case, a high number of Group A members owned only 1 car, fewer members owned 2 cars, even fewer owned 3, and so on, indicating data that is skewed right. An approximately normal distribution shows an increase in frequency followed by a decrease in frequency of approximately the same rate.

18. B: Weak correlation coefficients are those with absolute values close to 0. Since −0.1 has an absolute value of 0.1 and 0.1 is closer to 0 than any of the absolute values of the other correlation coefficients in the answer choices, it is the weakest.

19. C: The theoretical probability of rolling a number less than 4 is the same as the theoretical probability of rolling an even number; the probability is $\frac{1}{2}$. The expected number of rolls showing a number less than 4 is equal to the product of the total number of rolls (100) and the probability $\frac{1}{2}$. Thus, it is likely that 50 of the rolls will show a number less than 4, not 75 of the rolls.

20. A: The events are dependent, since the first marble was not replaced. The sample space of the second draw will decrease by 1 because there will be one less marble to choose. The number of possible red marbles for the second draw will also decrease by 1. Thus, the probability may be written as $P(A \text{ and } B) = \frac{8}{15} \times \frac{7}{14}$. The probability Carlos draws a red marble, does not replace it, and draws another red marble is $\frac{4}{15}$.

English Language Arts and Reading

1. B: The author describes Ethan as "striking" due to his "careless powerful look." While his deformities might be construed as making him ugly (A) or pathetic (C), this is not implied by the author. He is described as looking much older than his 52 years, so youthful (D) does not fit.

2. A: The word *tempered* here means "adjusted to conform." The townspeople adjusted their greetings to match Ethan's "grave mien." While a temper, or temperament, can be described as "angry" (B), "calm" (C), or "gloomy" (D), these do not align with the verb form in the passage, and therefore do not reflect the meaning "adjusted."

3. C: The author makes frequent reference to a "smash-up" from close to twenty-four years ago. The physical results of the accident (scarring, bent shoulders, and deformities) affect Ethan's daily life as he can no longer walk well. His face is described as "bleak and unapproachable," which may be due to depression. However, we cannot be sure from the passage that this possible depression is because of his physical limitations, no matter how likely it seems, so answer choice A is incorrect. Ethan is described as having "great height" that sets him apart, but the passage does not state that he is the tallest in town, so answer choice B is incorrect. The author notes that Ethan arrives punctually to pick up the mail but not that he particularly enjoys it. In fact, he seems uninterested, based on the way he puts the mail in his pocket without looking at it, so answer choice D is incorrect.

4. C: In the third paragraph, the author mentions that Ethan frequently picks up packages addressed to his wife that contain various "patent medications." The frequency and variety of medications that are uncommon enough to need to be sent by mail would likely indicate that she is in poor health. There is no indication from the passage that any of the other answer choices describe Ethan's wife as she is only mentioned in the context of receiving packages.

5. D: The last sentence of Passage 1 states that exercise can be "almost futile" for losing weight unless paired with a healthy diet. Passage 2 counters this assumption by stating that exercise is a necessary component of any weight loss program. Answer choices A and C are both mentioned in Passage 1, but the author of Passage 2 is not likely to disagree with them. Answer choice B is a statement made in Passage 2, not Passage 1.

6. A: Both authors mention that social media allows companies to interact with individuals. Although one sees that as more positive than the other does, the two would be likely to agree that the statement is true. Passage 1 indicates that social media has aided in advertising, while Passage 2 indicates that it has made advertising more challenging, so answer choice B is incorrect. The author of Passage 2 would likely agree with answer choice C, but the author of Passage 1 would likely not. Though Passage 1 indicates that advertising on social media costs less than traditional advertising, neither passage states that it is free, so answer choice D is incorrect.

7. B: The concepts in answer choices A and C are mentioned only briefly. The idea shown in choice D is discussed, but it is one of two subpoints that serve the main purpose, which is to discuss why the Amazon rainforest is a valuable area that should be protected.

8. C: Answer choice A is not a logical conclusion because there is no indication that Gardner ranked the intelligences in any way. Answer choice B cannot be concluded from the passage, as there is no mention of the value placed on intrapersonal intelligences in a traditional academic environment. No IQ tests (answer choice D) are mentioned at all, so we cannot conclude anything about them based on this passage. Answer choice C is the correct choice. Those with interpersonal intelligence interact well with others, so it is reasonable to assume they would perform well in a group setting.

9. B: The word *judicious* has to do with sound judgment. This does not mean being judgmental (A) but making wise decisions. Though being judicious make take time, it cannot be equated with "slow" (C), and it does not mean "new" (D).

10. D: The fourth sentence of the selection states that the cotton gin led to increased production of cotton. Answer choice A states the opposite. There is no mention of US independence (B) in the passage. While the passage mentions finding solutions to the boll weevil problem (D), these solutions did not result from the invention of the cotton gin.

11. B: *Sovereign* can have several different meanings, but in the phrase *sovereign nation*, it means "independent." In some contexts, *sovereign* can mean "having supreme power" (A), and as a noun, *sovereign* can refer to a type of British coin (C). Neither of these definitions make sense in this context. While the passage mentions a gold standard (D), "possessing a gold standard" is not a possible meaning of *sovereign*.

12. C: The concepts in answer choices A and B are touched upon only very briefly. Examples of passwords that shouldn't be used (D) are discussed, but only as part of the larger discussion in the passage that aims to outline important considerations related to passwords.

13. C: The final sentence of the passage lists potential secondary sources: books, research papers, and magazine articles (choices B, A, and D, respectively). Eyewitness interviews (C) are listed as an example of a primary source.

14. A: Answer choices B and C refer to topics that are mentioned only briefly. Memory and concentration are mentioned, but strategies for improving them (D) are not. The passage focuses mainly on discussing some of the major benefits of sleep, so that is the main purpose of the passage.

15. B: Answer choice B is the logical conclusion. The passage states, "The king controlled all of the land in his jurisdiction. He divided this among a few barons. The barons then divided up the land they were given and distributed it to knights." If the barons divided up their lands, it would stand to reason that each baron would distribute his land more than one knight. Therefore, there would have to be more knights than barons. Choice A seems to be suggested by the last sentence and could be a point made later in the work, after the passage. But it cannot be concluded from this passage alone. Whether knights had any duties to perform in exchange for their land (C) is never made clear. Choice D directly contradicts the passage.

16. B: Sentence 8 repeats information that has already been given in Sentence 5. Additionally, it is vague in that it does not explain how the tax works. The passage will still be clear without this sentence. Sentences 7 and 9 add valuable details, and Sentence 10 is not part of the third paragraph.

17. C: The term "they" is vague here since the group it refers to is not clearly identified. We can see from sentences 5 and 6 that the Stamp Act benefited the British and that the colonists hated it. So we can infer that the British passed the act, not the colonists (B). Choices A and D are illogical since a select group of customers or artisans does not pass laws.

18. A: The third paragraph describes how the Stamp Act works and how it affected Paul Revere's business. Choice A provides further details of how the act taxes the colonists, so it is the best choice. Choice B, C, and D are true historical details, but they do not fit as well in this paragraph since none of them add information on how the Stamp Act worked or affected colonists.

19. A: Choice A uses a comma correctly to separate an independent clause from an absolute phrase and retains the logical intent of the original sentences. Choice B fails to specify an antecedent for the pronoun "they" and confuses the logical intent of the original sentence. Choice C lacks a subject and verb in the clause following the comma. Choice D joins a compound predicate using a comma instead of *and*.

20. B: The two clauses in the sentence are contradictory; the first one makes a statement, and the second modifies it by adding new information. To reflect this, we need a word that shows this contrast, like "although." Choices A and C do not imply contrast. Choice D does show contrast but does not fit grammatically in the original sentence. It would need to be "His favorite ice cream flavor was chocolate; however, he enjoyed strawberry as well."

21. B: The original sentence has two independent clauses (stand-alone sentences) connected by a comma. This creates a comma splice. The clauses must be joined by a semicolon (as choice B does correctly), joined by a comma and a conjunction, or split into two sentences. Choice C uses the word "moreover" rather than a conjunction, so it is not grammatical. Choice D splits the clauses into two sentences but adds *as* to the beginning of the second, making it a dependent clause (incomplete sentence).

22. D: The sentence is a fragment as written. It lacks a verb to go with the subject, "Photography." Choices B and C likewise do not include a verb, so the sentence would still be a fragment if either one were used. Choice D adds a verb to make it a complete sentence.

23. C: The subject of the sentence is "Charles," which is singular. So even though a plural noun is introduced later ("dogs"), the possessive pronoun should be singular. Choice A is plural. Choice B is singular but impersonal, so it is not appropriate in this setting. Choice D does not fit grammatically.

24. C: From the first clause ("Running and leaping joyfully") we can infer that the intended subject is "the playing children," since leaves do not run and leap. So, to avoid a dangling participle, "children" needs to be the subject of the clause and be mentioned first. Choices A and B use "leaves" as the subject, so they are incorrect. Choice D is a fragment because it uses "playing" instead of "played" in the verb's place.

25. A: As written, the sentence is correct, introducing the subject ("Mia") with a participial phrase. Choice B would create a comma splice because it would combine two independent clauses using a comma. Choice C uses confusing wording that leaves the sentence's meaning in question. Choice D adds commas to create a participial phrase but uses "stopped" instead of "stopping."

26. D: Answer choice A is incorrect because *severely* is an adverb and not an adjective. Choices B and C are incorrect because *problem* instead of the grammatically correct *problems* is used. Choice D uses the correct, plural form *problems* and uses adjectives to describe the problems.

27. A: The sentence implies that *velocity* is used to indicate more than one value, which eliminates B and D. The phrase includes a verb whose subject is "velocity," which is singular, but "indicate" (not "indicates") in choice C would agree with a plural noun. Choice A agrees with the singular noun, and the *and* reflects that velocity is used to indicate more than one value.

28. B: Choice A is not grammatically correct because it uses *there* instead of *their*. The *to* indicates the companies are using these sites for a purpose. This would not be indicated by *and* (C). While choices B and D both use *services* and *products*, which agree with each other because they are plural, the *which* in D also does not show that the companies are using the sites for a purpose.

29. C: Answer choice C states that an autoclave is a tool used "to sterilize." Choices A and B, which begin with "to sterilizing" and "for sterilize," are not grammatically correct. Choice D refers to a single tool and needle or the generic idea of a surgical tool and hypodermic needle. Neither meaning would make sense in the sentence since "hospitals" is plural.

30. D: Answer choices A and C are incorrect because they would mean that the bizarre creatures are something other than electric eels. "A bizarre creature" in choice B does not agree with the plural "electric eels." Choice D is best because it is grammatically correct and identifies electric eels as the bizarre creatures being discussed in the sentence.

TSI Practice Test #2

Math

1. A combination lock uses a three-digit code. Each digit can be any one of the ten available integers 0–9. How many different combinations are possible?

A. 1,000
B. 30
C. 81
D. 100

2. The cost in dollars of shipping x computers to California for sale is $3{,}000 + 100x$. The amount received when selling these computers is $400x$ dollars. What is the least number of computers that must be shipped and sold so that the amount received is at least equal to the shipping cost?

A. 10
B. 15
C. 20
D. 25

3. If $\frac{3}{s} = 7$ and $\frac{4}{t} = 12$, then what is the value of $s - t$?

A. $-\frac{1}{7}$
B. $\frac{2}{12}$
C. $\frac{2}{7}$
D. $\frac{2}{21}$

4. If the average of 7 and x is equal to the average of 9, 4, and x, what is the value of x?

A. 4
B. 5
C. 6
D. 7

5. How many integers are solutions of the inequality $|x| < 4$?

A. An infinite number
B. 0
C. 3
D. 7

6. For what real number x is it true that $3(2x - 10) = x$?

A. -6
B. -5
C. 5
D. 6

7. Expand the following expression: $(y + 1)(y + 2)(y + 3)$

A. $y^3 + 3y + 2$
B. $3y^2 + 6y + 3$
C. $y^3 + 6y^2 + 11y + 6$
D. $8y^3 + 6y + 8$

8. Which of the following is *not* a factor of $x^3 - 3x^2 - 4x + 12$?

A. $x - 2$
B. $x + 2$
C. $x - 3$
D. $x + 3$

9. Simplify $\frac{x^6}{y^4} \times x^2y^3$.

A. x^4y
B. $\frac{x^4}{y}$
C. x^8y
D. $\frac{x^8}{y}$

10. Expand the following expression: $(x + 2)(x - 3)$

A. $x^2 - 1$
B. $x^2 - 6$
C. $x^2 - x - 6$
D. $x^2 - 5x - 1$

11. The formula for the volume of a sphere is $V = \frac{4}{3}\pi r^3$. If $r = \frac{3}{2}x$, what is the volume of the sphere in terms of x?

A. $2\pi x^3$
B. $\frac{9}{2}\pi x^3$
C. $\frac{27}{8}\pi x^3$
D. $\frac{4}{3}\pi x^3$

12. If $x - 2$ is the least of three consecutive even integers, what is the sum of the three integers?

A. $3x - 3$
B. x
C. $3x$
D. $x - 3$

13. Andi wants to put tile on her shower floor, which is 3 ft by 5.5 ft. If the tile costs $5.75 per square foot, how much will it cost her to buy the tile, rounded to the nearest dollar?

A. $17
B. $72
C. $95
D. $131

14. AC and BD are straight lines intersecting at point E. Angle BEC is 45°. What is the measure for angle AEB?

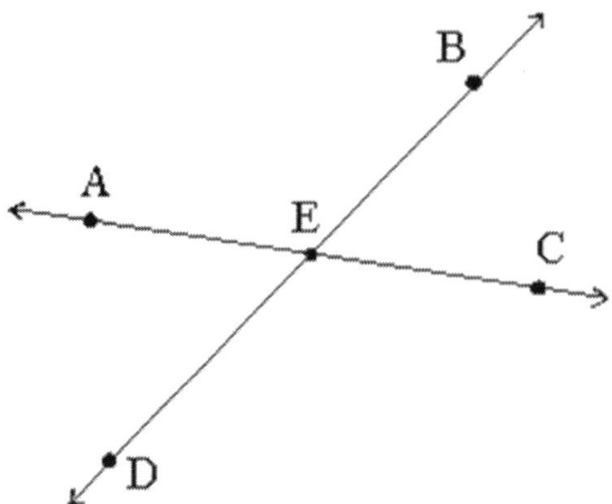

A. Angle AEB is 90°
B. Angle AEB is 115°
C. Angle AEB is 135°
D. Angle AEB is 180°

15. If the ratio of the measures of the three angles in a triangle are 2 : 6 : 10, what is the actual measure of the smallest angle?

A. 20 degrees
B. 40 degrees
C. 60 degrees
D. 80 degrees

16. If the area of a rectangular game board is 336 square inches and its perimeter is 76 inches, what is the length of each of the shorter sides?

A. 10 inches
B. 14 inches
C. 19 inches
D. 24 inches

17. Given the histograms shown below, which of the following statements is true?

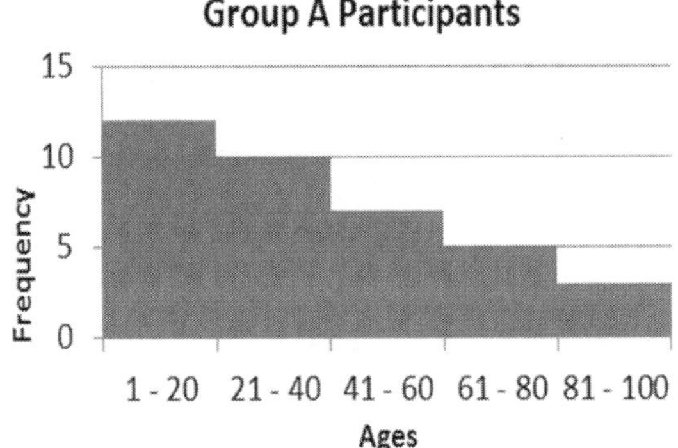

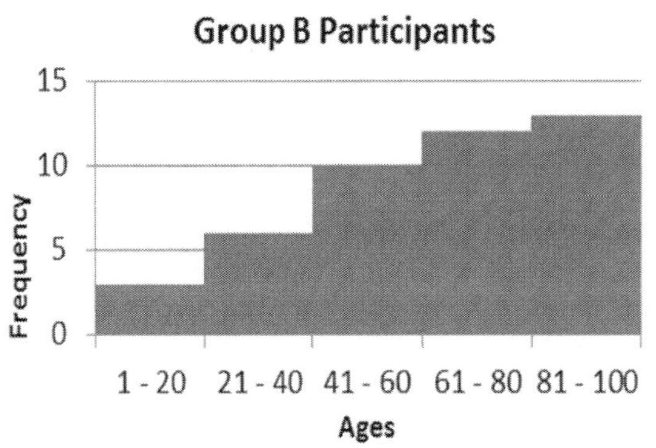

A. Group A is negatively skewed and has a mean that is less than the mean of Group B.
B. Group A is positively skewed and has a mean that is more than the mean of Group B.
C. Group B is negatively skewed and has a mean that is more than the mean of Group A.
D. Group B is positively skewed and has a mean that is less than the mean of Group A.

18. Which of the following best represents the line of best fit for the data shown in the scatter plot?

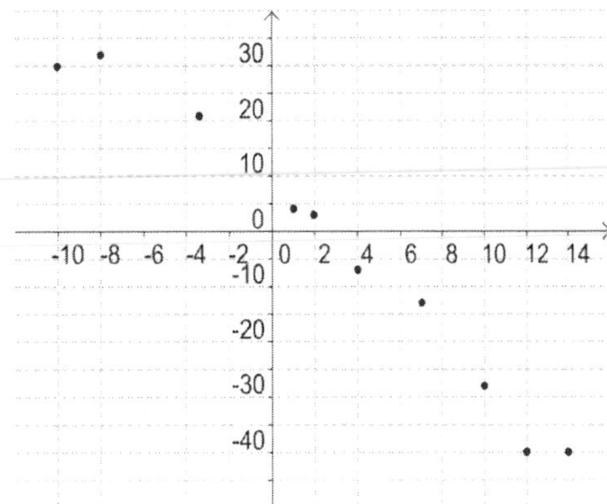

A. $y = -3.2x + 5.1$
B. $y = -2.4x + 10.3$
C. $y = -4.7x - 5.3$
D. $y = -8.2x + 3.4$

19. Drawing cards from a regular deck*, what is the probability that Ana draws a jack, replaces the card, and then draws an ace card?

*A regular deck of playing cards contains 52 unique cards, each belonging to a suit (*spades*, *hearts*, *diamonds*, or *clubs*) and having a number or letter (numbers 2-10, followed by J (*jack*), Q (*queen*), K (*king*), and A (*ace*)). There are 13 cards of each suit and 4 cards of each number or letter.

A. $\frac{1}{52}$
B. $\frac{3}{208}$
C. $\frac{1}{169}$
D. $\frac{17}{52}$

20. What is the expected value of the number on a single ball that is drawn from a bag containing 5 balls that are labeled 1–5?

A. 1.5
B. 2
C. 2.5
D. 3

English Language Arts and Reading

For questions 1–15, read each passage and then choose the best answer to the accompanying questions. Answer the questions on the basis of what is stated or implied in the passage(s).

The following passage is adapted from Herman Melville's, "Bartleby, the Scrivener," originally published in 1856. A scrivener is a scribe, one who copies documents by hand.

(1) "Bartleby! quick, I am waiting."

(2) I heard a slow scrape of his chair legs on the uncarpeted floor, and soon he appeared standing at the entrance of his hermitage.

(3) "What is wanted?" said he mildly.

(4) "The copies, the copies," said I hurriedly. (5) "We are going to examine them. (6) There"—and I held the document towards him.

(7) "I would prefer not to," he said, and gently disappeared behind the screen.

(8) For a few moments I was turned into a pillar of salt, standing at the head of my seated column of clerks. (9) Recovering myself, I advanced towards the screen, and demanded the reason for such extraordinary conduct.

(10) "*Why* do you refuse?"

(11) "I would prefer not to."

(12) With any other man I should have flown outright into a dreadful passion, scorned all further words, and thrust him ignominiously from my presence. (13) But there was something about Bartleby that not only strangely disarmed me, but in a wonderful manner touched and disconcerted me. (14) I began to reason with him.

(15) "These are your own copies we are about to examine. (16) It is labor saving to you, because one examination will answer for your four papers. (17) It is common usage. (18) Every copyist is bound to help examine his copy. (19) Is it not so? (20) Will you not speak? (21) Answer!"

(22) "I prefer not to," he replied in a flute-like tone. (23) It seemed to me that while I had been addressing him, he carefully revolved every statement that I made; fully comprehended the meaning; could not gainsay the irresistible conclusions; but, at the same time, some paramount consideration prevailed with him to reply as he did.

1. As used in sentence 13, "wonderful" most nearly means

A. Surprising
B. Glorious
C. Horrifying
D. Pleasurable

2. What does the author mean by "a pillar of salt" in sentence 8?

A. The narrator was filled with fury at Bartleby's refusal.
B. The narrator felt very bitter toward Bartleby.
C. The narrator was unable to move due to shock.
D. The narrator was deeply impressed by Bartleby's courage.

3. As used in sentence 23, "revolved" most nearly means

A. Turned
B. Spurned
C. Believed
D. Considered

4. How does the author use the narrator's character in this passage?

A. The narrator's excellent work ethic shows Bartleby's lack of character.
B. The narrator's confusion highlights Bartleby's superior intelligence.
C. The narrator's haste and temper emphasize Bartleby's unhurried, peaceful nature.
D. The narrator's constant talking explains why Bartleby was so quiet.

Use these two passages to answer the question that follows:

Passage 1

Throughout history, countless lives have been lost to hunger due to famine, drought, insects, and other disasters that destroy crops. A modern-day solution to this issue is GMO food. Plants can be genetically engineered to be resistant to disease and drought, as well as to produce more or to have extra nutrients. Growing genetically engineered crops even lowers the carbon footprint. Despite the concerns some have regarding changing plant DNA, the development of GMO food has already provided immense benefits throughout the world. Food can be produced more cheaply, allowing for greater distribution, and fewer pesticides are required. With this cure for an age-old problem, everyone benefits.

Passage 2

The advancement of GMO technology has allowed for greater production at less cost, which benefits both producers and consumers. However, the long-term risks may not be worth the short-term savings. While some foods are supposedly more nutritious in GMO form, many foods actually lose nutritional benefits. Another risk is the possibility of toxicity in GMO foods. Additionally, these foods may affect the immune system and cause allergic reactions because of using genes from other plants. For instance, soybeans were engineered with a gene from a Brazil nut, causing reactions in consumers who had nut allergies. Also, GMO foods could potentially be linked with cancer. The idea of stronger, cheaper crops is highly appealing, but is it worth the risk?

5. The author of Passage 2 would likely criticize the author of Passage 1 for

A. Prioritizing cost of growing crops over health concerns
B. Being concerned over the carbon footprint of farming
C. Worrying about allergic reactions while people are starving due to failed crops
D. Using unproven science to alter the world's food supply

Use these two passages to answer the question that follows:

Passage 1

Although reading is undoubtedly one of the best ways to improve a child's mind, not all books are created equal. It is vital to choose high-quality books that are well-written and have worthwhile content. In today's world, where anyone can independently publish, the market is awash with truly terrible books that are lacking in plot, writing quality, and everything else a decent book should contain. Good literature not only engages the reader but calls him or her to a high standard, inspiring him or her to attempt great things. Much of today's insipid "literature" does nothing for the reader except keep him or her mildly entertained for a matter of hours.

Passage 2

Reading—of any kind—is one of the best things a child can do. It not only teaches reading skills but develops the imagination, builds a long attention span, and gives the child valuable perspective as he or she looks at the world through someone else's eyes. Different children have different needs and learning styles, so it is impossible to define what a "good" book is for everyone. One child may thrive on biographies, while another may benefit most from graphic novels that help him or her to stay focused and develop a lifelong love of reading. No matter the level or type of book, reading has been shown to have valuable benefits for young minds, so it is important to find books that will engage each individual child.

6. The author of Passage 1 would probably agree with the author of Passage 2 that

A. Many books are very poorly written.
B. It is important to choose books that interest the reader.
C. The type of book is much less important than the fact that the child is reading.
D. Biographies are better than graphic novels.

7. Consider the following passage:

> A bird's feathers are extremely important. Birds in the wild preen (clean and smooth) their feathers on a regular basis. This is also true of most captive birds, but not for all of them—some do not preen their feathers at all. This problem is most common in birds that are taken from their mothers at a very young age and presumably did not learn how to preen properly. A more common problem among captive birds is excessive preening. Some birds may pull out large numbers of their feathers or bite them down to the skin. (Wild birds never exhibit this kind of behavior.) There are several suggestions to solve the problem of excessive preening. Bathing birds may help, and placing them in an area that has more activity to prevent boredom could be beneficial. However, these measures are often not sufficient to solve the problem.

What is the main purpose of this passage?

A. To give an overview of abnormal preening in birds
B. To compare captive birds to wild birds
C. To discuss why preening is important
D. To explain how excessive preening problems can be solved

8. Consider the following passage:

Hibernation in animals is a fascinating phenomenon, one that biologists do not yet understand fully. However, it is quite easy to understand why animals hibernate during the cold winter months. Food is scarce during this time. Herbivorous animals will find the winters extremely tough, because vegetation dies when winter arrives. Hibernation is essentially a way of dealing with this food shortage. Animals like birds rely on seeds and small insects for sustenance. Obviously, these will also be quite scarce in the winter when the ground becomes covered and frozen. Many birds address their upcoming food shortage in a different way: they migrate to warmer areas where their sources of food will be plentiful.

What is the main reason that animals hibernate?

A. To travel to a warmer area where food will be more plentiful
B. To cut down on their food consumption during the winter months
C. To avoid the harsh weather that occurs during the winter months
D. To avoid food shortages that occur during the winter months

9. Consider the following passage:

Caves are known for several things: darkness, bats, and stalactites. These stalactites are the result of decades or even centuries of slow formation. They are made of a wide range of substances: various minerals, mud, sand, and even rat urine. As limestone rock is eroded by water, the calcium carbonate and other substances are deposited, dripping slowly enough that they solidify. Stalagmites, on the other hand, are the corresponding growths on the floors of caves, slowly rising as minerals drip off of the ceilings. A cave's pH conditions must be precise for stalactites and stalagmites to form.

As used in the final sentence, "precise" most nearly means

A. Clearly stated
B. A particular measurement
C. Perfectly on time
D. Rigorously planned

10. Consider the following passage:

Horror films are a relatively new concept in entertainment, as film itself has only been in existence a little over a century. But terrifying an audience—at its own volition—is a long-standing tradition. Whether this means ghost stories around campfires or entire books written to spook readers, it points to human nature's fascination with fear. The Gothic novel rose to popularity in the mid-to-late eighteenth century, though it was predated by the "Graveyard Poets," a group of English poets who popularized the Gothic symbols of coffins, skulls, and cemeteries. It is thought that political unrest in England led to the birth of the Gothic novel, as readers could identify with feelings of fear and also find a sense of relief that the book-induced fear was fictional.

What can be inferred from this passage?

A. Book genres are usually sparked by political events or historical happenings.
B. Horror movies were among the first films to be made.
C. The Graveyard Poets wrote during or before the mid-1700s.
D. The Gothic novel was the first example of horror stories being written in novel form.

11. Consider the following passage:

At one time, the use of leeches to treat medical problems was quite common. If a person suffered from a snake bite or a bee sting, leeches were believed to be capable of removing the poison from the body if they were placed on top of the wound. They have also been used for bloodletting and to stop hemorrhages, although neither of these leech treatments would be considered acceptable by present-day physicians. Today, leeches are still used on a limited basis. Most often, leeches are used to drain blood from clogged veins. This results in little pain for the patient and also ensures the patient's blood will not clot while it is being drained.

What is the main purpose of this passage?

A. To discuss the benefits of using leeches to treat blocked veins
B. To give an overview of how leeches have been used throughout history
C. To compare which uses of leeches are effective and which are not
D. To explain how leeches can be used to remove poison from the body

12. Consider the following passage:

When online file-sharing programs emerged, the music industry changed forever. Perhaps the first widely used file-sharing program for music was Napster. It allowed users to sign up to use the service at no charge. Then they could download music files from other users all over the world by simply typing in what song or album they wanted. Obviously, this was bad news for music artists and record labels because they weren't making any profits from downloaded music. Eventually, Napster was shut down. While it later reinvented itself as a paid service, other free music-sharing sites cropped up almost immediately. Even though several sites and individual users have been sued or charged with crimes, there are still countless individuals who log onto these sites to obtain free music.

What is the main problem associated with file-sharing sites?

A. It is hard to locate users to criminally charge them.
B. There are too many of them currently in existence.
C. They prevent artists and labels from earning money.
D. They allow users to sign up for their services free of charge.

13. Consider the following passage:

The so-called anti-aging industry is worth a staggering amount of money in North America. Women are sold all sorts of creams and ointments, and are promised that these will make them look younger over time. Unfortunately, these claims are entirely false. Lotions cannot penetrate the inner layers of the skin, which is where wrinkles typically form. Therefore, no over-the-counter creams are effective at erasing lines or wrinkles.

Which of the following is true of the anti-aging industry?

A. It targets its products at men and women equally.
B. It sells products that are highly effective.
C. It is still a relatively small industry.
D. It sells goods that do not do what they promise.

14. Consider the following passage:

On April 30, 1803, the United States bought the Louisiana Territory from the French. Astounded and excited by the offer of a sale and all that it would mean, politicians needed less than a month to hear the offer and determine to buy the territory for $15 million. Right away the United States had more than twice the amount of land it had before, giving the country a better chance to become powerful. Leaders had to move military and governmental power into this region, but even as they did this, they had little knowledge about the area. They did not even really know where the land boundaries were, nor did they have any idea what number of people lived there. They needed to explore.

As used in the second sentence, "determine" most nearly means

A. Purposeful
B. Resolute
C. Debate
D. Decide

15. Consider the following passage:

There is a clear formula that many students are taught when it comes to writing essays. The first part of the writing is the introduction, which outlines what will be discussed in the work. It also includes the thesis statement. Next come the supporting paragraphs. Each paragraph contains a topic sentence, supporting evidence, and then a closing sentence that restates the point of the paragraph. Finally, the conclusion sums up the purpose of the paper and emphasizes that the thesis statement was proven.

What immediately follows a topic sentence?

A. A thesis statement is included.
B. Supporting evidence is presented.
C. The conclusion is stated.
D. The author outlines what will be discussed.

For questions 16–19, read the following early draft of an essay and then choose the best answer to the question or the best completion of the statement.

(1) For almost 30 years, the Berlin Wall divided Berlin in two. (2) On November 9, 1989, citizens from both sides of the city joined together to break down the wall and reunite the city. (3) Today, most of the wall has fallen, but a line of bricks snakes across the city, marking its old path.

(4) Although bombing during World War II destroyed most of Berlin's buildings, it has been rebuilt as a cultural center. (5) It has art, history, and science museums, as well as famous historical monuments.

(6) The majestic Brandenburg Gate was built in 1791 as a symbol of peace. (7) For many years, it was part of the Berlin Wall and reminded people of the division between East and West. (8) Today, the Brandenburg Gate symbolizes reunification and freedom. (9) Near the Brandenburg Gate is the Reichstag, the German parliament building. (10) It was built in 1894 and was at the center of many important events in German politics. (11) Today, visitors can take an elevator up to the sparkling glass dome at the top of the Reichstag for a view of the city.

(12) On June 26, 1963, President John F. Kennedy visited West Berlin. (13) His visit took place only a few years after the Berlin Wall was built, and tensions between the United States and communist

East Germany were running high. (14) He gave an inspiring speech about freedom and democracy to the people of democratic West Berlin that ended with words of unity. (15) He said, "Ich bin ein Berliner," meaning "I am a citizen of Berlin"; however, these words could also be interpreted as "I am a doughnut." (16) Though the audience knew what he meant, to this day, people laugh at the idea of Kennedy calling himself a doughnut. (17) The Germans in the audience appreciated President Kennedy's support, and cheered his message of freedom enthusiastically.

16. What could be deleted from sentence 2 without changing the meaning?

A. 1989
B. from both sides of the city
C. together
D. break down

17. In sentence 4, "it" could be replaced with which of the following to be more clear?

A. the city
B. the buildings
C. bombing
D. World War II

18. Which sentences could be removed from the passage because they provide unnecessary information?

A. Sentences 4–5
B. Sentences 6–8
C. Sentences 15–16
D. All of these sentences are necessary.

19. What is the most effective way to combine sentences 9 and 10?

A. Near the Brandenburg Gate is the Reichstag, the German parliament building, it was built in 1894 and was at the center of many important events in German politics.
B. Near the Brandenburg Gate is the Reichstag, the German parliament building; but it was built in 1894 and was at the center of many important events in German politics.
C. Near the Brandenburg Gate is the Reichstag, the German parliament building, that was built in 1894 and was at the center of many important events in German politics.
D. Near the Brandenburg Gate is the Reichstag, the German parliament building, which was built in 1894 and was at the center of many important events in German politics.

For questions 20–30, select the best version of the underlined part of the sentence. If you think the original sentence is best, choose the first answer.

20. Because <u>they have had</u> several inches of snow, the city looks clean and beautiful.

A. they have had
B. they had
C. it has had
D. it have had

21. *The Silver Mist* being the third book in the series, answers all the questions introduced in the first two books.

A. *Mist* being the
B. *Mist*, which is the
C. *Mist*, having been the
D. *Mist* the

22. After studying frantically for hours, the test was easier than Juan had anticipated.

A. the test was easier than Juan had anticipated
B. Juan had anticipated an easier test
C. the test, more so than Juan had anticipated, was easier
D. Juan found that the test was easier than he had anticipated

23. The Sugar Act was implemented in 1764 by England, it required individuals residing in the North American colonies to pay a tax on sugar as well as dyes and other goods.

A. The Sugar Act was implemented in 1764 by England, it required
B. Implemented in 1764 by England, the Sugar Act required
C. The Sugar Act, implemented in 1764 by England, it required
D. In 1764, implemented by England, the Sugar Act requires

24. Beth leaned forward, and stretched to reach a book on the shelf, wishing she were a few inches taller.

A. forward, and stretched
B. forward, and then stretching
C. forward, stretching
D. forward, and stretching

25. The thin cat crept forward slowly; it was ready to dash to safety at any sudden movement.

A. slowly; it was ready
B. slowly, it was ready
C. slowly; ready
D. slowly, and being ready

26. A key factor taken into account during city planning is where major services and amenities will be located.

A. A key factor taken into account during city planning is
B. Key factors taken into account during city planning is
C. A key factor taking into account during city planning is
D. Key factors, taken into accounting during city planning are

27. Jupiter with its numerous moons, and Great Red Spot, has been studied extensively by astronomers.

A. Jupiter with its numerous moons, and Great Red Spot,
B. Jupiter with, its numerous moons and Great Red Spot,
C. Jupiter, with its numerous moons and Great Red Spot,
D. Jupiter with, its numerous moons, and Great Red Spot,

28. Many gardeners are now making their own backyard compost, an activity that not only is cost-effective but also helps to cut down on landfill waste.

A. not only is cost-effective but also helps to cut down on landfill waste
B. not only is more cost-effective but also cuts down on landfill's waste
C. not only is cost-effective but also, helps to cut down on landfill waste
D. not only is done cost-effectively but is also cutting down on landfills wastes

29. The growth of the security industry can be large attributable to the fact that people are less trusting of others than they once were.

A. The growth of the security industry can be large attributable
B. The growing of the securities industry can be largely attributable
C. The growth on the security industry can be large attributed
D. The growth of the security industry can be largely attributed

30. Claude Monet was a famous painter who's well-known painting includes *San Giorgio Maggiore at Dusk* and *The Water Lily Pond*.

A. who's well-known painting includes
B. whose well-known painting including
C. whose well-known paintings include
D. who well-known paintings include

Essay

Preemptive war has long been discussed as an option to prevent certain countries that are viewed as dangerous or unstable from acquiring nuclear weapons. Please write a multiple-paragraph persuasive essay (approximately 350–500 words) discussing whether you support or oppose the idea of a preemptive war for this purpose.

Answers and Explanations for Test #2

Math

1. A: In this probability problem, there are three independent events (each digit of the code), each with ten possible outcomes (the numerals 0–9). Since the events are independent, the total number of possible outcomes equals the product of the possible outcomes for each of the three events. That is:

$$P = P_1 \times P_2 \times P_3 = 10 \times 10 \times 10 = 1{,}000$$

This result makes sense when we consider trying every possible code in sequence, beginning with the combinations 0-0-0, 0-0-1, 0-0-2, etc. In ascending order, the last three-digit combination would be 9-9-9. Although it may seem that there would be 999 possible combinations, there are in fact 1,000 when we include the initial combination, 0-0-0.

2. A: Setting the cost of shipping equal to the amount received gives us the equation $3{,}000 + 100x = 400x$. Subtract $100x$ from both sides to get $3{,}000 = 300x$, then divide both sides by 300 to see that $x = 10$.

3. D: Multiply both sides of the first equation by s to get $3 = 7s$. Then divide both sides by 7 to find that $s = \frac{3}{7}$. Multiply both sides of the second equation by t to get $4 = 12t$. Then divide both sides by 12 to find that $t = \frac{4}{12}$, which reduces to $\frac{1}{3}$. To find the difference, we must convert to a common denominator. In this case, the common denominator is 21. Multiplying by appropriate fractional equivalents of 1, we find that $\frac{3}{7}\left(\frac{3}{3}\right) = \frac{9}{21}$ and $\frac{1}{3}\left(\frac{7}{7}\right) = \frac{7}{21}$. Therefore, $s - t = \frac{9}{21} - \frac{7}{21} = \frac{2}{21}$.

4. B: The average of 7 and x is $7 + x$ divided by 2. The average of 9, 4, and x is $9 + 4 + x$ divided by 3. Thus, $\frac{7+x}{2} = \frac{13+x}{3}$. Cross-multiply: $3(7 + x) = 2(13 + x)$. This gives us $21 + 3x = 26 + 2x$. Solving for x yields $x = 26 - 21 = 5$.

5. D: There are seven integers whose absolute value is less than 4: –3, –2, –1, 0, 1, 2, 3.

6. D: To solve $3(2x - 10) = x$, first expand the left side by multiplying through by 3: $6x - 30 = x$. Therefore, $5x = 30$, and $x = 6$.

7. C: This question requires us to multiply three algebraic expressions. When multiplying more than two expressions, multiply any two expressions (using the FOIL method), and then multiply the result by the remaining expression. Start by multiplying the first two:

$$\begin{aligned}(y+1)(y+2) &= (y \times y) + (y \times 2) + (1 \times y) + (1 \times 2)\\ &= y^2 + 2y + y + 2\\ &= y^2 + 3y + 2\end{aligned}$$

Then multiply the result by the third expression:

$$(y^2 + 3y + 2)(y + 3) = (y^2 + 3y + 2)(y) + (y^2 + 3y + 2)(3)$$
$$= (y^3 + 3y^2 + 2y) + (3y^2 + 9y + 6)$$
$$= y^3 + 3y^2 + 3y^2 + 9y + 2y + 6$$
$$= y^3 + 6y^2 + 11y + 6$$

8. D: Note that the first two terms and the last two terms of $x^3 - 3x^2 - 4x + 12$ are each divisible by $x - 3$. Thus:

$$x^3 - 3x^2 - 4x + 12 = x^2(x - 3) - 4(x - 3) = (x^2 - 4)(x - 3)$$

The term $x^2 - 4$ is a difference of squares, and since $x^2 - a^2 = (x + a)(x - a)$, we know $x^2 - 4 = (x + 2)(x - 2)$. The full factorization of $x^3 - 3x^2 - 4x + 12$ is therefore $(x + 2)(x - 2)(x - 3)$. Thus, all the answer choices except $x + 3$ are factors.

Alternatively, instead of factoring the polynomial, we could have divided the polynomial $x^3 - 3x^2 - 4x + 12$ by the expression contained in each answer choice. Of the expressions listed, only $x + 3$ yields a nonzero remainder when divided into $x^3 - 3x^2 - 4x + 12$, so it is not a factor.

9. D: When variables are multiplied, their exponents are summed. First, move any variables out of the denominator by reversing the sign on their exponents:

$$\frac{x^6}{y^4} \times x^2y^3 = x^6y^{-4} \times x^2y^3$$

Next, group sets of like variables to make it easier to combine them accurately:

$$= (x^6x^2)(y^{-4}y^3)$$

Finally, sum the exponents and simplify:

$$= x^{6+2}y^{-4+3}$$
$$= x^8y^{-1}$$
$$= \frac{x^8}{y}$$

10. C: A method commonly taught to multiply binomials is the "FOIL" method, an acronym for *first, outer, inner, last*: multiply the first terms of each factor, then the outer terms, and so forth. Applied to $(x + 2)(x - 3)$, this yields:

$$(x)(x) + (x)(-3) + (2)(x) + (2)(-3) = x^2 - 3x + 2x - 6 = x^2 - x - 6$$

11. B: We can plug the value of r into the volume equation:

$$V = \frac{4}{3}\pi\left(\frac{3}{2}x\right)^3 = \frac{4}{3}\pi\left(\frac{3}{2}\right)^3 x^3 = \frac{4}{3}\pi\frac{27}{8}x^3 = \frac{9}{2}\pi x^3$$

12. C: Consecutive even integers increase by 2. So if the first integer is $x - 2$, the second is $x - 2 + 2 = x$, and the third is $x - 2 + 2 + 2 = x + 2$. Adding the three integers together yields: $x - 2 + x + x + 2 = 3x$.

13. C: We first calculate the square footage (or area) of the shower floor by multiplying the length by the width:

$$3 \times 5.5 = 16.5\ ft^2$$

We can then multiply the number of square feet by the cost per square foot to find the total cost:

$$16.5 \times 5.75 = 94.875$$

We round this to the nearest dollar to find that Andi's total cost is $95.

14. C: A straight line is 180°. Subtract to solve: 180° – 45° = 135°.

15. A: The sum of the measures of the three angles of any triangle is 180. The equation of the angles of this triangle can be written as $2x + 6x + 10x = 180$, or $18x = 180$. Therefore, $x = 10$. We multiply 2 by 10 to find that the measure of the smallest angle is 20°.

16. B: Using the formula for the perimeter of a rectangle, we know that $P = 2l + 2w$. Substituting the value given, we get $76 = 2l + 2w$ or $38 = l + w$. We can now solve for l: $38 - w = l$.

Using the formula for the area of a rectangle, we know that $A = l \times w$. Substituting the value given, we get $336 = l \times w$.

If we substitute the $38 - w$ we found in the first step for l, we get $(38 - w)w = 336$. Thus:

$$38w - w^2 = 336$$

$$0 = w^2 - 38w + 336$$

$$0 = (w - 14)(w - 24)$$

$$w = 14\ or\ 24$$

The shorter of these two possibilities is 14.

17. C: Group B is negatively skewed since there are more high scores. With more high scores, the mean for Group B will be higher.

18. A: The correlation is negative with a slope of approximately −3 and a y-intercept of approximately 5. Choices B and C can be eliminated, since a y-intercept of 10.3 is too high and a y-intercept of −5.3 is too low. Choice D may also be eliminated since the slope of −8.2 is too steep for the slope shown on the graph.

19. C: The probability of drawing a jack is $\frac{4}{52} = \frac{1}{13}$ because there are 4 jacks and a total of 52 cards. Likewise, the probability of drawing an ace is $\frac{4}{52}$. We can find the probability of independent events A and B using the formula $P(A \text{ and } B) = P(A) \times P(B)$. Thus, the probability she draws a jack, replaces it, and then draws an ace card may be represented as $P(A \text{ and } B) = \frac{1}{13} \times \frac{1}{13}$, which simplifies to $P(A \text{ and } B) = \frac{1}{169}$.

20. D: The expected value is equal to the sum of the products of each ball value and its probability. Thus, the expected value is $\left(1 \times \frac{1}{5}\right) + \left(2 \times \frac{1}{5}\right) + \left(3 \times \frac{1}{5}\right) + \left(4 \times \frac{1}{5}\right) + \left(5 \times \frac{1}{5}\right)$, which equals $\frac{15}{5} = 3$.

English Language Arts and Reading

1. A: *Wonderful*, as it is often used today, can mean "excellent" or "admirable" and carry a positive feeling (answer choices B and D). However, it can also mean "causing wonder," much like *marvelous* or *astonishing*. This meaning best fits the context here, which is slightly negative. Answer choice C is too extreme for the context.

2. C: To say that one is a pillar of salt is like saying that one has become "a statue." The narrator was so stunned by Bartleby's words that he was frozen in place momentarily. The other answer choices are understandable reactions, but they do not suggest the level of shock conveyed by "pillar of salt."

3. D: Sentence 23 states that Bartleby "revolved" everything the narrator said. In other words, he carefully considered the words. The literal meaning of "turned" (answer choice A) does not apply here. Answer choice B is incorrect because although Bartleby did not go along with the narrator's requests, he did not "spurn" them but rather seemed to agree with them. While Bartleby did seem to "believe" the narrator's statements (answer choice C), that is not the meaning here.

4. C: The author makes an effort to show that Bartleby is slow and quiet. He speaks "mildly," "gently," and "in a flute-like tone." In contrast, the narrator is hurried and impatient and admits that he is prone to flying "into a dreadful passion." These actions of the narrator serve as a foil to Bartleby, emphasizing Bartleby's nature by the contrast. While the narrator works busily, there is no real description of his work ethic, nor does the author seem to indicate that Bartleby was lacking in character, so answer choice A is incorrect. The narrator is confused at Bartleby's refusal to follow an order, but this does not indicate that Bartleby is more intelligent than he is, so answer choice B is incorrect. The narrator speaks much more than Bartleby does in this passage, but gives plenty of opportunity for Bartleby to answer, so this does not indicate that Bartleby was quiet because the narrator talked so much (answer choice D).

5. A: One of the arguments used in Passage 1 is the lowered cost of GMO farming. One objection that could potentially be raised by the author of Passage 2 is that these lowered costs are not worth the health risks. Passage 1 does discuss carbon footprint (answer choice B), but it does not make sense that the author of Passage 2 would object to this. Answer choice C might be a criticism that the author of Passage 1 would apply to Passage 2, not vice versa. Neither passage makes any mention of unproven science, so answer choice D is incorrect.

6. B: Passage 2 emphasizes that each reader has individual needs and that it is therefore important to find what will engage each individual rather than using the same reading list for everyone. Passage 1 agrees that "good literature ... engages the reader," although this author does not think all books have equal value. Answer choice A is an idea from Passage 1 that is not reflected in Passage 2. Answer choice C is an idea from Passage 2 that is disagreed with in Passage 1. Passage 2 mentions both biographies and graphic novels (answer choice D) but intentionally does not imply that one is better than the other.

7. A: Answer choice B is not correct, because wild birds are not discussed at length. Answer choice C is not really discussed, and D is touched upon only briefly. The passage focuses on lack of preening and excessive preening, which are both examples of abnormal preening behavior. The main purpose of the passage is to discuss abnormal preening in birds.

8. D: The passage states that "Herbivorous animals will find the winters extremely tough, because vegetation dies when winter arrives. Hibernation is essentially a way of dealing with this food shortage." Therefore, D is the correct answer. Answer choice A refers to the purpose of migration, not hibernation. Reducing food consumption (B) and avoiding harsh weather (C) are not mentioned.

9. B: The term "pH conditions" refers to the level of acid or base in the liquids in the cave. This can be described as a particular measurement. While the other answer choices may be possible meanings of *precise*, they do not fit in this context.

10. C: The passage states that the Gothic novel became popular in the mid-to-late eighteenth century, or the mid-to-late 1700s, and that the Graveyard Poets wrote before this. So we can infer that they wrote during or before the mid-1700s. While this genre was sparked by political events, it is not logical to assume that all genres came about in this way, so answer choice A is incorrect. There is no indication that horror movies were among the first films made, so answer choice B is incorrect. Likewise, there is no indication that horror stories were never put in novel form before the Gothic novel.

11. B: The ideas in answer choices A, C, and D are all mentioned in the passage, but they are part of the overall purpose, which is to give an overview of how leeches have been used throughout history.

12. C: The passage states that "Obviously, this was bad news for music artists and record labels because they weren't making any profits from downloaded music." Therefore, answer choice C is the correct choice. None of the other choices are identified as problems associated with file-sharing sites.

13. D: The passage states, "Women are sold all sorts of creams and ointments and are promised that these will make them look younger over time. Unfortunately, these claims are entirely false. Lotions cannot penetrate the inner layers of the skin, which is where wrinkles typically form." Therefore, these goods do not deliver what they promise. Targeting of men or women (A) is not mentioned. Answer choices B and C contradict the passage.

14. D: *Determine* in this context means "to decide or make up one's mind." Answer choices A and B are synonyms for *determined*, but are adjectives, not verbs, so they do not fit this context. While there was doubtless debate about making this decision, *debate* does not indicate a final decision as *determine* does, so answer choice C is incorrect.

15. B: The topic sentence is placed at the beginning of each supporting paragraph. Supporting evidence is presented after the topic sentence in each supporting paragraph. The passage states, "Next come the supporting paragraphs. Each paragraph contains a topic sentence, supporting evidence, and then a closing sentence that restates the point of the paragraph."

16. C: The word *together* reinforces the word *joined* but is not required, so *joined together* is slightly redundant. Choice A is incorrect because the year is required to help the reader know when these events are taking place. Choice B is incorrect because "from both sides of the city" tells the reader that citizens from both East Berlin and West Berlin participated. Choice D is incorrect because *break down* makes it clear that the wall was torn down.

17. A: The generic *it* is vague. From context, we can see that *it* refers to the city of Berlin that has been rebuilt. It does not make sense for "bombing" or "World War II" to be rebuilt, so answer choices C and D are incorrect. "The buildings" does not work grammatically since "has been" is singular, so answer choice B is incorrect.

18. C: Sentences 15 and 16 add an amusing anecdote about a historical event, but this information is not necessary in a history of Berlin, and it may even distract from the main purpose.

19. D: Two sentences can be combined in several ways. Answer choice A is a comma splice because it uses only a comma to combine the two clauses. Answer choice B uses a semicolon and a conjunction. Because the conjunction makes the second sentence into a dependent clause, the semicolon no longer works. Answer choice C incorrectly uses a comma with "that." The word *that* is used with essential clauses and cannot be introduced with a comma. Answer choice D adds "which" to the second sentence, turning it into a nonessential clause that is correctly introduced with a comma.

20. C: The subject of the sentence is "the city," which is singular. So the fitting pronoun is *it*, not *they*. Answer choice D is incorrect because "have had" agrees with a plural subject.

21. B: As written, the sentence is a fragment because "being" is not a finite verb, and the verb "answers" does not have a subject. Since the modifying phrase is a nonessential clause, it is appropriate to introduce it with a comma and "which." Answer choice C is incorrect because it implies that being the third book in the series is a past action rather than a present fact. Answer choice D would be correct if it included a comma before "the."

22. D: As written, the sentence has a dangling participle. The participial phrase "After studying frantically for hours" modifies the subject of the main clause. Because the subject is "test," it sounds as if the test studied frantically. Answer choice C has the same problem. Answer choice B puts "Juan" in the proper place as the subject, but changes the meaning. It is illogical that Juan would study frantically for hours if he had already been anticipating an easy test. Only answer choice D uses "Juan" as the subject and keeps the meaning unchanged.

23. B: The original sentence is a comma splice, connecting two independent clauses with a comma. Answer choice C would be correct if the word "it" were left out. Answer choice D uses awkward comma placement, and gives the impression that the Sugar Act is still in effect with "requires."

24. C: The comma in the original sentence is incorrect because a comma combined with a conjunction connects two independent clauses, not two verbs (in this case "leaned" and "stretched") that share a subject ("Beth"). Answer choices B and D are incorrect because they turn the "stretched" into a participial adverb, but they keep the conjunction "and." Answer choice C correctly uses "stretching" as a participial adverb and removes "and."

25. A: Each clause of this sentence is an independent clause—a stand-alone sentence. A semicolon is one correct way to join two independent clauses. Using a comma (answer choice B) creates a comma splice. Answer choice C removes "it was," which turns the second clause into a predicate, which cannot stand alone, so a semicolon is no longer appropriate. Answer choice D would be acceptable if "and being" were removed.

26. A: Answer choice B is incorrect because the plural "key factors" and the singular "is" do not agree. The "taking" in choice C makes it incorrect. Choice D has a misplaced comma. Choice A makes sense as the singular "A key factor" and "is" agree with each other.

27. C: Choice C is the only choice that has correctly placed commas. The phrase "with its numerous moons and Great Red Spot" is one piece of additional information modifying "Jupiter," and this is reflected in answer choice C.

28. A: Answer choice B is incorrect because of the singular possessive "landfill's" without an article as well as the comparative phrase "more cost-effective" without anything with which to compare it. Choice C has an unnecessary comma. Answer choice D is too wordy, and "landfills wastes" is both ungrammatical and awkward. Answer choice A is succinct, the comma is in the correct place, and it expresses the information is a clear way that is not awkward.

29. D: Answer choices A and C are incorrect because "large" is in front of "attributable" and "attributed." Both of these phrases are grammatically incorrect as *large* is an adjective and not an adverb, which is what we need here. Choice B uses "the growing of the securities industry," which is quite awkward and could refer to an entirely different industry. Choice D is best because it uses "the growth of the security industry" as well as the adverb "largely" before "attributed," which is grammatically correct.

30. C: The possessive form of the relative pronoun *who* is *whose*, so we can eliminate A and D. Two paintings are identified, so the plural of *painting* must be used. We can therefore eliminate choice B as well. Choice C uses the possessive form of *who* and the plural of *painting* in "whose well-known paintings," making it the correct choice.

TSI Practice Test #3

Math

1. If $2x + 3y = 13$ and $4x - y = 5$, then what is the value of $3x + 2y$?

A. 3
B. 6
C. 12
D. 24

2. If a movie reached the 90-minute mark 12 minutes ago, what minute mark had it reached m minutes ago?

A. $m - 102$
B. $m - 78$
C. $102 - m$
D. $78 - m$

3. If $x > 2,500$, then the value of $\frac{x}{1-2x}$ is closest to

A. $-\frac{50}{99}$
B. $-\frac{1}{2}$
C. $\frac{50}{99}$
D. $\frac{1}{2}$

4. If $520 \div x = 40n$, then which of the following is equal to nx?

A. 13
B. 26
C. 40
D. $13x$

5. If $a - 16 = 8b + 6$, what does $a + 3$ equal?

A. $b + 3$
B. $8b + 19$
C. $8b + 22$
D. $8b + 25$

6. Janice weighs x pounds. Elaina weighs 23 pounds more than Janice. June weighs 14 pounds more than Janice. In terms of x, what is the combined weight of the three girls minus 25 pounds?

A. $3x + 37$
B. $3x + 12$
C. $x + 12$
D. $3x - 25$

7. Max reads three books averaging 360 pages. Lucy reads five books averaging 200 pages. What is the average length of all the books that Max and Lucy read?

A. 212
B. 232
C. 260
D. 295

8. If $x > 2$, then what is the value of $\left(\frac{x^2-5x+6}{x+1}\right) \times \left(\frac{x+1}{x-2}\right)$?

A. $x + 1$
B. $x - 3$
C. $\frac{x^2+2x+1}{x-2}$
D. $\frac{x^2-2x-3}{x+1}$

9. What is $\frac{x^3+2x}{x+3}$ when $x = -1$?

A. $-\frac{3}{2}$
B. $-\frac{2}{3}$
C. $\frac{1}{2}$
D. $\frac{3}{4}$

10. $(x + 6)(x - 6) =$

A. $x^2 - 12x - 36$
B. $x^2 + 12x - 36$
C. $x^2 + 12x + 36$
D. $x^2 - 36$

11. Which of the following equations has a slope of 3 and a y-intercept of –2?

A. $-3x + y + 2 = 0$
B. $3x - y + 2 = 0$
C. $-2x + y - 3 = 0$
D. $2x + y + 3 = 0$

12. If an item with an original price of $25.98 is marked down by 25%, and a coupon for 20% off is additionally applied, what is the final price?

A. $19.49
B. $17.77
C. $15.59
D. $13.28

13. If $x + 2y = 3$ and $-x - 3y = 4$, then what is the value of x?

A. 1
B. 5
C. 7
D. 17

Use the figure below to answer question 14.

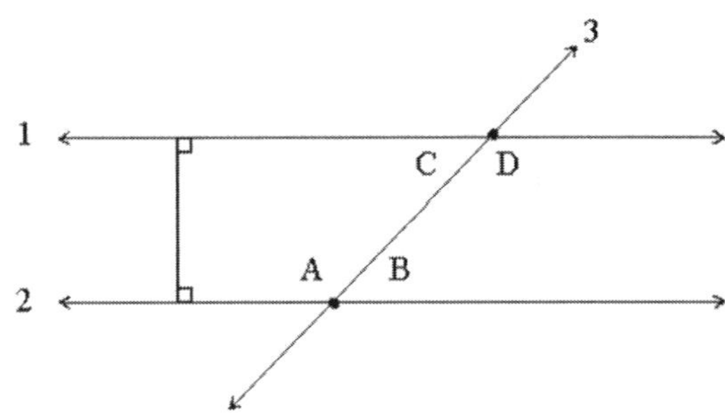

14. In the figure, which of the following is a pair of alternate interior angles?

A. Angle A and angle B
B. Angle A and angle C
C. Angle B and angle D
D. Angle A and angle D

15. In the following figure, if $\frac{b}{a+b+c} = \frac{3}{5}$, then what is the value of b?

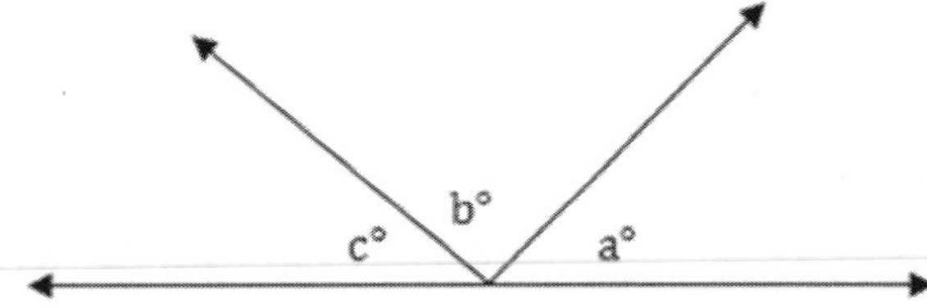

A. 60
B. 72
C. 108
D. 120

16. If the radius of circle O is one-quarter the diameter of circle P, what is the ratio of the circumference of circle O to the circumference of circle P?

A. $\frac{1}{4}$
B. $\frac{1}{2}$
C. 2
D. 4

17. Suppose two variables show a correlation of 0.9. Which of the following statements BEST describes the relationship?

A. The variables show a strong correlation.
B. The variables show some correlation, but it is neither weak nor strong.
C. The variables show a weak correlation.
D. The variables show a perfect correlation.

18. Edward draws a card from a regular deck*, does not replace it, and then draws another card. What is the probability that he draws a heart and then a spade?

*A regular deck of playing cards contains 52 unique cards, each belonging to a suit (*spades*, *hearts*, *diamonds*, or *clubs*) and having a number or letter (numbers 2-10, followed by J (*jack*), Q (*queen*), K (*king*), and A (*ace*)). There are 13 cards of each suit and 4 cards of each number or letter.

A. $\frac{1}{16}$
B. $\frac{1}{2}$
C. $\frac{1}{17}$
D. $\frac{13}{204}$

19. Suppose Ashley will receive a $6,000 scholarship if she chooses University A, a $4,500 scholarship if she chooses University B, and a $5,500 scholarship if she chooses University C. She has an equal probability of attending each of the universities. Which of the following BEST represents the expected value for the scholarship amount she will receive?

A. $4,833
B. $5,155
C. $5,333
D. $5,525

20. Nia spends $5 on a raffle ticket. If she is the winner, she will receive $500. A total of 250 raffle tickets were sold. What is the expected value of her raffle ticket?

A. –$2
B. –$3
C. –$5
D. –$7

English Language Arts and Reading

For questions 1–15, read each passage and then choose the best answer to the accompanying questions. Answer the questions on the basis of what is stated or implied in the passage(s).

The following passage is adapted from Charles Dickens, A Tale of Two Cities, *originally published in 1859.*

(1) "You have a visitor, you see," said Monsieur Defarge.

(2) "What did you say?"

(3) "Here is a visitor."

(4) The shoemaker looked up as before, but without removing a hand from his work.

(5) "Come!" said Defarge. (6) "Here is monsieur, who knows a well-made shoe when he sees one. (7) Show him that shoe you are working at. (8) Take it, monsieur."

(9) Mr. Lorry took it in his hand.

(10) "Tell monsieur what kind of shoe it is, and the maker's name."

(11) There was a longer pause than usual, before the shoemaker replied: "I forget what it was you asked me. (12) What did you say?"

(13) "I said, couldn't you describe the kind of shoe, for monsieur's information?"

(14) "It is a lady's shoe. (15) It is a young lady's walking-shoe. (16) It is in the present mode. (17) I never saw the mode. (18) I have had a pattern in my hand."

(19) He glanced at the shoe with some little passing touch of pride.

(20) "And the maker's name?" said Defarge.

(21) Now that he had no work to hold, he laid the knuckles of the right hand in the hollow of the left, and then the knuckles of the left hand in the hollow of the right, and then passed a hand across his bearded chin, and so on in regular changes, without a moment's intermission. (22) The task of recalling him from the vagrancy into which he always sank when he had spoken, was like recalling some very weak person from a swoon, or endeavouring, in the hope of some disclosure, to stay the spirit of a fast-dying man.

(23) "Did you ask me for my name?"

(24) "Assuredly I did."

(25) "One Hundred and Five, North Tower."

(26) "Is that all?"

(27) "One Hundred and Five, North Tower."

(28) With a weary sound that was not a sigh, nor a groan, he bent to work again.

1. The author implies that Defarge looks on the shoemaker with _______________.

A. admiration
B. disgust
C. sympathy
D. care

2. Which of the following is NOT a sign of the man's mental condition?

A. His inability to complete a thought
B. His identifying himself by a location instead of a name
C. The repetitive motion of his hands
D. His cheerful laughter

3. As used in sentence 16, "mode" most nearly means

A. Method of doing something
B. Something that happens more frequently than others
C. Style of fashion
D. Type of materials used

4. Why does the author say that the shoemaker returned to his task "with a weary sound that was not a sigh, nor a groan" (sentence 28)?

A. To show that his task is a particularly difficult and tiring one
B. To show that he does his work automatically and without much feeling
C. To show that he is sick of the job and does not want to continue
D. To show that he does not want Defarge or Mr. Lorry to see how tired he is

Use these two passages to answer the question that follows:

Passage 1

Most Americans are deficient in omega-3, a vital nutrient that can help in lowering inflammation, preventing depression, and supporting brain and eye function. While many foods, including eggs and various fruits, contain trace amounts of omega-3, the best source by far is oily fish such as salmon, tuna, and mackerel. Most of these fish are easily obtainable and include many health benefits along with the dose of omega-3. While some people have concern about heavy metals and pollutants that may be found in grocery store fish, the possibility of heavy metal poisoning from fish is nearly zero. Experts agree that the benefits of eating fish far outweigh the risks.

Passage 2

Omega-3 is a helpful nutrient, though not as valuable as proponents say. Claims that it can prevent cancer, stroke, and heart disease have not been substantiated. It does have benefits for the brain and eyesight, especially for growing children, but these benefits can be gotten easily and affordably from an omega-3 supplement. In other words, there is no need to risk the dangers of today's fishing industry. Due to pollution, and even more to unsanitary conditions in fish farms, most commercially available fish is not safe to consume. The benefits simply do not outweigh the risks of eating fish unless you catch it yourself from a pure mountain river.

5. Which of the following points would the authors of both passages likely agree with?

A. Omega-3 is beneficial for brain development.
B. Eating commercial fish is dangerous.
C. Pollutants are common in fish.
D. Fish have many other health benefits besides omega-3.

Use these two passages to answer the question that follows:

Passage 1

Fairy tales, fictional stories that involve magical occurrences and imaginary creatures like trolls, elves, giants, and talking animals, are found in similar forms throughout the world. This occurs when a story with an origin in a particular location spreads geographically to, over time, far-flung lands. All variations of the same story must logically come from a single source. As language, ideas, and goods travel from place to place through the movement of peoples, stories that catch human imagination travel as well through human retelling.

Passage 2

Fairy tales capture basic, fundamental human desires and fears. They represent the most essential form of fictionalized human experience: the bad characters are pure evil, the good characters are pure good, the romance of royalty (and of commoners becoming royalty) is celebrated, etc. Given the nature of the fairy tale genre, it is not surprising that many different cultures come up with similar versions of the same essential story.

6. Which of the following is not an example of something that the author of Passage 1 states might be found in a fairy tale?

A. Trolls
B. Witches
C. Talking animals
D. Giants

7. Consider the following passage:

> The importance of a comfortable workspace cannot be overstated. Developing a comfortable work environment is relatively simple for employers. Ergonomic chairs, large computer screens, personal desk space, and some level of privacy are all essential. This involves some expense, but not a great deal. Not surprisingly, employees are happier in this type of environment, but it is the employers who really benefit. Reduced sick time, higher levels of employee satisfaction, higher productivity, and more creativity have all been observed.

What is the main idea expressed in this passage?

A. A comfortable workspace is not as important as people say.
B. Developing a comfortable workspace is easy.
C. Establishing a comfortable workspace is not expensive.
D. Employers benefit greatly when they provide comfortable workspaces.

8. Consider the following passage:

Planning weddings is tough. One important part of the planning process is choosing bridesmaid dresses. Although there used to be a lot of rules when it came to picking out a color, many of them are not observed anymore. However, one that is still observed is that the bridesmaids should not wear the same color as the bride. The most popular colors for bridesmaid dresses in recent years have been white and black.

What can be concluded from this passage?

A. Picking dresses is the hardest part of planning a wedding.
B. Many brides are choosing to wear colors other than white.
C. Most bridesmaids are allowed to choose their own dresses.
D. Bridesmaids were not traditionally allowed to wear black.

9. Consider the following passage:

Those so-called green fuels may not be as environmentally friendly as once thought. For example, producing natural gas is a much more labor-intensive process than producing an equal amount of conventional gasoline. Also, producing natural gas involves burning fossil fuels. Transporting natural gas also involves burning fossil fuels.

Which of the following is a weakness of green fuels?

A. They are not as abundant as conventional fuels.
B. They require a lot more work to produce.
C. Burning them releases fossil fuels.
D. They must be transported greater distances.

10. Consider the following passage:

The media has done a lot to promote racism in North America. For example, it was found that the majority of crimes discussed on the nightly news featured African American suspects. However, when the total number of crimes committed in North America was examined, it was found that white people were also suspects 50 percent of the time.

What can be concluded from this passage?

A. There are more white criminals than African American criminals.
B. Most people believe that African Americans commit more crimes.
C. The media tends not to discuss many crimes that have white suspects.
D. The total number of crimes committed has decreased in the last several years.

11. Consider the following passage:

Many people feel that the use of stem cells in research is unethical. However, they fail to realize that such research could lead to cures for some of the world's most troubling diseases. For example, Parkinson's disease and multiple sclerosis (MS) could possibly be cured through the use of stem cells, and those with spinal cord injuries could possibly walk again. Therefore, it is entirely ethical to engage in stem cell research aimed at easing the suffering of those who have life-altering conditions.

What is the main purpose of this passage?

A. To explain the common belief that stem cell research is unethical
B. To discuss why the use of stem cells in research is ethical
C. To identify diseases that have been cured through stem cell research
D. To argue that not conducting stem cell research is unethical

12. Consider the following passage:

Many people do not know the difference between precision and accuracy. While accuracy means that something is correct, precision simply means that you are able to duplicate results and that they are consistent. For example, if a glass of liquid was 100 degrees, an accurate measurement would be one that was close to this temperature. However, if you measured the temperature five times, and came up with a measurement of exactly 50 degrees each time, your measurement would be extremely precise, but not accurate.

The term *accurate results* is most properly used to refer to results that ____________.

A. are correct
B. are consistent
C. can be duplicated
D. are measurable

13. Consider the following passage:

Cinnamon is perhaps the best known "sweet" spice, flavoring cookies, muffins, and many other sweets. It is sourced from the inner bark of certain trees. These are flowering evergreen trees that are carefully raised. The trees are grown for two years and are then cut. Immediately, before the stems can dry, the outer bark is scraped off and the inner bark is removed in long rolls that curl into tighter rolls (or "cinnamon sticks") as they dry. The trees regenerate from the roots, ready for another harvest in two more years. There are many varieties of cinnamon, grown in various countries, but each is flavored with the essential oil cinnamaldehyde.

As used in the third sentence, "raised" most nearly means

A. Cultivated
B. Lifted
C. On a higher level
D. Used for commercial purposes

14. Consider the following passage:

We all know that it is important to hydrate, but water is linked to a larger number of vital operations than many people realize. Inadequate water intake is extremely common—many people drink far less than the recommended eight glasses of water per day. A low intake can make it difficult for the body to regulate its temperature, lubricate joints, fight infection, and take nutrients to various cells. Mild dehydration can be characterized by a headache, feeling sluggish, and waking up tired. More severe dehydration may cause dizziness, dark urine, rapid heartbeat, and fainting.

Which of the following is NOT a symptom of mild dehydration?

A. Feeling sluggish
B. Tiredness upon waking
C. Rapid heartbeat
D. Headache

15. Consider the following passage:

Millions of dollars are spent yearly on perfume, scented candles, bath products, and other scented products. Why are so many willing to spend hard-earned money just for a pleasant smell? The answer is that scent is more than just pleasant; it has a strong physical and emotional effect. Certain scents like lavender may help calm someone in a stressful situation. Scent also has a very strong connection to memory, triggering an emotional reaction when someone smells the perfume her mother used to wear or a pie like her grandmother often baked. Each person's scent receptors differ, leading some people to prefer more floral perfumes while others enjoy musky scents and still others like citrus.

Scent is closely linked with ________.

A. stress
B. family
C. personality
D. memory

For questions 16–19, read the following early draft of an essay and then choose the best answer to the question or the best completion of the statement.

(1) Mrs. Conwer, the Jackson High principal, announced last week that Jackson High is considering a student dress code. (2) She is saying that some of the outfits students are wearing to school are being distracting and inappropriate. (3) For example, she says that some of the boys like to wear their pants too low and that some of the girls like to wear very short skirts. (4) I don't see anything wrong with these. (5) This is only Mrs. Conwer's opinion, and I think there are several reasons why it is important that Jackson High does not have a dress code.

(6) High school students are teenagers. (7) The teen years are a time in life when you are exploring new things and learning about yourself. (8) Many teens also like to express themselves. (9) For example, some people I know keep a blog where they write about things that are important to them. (10) Other people play in a band and can express themselves through music. (11) A lot of teens express themselves through fashion. (12) Since many teens start earning their own money, they can buy their own clothes and choose the fashions that they want. (13) If Jackson High adopts a dress code, the students won't be able to express themselves. (14) Self-expression is important and is often taught at Jackson High. (15) Ms. Riley, my dance teacher, tells me to express myself through dance. (16) Mr. Hunter, my English teacher, tells me to express myself through writing. (17) Taking away expression through fashion is hypocritical because it goes against what is taught in many classes.

(18) A dress code at Jackson High will never please everyone. (19) Who gets to decide what is appropriate and what is not? (20) What happens if the students disagree with the code? (21) In school, we learn about respecting different opinions and making compromises. (22) However, if Mrs. Conwer or just a couple of teachers choose the dress code, they will be ignoring them. (23) Jackson High should stop ignoring the lessons that we learn in our classes every day. (24) Teachers should show us, the students, how people are supposed to dress in the real world when they have jobs, explain why certain choices might be inappropriate, and then let us make our own decisions. (25) That's what we learn in all our classes, and that's how it should be for the dress code.

16. What is the most effective way to rewrite sentence 2?

A. Some of the outfits students wear to school, she is saying, are distracting and not appropriate.
B. The outfits are distracting and inappropriate, she says, that students wear to school.
C. She says some of the outfits that students wear to school are distracting and inappropriate.
D. She says that it is distracting and inappropriate that students wear outfits to school.

17. Which of the following sentences is unnecessary and could be removed from the passage?

A. Sentence 4
B. Sentence 5
C. Sentence 13
D. Sentence 19

18. What is the most effective way to combine sentences 11 and 12?

A. A lot of teens express themselves through fashion, and since many teens start earning their own money, they can buy their own clothes and choose the fashions that they want.
B. A lot of teens express themselves through fashion and since many teens start earning their own money, they can buy their own clothes and choose the fashions that they want.
C. A lot of teens express themselves through fashion, but since many teens start earning their own money, they can buy their own clothes and choose the fashions that they want.
D. A lot of teens express themselves through fashion but since many teens start earning their own money, they can buy their own clothes and choose the fashions that they want.

19. Which of the following is the best replacement for the vague "them" in sentence 22 (reproduced below)?

However, if Mrs. Conwer or just a couple of teachers choose the dress code, they will be ignoring them.

A. the teachers' wisdom
B. the students' voices
C. the dress code's details
D. the administration's authority

For questions 20–30, select the best version of the underlined part of the sentence. If you think the original sentence is best, choose the first answer.

20. If he stops to consider the ramifications of this decision, <u>it is probable that he will rethink his original decision a while longer</u>.

A. it is probable that he will rethink his original decision a while longer
B. he will rethink his original decision over again
C. he will probably rethink his original decision
D. he will most likely rethink his original decision for a bit

21. "When you get <u>older," she said "you will no doubt</u> understand what I mean."

A. older," she said "you will no doubt
B. older" she said "you will no doubt
C. older," she said, "you will no doubt
D. older," she said "you will not

22. <u>Dr. Anderson strolled past the nurses examining a bottle of pills</u>.

A. Dr. Anderson strolled past the nurses examining a bottle of pills.
B. Dr. Anderson strolled past the nurses to examining a bottle of pills.
C. Examining a bottle of pills Dr. Anderson strolled past the nurses.
D. Examining a bottle of pills, Dr. Anderson strolled past the nurses.

23. Karl and Henry <u>raced to the reservoir, climbed the ladder, and then they dove into</u> the cool water.

A. raced to the reservoir, climbed the ladder, and then they dove into
B. first raced to the reservoir, climbed the ladder, and then they dove into
C. raced to the reservoir, they climbed the ladder, and then dove into
D. raced to the reservoir, climbed the ladder, and dove into

24. Did either Tracy or Vanessa realize that her degree would be so valuable to future employers?

A. Tracy or Vanessa realize that her degree would be
B. Tracy or Vanessa realize that each of their degree was
C. Tracy or Vanessa realize that her or her degree would be
D. Tracy or Vanessa realize that their degree would be

25. The Burmese python is a large species of snake, it is native to parts of southern Asia although it has recently begun infesting the Florida Everglades.

A. snake, it is native
B. snake, that is native
C. snake that is native
D. snake, it's native

26. In the wild, the Burmese python typically grows to around 12 feet in length, but in captivity the snake often grow much longer than that, to upwards of 15 or 20 feet in length.

A. the snake often grow
B. the snakes often grow
C. the snake often will be growing
D. the snakes, often grow

27. A new bill was recently passed; they put increased regulations on businesses to protect the environment.

A. passed; they put
B. passed, and put
C. passed, they have put
D. passed; it put

28. Luis paused to think before he spoke, Luis carefully stated his opinion to the board.

A. Luis paused to think
B. He paused, thinking
C. Pausing to think
D. Pausing, Luis thought

29. As the wind gusted loudly, and leaves tumbled off the branches, drifting to the ground.

A. loudly, and leaves tumbled off the branches
B. loud, and leaves tumbled off the branches
C. loudly, the tumbling leaves off the branches
D. loudly, leaves tumbled off the branches

30. Barking loudly, the man stumbled forward as the dog tugged on the leash.

A. the man stumbled forward as the dog tugged on the leash
B. the dog tugged on the leash as the man stumbled forward
C. the man stumbled forward, tugged by the dog on the leash
D. the dog, stumbling forward, tugged the man on the leash.

Essay

Wiretapping and spying policies of the National Security Agency have been a topic of interest lately, with much discussion taking place over the need for security as it relates to the right to individual privacy. Please write a multiple-paragraph persuasive essay (approximately 350–500 words) discussing whether you support or oppose government collection of private data for the purpose of national security.

Answers and Explanations for Test #3

Math

1. C: Solving for y in the second equation gives $y = 4x - 5$. If we plug this into the first equation, we get $2x + 3(4x - 5) = 13$, which expands to $2x + 12x - 15 = 13$. Solving for this equation gives us $14x = 28$, or $x = 2$. Then we plug the value of x into either equation to solve for y: $y = 3$. Therefore, $3x + 2y = 3(2) + 2(3) = 12$.

2. C: The movie is now at the 102-minute mark $(90 + 12 = 102)$. Therefore, m minutes ago, it had reached the $(102 - m)$ mark.

3. B: For all large values of x, the value of $\frac{x}{1-2x}$ will be very close to the value of $\frac{x}{-2x} = -\frac{1}{2}$. Answer choice A represents the value of $\frac{x}{1-2x}$ when $x = 50$. When $x = 100$, the value of $\frac{x}{1-2x}$ is already closer to $-\frac{1}{2}$ than it is to $-\frac{50}{99}$, and it grows continuously closer to $-\frac{1}{2}$ as x increases, so answer choice A cannot by correct.

4. A: If $520 \div x = 40n$, then

$$40nx = 520$$
$$nx = 13$$

5. D: Isolate a: $a = 8b + 6 + 16$. Thus, $a = 8b + 22$. Next, add 3 to both side of the equation:

$$a + 3 = 8b + 22 + 3$$
$$= 8b + 25$$

6. B: Translate this word problem into a mathematical equation. Let Janice's weight equal x. Let Elaina's weight equal $x + 23$. Let June's weight equal $x + 14$. Add all three weights together and subtract 25 pounds:

$$= x + x + 23 + x + 14 - 25$$
$$= 3x + 37 - 25$$
$$= 3x + 12$$

7. C: To find the average, we need to add up each part and divide by the number of parts. If Max reads three books and Lucy reads five books, there are eight books in total. We can find the total number of pages by multiplying 360 by 3 and 200 by 5, and then dividing the sum by 8:

$$\frac{360 \times 3 + 200 \times 5}{8} = \frac{1{,}080 + 1{,}000}{8} = \frac{2{,}080}{8} = 260$$

8. B: $\left(\frac{x^2-5x+6}{x+1}\right) \times \left(\frac{x+1}{x-2}\right) = \frac{(x^2-5x+6)\times(x+1)}{(x+1)\times(x-2)}$. Before carrying out the multiplication of the polynomials, notice that there is a factor of $x + 1$ in both the numerator and denominator, so the expression reduces to $\frac{x^2-5x+6}{x-2}$. We can simplify further by factoring the numerator.

One way to factor a quadratic expression with a leading coefficient of 1 is to look for two numbers that add up to the coefficient of x (in this case -5) and multiply to the constant term (in this case 6).

Two such numbers are -2 and -3: $(-2) + (-3) = -5$ and $(-2) \times (-3) = 6$. So $x^2 - 5x + 6 = (x-2)(x-3)$. That means $\frac{x^2-5x+6}{x-2} = \frac{(x-2)(x-3)}{x-2}$. The $x - 2$ in the numerator and denominator can cancel, so we are left with just $x - 3$. (Note that if $x = -1$ or $x = 2$, the obtained simplified expression would not be true: either value of x would result in a denominator of zero in the original expression, so the whole expression would be undefined. Therefore, it is necessary to state that these values of x are excluded from the domain. For a domain of $x > 2$, both $x = -1$ and $x = 2$ would be excluded.)

9. A: To evaluate $\frac{x^3+2x}{x+3}$ at $= -1$, substitute in -1 for x in the expression: $\frac{(-1)^3+2(-1)}{(-1)+3} = \frac{(-1)+(-2)}{2} = \frac{-3}{2} = -\frac{3}{2}$.

10. D: Use the rule that states that $(a + b)(a - b) = a^2 - b^2$, or multiply the bionomials using the FOIL method: multiply together the *first* term of each factor, then the *outer* terms, then the *inner* terms, and finally the *last* terms. Then add the products together.

$$\begin{aligned}(x+6)(x-6) &= x \times x + x \times (-6) + 6 \times x + 6 \times (-6) \\ &= x^2 - 6x + 6x - 36 \\ &= x^2 - 36\end{aligned}$$

11. A: In the equation $y = mx + b$, m is the slope and b is the y-intercept. So we can insert 3 for m and –2 for b in the equation: $y = 3x - 2$. We can see that all of the answer choices have the variables and constants on the left side of the equation, so we rewrite our equation by subtracting $3x$ from each side and adding 2 to each side:

$$-3x + y + 2 = 0$$

12. C: An item is first marked down by 25% and then by an additional 20%. If 25% is taken off the price, the remaining cost is 75% of the original price, so we can calculate the first markdown: $25.98(0.75) = 19.485$. If 20% is taken off this price, the remaining cost is 80% of this price, so we can calculate the second and final markdown: $19.485(0.8) = 15.588$. We round to the hundredths place to find the final cost: \$15.59.

13. D: There are several ways to solve a system of equations like this. Likely the simplest is by elimination. We add the two equations together to cancel out the x-values:

$$\begin{aligned}(x + 2y = 3) + (-x - 3y = 4) \\ x + 2y - x - 3y = 3 + 4 \\ -y = 7 \\ y = -7\end{aligned}$$

Now, putting that value for y back into one of the original equations, we get:

$$\begin{aligned}x + 2(-7) &= 3 \\ x - 14 &= 3 \\ x &= 17\end{aligned}$$

14. D: The degree measurement for alternate interior angles is exactly the same. In the figure, there are two pairs of alternate interior angles: B and C; A and D.

15. C: The angles a, b, and c form a straight line, so $a + b + c = 180$. Substituting 180 for $a + b + c$ in the proportion, we have: $\frac{b}{180} = \frac{3}{5}$. By cross-multiplying, we can solve for b: $5b = 3(180)$ or $b = 108$.

16. B: The radius of circle O is one-fourth the diameter of circle P. The diameter is twice the radius, or $d = 2r$. This means that the radius of circle O is half of the radius of circle P, or $\mathrm{r}_O = \frac{1}{4}(2\mathrm{r}_P) = \frac{1}{2}\mathrm{r}_P$. The circumference of circle P is: $2\pi\mathrm{r}_P$. The circumference of circle O is: $2\pi\mathrm{r}_O = 2\pi(\frac{1}{2}\mathrm{r}_P) = \pi\mathrm{r}_P$. Since circle P's circumference is twice that of circle O, the ratio of circle O's circumference to circle P's is $\frac{\pi\mathrm{r}_P}{2\pi\mathrm{r}_P} = \frac{1}{2}$.

17. A: A correlation of 0.9 is a strong correlation because it is close to 1. Recall that the closer a correlation coefficient is to −1 or 1, the stronger the correlation. A correlation of −1 or 1 is perfect.

18. D: Since he does not replace the first card, the events are dependent. The sample space will decrease by 1 for the second draw because there will be one less card to choose from. Thus, the probability may be written as $P(A \text{ and } B) = \frac{13}{52} \times \frac{13}{51}$, or $P(A \text{ and } B) = \frac{169}{2{,}652}$, which simplifies to $\frac{13}{204}$.

19. C: The expected value is the sum of the products of the scholarship amounts and probability she will attend each college, or $\frac{1}{3}$. Thus, the expected value is $\left(6{,}000 \times \frac{1}{3}\right) + \left(4{,}500 \times \frac{1}{3}\right) + \left(5{,}500 \times \frac{1}{3}\right)$, which equals approximately 5,333. So, she can expect to receive $5,333.

20. B: The expected value is found by multiplying the value of each possible outcome by its probability to occur, and then summing all of these products. In this case, there are only two possible outcomes: winning and not winning. The value of winning is $495 ($500 minus the price of the $5 ticket), and the probability of winning is $\frac{1}{250}$. The value of not winning is −$5 (the price of the ticket), and the probability of losing is $\frac{249}{250}$. Written mathematically, the expected value is $\left(495 \times \frac{1}{250}\right) + \left((-5) \times \frac{249}{250}\right)$, which equals $\frac{495}{250} - \frac{1{,}245}{250} = \frac{-750}{250} = -3$. Thus, Nia's expected value is −$3.

English Language Arts and Reading

1. D: Defarge introduces the shoemaker to the visitor, converses with the shoemaker despite the shoemaker's difficulty replying, and tries to help the shoemaker showcase his work for Mr. Lorry. So it is reasonable to infer that Defarge cares for him to some degree, and isn't disgusted with him (B). On the other hand, Defarge is surprisingly neutral about the shoemaker's mental condition, as if he is merely demonstrating the problem to Mr. Lorry, so we do not get the sense that Defarge is sympathetic (C). The author does not say anything to suggest that Defarge looks up to the shoemaker (A).

2. D: The man does not laugh in this passage. Choice A is clearly stated in the passage. He has lapses in conversation with Mr. Lorry. It is also clear in the passage that the man has no remembrance of a given personal name, another sign of his mental condition, so choice B can be eliminated. The repeated motion of his hands when they do not hold the shoe is a telling sign of derangement, so choice C is incorrect.

3. C: *Mode* has several meanings, but the one that makes sense in this context is a popular style or fashion. Answer choices A and B are alternate definitions that do not fit this context. Answer choice D is not a possible meaning of *mode*.

4. B: The passage suggests that the shoemaker does not put much emotion into his work, and that he rather uses it to occupy his deteriorating mind. So it makes sense that he is "weary," but that he does not mind continuing to work (C). Shoemaking seems to be his normal work, and there is no reason to assume this shoe is more difficult than any other (A). Defarge and Mr. Lorry do not seem strict or cruel, so the shoemaker would have no reason to hide his weariness or attitude about the work from them (D).

5. A: Passage 1 mentions that omega-3 is important for brain function, and Passage 2 agrees that it has benefits for the brains of growing children. While Passage 2 agrees with answer choice B, Passage 1 does not. Passage 2 agrees that pollutants are common in fish (C), while Passage 1 downplays the concern. Passage 1 states that fish have many additional health benefits (D), but Passage 2 makes no mention of it, and encourages people to use an omega-3 supplement rather than eating fish.

6. B: The author never mentions witches in the passage. The others are listed in the first sentence.

7. D: The main idea discussed in the passage is that employers benefit the most from establishing a comfortable workspace. The author points out that it is not extremely expensive, and then identifies all the benefits for employers. Answer choice A directly opposes the opening sentence. Answer choices B and C are consistent with the passage, but they are not the main idea.

8. B: It can be concluded that many brides are choosing to wear colors other than white based on two statements in the passage. First, we know that bridesmaids should not wear the same color as the bride. Secondly, it is stated that white is a popular color for bridesmaid dresses. Since the color of the bridesmaid dress and the bride's dress should not be the same, the bride's dress will not be white if the bridesmaid dress is white. While picking dresses is an "important part" of wedding planning, the passage does not state that it is the hardest part (A). There is nothing in the passage about bridesmaids choosing their own dresses (C) or avoiding black (D).

9. B: Many green fuels require more work to produce than conventional fuels. The passage states, "producing natural gas is a much more labor-intensive process than producing an equal amount of conventional gasoline. Also, producing natural gas involves burning fossil fuels." There is no evidence to support answer choice A or D. Answer choice C looks promising, but the passage does not mention that burning the green fuels produces fossil fuels, but rather that producing and transporting them uses fossil fuels.

10. C: This conclusion can be made based on two statements. First, the passage states that "the majority of crimes discussed on the nightly news featured African American suspects." Second, "it was found that white people were also suspects 50 percent of the time." Therefore, if half of all suspects are white, but the majority of suspects on the news are African American, it is reasonable to conclude that the news does not report as many crimes that involve white suspects. Answer choice A is incorrect because 50 percent is not a majority, and because the passage tells us about suspects, not necessarily about criminals. The passage does not make any comment on what people believe (B) or the total number of crimes (D).

11. B: The main purpose of the passage is to discuss why the use of stem cells in research is ethical. The author states that many people feel it is unethical (A), but this statement merely draws attention to the main claim of the passage. The passage does say that some diseases and injuries may be cured through stem cell research, but it does not claim that this has already been achieved (C) or that it is unethical not to conduct stem cell research (D).

12. A: Accuracy is the same as correctness. The passage states "accuracy means that something is correct" and "if a glass of liquid was 100 degrees, an accurate measurement would be one that was close to this temperature." Consistency (B) refers to precision rather than accuracy, as does a result that can be duplicated (C). Both accurate and precise results are measurable (D).

13. A: Sentence 3 discusses the trees that are raised, or cultivated, to obtain cinnamon. *Raised* can have a literal meaning of being lifted (B) or of being on a higher level, like a raised garden bed (C), but neither meaning is the case here. While answer choice D makes sense in context, it is not a possible meaning of the word *raised.*

14. C: The passage lists the symptoms of mild dehydration as headache, feeling sluggish, and waking up tired. Rapid heartbeat is a symptom of more severe dehydration.

15. D: The passage states that "scent also has a very strong connection with memory." It mentions that certain scents may be able to help with stress, not that scent and stress are linked (A). It also mentions potential scents associated with family that may trigger an emotional reaction, but it does not state that family and scent are connected (B). Finally, the passage mentions that different people have different scent preferences based on their physiological makeup, but it does not say that personality is connected to scent (C).

16. C: This version begins with a subject and verb and is followed by a clause. It is also clear and concise. Choice A is incorrect because the order of information is unusual and does not flow well with the previous sentence. Sentence 2 should ideally begin with "She says" because it is the school principal's opinion being expressed. Furthermore, choice A uses *not appropriate* where *inappropriate* would be more effective. Choice B is incorrect because the clause "that students wear to school" should come immediately after "outfits." Choice D is incorrect because the word order changes the meaning to suggest that all outfits are distracting and inappropriate.

17. A: Sentence 4 makes a statement that doesn't add anything to the argument. It is obvious that the author doesn't agree with Mrs. Conwer's statement, so it is not necessary to write a whole sentence just to say so. Sentence 5 is important to the essay because it sets the essay up for the author's list of arguments. Sentence 13 is necessary because it draws the conclusion from the previous two sentences. Sentence 19 is necessary because it brings up an important point.

18. A: Answer choice A uses correct punctuation and a logical conjunction. When conjunctions *and* and *but* connect two independent clauses (meaning that these clauses can stand on their own as sentences), there must be a comma before the conjunction. Therefore, choices B and D are incorrect because they are missing this comma. While choice C does have a comma before the conjunction, it uses the conjunction *but* rather than *and*. *But* implies that the two clauses contradict each other. *And* is a better choice because the two clauses are connected and support each other.

19. B: In the original sentence, it is unclear what "them" refers to. Using logic and context, we can reason that the object pronoun must refer to the students, since Mrs. Conwer and the teachers are the subject. It does not make sense to say that the principal and teachers would be ignoring other teachers or the administration, so answer choices A and D are incorrect. Answer choice C does not make sense either, as creating a dress code does not ignore a dress code's details.

20. C: The original sentence (choice A) is redundant and wordy. Choice B is also redundant and changes the meaning by declaring that he "will" rethink his decision, rather than that he will likely rethink it. Choice D is redundant because of "for a bit."

21. C: The syntax of the original sentence is fine, but a comma after "said" and before the open-quotation mark is required. Choice C is the only one that includes this comma.

22. D: Choice A is incorrect because the sentence needs a comma after "nurses." Choice B incorrectly adds the word *to*, which does not match the verb form. Choice C also omits a necessary comma after *pills*. Only choice D is grammatically correct.

23. D: When there is more than one verb phrase, we write them in a parallel structure that uses commas and *and* the way a list does. In this case, the verb phrases should be written as "raced to the reservoir, climbed the ladder, and dove into." Choices A, B, and C each include the subject "they" with one of the verb phrases, creating an inconsistent parallel structure.

24. A: The singular pronoun *her* and singular noun *degree* are grammatically correct. The subjects, "Tracy" and "Vanessa," are connected by "or" and refer to two women, each of whom has her own degree. Choices B and D use "their degree," which would suggest the women share one degree (also eliminating the need for "each of" in B). B also uses "was" rather than "would be," which disagrees with "future employers." Choice C is awkward and unclear.

25. C: The original sentence is a comma splice, connecting two independent clauses (complete sentences) with a comma rather than a semicolon or period. Answer choice B is incorrect because *that* is not set off with commas when used for essential information as it is here. Answer choice D uses the correct contraction for "it is" but again uses a comma instead of a semicolon or period. Answer choice C correctly uses *that* for an essential clause that does not need commas.

26. B: Answer choice A uses a singular subject with a plural verb. Answer choice C is awkward and unnecessarily wordy. Answer choice D incorrectly places a comma after "snakes," interrupting the sentence flow.

27. D: The sentence has a singular subject in the first clause ("bill"), but choice A uses a plural subject in the second ("they"). Answer choice B incorrectly uses a comma before a dependent clause. Answer choice C connects two independent clauses with a comma, creating a comma splice. Also, like choice A, it uses a plural pronoun rather than a singular one. Answer choice D correctly connects the two independent clauses with a semicolon and uses a singular subject to match "bill."

28. C: Answer choice A leads to both a comma splice (two independent clauses connected by a comma) and the repetitive use of "Luis." Answer choice B also causes a comma splice as both clauses are independent, which is also the case with answer choice D. Answer choice C makes the first clause dependent (no longer a standalone sentence) so that a comma is appropriate, and also eliminates one of the proper nouns.

29. D: The original sentence is a fragment, with multiple dependent clauses strung together, so choice A is not correct. Answer choice B leaves the sentence as a fragment and awkwardly uses *loud* instead of *loudly*. Answer choice C also leaves the sentence as a fragment, and the rearrangement of the middle clause is confusing. Answer choice D turns the middle clause into an independent clause, making a complete sentence.

30. B: As written, this sentence has a dangling participle. The first clause clearly refers to the dog, not the man, so the dog needs to be mentioned before the man in the second clause. Thus answer choices A and C are incorrect. Answer choice D uses awkward wording and also states that the dog stumbled forward, which is unlikely. Only answer choice B mentions the dog first while being clear and logical.

TSI Practice Test #4

Math

1. A regular toilet uses 3.2 gallons of water per flush. A low-flow toilet uses 1.6 gallons of water per flush. What is the difference between the number of gallons used by the regular toilet and the low-flow toilet after 375 flushes?

A. 100 gallons
B. 525 gallons
C. 600 gallons
D. 1,200 gallons

2. Solve for n in the following equation: $4n - p = 3r$

A. $\frac{3r}{4} - p$
B. $p + 3r$
C. $\frac{3r}{4} + p$
D. $\frac{3r}{4} + \frac{p}{4}$

3. What is $|x| + |x - 2|$ when $x = 1$?

A. 0
B. 1
C. 2
D. 3

4. Which of the following inequalities is correct?

A. $\frac{1}{3} < \frac{2}{7} < \frac{5}{12}$
B. $\frac{2}{7} < \frac{1}{3} < \frac{5}{12}$
C. $\frac{5}{12} < \frac{2}{7} < \frac{1}{3}$
D. $\frac{5}{12} < \frac{1}{3} < \frac{2}{7}$

5. If $6q + 3 = 8q - 7$, what is q?

A. $-\frac{5}{7}$
B. $\frac{5}{7}$
C. 5
D. -7

6. A communications company charges \$5.00 for the first 10 minutes of a call and \$1.20 for each minute thereafter. Which of the following equations correctly relates the price in dollars, d, to the number of minutes, m (when $m \geq 10$)?

A. $d = 5 + 1.2m$
B. $d = 5 + 1.2(m - 10)$
C. $d = 5m + 1.2(m + 10)$
D. $d = (m + 10)(5 + 1.2)$

7. Simplify the following: $\frac{x^2}{y^2} + \frac{x}{y^3}$

A. $\frac{x^3+x}{y^3}$
B. $\frac{x^2+xy}{y^3}$
C. $\frac{x^2y+xy}{y^3}$
D. $\frac{x^2y+x}{y^3}$

8. How many solutions are there to the equation $|x^2 - 2| = x$?

A. 0
B. 1
C. 2
D. 4

9. Which of the following is the factored form of the expression $x^2 - 3x - 40$?

A. $(x - 8)(x + 5)$
B. $(x - 7)(x + 4)$
C. $(x + 10)(x - 4)$
D. $(x + 6)(x - 9)$

10. Given the equation $2^x = 64$, what is the value of *x*?

A. 4
B. 5
C. 6
D. 7

11. In the figure below, angles *b* and *d* are equal. What is the degree measure of angle *d*?

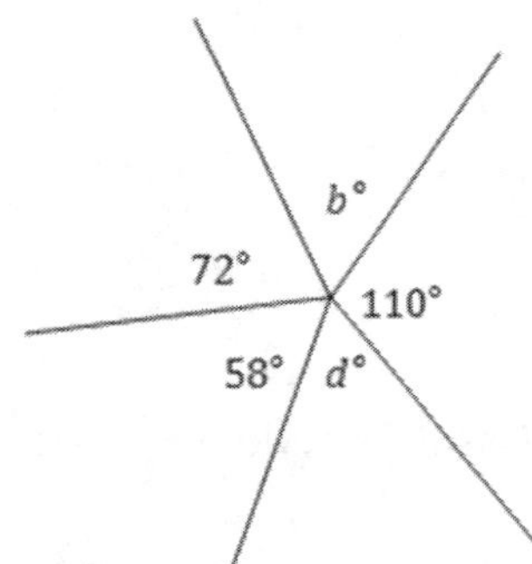

A. 120°
B. 80°
C. 60°
D. 30°

12. What is the area of the parallelogram in the figure pictured below?

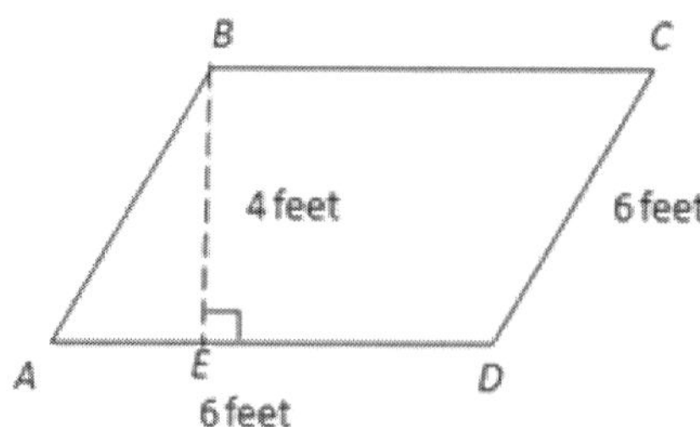

A. 10 square feet
B. 16 square feet
C. 24 square feet
D. 36 square feet

13. What is the slope of the line in the graph below?

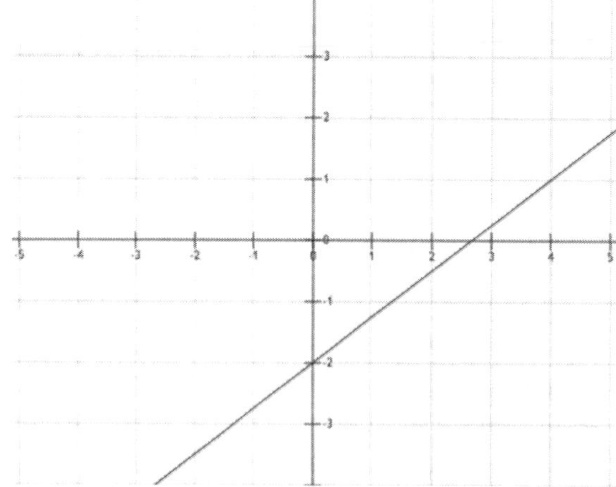

A. $\frac{4}{3}$
B. $-\frac{4}{3}$
C. $\frac{3}{4}$
D. $-\frac{3}{4}$

14. If a number is increased by 30% and then decreased by 25%, how does the final number differ from the original?

A. It is 5% greater than the original.
B. It is 7.5% greater than the original.
C. It is the same as the original.
D. It is 2.5% less than the original.

15. A building has a number of floors of equal height, as well as a 30-foot spire above them all. If the height of each floor in feet is *h*, and there are *n* floors in the building, which of the following represents the building's total height in feet?

A. $n + h + 30$
B. $nh + 30$
C. $30n + h$
D. $30h + n$

16. Which of the following figures show parallelogram $WXYZ$ being carried onto its image $W'X'Y'Z'$ by a reflection across the *x*-axis?

A.

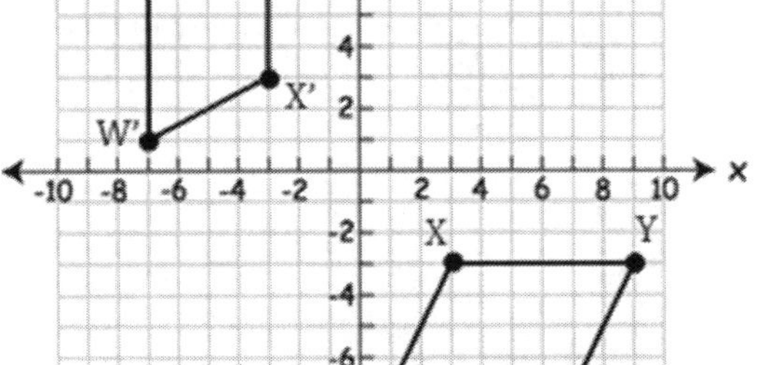

B.

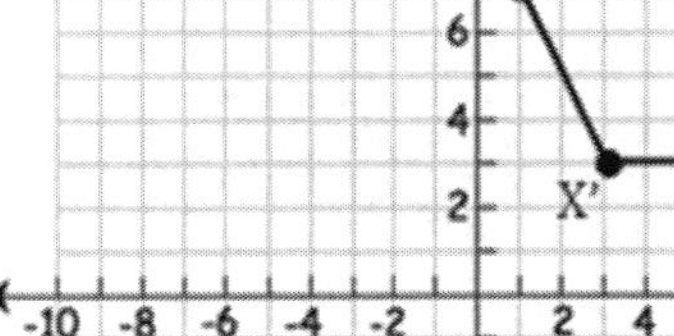

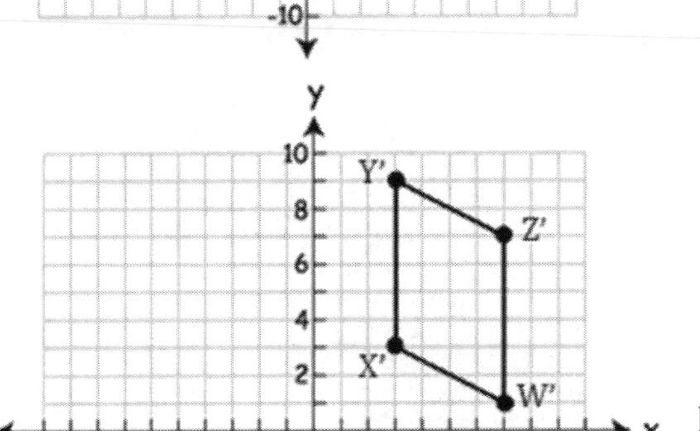

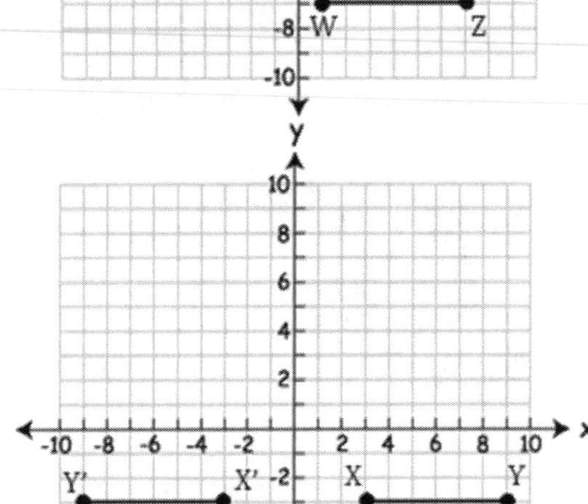

C.

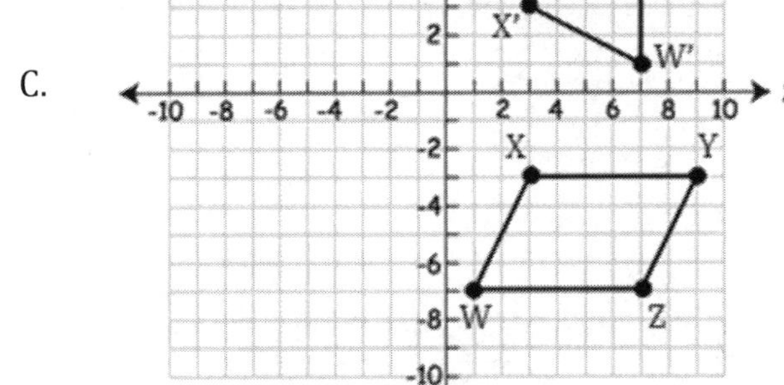

D.

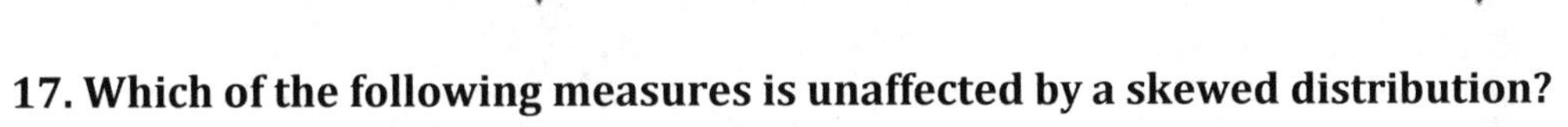

17. Which of the following measures is unaffected by a skewed distribution?

A. Mean
B. Median
C. Standard deviation
D. Range

18. Which of the following correlation coefficients represents a weak correlation?

A. −0.9
B. 0.2
C. −0.7
D. 0.8

19. Elisha spins a spinner with 8 equally spaced sections labeled 1–8. What is the probability that the spinner lands either on a number greater than 5 or on 2?

A. $\frac{3}{64}$
B. $\frac{1}{2}$
C. $\frac{1}{8}$
D. $\frac{3}{8}$

20. A bag contains 2 red marbles, 3 blue marbles, and 5 green marbles. What is the probability Gitta draws a red marble, does not replace it, and then draws another red marble?

A. $\frac{1}{25}$
B. $\frac{1}{45}$
C. $\frac{2}{45}$
D. $\frac{14}{45}$

English Language Arts and Reading

For questions 1–15, read each passage and then choose the best answer to the accompanying questions. Answer the questions on the basis of what is stated or implied in the passage(s).

Leaving

(1) Even though Martin and Beth's steps were muffled by the falling snow, Beth could still hear the faint crunch of leaves underneath. (2) The hushed woods had often made Beth feel safe and at peace, but these days they just made her feel lonely.

(3) "I'm glad we decided to hike the trail, Martin. (4) It's so quiet and pretty."

(5) "Sure."

(6) Beth couldn't understand how it happened, but over the past few months this silence had grown between them, weighing down their relationship. (7) Of course, there was that thing with Mary, but Beth had forgiven Martin. (8) They moved on. (9) It was in the past.

(10) "Do you want to see a movie tonight?" asked Beth. (11) "There's a new one showing at the downtown theater."

(12) "Whatever you want."

(13) She wanted her husband back. (14) She wanted the laughter and games. (15) She wanted the late-night talks over coffee. (16) She wanted to forget Mary and Martin together. (17) She wanted to feel some sort of rapport again.

(18) "Is everything alright, Martin?"

(19) "I'm fine. (20) Just tired."

(21) "We didn't have to come; we could have stayed at home."

(22) "It's fine."

(23) Beth closed her eyes, tilted her head back, and breathed in the crisp air. (24) "Fine" once meant "very good," or "precious." (25) Now, it is a meaningless word, an excuse not to tell other people what's on your mind. (26) "Fine" had hung in the air between them for months now, a softly falling word that hid them from each other. (27) Beth wasn't even sure she knew Martin anymore, but she was confident that it was only a matter of time before everything was not "fine," only a matter of time before he told her...

(28) "I have to leave."

(29) "Huh? (30) What?"

(31) "I got a page. (32) My patient is going into cardiac arrest."

(33) "I wish you didn't have to leave."

(34) "I'm sorry, but I have to go."

(35) "I know."

1. It is reasonable to infer that Martin and Beth's relationship is strained because

A. Martin recently lost his job
B. Martin was unfaithful to Beth
C. Martin works too much
D. Martin does not want to go to the movies

2. Based on the passage, it is reasonable to infer that Martin is a ______________.

A. mechanic
B. medical doctor
C. dentist
D. film director

3. As used in sentence 17, "rapport" most nearly means

A. A close relationship
B. A sense of well-being
C. A common goal
D. Loneliness

4. Sentences 10–17 suggest which of the following?

A. Beth particularly enjoys movies and is excited about the new one.
B. Martin does not like movies and is hoping Beth will decide against seeing it.
C. Beth hopes doing an activity together will help their struggling relationship.
D. Martin is tired of arguing over what to do and is willing to let Beth make the decision.

Use these two passages to answer the question that follows:

Passage 1

Daylight Saving Time began with the goal of conservation. Benjamin Franklin suggested it as a method of saving on candles. It was used during both World Wars to save energy for military needs. Although DST's potential to save energy was a primary reason behind its implementation, research into its effects on energy conservation are contradictory and unclear. Beneficiaries of DST include all activities that can benefit from more sunlight after working hours, such as shopping and sports. A 1984 issue of *Fortune* magazine estimated that a seven-week extension of DST would yield an additional $30 million for 7-Eleven stores. Public safety may be increased by the use of DST: some research suggests that traffic fatalities may be reduced when there is additional afternoon sunlight.

Passage 2

Daylight Saving Time complicates timekeeping and some computer systems. Tools with built-in timekeeping functions, such as medical devices, can be affected negatively. Agricultural and evening entertainment interests have historically opposed DST. Furthermore, DST can affect health, both positively and negatively. It provides more afternoon sunlight in which to get exercise. It also impacts sunlight exposure; this is good for getting vitamin D, but bad in that it can increase skin cancer risk. Also, DST may disrupt sleep, leading to increased deadly traffic accidents in the days after time change. The sudden change to darkness coming earlier in the evening after the autumn time change has been linked to depression.

5. The authors of the two passages disagree on

A. Why DST was implemented
B. The fact that DST complicates several things
C. Whether sunlight has benefits
D. Whether time change increases or decreases traffic fatalities

Use these two passages to answer the question that follows:

Passage 1

Many children who have never felt that they truly belonged find, for the first time, a sense of purpose and worth in sports. Children from a troubled home environment can flourish in the stability and order of sports, as well as by having teammates who care about them and a coach who encourages them. Children from any background can learn the valuable lessons of working together, pushing through challenging circumstances, and being graceful in losing as well as winning. Of course, the physical benefits of exercise are a bonus. Countless adults can look back at their time in sports as a pivotal experience that influenced the course of their lives.

Passage 2

Today's children and teens are exhausted. No longer free to simply play or relax at home in the hours not taken up by school and family, they are enrolled in an endless list of programs. Many of these are sports. There is ever-increasing pressure for students to be well-rounded and not simply to play sports but to spend endless hours practicing, working with personal trainers and continually striving to become superior athletes. Young people are waking up early for before-school practices and staying late after school for more training. Family schedules revolve around practices and games, and family dinners are rare. Additionally, students are so busy with sports that they don't have time to try other activities or explore possible career paths.

6. The author of Passage 1 would likely disagree with the assertion of Passage 2 that

A. Children need the time at home with family that sports take away from.
B. Sports have physical health benefits.
C. Sports often take a lot of practice and training.
D. Today's students are under too much pressure to perform well.

7. Consider the following passage:

> Literacy rates are lower today than they were 15 years ago. Then, most people learned to read through the use of phonics. Today, whole-language programs are favored by many educators. While phonics methods focus on teaching sounds of individual letters and blends, whole-language programs use the individual words as whole pieces of information, teaching children to recognize words and associate them with their meanings rather than sound them out.

What can be concluded from this passage?

A. Whole language is more effective at teaching people to read than phonics.
B. Phonics is more effective at teaching people to read than whole language.
C. Literacy rates will probably continue to decline over the next 15 years.
D. The definition of what it means to be literate is much stricter now.

8. Consider the following passage:

> George Washington was a remarkable man. He was born in 1732. Shortly before becoming the president of the United States in 1789, Washington was an important leader in the American Revolutionary War from 1775 to 1783. After retiring, he returned to his home in Mount Vernon in 1797. A short time later, John Adams made him commander-in-chief of the United States Army again. This was done in the anticipation that the country might go to war with France.

Which of the following happened soonest after Washington served as a leader in the American Revolutionary War?

A. Washington returned to Mount Vernon.
B. Washington was made commander-in-chief of the U.S. Army.
C. Washington became the President of the United States.
D. Washington decided to go into retirement.

9. Consider the following passage:

> During the 1970s, a new type of pet became popular in North America. Although they were actually just brine shrimp, they were marketed as "Sea-Monkeys." These animals don't actually look like monkeys at all, but they were branded as such due to their long tails. When Sea-Monkeys first began to be sold in the United States, they were sold under the brand name Instant Life. Later, when they became known as Sea-Monkeys, the cartoon drawings that were featured in comic books showed creatures that resembled humans more than shrimp. The creative marketing of these creatures can only be described as genius, and at the height of their popularity in the 1970s, they could be found in as many as one in five homes.

Which of the following can be inferred based on the information in the passage?

A. Sea-Monkeys were more popular when they were marketed as "Instant Life."
B. Sea-Monkeys wouldn't have been as popular if they had been marketed as "brine shrimp."
C. Most people thought they were actually purchasing monkeys that lived in the sea.
D. There are more homes today that have Sea-Monkeys than there were in the 1970s.

10. Consider the following passage:

> Before the battle between CDs and MP3s, there was a rivalry during the 1960s between the four-track and the eight-track tape. Four-track tapes were invented in the early 1960s by Earl Muntz, an entrepreneur from California. Later, Bill Lear designed the eight-track tape. This latter invention was similar in size to the four-track tape, but it could store and play twice as many songs. Lear had close ties with the motor company Ford, and he convinced them to include eight-track players in their vehicles, which definitely helped the eight-track tape to achieve a high level of popularity. Soon after, they were introduced into homes, and the four-track tape all but disappeared.

Which of the following describes a key difference between the four-track tape and the eight-track tape?

A. The four-track tape was much larger than the eight-track tape.
B. The eight-track tape cost a lot more to produce than the four-track tape.
C. The eight-track tape could hold more songs than the four-track tape.
D. The four-track tape was usually included in Ford vehicles.

11. Consider the following passage:

It is natural for humans to have fears, but when those fears are completely irrational and begin to interfere with everyday activities they are known as "phobias." Agoraphobia is a serious phobia, and it can be devastating for those who suffer from it. Contrary to popular belief, agoraphobia is not simply a fear of open spaces. Rather, a person with agoraphobia may fear being in any place that he or she feels is unsafe. Depending on the severity of the condition, a person with agoraphobia might fear going to the mall, walking down the street, or even walking to the mailbox. Often, a person with agoraphobia will view his or her home as the safest possible place to be, and the person may even be reluctant to leave the home at all. Treatments for this condition include medication and behavioral therapy.

Where would a person with agoraphobia likely feel the safest?

A. In their yard
B. In their home
C. In a mall
D. In the woods

12. Consider the following passage:

The butterfly effect is a mathematical concept that is somewhat poorly understood, primarily because it is interpreted and presented incorrectly by the popular media. It refers to systems, and how initial conditions can influence the ultimate outcome of an event. The best way to understand the concept is through an example. You have two rubber balls. There are two inches between them, and you release them. Where will they end up? Well, that depends. If they're in a sloped, sealed container, they will end up two inches away from each other at the end of the slope. If it's the top of a mountain, however, they may end up miles away from each other. They could bounce off rocks; one could get stuck in a snowbank while the other continues down the slope; one could enter a river and be swept away. This fact, that even a tiny initial difference can have a significant overall impact, is what the "butterfly effect" actually refers to.

What is the main purpose of this passage?

A. To discuss what could happen to two rubber balls released on top of a mountain
B. To show why you can predict what will happen to two objects in a sloped, sealed container
C. To discuss the primary reason why the butterfly effect is a poorly understood concept
D. To give an example of how small changes at the beginning of an event can have large effects

13. Consider the following passage:

> Does an apple a day really "keep the doctor away"? Well, it can definitely help. Apples are high in fiber, which helps keep digestion working smoothly and encourages gut flora. They also contain polyphenols, which help lower risk of heart disease and support brain function and digestion. Eating apples regularly has been linked to lower rates of asthma and diabetes as well as higher bone density. Apples may even help guard against Alzheimer's disease and mental decline. So while they don't guarantee protection from all disease, apples can play a valuable role in a person's health goals.

As used in the third sentence, "encourage" most nearly means

A. Reassure
B. Cause
C. Promote
D. Eliminate

14. Consider the following passage:

> We may think of archaeology as a modern pursuit, but the first known archaeologist was King Nabonidus of the Neo-Babylon Empire, over 2,500 years ago. He led multiple excavations to explore ancient Mesopotamian ruins. In the 1800s, stratigraphy was developed, which considers the fact that civilizations are often discovered in successive strata, buried beneath each other. Today, remote sensing instruments are used to examine an area before excavation, minimizing the damage of digging.

As used in the third sentence, "strata" most nearly means

A. Layers
B. Civilizations
C. Cities
D. Excavations

15. Consider the following passage:

> To increase your calcium intake, include milk at meals, preferably fat-free or low-fat milk. If you usually drink whole milk, try switching gradually to fat-free milk to lower saturated fat and calories. Try reduced fat (2 percent), then low-fat (1 percent), and finally fat-free (skim). When making oatmeal or hot cereal, use fat-free or low-fat milk instead of water. Yogurt is an excellent way to include calcium: eat it as a snack, make a fruit or veggie dip from yogurt, or make yogurt smoothies in a blender. If you cannot or prefer not to have dairy products, choose calcium-fortified juices, cereals, breads, and beverages.

How can you reduce your intake of saturated fat and calories from milk?

A. Add fat-free milk to oatmeal instead of water.
B. Switch to fat-free milk.
C. Drink calcium-fortified juice.
D. Make yogurt dip.

For questions 16–19, read the following early draft of an essay and then choose the best answer to the question or the best completion of the statement.

(1) After Orville and Wilbur Wright flew their first airplane in 1903, the age of flying slowly began. (2) During the war, the American public loved hearing stories about the daring pilots and their air fights. (3) But after the war ended, many Americans thought that men and women belonged on the ground and not in the air.

(4) In the years after the war and through the Roaring Twenties, America's pilots found themselves without jobs. (5) Some of them gave up flying altogether. (6) But other pilots found new and creative things to do with their airplanes. (7) Pilot Casey Jones used his airplane to help get news across the country. (8) When a big news story broke, Jones flew news photos to newspapers in different cities. (9) Other pilots took people for short airplane rides, often charging five dollars for a five-minute ride (by comparison, a loaf of bread cost about ten cents in 1920).

(10) During the 1920s, the U.S. Post Office developed airmail. (11) Before airmail, the post traveled on trains and could take weeks to reach a destination. (12) Flying for the post office was dangerous work. (13) Early pilots didn't have sophisticated instruments or safety equipment on their planes. (14) Many of them had to bail out and use their parachutes when their planes iced up in the cold air or had other trouble.

(15) The most famous pilot of the 1920s, Charles A. Lindbergh, began as a postal pilot. (16) In May 1927, he participated in an air race to fly across the Atlantic Ocean. (17) The prize was $25,000, but the dangers were extensive. (18) Named Nungesser and Coli, two French pilots had recently tried to fly across the Atlantic but disappeared.

(19) The newspapers called Charles Lindbergh the "dark horse" to win the race. (20) He had already set a record by making the fastest solo flight between St. Louis, Missouri, and San Diego, California. (21) Lindbergh's record-setting flight took 23 hours and 15 minutes; today, a flight between St. Louis and San Diego takes about four hours.

(22) After several weather delays, Lindbergh took off in his small plane, the *Spirit of St. Louis*, on May 20, 1927. (23) He made it across the Atlantic Ocean and arrived in France after 33 hours and 30 minutes of nonstop flight; today, a flight from New York to Paris would take about seven hours.

(24) The flight was taxing. (25) Because Lindbergh flew alone, he had to stay awake for the entire trip. (26) He knew that he couldn't have made it across without a great plane. (27) He said, "I feel that the monoplane was as much a part of the trip as myself."

(28) Lindbergh's trip set off a golden age for aviation. (29) The same people who were nervous about airplanes at the beginning of the 1920s came out by the thousands to cheer Lindbergh. (30) The age of pilots doing odd jobs and dangerous stunt work had ended.

16. What's the most effective way to rewrite sentence 18?

A. Two French pilots, named Nungesser and Coli, had recently tried to fly across the Atlantic but disappeared.
B. Two French pilots Nungesser and Coli had recently tried to fly across the Atlantic but disappeared.
C. Recently having tried to fly across the Atlantic but disappeared, two French pilots were named Nungesser and Coli.
D. No change

17. Which of the following statements would be best to add to the first paragraph?

A. The Wright brothers made history in North Carolina with their plane, the *Wright Flyer*.
B. Many new pilots learned how to fly in World War I, which the United States joined in 1917.
C. Many other inventors had been working on flying machines, but the Wright brothers were the first to develop the technology.
D. Some pilots used their training to become stuntmen.

18. How could sentences 26 and 27 best be combined?

A. He knew that he couldn't have made it across without a great plane and he said, "I feel that the monoplane was as much a part of the trip as myself."
B. He knew that he couldn't have made it across without a great plane, he said, "I feel that the monoplane was as much a part of the trip as myself."
C. He knew that he couldn't have made it across without a great plane and says, "I feel that the monoplane was as much a part of the trip as myself."
D. He knew that he couldn't have made it across without a great plane and said, "I feel that the monoplane was as much a part of the trip as myself."

19. What transition could be added at the beginning of sentence 28?

A. In conclusion
B. Furthermore
C. Therefore
D. Additionally

For questions 20–30, select the best version of the underlined part of the sentence. If you think the original sentence is best, choose the first answer.

20. Despite their lucky escape, <u>Jason and his brother could not hardly enjoy themselves</u>.

A. Jason and his brother could not hardly enjoy themselves
B. Jason and his brother could hardly enjoy themselves
C. Jason and Jason's brother could not hardly enjoy themselves
D. Jason and his brother could not enjoy them

21. Stew recipes call <u>for rosemary, parsley, thyme, and these sort of herbs</u>.

A. for rosemary, parsley, thyme, and these sort of herbs
B. for: rosemary; parsley; thyme; and these sort of herbs
C. for rosemary, parsley, thyme, and these sorts of herbs
D. for rosemary, parsley, thyme, and this sorts of herbs

22. Mr. King, <u>an individual of considerable influence, created a personal fortune and gave back</u> to the community.

A. an individual of considerable influence, created a personal fortune and gave back
B. an individual of considerable influence, he created a personal fortune and gave back
C. an individual of considerable influence created a personal fortune and gave back
D. an individual of considerable influence, created a personal fortune and gave it back

23. <u>She is the person whose opinion matters the most</u>.

A. She is the person whose opinion matters the most.
B. She is the person to whom her opinion matters the most.
C. She is the person her opinion matters the most.
D. She is the person for whom her opinion matters the most.

24. Minerals are nutritionally significant elements <u>that assist to make your body</u> work properly.

A. that assist to make your body
B. that help your body
C. that making your body
D. that work to make your body

25. Preying on local birds and wildlife, <u>the alligator, the most</u> prolific predator in the Florida Everglades.

A. the alligator, the most
B. the alligator; the most
C. the alligator is the most
D. the alligator. The most

26. <u>While</u> the alligator is generally predator rather than prey, Burmese pythons have been known to swallow full-grown alligators whole.

A. While
B. Because
C. Accordingly
D. However

27. <u>Reading, being one of the most important activities</u> for child development, libraries are an invaluable resource.

A. Reading, being one of the most important activities
B. As reading is one of the most important activities
C. One of the most important activities being reading
D. Reading, one of the most important activities

28. Although oranges and grapefruits are high in <u>vitamin C; thus kiwifruit</u> has an even higher amount.

A. vitamin C; thus kiwifruit
B. vitamin C—thus kiwifruit
C. vitamin C. Kiwifruit
D. vitamin C, kiwifruit

29. Waiting to finish her lunch after the business call, <u>the apple was set on Juliet's desk</u>.

A. the apple was set on Juliet's desk
B. Juliet set the apple on her desk
C. Juliet, setting the apple on her desk
D. the apple, being set on Juliet's desk

30. Motorcycles, <u>with its smaller profile than automobiles</u>, tend to have excellent fuel efficiency.

A. with its smaller profile than automobiles
B. having it's smaller profile than automobiles
C. with their smaller profiles than automobiles
D. having a smaller profile than automobiles

Essay

There is an ongoing struggle between those who would like to develop the oil reserves in Alaska and the Gulf of Mexico to help the US gain energy independence and those who oppose doing so because of possible environmental consequences. Please write a multiple-paragraph persuasive essay (approximately 350–500 words) discussing whether you support or oppose developing the oil reserves.

Answers and Explanations for Test #4

Math

1. C: To solve this problem, first calculate how many gallons each toilet uses in 375 flushes:

$$3.2 \times 375 = 1{,}200 \text{ gallons}$$

$$1.6 \times 375 = 600 \text{ gallons}$$

The problem is asking for the difference, so find the difference between the regular toilet and the low-flow toilet: $1{,}200 - 600 = 600$ gallons. Note that you could also find the difference in water use for one flush, and then multiply that amount by 375:

$$3.2 - 1.6 = 1.6 \text{ gallons}$$

$$1.6 \times 375 = 600 \text{ gallons}$$

2. D: To solve for n, you have to isolate that variable by putting all of the other terms of the equation, including coefficients, integers, and variables on the other side of the equal sign.

Add p to each side of the equation:

$$\begin{aligned} 4n - p &= 3r \\ 4n - p + p &= 3r + p \\ 4n &= 3r + p \end{aligned}$$

Divide each term by 4:

$$\begin{aligned} \frac{4n}{4} &= \frac{3r}{4} + \frac{p}{4} \\ n &= \frac{3r}{4} + \frac{p}{4} \end{aligned}$$

3. C: Substitute and simplify as follows:

$$\begin{aligned} |x| + |x - 2| &= |1| + |1 - 2| \\ &= |1| + |-1| \\ &= 1 + 1 \\ &= 2 \end{aligned}$$

4. B: One way to compare fractions is to convert them to equivalent fractions with common denominators. In this case, the lowest common denominator of the three fractions is $7 \times 12 = 84$. Convert each of the fractions to this denominator: $\frac{1}{3} = \frac{1\times28}{3\times28} = \frac{28}{84}$, $\frac{2}{7} = \frac{2\times12}{7\times12} = \frac{24}{84}$, and $\frac{5}{12} = \frac{5\times7}{12\times7} = \frac{35}{84}$. Since $24 < 28 < 35$, it must be the case that $\frac{2}{7} < \frac{1}{3} < \frac{5}{12}$.

5. C: Rearrange the equation to isolate q:

$$6q + 3 = 8q - 7$$
$$3 + 7 = 8q - 6q$$
$$10 = 2q$$
$$q = 5$$

6. B: The charge is \$1.20 for each minute after the first ten minutes. The number of minutes after the first ten minutes is $m - 10$, so \$1.20 per minute charged for the part of the phone call exceeding 10 minutes is $1.2(m - 10)$. Adding this to the \$5.00 charge for the first ten minutes gives $d = 5 + 1.2(m - 10)$.

7. D: To add the two fractions, first rewrite them with the least common denominator, which is in this case y^3. This is already the denominator in $\frac{x}{y^3}$, and we can rewrite $\frac{x^2}{y^2}$ as $\frac{x^2 \times y}{y^2 \times y} = \frac{x^2 y}{y^3}$. Thus, $\frac{x^2}{y^2} + \frac{x}{y^3} = \frac{x^2 y}{y^3} + \frac{x}{y^3} = \frac{x^2 y + x}{y^3}$.

8. C: To solve an equation with an absolute value like $|x^2 - 2| = x$, we need to treat it as two separate cases. If $x^2 - 2$ is positive, then $|x^2 - 2| = x^2 - 2$. The equation then becomes $x^2 - 2 = x$, which can be rewritten as $x^2 - x - 2 = 0$. If $x^2 - 2$ is negative, then $|x^2 - 2| = -(x^2 - 2)$, and the equation becomes $-(x^2 - 2) = x$, which we can rewrite as $x^2 + x - 2 = 0$. We will need to examine both of these equations.

We can factor $x^2 - x - 2 = 0$ by finding two numbers that sum to the coefficient of x (–1) and multiply to the constant term (–2). The two qualifying numbers are 1 and –2; thus, this equation factors to $(x + 1)(x - 2) = 0$, yielding the solutions $x = -1$ and $x = 2$.

We can factor $x^2 + x - 2 = 0$ in the same way. In this case, the two qualifying numbers are –1 and 2; thus, this equation factors to $(x - 1)(x + 2) = 0$, yielding the solutions $x = 1$ and $x = -2$.

From solving these two equations, we have solutions of $x = -2, -1, 1, 2$, but this method of solving absolute value equations can yield invalid solutions. We must verify that our solutions are valid.

Notice that in the original equation, x is set equal to an absolute value. By definition, this means that x cannot be a negative number, which eliminates two of our possible solutions. We can verify the positive values by plugging them into the original equation:

$$|1^2 - 2| = |-1| = 1; \quad |2^2 - 2| = |2| = 2$$

Since $x = 1$ and $x = 2$ are both valid, we can see that there are two solutions to the equation.

9. A: The expression may be factored as $(x - 8)(x + 5)$. The factorization may be checked by distributing each term in the first factor to each term in the second factor. Doing so gives $x^2 + 5x - 8x - 40$, which can be rewritten as $x^2 - 3x - 40$.

10. C: The power to which 2 is raised to give 64 is 6; $2^6 = 64$ because $2 \times 2 \times 2 \times 2 \times 2 \times 2 = 64$. Thus, $x = 6$.

11. C: Angles around a point add up to 360 degrees. Add the degrees of the given angles: 72° + 110° + 58° = 240°. Then subtract this from 360 degrees: 360° – 240° = 120°. Remember to divide 120 in half, since the question is asking for the degree measurement of one angle, angle d, among two equal angles that add up to 120.

12. C: The area of a parallelogram is base times height or $A = bh$, where b is the length of a side and h is the length of an altitude to that side. In this problem, $A = 6 \times 4$; $A = 24$. Remember, use the length of BE, not the length of CD for the height.

13. C: Slope can be calculated as change in y over change in x, or rise over run. We can see that the line passes through the points (0, –2) and (4, 1). So the y-value changes by positive 3 and the x-value changes by positive 4 between these two points. The slope can be found by dividing these two values: $\frac{3}{4}$.

14. D: We can choose a value for the original number and calculate the increase and decrease. For example, we can let the original value equal 100. We increase this by 30% by multiplying by 1.3: $100(1.3) = 130$. Then we decrease it by 25% by multiplying by 0.75: $130(0.75) = 97.5$. This is 2.5 less than 100, and 2.5 out of 100 is 2.5%, so the final value is 2.5% less than the original.

15. B: If there are n floors, and each floor has a height of h feet, then to find the total height of the floors, we just multiply the number of floors by the height of each floor: nh. To find the total height of the building, we must also add the height of the spire, 30 feet. So the building's total height in feet is $nh + 30$.

16. B: A reflection is a transformation producing a mirror image. A figure reflected over the x-axis will have its vertices in the form (x, y) transformed to $(x, -y)$. The point W at (1,–7) reflects to W' at (1,7), and so on. Only answer choice C shows $WXYZ$ being carried onto its image $W'X'Y'Z'$ by a reflection across the x-axis. Choice A shows a reflection across the line $y = x$. Choice C shows a 90° counterclockwise rotation about the origin. Choice D shows a reflection across the y-axis.

17. B: The median is unaffected by a skewed distribution (i.e., by extreme outliers). The median represents the value that 50 percent of the scores fall above and 50 percent of the scores fall below. The mean, standard deviation, and range are all impacted by non-normal data.

18. B: Correlation coefficients range from −1 to 1, with values close to −1 or 1 representing strong relationships. Thus, a correlation coefficient of 0.2 represents a weak correlation because it is close to 0 rather than 1.

19. B: The probability of mutually exclusive events A or B occurring may be written as $P(A \text{ or } B) = P(A) + P(B)$. The probability of obtaining a number greater than 5 is $\frac{3}{8}$ because 3 of the 8 sections are greater than 5 (6, 7, 8). The probability of obtaining a 2 is $\frac{1}{8}$ because this refers to 1 of the 8 sections. Thus, $P(A \text{ or } B) = \frac{3}{8} + \frac{1}{8}$ or $\frac{1}{2}$.

20. B: The events are dependent since the first marble was not replaced. The sample space of the second draw will decrease by 1 because there will be one less marble to choose from. The number of possible red marbles for the second draw will also decrease by 1. Thus, the probability may be written as $P(A \text{ and } B) = \frac{2}{10} \times \frac{1}{9}$. Thus, the probability Gitta draws a red marble, does not replace it, and draws another red marble is $\frac{2}{90}$ or $\frac{1}{45}$.

English Language Arts and Reading

1. B: Although the passage is not explicit about why Martin and Beth's relationship is strained, by eliminating all but one of the answer choices, we can easily find the right answer. Choice A can be eliminated because Martin has not lost his job—he receives a work-related page at the end of the passage. Choice B is not contradicted by the passage, but all that the reader is told is that Beth has forgiven Martin for "that thing with Mary." Choices C and D can be eliminated because Beth expects Martin to leave her, which would not be explained by his workload or movie preferences. The best choice, then, is B.

2. B: This question asks the reader to make a conclusion based on details from the passage. The reader knows that (1) Martin wears a pager for his job, (2) he has patients, and (3) one of his patients is going into cardiac arrest. Choices A and D can be eliminated because mechanics and film directors do not see patients. Choice C seems like a possibility. After all, dentists see patients. But choice B is the best choice because, if a person goes into cardiac arrest, it is more likely that a medical doctor rather than a dentist would be paged.

3. A: This question asks for the best definition of "rapport" in the passage. A rapport is a relationship based on mutual understanding. In light of this definition, Choice A is a good answer even though it is not an exact match. Choice B can be eliminated because it does not describe a relationship. Choice C can be eliminated because, though a rapport may involve a common goal, the word *rapport* itself does not imply "a common goal." Choice D can be eliminated because loneliness has nothing to do with the definition of *rapport*.

4. C: The passage centers around the couple's marital struggles and Beth's desire for renewed closeness. She was happy to take a walk with Martin and suggests another activity they could do together, hoping for "rapport." She doesn't seem to particularly care whether this is through a movie or something else, so choice A is incorrect. Martin doesn't seem to have any opinion on movies, positive or negative, so choice B is incorrect. Martin does offer to let Beth make the decision, but there is no evidence that they have been arguing over what to do, so choice D is incorrect.

5. D: Passage 1 explains the reasoning behind Daylight Saving Time, while Passage 2 does not mention it, so answer choice A is incorrect. Passage 2 states that DST causes complications, and Passage 1 does not dispute this, so answer choice B is incorrect. Both passages agree that sunlight has benefits, whether for health or business, so answer choice C is incorrect. Passage 1 states that DST may lead to reduced traffic fatalities because of the extra light, while Passage 2 states that the time change may be linked to increased traffic fatalities because of the lost sleep.

6. A: Passage 2 states that children need family time and time at home, but that sports come at a cost to this. On the other hand, Passage 1 states that sports provide an escape from a troubled home life for some children. Answer choice B is incorrect because Passage 1 is the one that states that sports have physical benefits. Answer choices C and D are assertions from Passage 2, but the author of Passage 1 is not likely to disagree with them.

7. B: It can be concluded that phonics is a more effective way to learn to read for two reasons. First, the passage states that literacy rates are lower now than they were 15 years ago, meaning that more people knew how to read 15 years ago. Then the passage states that phonics was the main way people learned how to read at the time. Based on these two facts, it can be concluded that phonics is more effective. Choice A is incorrect because it states the opposite. Choice C cannot be inferred from the passage, nor can choice D.

8. C: The passage states, "Shortly before becoming the president of the United States in 1789, Washington was an important leader in the American Revolutionary War from 1775 to 1783." Retiring (D) and returning to Mount Vernon (A) came after this. Washington being made commander-in-chief for the second time is the last event in the passage.

9. B: In describing the marketing of Sea-Monkeys, the author describes it as creative genius, and attributes their popularity to the drawings and advertisements that appeared in comic books. It is reasonable to conclude that without the (somewhat misleading) branding and ads, they wouldn't have been as popular. Marketing them under the less exciting name "brine shrimp" likely wouldn't have resulted in as many sales. The passage does not mention whether "Instant Life" or "Sea-Monkeys" was a more popular name (A). While the passage does mention "creative marketing" that showed drawings different from the actual creatures, it does not say that people thought they were buying actual monkeys (C). The passage states that Sea-Monkeys were "at the height of their popularity" in the 1970s, so it is unreasonable to think that more homes have them today (D).

10. C: Choice A is incorrect because the passage states they were similar in size. The cost of production is not mentioned, eliminating choice B as a possibility. Choice D is incorrect because it was the eight-track tape that was included in these vehicles. Choice C is correct because the passage states the eight-track tape could store and play twice as many songs.

11. B: The passage states that, "Often, a person with agoraphobia will view his or her home as the safest possible place to be, and the person may even be reluctant to leave the home at all," making B the correct choice. Being in the yard (A) or on the sidewalk (D) can be inferred as causing fear ("walking to the mailbox"). Being at the mall (C) also is listed as a possible cause of fear.

12. D: Choices B and C are only briefly mentioned, allowing them to be eliminated as possibilities. Although the passage does discuss what could happen to two balls released at the top of a mountain, that is not the purpose of the passage, so choice A can be eliminated. The purpose is to show how small differences (in this case two inches between two rubber balls) can have large effects. This is essentially what the butterfly effect is, and the purpose of the passage is to give an example to demonstrate this principle.

13. C: *Encourage* can have several meanings, such as "reassure" (A), but in context we can see that it means to promote or stimulate. Answer choice B is too strong a word; fiber assists with the growth of gut flora but cannot be said to cause it. Answer choice D is the opposite of the correct meaning.

14. A: *Strata* refers to the layers that archaeologists have found that contain artifacts from different time periods corresponding to the time periods associated with specific layers. The other answer choices are related to the topic but do not fit the definition.

15. B: The second sentence recommends that those who drink whole milk gradually switch to fat-free milk to lower the amount of saturated fat and calories they consume from milk. The other choices are mentioned in the passage but not as ways to lower saturated fat and calories.

16. A: The word order in answer choice A best conveys the meaning of the sentence concisely. Choice B is incorrect because "Nungesser and Coli" is a nonessential phrase and needs to be separated from the rest of the sentence with commas. Choice C inverts the order of the sentence and makes it more awkward; it is better to have a simple subject and verb at the beginning of a sentence. Choice D is incorrect because the word order confuses the sentence's meaning.

17. B: The first paragraph introduces the subject of flight and discusses how the war—and its end—affected pilots. Answer choice B fits best because it gives needed background: what war is being discussed and that the war was the reason so many people became pilots. Answer choices A and C are not useful because the Wright brothers were mentioned only to introduce the topic; the passage is not about them. Answer choice D would fit better in the second paragraph.

18. D: This answer choice uses the correct punctuation and verb tense. Choice A is incorrect because the conjunction *and* separates two independent clauses; when the conjunction is used in this way, a comma must come before it. Choice B is incorrect because there is no conjunction between the two independent clauses, making the answer choice a comma splice. Choice C is incorrect because the passage is written in the past tense but "says" is in the present tense.

19. A: This is the best answer choice because *in conclusion* is used for introducing concluding paragraphs. Choices B and D are incorrect. The words *furthermore* and *additionally* indicate that an additional argument will be made, but sentence 28 begins a concluding paragraph where no more arguments will be added. Choice C is incorrect because the word *therefore* should be used as a conclusion to a specific point rather than the conclusion of an entire essay.

20. B: The combination of *hardly* and *not* constitutes a double negative, so answer choices A and C are incorrect. Answer choice D is incorrect because "them" refers to some unknown objects rather than "Jason and his brother."

21. C: The plural demonstrative adjective *these* should be used with the plural noun *sorts*. Choices A and B make the noun singular in "sort," and choice D makes the demonstrative adjective singular in "this."

22. A: This sentence contains an appositive that gives extra information and is set off with commas. Therefore, the subject ("Mr. King,") and the predicate (beginning with "created") should be a complete sentence that makes sense without the portion set off by commas. Choice B adds "he," which is not grammatically correct because "Mr. King" is already the subject. Choice C omits the second comma, not setting off the nonessential phrase "an individual of considerable influence." Choice D changes the meaning by saying that Mr. King literally gave his fortune to the community, but "give back" in the original simply means he contributed to the community in some way.

23. A: In this sentence, *whose* is the appropriate possessive pronoun to modify *opinion*. Choices B and D are grammatically correct, but they are awkward and change the meaning. Choice C combines two independent clauses with no punctuation, so it is incorrect.

24. B: Answer choice B is a clear and efficient revision. Answer choice A keeps the meaning but is awkward. Answer choice C uses "making," which would be a noun or a participle rather than the necessary verb form *make*. Answer choice D would put the word *work* into the sentence twice. It is not grammatically incorrect and has a similar meaning, but the repetition of *work* is awkward.

25. C: As written, the sentence is a fragment because it has no verb. Only answer choice C adds a verb to make a complete sentence.

26. A: The second part of the sentence adds contrasting information to the first, so the conjunction at the beginning of the first clause needs to reflect this. Answer choices B and C use words that signify agreeing information rather than contrasting information, so they do not fit. Also, choice C is an adverb, not a conjunction, so it does not fit grammatically. Answer choice D signifies a contrast, but like choice C it does not fit grammatically.

27. B: The original sentence uses a nonessential participle clause to modify the subject "reading," but then uses another noun, "libraries," which is grammatically incorrect. Choice B correctly turns the participle clause into a dependent clause. Choice C would correctly use a participle, but it leaves an awkward wording that confuses the meaning. Choice D, like choice A, leaves the original sentence with two nouns instead of one subject.

28. D: In choices A and B, "thus" is unnecessary and incorrect, especially because it is combined with "although," so these choices are incorrect. The first clause is not a complete sentence, so it cannot be separated as in answer choice C. Answer choice D correctly combines the dependent and independent clauses with a comma and eliminates "thus."

29. B: As written, the sentence has a dangling participle. The implied subject of "waiting" in the first clause is Juliet, not the apple, so Juliet needs to be mentioned first in the main clause, followed by "apple" as the object. Thus answer choices A and D are incorrect. Answer choice C is incorrect because it lacks a verb.

30. C: The subject ("motorcycles") is plural, so the rest of the sentence needs to match. Only answer choice C uses "their" to signify the plural nature; each of the other answer choices uses a singular pronoun. Additionally, answer choice B incorrectly uses "it's," which is a contraction of *it is*, not the possessive form *its*.

TSI Practice Test #5

Math

1. Which of the following graphs represents the inequality $-2 < x \leq 4$?

A.
-3 -2 -1 0 1 2 3 4 5

B.
-3 -2 -1 0 1 2 3 4 5

C.
-3 -2 -1 0 1 2 3 4 5

D.
-3 -2 -1 0 1 2 3 4 5

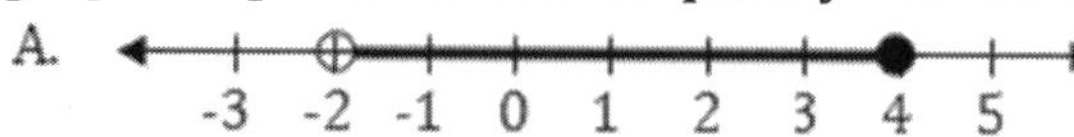

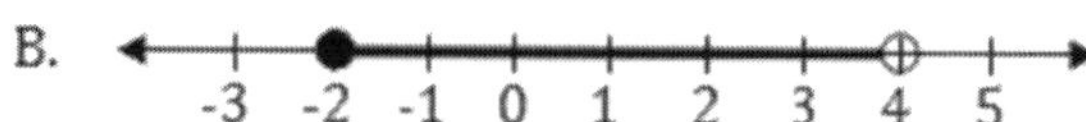

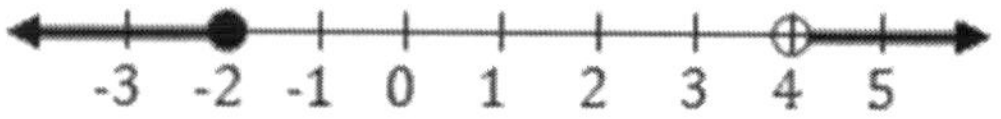

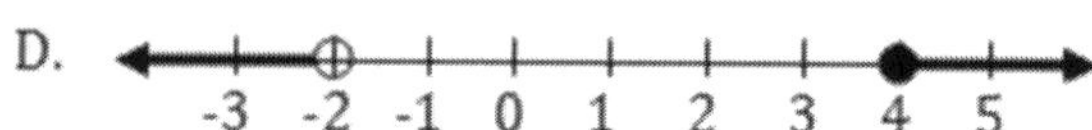

2. Which of the following is equivalent to $3 - 2x < 5$?

A. $x < 1$
B. $x > 1$
C. $x < -1$
D. $x > -1$

3. An exam has 30 questions. A student gets 1 point for each correctly answered question and loses $\frac{1}{2}$ point for each incorrectly answered question. The student neither gains nor loses any points for a question left blank. If C is the number of questions a student gets right and B is the number of questions the student leaves blank, which of the following represents the student's score on the exam?

A. $C - \frac{1}{2}B$
B. $C - \frac{1}{2}(30 - B)$
C. $C - \frac{1}{2}(30 - B - C)$
D. $(30 - C) - \frac{1}{2}(30 - B)$

4. Every person attending a meeting hands out a business card to every other person at the meeting. If a total of 30 cards are handed out, how many people are at the meeting?

A. 5
B. 6
C. 10
D. 15

5. Which of the following is equal to this expression: $x(y - 2) + y(3 - x)$?

A. $xy + y$
B. $-2x + 3y$
C. $2xy - 2x + 3y$
D. $xy + 3y - x - 2$

6. At a school carnival, three students spend an average of $10. Six other students spend an average of $4. What is the average amount of money spent by all nine students?

A. $5
B. $6
C. $7
D. $8

7. The formula for finding the volume of a cone is $V = \frac{1}{3}\pi r^2 h$. Which of the following equations is correctly solved for *r*?

A. $r = \frac{1}{3}\pi h$
B. $r = \sqrt{\frac{3V}{\pi h}}$
C. $r = \frac{3V}{\pi h}$
D. $r = V - \frac{1}{3}\pi h$

8. Given the equation: $\frac{2}{x+4} = \frac{3}{x}$, what is the value of *x*?

A. 10
B. 12
C. −12
D. −14

9. What is the solution to the equation: $4\sqrt{x} + 8 = 24$?

A. $x = 2$
B. $x = 4$
C. $x = 12$
D. $x = 16$

10. Which of the following represents the solution to the following system of linear equations:

$$5x + 9y = -7$$
$$2x - 4y = 20$$

A. $x = 3, y = 2$
B. $x = 4, y = 3$
C. $x = 4, y = -3$
D. $x = 3, y = -2$

11. Michaela can finish 3 problems in 10 minutes. How many problems can she complete in 3 hours?

A. 90
B. 54
C. 18
D. 9

12. In the figure pictured below, find the value of x:

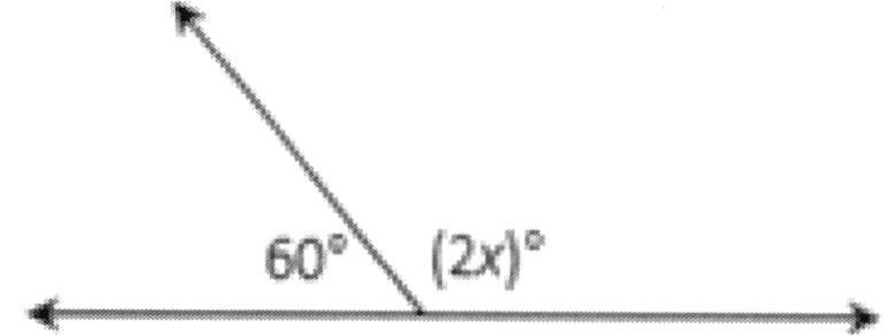

A. 30
B. 60
C. 100
D. 120

13. If 120 customers purchased coffee today, and this is $\frac{1}{4}$ less than yesterday, how many people purchased coffee yesterday?

A. 90
B. 150
C. 160
D. 240

14. What is the slope of the line described by the equation $5 - 3y = 2x + 8$?

A. $-\frac{2}{3}$
B. $\frac{2}{3}$
C. 2
D. -1

15. Examine the triangles below:

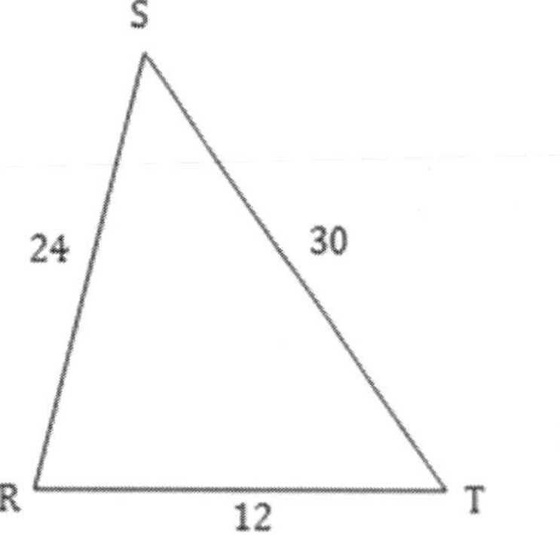

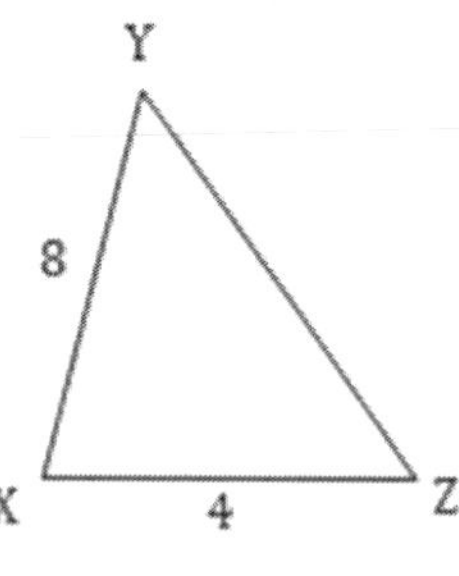

In order for ΔRST to be similar to ΔXYZ, what must the length of $\overline{YZ}$ be?

A. 10
B. 14
C. 15
D. 22

16. Two hikers start at a ranger station and leave at the same time. One hiker heads due west at 3 miles/hour. The other hiker heads due north at 4 miles/hour. How far apart are the hikers after 2 hours of hiking?

A. 5 miles
B. 7 miles
C. 10 miles
D. 14 miles

17. Which frequency table is represented by the histogram shown below?

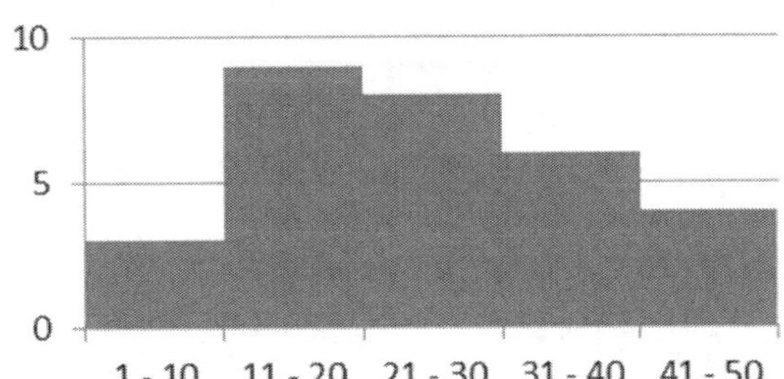

A.

Interval	Frequency
1 – 10	3
11 – 20	9
21 – 30	8
31 – 40	6
41 – 50	4

B.

Interval	Frequency
1 – 10	3
11 – 20	8
21 – 30	8
31 – 40	6
41 – 50	3

C.

Interval	Frequency
1 – 10	3
11 – 20	9
21 – 30	8
31 – 40	5
41 – 50	4

D.

Interval	Frequency
1 – 10	2
11 – 20	9
21 – 30	8
31 – 40	6
41 – 50	4

18. Abram rolls a 6-sided die with each side labeled 1–6. What is the probability he rolls an even number or a number greater than 4?

A. $\frac{2}{3}$
B. $\frac{1}{6}$
C. $\frac{3}{4}$
D. $\frac{5}{6}$

19. What is the expected value of spinning a spinner with 10 equally spaced sections labeled 1–10?

A. 4.5
B. 5
C. 5.5
D. 6

20. Amanda rolls a 6-sided die. She will lose $6 if the die lands on 3 or 5. She will win $3 if the die lands on 1 or 2. She will lose $9 if the die lands on 4 or 6. What is the expected value?

A. −$2
B. −$4
C. −$5
D. −$6

English Language Arts and Reading

For questions 1–15, read each passage and then choose the best answer to the accompanying questions. Answer the questions on the basis of what is stated or implied in the passage(s).

This passage is adapted from H. G. Wells, The Invisible Man, *originally published in 1897.*

(1) The stranger came early in February, one wintry day, through a biting wind and a driving snow, the last snowfall of the year, over the down, walking from Bramblehurst railway station, and carrying a little black portmanteau in his thickly gloved hand. (2) He was wrapped up from head to foot, and the brim of his soft felt hat hid every inch of his face but the shiny tip of his nose; the snow had piled itself against his shoulders and chest, and added a white crest to the burden he carried. (3) He staggered into the "Coach and Horses" more dead than alive, and flung his portmanteau down. (4) "A fire," he cried, "in the name of human charity! (5) A room and a fire!" (6) He stamped and shook the snow from off himself in the bar, and followed Mrs. Hall into her guest parlour to strike his bargain. (7) And with that much introduction, that and a couple of sovereigns flung upon the table, he took up his quarters in the inn.

(8) Mrs. Hall lit the fire and left him there while she went to prepare him a meal with her own hands. (9) A guest to stop at Iping in the wintertime was an unheard-of piece of luck, let alone a guest who was no "haggler," and she was resolved to show herself worthy of her good fortune. (10) As soon as the bacon was well under way, and Millie, her lymphatic maid, had been brisked up a bit by a few deftly chosen expressions of contempt, she carried the cloth, plates, and glasses into the parlour and began to lay them with the utmost éclat. (11) Although the fire was burning up briskly, she was surprised to see that her visitor still wore his hat and coat, standing with his back to her and staring out of the window at the falling snow in the yard. (12) His gloved hands were clasped behind him, and he seemed to be lost in thought. (13) She noticed that the melting snow that still sprinkled his shoulders dripped upon her carpet. (14) "Can I take your hat and coat, sir?" she said, "and give them a good dry in the kitchen?"

(15) "No," he said without turning.

(16) She was not sure she had heard him, and was about to repeat her question.

(17) He turned his head and looked at her over his shoulder. (18) "I prefer to keep them on," he said with emphasis, and she noticed that he wore big blue spectacles with sidelights, and had a bush side-whisker over his coat-collar that completely hid his cheeks and face.

(19) "Very well, sir," she said. (20) "As you like. In a bit the room will be warmer."

(21) He made no answer, and had turned his face away from her again, and Mrs. Hall, feeling that her conversational advances were ill-timed, laid the rest of the table things in a quick staccato and whisked out of the room. (22) When she returned he was still standing there, like a man of stone, his back hunched, his collar turned up, his dripping hat-brim turned down, hiding his face and ears completely.

1. What can be deduced about the stranger from his interaction with Mrs. Hall?

A. He is emotionless and has difficulty engaging in conversation.
B. He is ill or injured, and thus it is physically painful for him to speak.
C. He is extremely shy and attempts to avoid human interaction whenever possible.
D. He is trying to hide something and thus attempting to discourage conversation.

2. As used in sentence 10, the word "lymphatic" most nearly means

A. Sluggish
B. Sloppy
C. Stingy
D. Sullen

3. Why does the author emphasize that Mrs. Hall prepares the stranger's meal "with her own hands" (sentence 8)?

A. To show that she ran a humble business and served all the patrons herself
B. To show that his business was important to her, so she was making sure the food was prepared correctly
C. To show that she was a hardworking businesswoman, not merely an innkeeper
D. To show that she was capable and skilled, and deserving of more respect than the stranger offered

4. Based on context, what underlying reason might Mrs. Hall have in asking to take the guest's coat and hat in sentence 14?

A. She wants him to be as comfortable as possible.
B. She wants to know what he looked like.
C. She wants to protect her carpet from the moisture.
D. She wants to check the pockets for loose change.

Use these two passages to answer the question that follows:

Passage 1

Working from home has changed American business. The advantages are nearly endless. Overhead is less without the need for business offices. Employees are happier because they can be more comfortable in their own homes and save time and gas money spent on commuting—and happy employees are more productive. Pollution drops as fewer people are on the road. Tasks can be completed efficiently without the distractions of workplace gossip and drama. And thanks to technology, employees can be available at a moment's notice not only to their employers but to clients as well, so there is really no need to gather in person. Remote work is the future of business ... and a bright future it is.

Passage 2

Working from home has changed American business. Due to technological advances, more and more people have moved operations to their own homes. While much of the work can still be completed, this is not a good long-term solution. Online meetings (which are often rife with technological difficulties) cannot replace the camaraderie and creative sharing of in-person meetings that result in new ideas and a motivated team. Working from home means navigating the challenges of sharing a workspace with family members, resulting in interruptions and other distractions, not to mention the lack of accountability. Motivation is lowered when employees are working outside the office dynamics. It simply does not work for a team to be remote permanently.

5. Which of the following points would the authors of both passages likely agree with?

A. Employees appreciate being able to be at home where they are more comfortable.
B. It is difficult to truly relate to coworkers and clients when all meetings take place online.
C. Technology has made it possible to complete more tasks remotely than previously could be.
D. Remote work has been challenging to implement, but many companies are now reaping the rewards.

Use these two passages to answer the question that follows:

Passage 1

Gardening offers an excellent way to lower your grocery bill. Additionally, you can increase your nutritional intake by eating fresh produce, not fruits and veggies that have been shipped to stores to sit on shelves for days or weeks. You can avoid all the pesticides and preservatives by growing your own food. While some crops may be finicky, many are easy to grow, even if you have zero experience. A little effort and a small space—you can even garden in pots if you don't have a yard—can yield amazing benefits!

Passage 2

While many enjoy the hobby of gardening, keep in mind that it is just that: a hobby. After paying for seeds (or plants), fertilizer, and the myriad of other gardening necessities, you are not going to save money on your grocery bill. Further, if you don't use a pesticide, your "organic" garden will be a feast for insects, not for you. Even if you buy all the supplies and spray for pests, there's no guarantee that your garden won't fail, because plants are finicky. But for those who want a challenge and are willing to work hard, gardening can be a rewarding hobby. It can be therapeutic to work the ground and satisfying to see the results.

6. The author of Passage 2 would probably say that the author of Passage 1

A. Does not accurately convey the challenges of gardening
B. Is overly pessimistic concerning gardening
C. Has never planted a garden before
D. Has an unusual talent for gardening

7. Consider the following passage:

> Wells provide water for drinking, bathing, and cleaning to many people across the world. When wells are being dug, there are several issues that must be taken into account to minimize the chance of potential problems down the road. First, it's important to be aware that groundwater levels differ depending on the season. In general, groundwater levels will be higher during the winter. So if a well is being dug during the winter, it should be deep enough to remain functional during the summer, when water levels are lower. Well water that is used is replaced by melting snow and rain. If the well owners are using the water faster than it can be replaced, however, the water levels will be lowered. The only way to remedy this, aside from waiting for the groundwater to be replenished naturally, is to deepen the well.

What can be concluded from this passage?

A. It is better to have a well that is too deep than one that is too shallow.
B. Most well owners will face significant water shortages every year.
C. Most people who dig wells during the winter do not make them deep enough.
D. Well water is safe to use for bathing and cleaning but is not suitable for drinking.

8. Consider the following passage:

Today's low-fat craze has led many people to assume that all fats are unhealthy, but this is simply not the case. Fat is an essential component of any healthy diet because it provides energy and helps the body process nutrients. While all fats should be consumed in moderation, there are good and bad fats. Good fats are what are known as unsaturated fats. They are found in olive oil, fatty fish like salmon, and nuts. Bad fats are saturated and trans fats. They are found in foods like butter, bacon, and ice cream. Consumption of foods that contain trans or saturated fats should be restricted or avoided altogether.

What is the main purpose of this passage?

A. To explain why fat is important for the body
B. To discuss some of the main sources of good fats
C. To talk about the different types of fats
D. To discuss examples of foods that should be avoided

9. Consider the following passage:

Satire is a genre that originated in the ancient world and is still popular today. Although satire is often humorous, its purposes and intentions go well beyond simply making people laugh. Satire is a way for a playwright, author, or other artist to criticize society, human nature, and individuals that he or she holds in contempt. Satire as we know it today developed in ancient Greece and Rome. There were three main types. One type, Menippean satire, focused on criticizing aspects of human nature. This was done by introducing stereotypical, one-dimensional characters. Horatian satire can be viewed as gentle satire. It made fun of people and their habits but in a way that was not offensive. Juvenalian satire was written is such a way that the audience would experience feelings of disgust and aversion when they saw the characters and their actions. Some of the most popular satires today are fake news shows, like the *Daily Show* and the *Colbert Report*, and satirical comic strips like *Doonesbury*.

As used in the eighth sentence, "gentle" most nearly means

A. Careful not to break
B. Not angry
C. Chivalrous
D. Not harsh

10. Consider the following passage:

Many people believe that how we express our feelings is mainly determined by our upbringing and culture. Undoubtedly, this is true in some cases. In North America, for example, it is customary to shake hands when we meet somebody to express acceptance, whereas in other countries it may be customary to bow slightly. Many feelings, however, are expressed in similar ways by people all over the world. These emotions include fear, anger, happiness, disgust, and sorrow. For example, if a person is experiencing fear, his or her eyes will widen and the pupils will dilate. This reaction is largely involuntary. The finding that people express many feelings in a similar manner, regardless of where they are from, indicates that facial expressions are influenced more by evolution than culture.

What can be concluded from this passage?

A. People often cannot hide what they are feeling.
B. People from other parts of the world express happiness differently.
C. Fear is the only emotion that is felt by everybody in the world.
D. Acceptance is a feeling invented by humans.

11. Consider the following passage:

Cities are typically warmer than the surrounding countryside, a phenomenon known as the "heat island effect." There are numerous causes of this phenomenon, including emissions from cars and buildings, which create a mini greenhouse effect. In rural areas, the standing water in marshes and ponds evaporates, which cools the air slightly. This does not occur to the same extent in the city. The tall buildings in the center of most cities block winds that would provide some relief from the excessive heat. Finally, the colors and materials of most roads and buildings absorb rather than reflect heat. Although planting trees and using building materials that reflect heat may alleviate the problem somewhat, it will by no means eliminate it.

What is the main purpose of this passage?

A. To talk about how the problem of heat islands can be solved
B. To argue that cities should make an effort to plant more trees
C. To present the major causes of the problem of heat islands
D. To contrast the city environment to that of the countryside

12. Consider the following passage:

Marsupials resemble mammals in a number of ways. For one thing, they are warm-blooded creatures. They have hair, and the mothers feed their young by producing milk. However, one thing that separates marsupials from mammals is that marsupials' young are born when they are not yet fully developed. Most are born after only about four or five weeks. They finish their development in the pouch of their mother. Some of the more commonly known marsupials are koalas, kangaroos, and opossums. They are a diverse group, with many members having little in common besides their reproductive traits.

Which of the following describes a major difference between marsupials and mammals?

A. Marsupials have hair, while mammals do not.
B. Mammals are a much more diverse group than marsupials.
C. Marsupials are born at an earlier stage of development.
D. Mammals feed their young by producing milk.

13. Consider the following passage:

Grapes are one of the oldest cultivated fruits. Hieroglyphics show that Egyptians were involved in grape and wine production. Also, the early Romans were known to have developed many grape varieties. Grapes have been grown in California for more than 200 years. Its tradition of viticulture (growing grapes) began in 1769 when Spanish friars established missions throughout the state. The boom in grapes planted for eating arose in the early 1800s. William Wolfskill, founder of California's citrus industry, planted the first table grape vineyard in 1839 near Los Angeles. By the 1850s, the United States had officially acquired California from Mexico, and 80,000 gold prospectors had moved to the region, a few of them realizing that there was money in grapes as well as in gold.

What is the primary topic of the passage?

A. How Egyptians grew wine grapes
B. How grapes were used in ancient times
C. William Wolfskill's life as a farmer
D. The history of growing grapes in California

14. Consider the following passage:

Most scientists agree that while the scientific method is an invaluable methodological tool, it is not a perfect method for arriving at objectively true universals. A scientist may be interested in demonstrating that all members of a given category *x* are also members of a given category *y*. However, a hypothesis of the form "all *x* are also *y*" cannot be proven true by observing instances of x and demonstrating that they are also y because it is possible that at some point in the past, there existed an *x* that was not *y*, or that at some point in the future, there will exist an *x* that is not *y*. It is expected that there may be rare "disconfirming" occurrences since the hypothesis is only stated as a likelihood rather than a certainty. Thus scientific hypotheses are frequently confirmed as probabilities rather than universal truths.

As used in the second-to-last sentence, "disconfirming" most nearly means

A. Proving
B. Dissipating
C. Distilling
D. Disproving

15. Consider the following passage:

Harriet Tubman was a runaway slave from Maryland who became known as the "Moses of her people." Over the course of 10 years, and at great personal risk, she led hundreds of slaves to freedom along the Underground Railroad, a secret network of safehouses where runaway slaves could stay on their journey north to freedom. During the Civil War, she was a spy for the federal forces in South Carolina, as well as a nurse. She later became a leader in the abolitionist movement.

What is the primary topic of the passage?

A. Slaves in the Civil War
B. How slaves escaped along the Underground Railroad
C. Harriet Tubman's actions as an abolitionist
D. Harriet Tubman's life history

For questions 16–19, read the following early draft of an essay and then choose the best answer to the question or the best completion of the statement.

(1) I had the same teacher for both third and fourth grades, which were difficult years for me. (2) My teacher and I did not get along, and I don't think she liked me. (3) Every day, I thought she was treating me unfairly and being mean. (4) Because I felt that way, I acted out and stopped doing my work. (5) In the middle of fourth grade, my family moved to a new town, and I had Mr. Shanbourne as my new teacher.

(6) From the very first day in Mr. Shanbourne's class, I was on guard. (7) I was expecting to hate my teacher and for him to hate me back when I started his class. (8) Mr. Shanbourne took me by surprise right away when he asked me if I wanted to stand up and introduce myself. (9) I said no, probably in a surly voice, and he just nodded and began teaching the first lesson of the day.

(10) I wasn't sure how to take this. (11) My old teacher forced me to do things and gave me detention if I didn't. (12) He obviously didn't believe in detention, and I tried him! (13) During my first two weeks at my new school I did my best to get in trouble. (14) I zoned out in class, turned work in late, talked during lectures, and handed in assignments after the due date. (15) Mr. Shanbourne just nodded.

(16) Finally one day Mr. Shanbourne asked me to stay in during recess. (17) *This is it*, I thought—I was going to get in trouble, get the detention my ten-year-old self had practically been begging for. (18) After all of the other kids ran outside, I walked up to Mr. Shanbourne's desk.

(19) "How are you doing, Alberto?" he said.

(20) I mumbled something.

(21) He told me he was disappointed in my behavior over the last two weeks. (22) I had expected this and just took it, waiting for detention. (23) Then Mr. Shanbourne took me by surprise. (24) He told me that even though he didn't know me very well, he believed I could be a hard worker and that I could be successful in his class. (25) He asked me how he could help me listen better and turn my work in on time.

(26) I told him I had to think about it and rushed out to recess. (27) My answer may have seemed rude, but I was stunned. (28) I hadn't had a teacher in years who seemed to care about me and said he believed in my abilities. (29) I'll never forget how Mr. Shanbourne helped me, and I hope he'll never forget me either.

16. What is the most effective way to revise sentence 7 (reproduced below)?

I was expecting to hate my teacher and for him to hate me back when I started his class.

A. I started his class expecting my teacher to hate me back and for me to hate him.
B. Expecting to hate my teacher, I started his class expecting him to hate me back.
C. Starting his class expecting to hate my teacher, I also expected to hate him back.
D. I started his class expecting to hate my teacher and for him to hate me back.

17. What is the most effective way to combine sentences 10 and 11 (reproduced below)?

I wasn't sure how to take this. My old teacher forced me to do things and gave me detention if I didn't.

A. I wasn't sure how to take this, and my old teacher forced me to do things and gave me detention if I didn't.
B. I wasn't sure how to take this, although my old teacher forced me to do things and gave me detention if I didn't.
C. I wasn't sure how to take this because my old teacher forced me to do things and gave me detention if I didn't.
D. I wasn't sure how to take this as a result of my old teacher forced me to do things and gave me detention if I didn't.

18. In sentence 12, "he" should be replaced with which of the following to be more clear?

A. My old teacher
B. Mr. Shanbourne
C. Alberto
D. My classmate

19. Which phrase, if any, can be deleted from sentence 14 (reproduced below) without changing the meaning of the sentence?

I zoned out in class, turned work in late, talked during lectures, and handed in assignments after the due date

A. zoned out in class
B. turned work in late
C. talked out in class
D. No change

For questions 20–30, select the best version of the underlined part of the sentence. If you think the original sentence is best, choose the first answer.

20. Several theories <u>about what caused dinosaurs to have extinction exist</u>, but scientists are still unable to reach a concrete conclusion.

A. about what caused dinosaurs to have extinction exist
B. about what caused dinosaurs to become extinct exist
C. about the causes of the dinosaur extinction exists
D. in regards to the extinction cause of dinosaurs exist

21. <u>Although most persons</u> prefer traditional pets, like cats and dogs, others gravitate towards exotic animals, like snakes and lizards.

A. Although most persons
B. Because most people
C. While most people
D. Maybe some persons

22. It is important that software companies offer tech support <u>to customers who are encountering problems</u>.

A. to customers who are encountering problems
B. because not all customers encounter problems
C. with customers who encounter problems
D. to customer who is encountering difficulties

23. The fact <u>that children eat high-fat diets and watch excessive amount of television are a cause of concern</u> for many parents.

A. that children eat high-fat diets and watch excessive amount of television are a cause of concern
B. the children eat high-fat diets and watches excessive amount of television are a cause of concern
C. is children eat high-fat diets and watch excessive amount of television is a cause for concern
D. that children eat high-fat diets and watch excessive amounts of television is a cause for concern

24. <u>Contrarily to popular beliefs</u>, bats do not actually entangle themselves in the hair of humans on purpose.

A. Contrarily to popular beliefs
B. Contrary to popular belief
C. Contrary to popularity belief
D. Contrary to popular believing

25. Mitosis is the process of cell <u>division; if there are</u> errors during this process, it can result in serious complications.

A. division; if there are
B. division; however if there are
C. division but if, there are
D. division. However if there are

26. After months of struggling with the decision, <u>biology was finally chosen as Sharon's major</u>.

A. biology was finally chosen as Sharon's major
B. Sharon was finally chosen as a biology major
C. biology as Sharon's major was finally chosen
D. Sharon finally chose biology as her major

27. Small business owners must compete with larger stores by providing excellent service, because department store prices are simply too low <u>for him to match</u>.

A. for him to match
B. for him, matching
C. for them to match
D. for them, matching

28. Ants are fascinating creatures, <u>although</u> some of their unique characteristics are their strength, organizational skills, and construction abilities.

A. although
B. but
C. while
D. and

29. <u>At the book club meeting on Thursday afternoon</u>, the book club decided on their next biography.

A. At the book club meeting on Thursday afternoon
B. At their meeting on Thursday afternoon
C. At the meeting for the book club on Thursday afternoon
D. On Thursday afternoon, at the book club meeting

30. *The Fir Wood*, <u>being the first book in the series</u>, has sold more copies than any of the author's other works.

A. being the first book in the series
B. it is the first book in the series
C. the first book in the series
D. that is the first book in the series

Essay

In the United States, congressional elections are decided by majority vote, with the candidate who receives over 50 percent of the vote winning the entire seat. However, in many other countries, the election system is proportional, with parties receiving a particular number of seats based on the percentage of the vote they receive. Please write a multiple-paragraph persuasive essay (approximately 350–500 words) discussing which system you believe to be better and why.

Answers and Explanations for Test #5

Math

1. A: When graphing an inequality, a solid circle at an endpoint means that the number at that endpoint is included in the range, while a hollow circle means it is not. Since the inequality says that x is strictly greater than –2, the circle at –2 should be hollow; since the inequality says that x is less than or equal to 4, the circle at 4 should be solid. $-2 < x \leq 4$ indicates that x is between –2 and 4, so the area between the circles should be shaded.

2. D: To simplify the inequality $3 - 2x < 5$, we can first subtract 3 from both sides: $3 - 2x - 3 < 5 - 3 \Rightarrow -2x < 2$. Now we can divide both sides of the inequality by -2. When an inequality is multiplied or divided by a negative number, its direction changes ($<$ becomes $>$, $\leq$ becomes $\geq$, and vice versa). So $-2x < 2$ becomes $\frac{-2x}{-2} > \frac{2}{-2}$, or $x > -1$.

3. C: If the exam has 30 questions, and the student answered C questions correctly and left B questions blank, then the number of questions the student answered incorrectly must be $30 - B - C$. The student gets 1 point for each correct question, or $1 \times C = C$ points, and loses $\frac{1}{2}$ point for each incorrect question, or $\frac{1}{2}(30 - B - C)$ points. Since the blank questions do not affect the student's score, one way to express his total score is $C - \frac{1}{2}(30 - B - C)$.

4. B: Call the number of people present at the meeting x. If each person hands out a card to every other person (that is, every person besides himself), then each person hands out $x - 1$ cards. The total number of cards handed out is therefore $x(x - 1)$. Since we are told there are a total of 30 cards handed out, we have the equation $x(x - 1) = 30$, which we can rewrite as the quadratic equation $x^2 - x - 30 = 0$. We can solve this equation by factoring the quadratic expression. One way to do this is to find two numbers that add up to the coefficient of x (in this case -1) and that multiply to the constant term (in this case -30). Those two numbers are 5 and -6. Our factored equation is therefore $(x + 5)(x - 6) = 0$. To make the equation true, one or both of the factors must be zero: either $x + 5 = 0$, in which case $x = -5$, or $x - 6 = 0$, in which case $x = 6$. Obviously, the number of people at the meeting cannot be negative, so the second solution, $x = 6$, must be correct.

5. B: First, let's distribute the x and y that are outside the parentheses and then combine like terms:

$$\begin{aligned} x(y - 2) + y(3 - x) &= (xy - 2x) + (3y - xy) \\ &= -2x + 3y + xy - xy \\ &= -2x + 3y \end{aligned}$$

6. B: The average is the total amount spent divided by the number of students. The first three students spend an average of \$10, so the total amount they spend is $3 \times \$10 = \$30$. The other six students spend an average of \$4, so the total amount they spend is $6 \times \$4 = \$24$. The total amount spent by all nine students is $\$30 + \$24 = \$54$, and the average amount they spend is $\$54 \div 9 = \$6$.

7. B: Dividing both sides of the equation by $\frac{1}{3}\pi h$ gives $r^2 = \frac{V}{\frac{1}{3}\pi h} = \frac{3V}{\pi h}$. We can then solve for r by taking the square root of both sides, which gives us $r = \sqrt{\frac{3V}{\pi h}}$.

8. C: We can cross-multiply to obtain: $2x = 3(x + 4)$ or $2x = 3x + 12$. Solving for x gives $x = -12$.

9. D: The radical equation may be solved by first subtracting 8 from both sides of the equation. Doing so gives $4\sqrt{x} = 16$. Dividing both sides of the equation by 4 gives $\sqrt{x} = 4$. Squaring both sides gives $x = 16$.

10. C: Using the method of elimination to solve the system of linear equations, each term in the top equation may be multiplied by −2, while each term in the bottom equation may be multiplied by 5. Doing so produces two new equations with x-terms that will add to 0. The sum of $-10x - 18y = 14$ and $10x - 20y = 100$ may be written as $-38y = 114$, so $y = -3$. When we substitute the y-value of −3 into the top, the original equation gives $5x + 9(-3) = -7$. Solving for x gives $x = 4$. Thus, the solution is $x = 4, y = -3$.

11. B: We need to find how many problems Michaela can finish in 3 hours, so we start with converting the 3 hours to minutes. Because 1 hour is 60 minutes, 3 hours is $3(60) = 180$ minutes. We can set up a ratio: $\frac{3\ problems}{10\ minutes} = \frac{x\ problems}{180\ minutes}$. To solve for x, we cross-multiply and divide: $10x = 3(180)$, so $x = \frac{3(180)}{10} = 54$.

12. B: Angles that form a straight line add up to 180 degrees. Such angles are sometimes referred to as being "supplementary."

$$60 + 2x = 180$$
$$2x = 120$$
$$x = 60$$

13. C: If 120 is $\frac{1}{4}$ less than yesterday's number, we can write this as: $120 = y - \frac{1}{4}y$, where y is yesterday's number. We combine terms on the right to solve: $120 = \frac{3}{4}y$, so $y = 120\left(\frac{4}{3}\right) = 160$.

14. A: The slope is the variable in front of the x when the equation is in the following form: $y = mx + b$. We rewrite the equation $5 - 3y = 2x + 8$ by subtracting 5 from both sides and then dividing both sides by −3: $\frac{-3y}{-3} = \frac{2x+8-5}{-3} \rightarrow y = -\frac{2}{3}x - 1$. The slope is the number in front of the x, which is $-\frac{2}{3}$.

15. A: If two triangles are similar, then all pairs of corresponding sides are proportional. For ΔRST to be similar to ΔXYZ, we need $\frac{RS}{XY} = \frac{RT}{XZ} = \frac{ST}{YZ}$. Substituting the numbers from the figure in for those values gives $\frac{24}{8} = \frac{12}{4} = \frac{30}{YZ}$. Simplifying the fractions results in $\frac{3}{1} = \frac{3}{1} = \frac{30}{YZ}$. Therefore, in order for the triangles to be similar, we need $\frac{3}{1} = \frac{30}{YZ}$. After cross-multiplying the terms, it becomes $3(YZ) = 30(1)$, so $3(YZ) = 30$. Divide both sides by 3 to get $YZ = 10$.

16. C: Hiking due west at 3 miles/hour, the first hiker will have gone 6 miles after 2 hours. Hiking due north at 4 miles/hour, the second hiker will have gone 8 miles after 2 hours. Since one hiker headed west and the other headed north, their distance from each other can be drawn as:

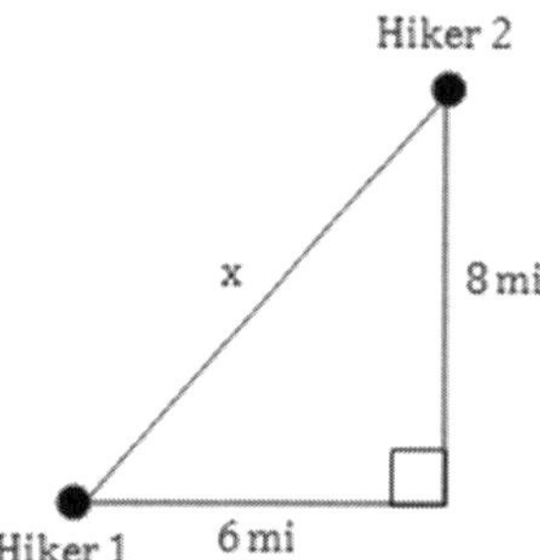

Since the distance between the two hikers is the hypotenuse of a right triangle, and since we know the lengths of the two legs of the right triangle, we can use the Pythagorean theorem $(a^2 + b^2 = c^2)$ to find the value of x. Therefore, $6^2 + 8^2 = x^2 \Rightarrow 36 + 64 = x^2 \Rightarrow 100 = x^2 \Rightarrow 10 = x$.

17. A: The frequency table in choice A correctly shows the frequencies represented by the histogram. The frequencies of values falling between 1 and 10 is 3, between 11 and 20 is 9, between 21 and 30 is 8, between 31 and 40 is 6, and between 41 and 50 is 4.

18. A: The probability of non-mutually exclusive events A and B occurring may be written as $P(A \text{ or } B) = P(A) + P(B) - P(A \text{ and } B)$. There are 3 even numbers on the die, so the probability of rolling an even number is $\frac{3}{6}$. There are 2 numbers greater than 4, so this probability is $\frac{2}{6}$. There is 1 number, 6, that is both even and greater than 4, so this probability is $\frac{1}{6}$. Thus, $P(A \text{ or } B) = \frac{3}{6} + \frac{2}{6} - \frac{1}{6} = \frac{2}{3}$.

19. C: The expected value is equal to the sum of a series of products, each of which is the product of a number's value and the probability of rolling that number. Thus, the expected value is $\left(1 \times \frac{1}{10}\right) + \left(2 \times \frac{1}{10}\right) + \left(3 \times \frac{1}{10}\right) + \left(4 \times \frac{1}{10}\right) + \left(5 \times \frac{1}{10}\right) + \left(6 \times \frac{1}{10}\right) + \left(7 \times \frac{1}{10}\right) + \left(8 \times \frac{1}{10}\right) + \left(9 \times \frac{1}{10}\right) + \left(10 \times \frac{1}{10}\right)$. The expected value is 5.5.

20. B: The expected value is equal to the sum of the products of the probabilities and the amount Amanda will lose or win. Each probability is equal to $\frac{2}{6}$. Thus, the expected value may be written as $\left(-6 \times \frac{2}{6}\right) + \left(3 \times \frac{2}{6}\right) + \left(-9 \times \frac{2}{6}\right)$. Thus, the expected value is –$4.

English Language Arts and Reading

1. D: The stranger makes a clear effort to keep conversation to a minimum. He does not haggle over the price, and he gives short responses—or none at all—to Mrs. Hall's questions. Additionally, he keeps his hat and coat on, hiding any view of his body from her. The reader can infer that he is being secretive and intentionally cutting conversation short for this purpose. We cannot suppose he is emotionless (A) after his impassioned opening remarks (sentences 4 and 5). There is no evidence that speech is physically painful (B) or that he is painfully shy (C).

2. A: The word *lymphatic* is an adjective that is used to mean "sluggish" or "lacking energy." Though it is not a common term today, we can infer the meaning from context. Mrs. Hall "brisked up" Millie using "expressions of contempt," implying that Millie is being slow or lazy, so Mrs. Hall chides her. While sloppy (B), stingy (C), and sullen (D) all have negative connotations, they do not fit the context clues.

3. B: Sentence 9 best explains Mrs. Hall's motivation: "she was resolved to show herself worthy of her good fortune." She has just received an unexpected and high-paying guest and wants to make sure that everything is perfect for him. There is no evidence that she does all the serving herself normally (A); rather, the author seems to emphasize that it is unusual for her to do it herself. She is likely hardworking (C), especially in contrast to her servant Millie, but that is not the author's point. Nor does the author imply that she deserves more respect than the stranger offers purely because of her skills (D), though she may indeed be disappointed at the apparent lack of respect.

4. C: In sentence 13 the author notes that Mrs. Hall sees that melted snow is dripping off of the guest's coat onto her carpet, and she then asks to take his coat and hat into the kitchen to dry them. The reader can infer that she is concerned for her carpet. She does want her guest to be comfortable (A), but this is an apparent reason, not an underlying one. A comfortable guest would be likely stay longer and pay more. She may well wonder what he looks like (B), but the passage does not give strong evidence of this. Likewise, there is no evidence that she wanted to steal from his pockets (D).

5. C: Both passages refer to the way technology has enabled remote work in today's world. The author of Passage 1 would agree with choice A, but the author of Passage 2 states that working from home can be challenging rather than comfortable due to interruptions and other distractions. The author of Passage 2 would likely agree with choice B, but the author of Passage 1 makes no statement about difficulties of relating to others online. Neither passage seems to fully agree with choice D.

6. A: The author of Passage 2 takes issue with several of the statements from Passage 1, indicating that they oversimplify gardening and its difficulties. Choice B is something that the author of Passage 1 might say about the author of Passage 2, not vice versa. Choice C is too strong a statement: the author of Passage 2 might question the other's experience, but we can't assume that he or she would make this claim. Choice D is unrealistic; the author of Passage 2 does not show admiration but skepticism.

7. A: The passage discusses two problems that can occur with wells. Both of the problems mentioned are associated with wells that are too shallow; there is no mention of problems associated with wells that are too deep. Therefore, it seems safe to conclude that an overly deep well would be more desirable than an overly shallow one. The passage does not indicate that most well owners have water shortages every year (choice B). Rather, it discusses how to deal with or avoid a shortage. Nor does the passage imply that most wells dug during the winter are not deep enough (choice C), though it advises to plan ahead for summer. Choice D is contradicted in the first sentence.

8. C: The topic in choice A is mentioned only briefly in the passage. Ideas from choices B and D are mentioned as well, not only as pieces of information in a framework that serves the overall purpose of the passage: to discuss the different types of fats, both good and bad.

9. D: Gentle satire is defined in the ninth sentence as "not offensive." The best synonym for this in the choices would be "not harsh." Choices A, B, and C are all possible meanings of the word *gentle*, but they do not fit the context of this passage.

10. A: Answer choice B is incorrect because the passage states that happiness is expressed similarly by people all over the world. Choice C is incorrect because the passage states that there are many emotions felt and expressed by people all over the world. Choice D is incorrect because, although people may express acceptance differently, we cannot conclude that it is not a natural emotion. We can conclude that people aren't always able to hide what they are feeling (A) because of the statement in the passage that the facial expressions associated with emotions like fear are largely involuntary.

11. C: Choice C is the correct answer because the passage mainly focuses on discussing the causes of heat islands. The ideas in choices A, B, and D are touched upon only in passing.

12. C: Answer choices A and D are incorrect because the passage states that marsupials and mammals both have hair and both feed their young with milk. Choice B can be eliminated, because while the diversity of marsupials is mentioned in the passage, that of mammals is not. Choice C is the correct choice, as the passage states that "one thing that separates marsupials from mammals is that their young are born when they are not yet fully developed."

13. D: Answer choice D best summarizes what this passage is mainly about. Egypt (A), ancient times (B), and William Wolfskill (C) are briefly mentioned, but are not the main subject.

14. D: To answer this question, it is helpful to break the word apart. From the passage, it is clear that *confirming* is synonymous with *proving*. The prefix *dis-* means "do the opposite of." So we can infer that *disconfirming* means "doing the opposite of confirming," and therefor refers to *disproving*. Choice A is inappropriate because it is an antonym of *disconfirming*. Choice B is inappropriate because *dissipating* means "breaking or spreading apart." Choice C is inappropriate because *distilling* means "purifying or breaking down."

15. D: Answer choice D best summarizes the main topic discussed here. While choice C is a fact given about Tubman in the passage, it is not the main focus. Choices A and B are not discussed in the passage.

16. D: Answer choice D uses proper word order to get the point across. This sentence begins with a subject and verb and follows the verb with two objects. Choice A is incorrect because the phrases "my teacher to hate me back" and "for me to hate him" are written in reverse order. It is more logical for "for me to hate him" to be written first. Choice B is incorrect because the subject and verb separate Alberto's two emotions ("expecting to hate my teacher" and "expecting him to hate me back"). This separation makes the sentence more difficult to read and understand. Choice C is incorrect because it repeats that Alberto expected to hate Mr. Shanbourne.

17. C: The word *because* combines the sentence by showing that the second clause is an explanation for the first clause. Choice A is incorrect because the conjunction *and* doesn't show how the two clauses are connected. Choice B is incorrect because the word *although* implies contrast rather than explanation. While *as a result of* has a similar meaning to *because* and could be used to effectively combine the sentences, choice D is incorrect because the verbs *forced* and *gave* should be changed to *forcing* and *giving* in order for *as a result of* to be used correctly.

18. B: Although the subject of the previous sentence is "my old teacher," we can see from context that this sentence has a new subject. The only logical subject for this sentence is "Mr. Shanbourne," since we see that it is someone who doesn't believe in detention but apparently has the power to give it. The old teacher definitely did believe in it, and neither Alberto nor his classmates have the power to give it, even if that made sense in context.

19. B: The phrase "turned work in late" is redundant with the phrase "handed in assignments after the due date"; only one of these two phrases needs to be in the sentence. Choices A and C are incorrect because both phrases add unique information to the sentence. Choice D is incorrect because the sentence has two redundant phrases, and one of them should be deleted.

20. B: The phrase "to have extinction" in choice A is grammatically incorrect. In choice C, "causes" is plural, and *exist* should be used rather than *exists*. D is not the best choice because it is awkward. Choice B sounds the best and is also grammatically correct.

21. C: C is the best answer because *while* indicates a side-by-side comparison, so it fits in this case, and it is a subordinating conjunction, so it is grammatically correct.

22. A: A is the best answer because it denotes the party to whom companies are offering tech support and because the verb "are" agrees with the noun "customers." Choice B does not make sense. Choice C is incorrect because it uses *with* instead of *to*. Choice D is missing the article *a* before "customer."

23. D: D is the best choice. The phrases "high-fat diets" and "excessive amounts of television" agree with each other because they are both plural. The subject of "is" is the singular "fact," so these also agree with each other in number.

24. B: This is a well-known phrase meaning "despite what most people believe." The word *contrarily* in choice A makes it incorrect. "Popularity" in choice C is incorrect, and "believing" in choice D is incorrect.

25. A: On both sides of the punctuation is an independent clause—a stand-alone sentence. The proper way to join these is with a semicolon, a period, or a comma followed by a conjunction. As written, the sentence is correct. Choices B and D join the two clauses with *however*, which can work, but this word must be followed by a comma, so these choices are incorrect. Choice C adds a conjunction but incorrectly places a comma after "if."

26. D: To avoid a dangling participle, the subject of the underlined part must be the word that the phrase "after months of struggling with the decision" applies to. Biology, obviously, did not struggle with a decision for months. So answer choices A and C cannot be correct. Choice B does not make sense as Sharon chooses a major rather than being chosen. Only choice D is logical and grammatically correct.

27. C: The subject of the sentence is "owners," which is plural, so the underlined portion must match this. Thus answer choices A and B are incorrect. Choice D is incorrect because it uses the wrong form of the verb *match*. Choice C uses a plural noun and includes the correct form of the verb *match*.

28. D: The part of the sentence after the underlined portion explains the first part, or adds details to it. So the connecting word needs to show agreement. Choices A, B, and C are contrast words, so they do not fit. Only choice D shows agreement.

29. B: The subject of the sentence is clear in the portion that is not underlined. It is not necessary (and is redundant) to state it in the underlined portion. So choice B is correct because it is clear and concise, while all the others restate the subject.

30. C: The underlined phrase modifies "*The Fir Wood*." This phrase should not be introduced with a participle (A), because that would mean the phrase shows a reason or explanation for the rest of the sentence. Being the first book in the series does not have any obvious relation to selling more copies. Choice B creates a comma splice by turning the underlined phrase into an independent clause. Choice D incorrectly uses *that* instead of *which* for a nonessential clause.

How to Overcome Test Anxiety

Just the thought of taking a test is enough to make most people a little nervous. A test is an important event that can have a long-term impact on your future, so it's important to take it seriously and it's natural to feel anxious about performing well. But just because anxiety is normal, that doesn't mean that it's helpful in test taking, or that you should simply accept it as part of your life. Anxiety can have a variety of effects. These effects can be mild, like making you feel slightly nervous, or severe, like blocking your ability to focus or remember even a simple detail.

If you experience test anxiety—whether severe or mild—it's important to know how to beat it. To discover this, first you need to understand what causes test anxiety.

Causes of Test Anxiety

While we often think of anxiety as an uncontrollable emotional state, it can actually be caused by simple, practical things. One of the most common causes of test anxiety is that a person does not feel adequately prepared for their test. This feeling can be the result of many different issues such as poor study habits or lack of organization, but the most common culprit is time management. Starting to study too late, failing to organize your study time to cover all of the material, or being distracted while you study will mean that you're not well prepared for the test. This may lead to cramming the night before, which will cause you to be physically and mentally exhausted for the test. Poor time management also contributes to feelings of stress, fear, and hopelessness as you realize you are not well prepared but don't know what to do about it.

Other times, test anxiety is not related to your preparation for the test but comes from unresolved fear. This may be a past failure on a test, or poor performance on tests in general. It may come from comparing yourself to others who seem to be performing better or from the stress of living up to expectations. Anxiety may be driven by fears of the future—how failure on this test would affect your educational and career goals. These fears are often completely irrational, but they can still negatively impact your test performance.

Review Video: 3 Reasons You Have Test Anxiety
Visit mometrix.com/academy and enter code: 428468

Elements of Test Anxiety

As mentioned earlier, test anxiety is considered to be an emotional state, but it has physical and mental components as well. Sometimes you may not even realize that you are suffering from test anxiety until you notice the physical symptoms. These can include trembling hands, rapid heartbeat, sweating, nausea, and tense muscles. Extreme anxiety may lead to fainting or vomiting. Obviously, any of these symptoms can have a negative impact on testing. It is important to recognize them as soon as they begin to occur so that you can address the problem before it damages your performance.

Review Video: 3 Ways to Tell You Have Test Anxiety
Visit mometrix.com/academy and enter code: 927847

The mental components of test anxiety include trouble focusing and inability to remember learned information. During a test, your mind is on high alert, which can help you recall information and stay focused for an extended period of time. However, anxiety interferes with your mind's natural processes, causing you to blank out, even on the questions you know well. The strain of testing during anxiety makes it difficult to stay focused, especially on a test that may take several hours. Extreme anxiety can take a huge mental toll, making it difficult not only to recall test information but even to understand the test questions or pull your thoughts together.

Review Video: How Test Anxiety Affects Memory
Visit mometrix.com/academy and enter code: 609003

Effects of Test Anxiety

Test anxiety is like a disease—if left untreated, it will get progressively worse. Anxiety leads to poor performance, and this reinforces the feelings of fear and failure, which in turn lead to poor performances on subsequent tests. It can grow from a mild nervousness to a crippling condition. If allowed to progress, test anxiety can have a big impact on your schooling, and consequently on your future.

Test anxiety can spread to other parts of your life. Anxiety on tests can become anxiety in any stressful situation, and blanking on a test can turn into panicking in a job situation. But fortunately, you don't have to let anxiety rule your testing and determine your grades. There are a number of relatively simple steps you can take to move past anxiety and function normally on a test and in the rest of life.

Review Video: How Test Anxiety Impacts Your Grades
Visit mometrix.com/academy and enter code: 939819

Physical Steps for Beating Test Anxiety

While test anxiety is a serious problem, the good news is that it can be overcome. It doesn't have to control your ability to think and remember information. While it may take time, you can begin taking steps today to beat anxiety.

Just as your first hint that you may be struggling with anxiety comes from the physical symptoms, the first step to treating it is also physical. Rest is crucial for having a clear, strong mind. If you are tired, it is much easier to give in to anxiety. But if you establish good sleep habits, your body and mind will be ready to perform optimally, without the strain of exhaustion. Additionally, sleeping well helps you to retain information better, so you're more likely to recall the answers when you see the test questions.

Getting good sleep means more than going to bed on time. It's important to allow your brain time to relax. Take study breaks from time to time so it doesn't get overworked, and don't study right before bed. Take time to rest your mind before trying to rest your body, or you may find it difficult to fall asleep.

Review Video: The Importance of Sleep for Your Brain
Visit mometrix.com/academy and enter code: 319338

Along with sleep, other aspects of physical health are important in preparing for a test. Good nutrition is vital for good brain function. Sugary foods and drinks may give a burst of energy but this burst is followed by a crash, both physically and emotionally. Instead, fuel your body with protein and vitamin-rich foods.

Also, drink plenty of water. Dehydration can lead to headaches and exhaustion, especially if your brain is already under stress from the rigors of the test. Particularly if your test is a long one, drink water during the breaks. And if possible, take an energy-boosting snack to eat between sections.

Review Video: How Diet Can Affect your Mood
Visit mometrix.com/academy and enter code: 624317

Along with sleep and diet, a third important part of physical health is exercise. Maintaining a steady workout schedule is helpful, but even taking 5-minute study breaks to walk can help get your blood pumping faster and clear your head. Exercise also releases endorphins, which contribute to a positive feeling and can help combat test anxiety.

When you nurture your physical health, you are also contributing to your mental health. If your body is healthy, your mind is much more likely to be healthy as well. So take time to rest, nourish your body with healthy food and water, and get moving as much as possible. Taking these physical steps will make you stronger and more able to take the mental steps necessary to overcome test anxiety.

Mental Steps for Beating Test Anxiety

Working on the mental side of test anxiety can be more challenging, but as with the physical side, there are clear steps you can take to overcome it. As mentioned earlier, test anxiety often stems from lack of preparation, so the obvious solution is to prepare for the test. Effective studying may be the most important weapon you have for beating test anxiety, but you can and should employ several other mental tools to combat fear.

First, boost your confidence by reminding yourself of past success—tests or projects that you aced. If you're putting as much effort into preparing for this test as you did for those, there's no reason you should expect to fail here. Work hard to prepare; then trust your preparation.

Second, surround yourself with encouraging people. It can be helpful to find a study group, but be sure that the people you're around will encourage a positive attitude. If you spend time with others who are anxious or cynical, this will only contribute to your own anxiety. Look for others who are motivated to study hard from a desire to succeed, not from a fear of failure.

Third, reward yourself. A test is physically and mentally tiring, even without anxiety, and it can be helpful to have something to look forward to. Plan an activity following the test, regardless of the outcome, such as going to a movie or getting ice cream.

When you are taking the test, if you find yourself beginning to feel anxious, remind yourself that you know the material. Visualize successfully completing the test. Then take a few deep, relaxing breaths and return to it. Work through the questions carefully but with confidence, knowing that you are capable of succeeding.

Developing a healthy mental approach to test taking will also aid in other areas of life. Test anxiety affects more than just the actual test—it can be damaging to your mental health and even contribute to depression. It's important to beat test anxiety before it becomes a problem for more than testing.

Review Video: Test Anxiety and Depression
Visit mometrix.com/academy and enter code: 904704

Study Strategy

Being prepared for the test is necessary to combat anxiety, but what does being prepared look like? You may study for hours on end and still not feel prepared. What you need is a strategy for test prep. The next few pages outline our recommended steps to help you plan out and conquer the challenge of preparation.

Step 1: Scope Out the Test

Learn everything you can about the format (multiple choice, essay, etc.) and what will be on the test. Gather any study materials, course outlines, or sample exams that may be available. Not only will this help you to prepare, but knowing what to expect can help to alleviate test anxiety.

Step 2: Map Out the Material

Look through the textbook or study guide and make note of how many chapters or sections it has. Then divide these over the time you have. For example, if a book has 15 chapters and you have five days to study, you need to cover three chapters each day. Even better, if you have the time, leave an extra day at the end for overall review after you have gone through the material in depth.

If time is limited, you may need to prioritize the material. Look through it and make note of which sections you think you already have a good grasp on, and which need review. While you are studying, skim quickly through the familiar sections and take more time on the challenging parts. Write out your plan so you don't get lost as you go. Having a written plan also helps you feel more in control of the study, so anxiety is less likely to arise from feeling overwhelmed at the amount to cover.

Step 3: Gather Your Tools

Decide what study method works best for you. Do you prefer to highlight in the book as you study and then go back over the highlighted portions? Or do you type out notes of the important information? Or is it helpful to make flashcards that you can carry with you? Assemble the pens, index cards, highlighters, post-it notes, and any other materials you may need so you won't be distracted by getting up to find things while you study.

If you're having a hard time retaining the information or organizing your notes, experiment with different methods. For example, try color-coding by subject with colored pens, highlighters, or post-it notes. If you learn better by hearing, try recording yourself reading your notes so you can listen while in the car, working out, or simply sitting at your desk. Ask a friend to quiz you from your flashcards, or try teaching someone the material to solidify it in your mind.

Step 4: Create Your Environment

It's important to avoid distractions while you study. This includes both the obvious distractions like visitors and the subtle distractions like an uncomfortable chair (or a too-comfortable couch that makes you want to fall asleep). Set up the best study environment possible: good lighting and a comfortable work area. If background music helps you focus, you may want to turn it on, but otherwise keep the room quiet. If you are using a computer to take notes, be sure you don't have any other windows open, especially applications like social media, games, or anything else that could distract you. Silence your phone and turn off notifications. Be sure to keep water close by so you stay hydrated while you study (but avoid unhealthy drinks and snacks).

Also, take into account the best time of day to study. Are you freshest first thing in the morning? Try to set aside some time then to work through the material. Is your mind clearer in the afternoon or evening? Schedule your study session then. Another method is to study at the same time of day that you will take the test, so that your brain gets used to working on the material at that time and will be ready to focus at test time.

Step 5: Study!

Once you have done all the study preparation, it's time to settle into the actual studying. Sit down, take a few moments to settle your mind so you can focus, and begin to follow your study plan. Don't give in to distractions or let yourself procrastinate. This is your time to prepare so you'll be ready to fearlessly approach the test. Make the most of the time and stay focused.

Of course, you don't want to burn out. If you study too long you may find that you're not retaining the information very well. Take regular study breaks. For example, taking five minutes out of every hour to walk briskly, breathing deeply and swinging your arms, can help your mind stay fresh.

As you get to the end of each chapter or section, it's a good idea to do a quick review. Remind yourself of what you learned and work on any difficult parts. When you feel that you've mastered the material, move on to the next part. At the end of your study session, briefly skim through your notes again.

But while review is helpful, cramming last minute is NOT. If at all possible, work ahead so that you won't need to fit all your study into the last day. Cramming overloads your brain with more information than it can process and retain, and your tired mind may struggle to recall even previously learned information when it is overwhelmed with last-minute study. Also, the urgent nature of cramming and the stress placed on your brain contribute to anxiety. You'll be more likely to go to the test feeling unprepared and having trouble thinking clearly.

So don't cram, and don't stay up late before the test, even just to review your notes at a leisurely pace. Your brain needs rest more than it needs to go over the information again. In fact, plan to finish your studies by noon or early afternoon the day before the test. Give your brain the rest of the day to relax or focus on other things, and get a good night's sleep. Then you will be fresh for the test and better able to recall what you've studied.

Step 6: Take a practice test

Many courses offer sample tests, either online or in the study materials. This is an excellent resource to check whether you have mastered the material, as well as to prepare for the test format and environment.

Check the test format ahead of time: the number of questions, the type (multiple choice, free response, etc.), and the time limit. Then create a plan for working through them. For example, if you have 30 minutes to take a 60-question test, your limit is 30 seconds per question. Spend less time on the questions you know well so that you can take more time on the difficult ones.

If you have time to take several practice tests, take the first one open book, with no time limit. Work through the questions at your own pace and make sure you fully understand them. Gradually work up to taking a test under test conditions: sit at a desk with all study materials put away and set a timer. Pace yourself to make sure you finish the test with time to spare and go back to check your answers if you have time.

After each test, check your answers. On the questions you missed, be sure you understand why you missed them. Did you misread the question (tests can use tricky wording)? Did you forget the information? Or was it something you hadn't learned? Go back and study any shaky areas that the practice tests reveal.

Taking these tests not only helps with your grade, but also aids in combating test anxiety. If you're already used to the test conditions, you're less likely to worry about it, and working through tests until you're scoring well gives you a confidence boost. Go through the practice tests until you feel comfortable, and then you can go into the test knowing that you're ready for it.

Test Tips

On test day, you should be confident, knowing that you've prepared well and are ready to answer the questions. But aside from preparation, there are several test day strategies you can employ to maximize your performance.

First, as stated before, get a good night's sleep the night before the test (and for several nights before that, if possible). Go into the test with a fresh, alert mind rather than staying up late to study.

Try not to change too much about your normal routine on the day of the test. It's important to eat a nutritious breakfast, but if you normally don't eat breakfast at all, consider eating just a protein bar. If you're a coffee drinker, go ahead and have your normal coffee. Just make sure you time it so that the caffeine doesn't wear off right in the middle of your test. Avoid sugary beverages, and drink enough water to stay hydrated but not so much that you need a restroom break 10 minutes into the test. If your test isn't first thing in the morning, consider going for a walk or doing a light workout before the test to get your blood flowing.

Allow yourself enough time to get ready, and leave for the test with plenty of time to spare so you won't have the anxiety of scrambling to arrive in time. Another reason to be early is to select a good seat. It's helpful to sit away from doors and windows, which can be distracting. Find a good seat, get out your supplies, and settle your mind before the test begins.

When the test begins, start by going over the instructions carefully, even if you already know what to expect. Make sure you avoid any careless mistakes by following the directions.

Then begin working through the questions, pacing yourself as you've practiced. If you're not sure on an answer, don't spend too much time on it, and don't let it shake your confidence. Either skip it and come back later, or eliminate as many wrong answers as possible and guess among the remaining ones. Don't dwell on these questions as you continue—put them out of your mind and focus on what lies ahead.

Be sure to read all of the answer choices, even if you're sure the first one is the right answer. Sometimes you'll find a better one if you keep reading. But don't second-guess yourself if you do immediately know the answer. Your gut instinct is usually right. Don't let test anxiety rob you of the information you know.

If you have time at the end of the test (and if the test format allows), go back and review your answers. Be cautious about changing any, since your first instinct tends to be correct, but make sure you didn't misread any of the questions or accidentally mark the wrong answer choice. Look over any you skipped and make an educated guess.

At the end, leave the test feeling confident. You've done your best, so don't waste time worrying about your performance or wishing you could change anything. Instead, celebrate the successful completion of this test. And finally, use this test to learn how to deal with anxiety even better next time.

Review Video: 5 Tips to Beat Test Anxiety
Visit mometrix.com/academy and enter code: 570656

Important Qualification

Not all anxiety is created equal. If your test anxiety is causing major issues in your life beyond the classroom or testing center, or if you are experiencing troubling physical symptoms related to your anxiety, it may be a sign of a serious physiological or psychological condition. If this sounds like your situation, we strongly encourage you to seek professional help.

How to Overcome Your Fear of Math

Not again. You're sitting in math class, look down at your test, and immediately start to panic. Your stomach is in knots, your heart is racing, and you break out in a cold sweat. You're staring at the paper, but everything looks like it's written in a foreign language. Even though you studied, you're blanking out on how to begin solving these problems.

Does this sound familiar? If so, then you're not alone! You may be like millions of other people who experience math anxiety. Anxiety about performing well in math is a common experience for students of all ages. In this article, we'll discuss what math anxiety is, common misconceptions about learning math, and tips and strategies for overcoming math anxiety.

What Is Math Anxiety?

Psychologist Mark H. Ashcraft explains math anxiety as a feeling of tension, apprehension, or fear that interferes with math performance. Having math anxiety negatively impacts people's beliefs about themselves and what they can achieve. It hinders achievement within the math classroom and affects the successful application of mathematics in the real world.

Symptoms and Signs of Math Anxiety

To overcome math anxiety, you must recognize its symptoms. Becoming aware of the signs of math anxiety is the first step in addressing and resolving these fears.

Negative Self-Talk

If you have math anxiety, you've most likely said at least one of these statements to yourself:

- "I hate math."
- "I'm not good at math."
- "I'm not a math person."

The way we speak to ourselves and think about ourselves matters. Our thoughts become our words, our words become our actions, and our actions become our habits. Thinking negatively about math creates a self-fulfilling prophecy. In other words, if you take an idea as a fact, then it will come true because your behaviors will align to match it.

Avoidance

Some people who are fearful or anxious about math will tend to avoid it altogether. Avoidance can manifest in the following ways:

- Lack of engagement with math content
- Not completing homework and other assignments
- Not asking for help when needed
- Skipping class
- Avoiding math-related courses and activities

Avoidance is one of the most harmful impacts of math anxiety. If you steer clear of math at all costs, then you can't set yourself up for the success you deserve.

Lack of Motivation

Students with math anxiety may experience a lack of motivation. They may struggle to find the incentive to get engaged with what they view as a frightening subject. These students are often overwhelmed, making it difficult for them to complete or even start math assignments.

Procrastination

Another symptom of math anxiety is procrastination. Students may voluntarily delay or postpone their classwork and assignments, even if they know there will be a negative consequence for doing so. Additionally, they may choose to wait until the last minute to start projects and homework, even when they know they need more time to put forth their best effort.

Physiological Reactions

Many people with a fear of math experience physiological side effects. These may include an increase in heart rate, sweatiness, shakiness, nausea, and irregular breathing. These symptoms make it difficult to focus on the math content, causing the student even more stress and fear.

Strong Emotional Responses

Math anxiety also affects people on an emotional level. Responding to math content with strong emotions such as panic, anger, or despair can be a sign of math anxiety.

Low Test Scores and Performance

Low achievement can be both a symptom and a cause of math anxiety. When someone does not take the steps needed to perform well on tests and assessments, they are less likely to pass. The more they perform poorly, the more they accept this poor performance as a fact that can't be changed.

Feeling Alone

People who experience math anxiety feel like they are the only ones struggling, even if the math they are working on is challenging to many people. Feeling isolated in what they perceive as failure can trigger tension or nervousness.

Feeling of Permanency

Math anxiety can feel very permanent. You may assume that you are naturally bad at math and always will be. Viewing math as a natural ability rather than a skill that can be learned causes people to believe that nothing will help them improve. They take their current math abilities as fact and assume that they can't be changed. As a result, they give up, stop trying to improve, and avoid engaging with math altogether.

Lack of Confidence

People with low self-confidence in math tend to feel awkward and incompetent when asked to solve a math problem. They don't feel comfortable taking chances or risks when problem-solving because they second-guess themselves and assume they are incorrect. They don't trust in their ability to learn the content and solve problems correctly.

Panic

A general sense of unexplained panic is also a sign of math anxiety. You may feel a sudden sense of fear that triggers physical reactions, even when there is no apparent reason for such a response.

Causes Of Math Anxiety

Math anxiety can start at a young age and may have one or more underlying causes. Common causes of math anxiety include the following:

The Attitude of Parents or Guardians

Parents often put pressure on their children to perform well in school. Although their intentions are usually good, this pressure can lead to anxiety, especially if the student is struggling with a subject or class.

Perhaps your parents or others in your life hold negative predispositions about math based on their own experiences. For instance, if your mother once claimed she was not good at math, then you might have incorrectly interpreted this as a predisposed trait that was passed down to you.

Teacher Influence

Students often pick up on their teachers' attitudes about the content being taught. If a teacher is happy and excited about math, students are more likely to mirror these emotions. However, if a teacher lacks enthusiasm or genuine interest, then students are more inclined to disengage.

Teachers have a responsibility to cultivate a welcoming classroom culture that is accepting of mistakes. When teachers blame students for not understanding a concept, they create a hostile classroom environment where mistakes are not tolerated. This tension increases student stress and anxiety, creating conditions that are not conducive to inquiry and learning. Instead, when teachers normalize mistakes as a natural part of the problem-solving process, they give their students the freedom to explore and grapple with the math content. In such an environment, students feel comfortable taking chances because they are not afraid of being wrong.

Students need teachers that can help when they're having problems understanding difficult concepts. In doing so, educators may need to change how they teach the content. Since different people have unique learning styles, it's the job of the teacher to adapt to the needs of each student. Additionally, teachers should encourage students to explore alternate problem-solving strategies, even if it's not the preferred method of the educator.

Fear of Being Wrong

Embarrassing situations can be traumatic, especially for young children and adolescents. These experiences can stay with people through their adult lives. Those with math anxiety may experience a fear of being wrong, especially in front of a group of peers. This fear can be paralyzing, interfering with the student's concentration and ability to focus on the problem at hand.

Timed Assessments

Timed assessments can help improve math fluency, but they often create unnecessary pressure for students to complete an unrealistic number of problems within a specified timeframe. Many studies have shown that timed assessments often result in increased levels of anxiety, reducing a student's overall competence and ability to problem-solve.

Debunking Math Myths

There are lots of myths about math that are related to the causes and development of math-related anxiety. Although these myths have been proven to be false, many people take them as fact. Let's go over a few of the most common myths about learning math.

Myth: Men Are Better at Math Than Women

Math has a reputation for being a male-dominant subject, but this doesn't mean that men are inherently better at math than women. Many famous mathematical discoveries have been made by women. Katherine Johnson, Dame Mary Lucy Cartwright, and Marjorie Lee Brown are just a few of the many famous women mathematicians. Expecting to be good or bad at math because of your gender sets you up for stress and confusion. Math is a skill that can be learned, just like cooking or riding a bike.

Myth: There Is Only One Good Way to Solve Math Problems

There are many ways to get the correct answer when it comes to math. No two people have the same brain, so everyone takes a slightly different approach to problem-solving. Moreover, there isn't one way of problem-solving that's superior to another. Your way of working through a problem might differ from someone else's, and that is okay. Math can be a highly individualized process, so the best method for you should be the one that makes you feel the most comfortable and makes the most sense to you.

Myth: Math Requires a Good Memory

For many years, mathematics was taught through memorization. However, learning in such a way hinders the development of critical thinking and conceptual understanding. These skill sets are much more valuable than basic memorization. For instance, you might be great at memorizing mathematical formulas, but if you don't understand what they mean, then you can't apply them to different scenarios in the real world. When a student is working from memory, they are limited in the strategies available to them to problem-solve. In other words, they assume there is only one correct way to do the math, which is the method they memorized. Having a variety of problem-solving options can help students figure out which method works best for them. Additionally, it provides students with a better understanding of how and why certain mathematical strategies work. While memorization can be helpful in some instances, it is not an absolute requirement for mathematicians.

Myth: Math Is Not Creative

Math requires imagination and intuition. Contrary to popular belief, it is a highly creative field. Mathematical creativity can help in developing new ways to think about and solve problems. Many people incorrectly assume that all things are either creative or analytical. However, this black-and-white view is limiting because the field of mathematics involves both creativity and logic.

Myth: Math Isn't Supposed To Be Fun

Whoever told you that math isn't supposed to be fun is a liar. There are tons of math-based activities and games that foster friendly competition and engagement. Math is often best learned through play, and lots of mobile apps and computer games exemplify this.

Additionally, math can be an exceptionally collaborative and social experience. Studying or working through problems with a friend often makes the process a lot more fun. The excitement and satisfaction of solving a difficult problem with others is quite rewarding. Math can be fun if you look for ways to make it more collaborative and enjoyable.

Myth: Not Everyone Is Capable of Learning Math

There's no such thing as a "math person." Although many people think that you're either good at math or you're not, this is simply not true. Everyone is capable of learning and applying mathematics. However, not everyone learns the same way. Since each person has a different learning style, the trick is to find the strategies and learning tools that work best for you. Some people learn best through hands-on experiences, and others find success through the use of visual aids. Others are auditory learners and learn best by hearing and listening. When people are overwhelmed or feel that math is too hard, it's often because they haven't found the learning strategy that works best for them.

Myth: Good Mathematicians Work Quickly and Never Make Mistakes

There is no prize for finishing first in math. It's not a race, and speed isn't a measure of your ability. Good mathematicians take their time to ensure their work is accurate. As you gain more experience and practice, you will naturally become faster and more confident.

Additionally, everyone makes mistakes, including good mathematicians. Mistakes are a normal part of the problem-solving process, and they're not a bad thing. The important thing is that we take the time to learn from our mistakes, understand where our misconceptions are, and move forward.

Myth: You Don't Need Math in the Real World

Our day-to-day lives are so infused with mathematical concepts that we often don't even realize when we're using math in the real world. In fact, most people tend to underestimate how much we do math in our everyday lives. It's involved in an enormous variety of daily activities such as shopping, baking, finances, and gardening, as well as in many careers, including architecture, nursing, design, and sales.

Tips and Strategies for Overcoming Math Anxiety

If your anxiety is getting in the way of your level of mathematical engagement, then there are lots of steps you can take. Check out the strategies below to start building confidence in math today.

Focus on Understanding, Not Memorization

Don't drive yourself crazy trying to memorize every single formula or mathematical process. Instead, shift your attention to understanding concepts. Those who prioritize memorization over conceptual understanding tend to have lower achievement levels in math. Students who memorize may be able to complete some math, but they don't understand the process well enough to apply it to different situations. Memorization comes with time and practice, but it won't help alleviate math anxiety. On the other hand, conceptual understanding will give you the building blocks of knowledge you need to build up your confidence.

Replace Negative Self-Talk with Positive Self-Talk

Start to notice how you think about yourself. Whenever you catch yourself thinking something negative, try replacing that thought with a positive affirmation. Instead of continuing the negative thought, pause to reframe the situation. For ideas on how to get started, take a look at the table below:

Instead of thinking...	Try thinking...
"I can't do this math." "I'm not a math person."	"I'm up for the challenge, and I'm training my brain in math."
"This problem is too hard."	"This problem is hard, so this might take some time and effort. I know I can do this."
"I give up."	"What strategies can help me solve this problem?"
"I made a mistake, so I'm not good at this."	"Everyone makes mistakes. Mistakes help me to grow and understand."
"I'll never be smart enough."	"I can figure this out, and I am smart enough."

Practice Mindfulness

Practicing mindfulness and focusing on your breathing can help alleviate some of the physical symptoms of math anxiety. By taking deep breaths, you can remind your nervous system that you are not in immediate danger. Doing so will reduce your heart rate and help with any irregular breathing or shakiness. Taking the edge off of the physiological effects of anxiety will clear your mind, allowing your brain to focus its energy on problem-solving.

Do Some Math Every Day

Think about learning math as if you were learning a foreign language. If you don't use it, you lose it. If you don't practice your math skills regularly, you'll have a harder time achieving comprehension and fluency. Set some amount of time aside each day, even if it's just for a few minutes, to practice. It might take some discipline to build a habit around this, but doing so will help increase your mathematical self-assurance.

Use All of Your Resources

Everyone has a different learning style, and there are plenty of resources out there to support all learners. When you get stuck on a math problem, think about the tools you have access to, and use them when applicable. Such resources may include flashcards, graphic organizers, study guides, interactive notebooks, and peer study groups. All of these are great tools to accommodate your individual learning style. Finding the tools and resources that work for your learning style will give you the confidence you need to succeed.

Realize That You Aren't Alone

Remind yourself that lots of other people struggle with math anxiety, including teachers, nurses, and even successful mathematicians. You aren't the only one who panics when faced with a new or challenging problem. It's probably much more common than you think. Realizing that you aren't alone in your experience can help put some distance between yourself and the emotions you feel about math. It also helps to normalize the anxiety and shift your perspective.

Ask Questions

If there's a concept you don't understand and you've tried everything you can, then it's okay to ask for help! You can always ask your teacher or professor for help. If you're not learning math in a traditional classroom, you may want to join a study group, work with a tutor, or talk to your friends. More often than not, you aren't the only one of your peers who needs clarity on a mathematical concept. Seeking understanding is a great way to increase self-confidence in math.

Remember That There's More Than One Way To Solve A Problem

Since everyone learns differently, it's best to focus on understanding a math problem with an approach that makes sense to you. If the way it's being taught is confusing to you, don't give up. Instead, work to understand the problem using a different technique. There's almost always more than one problem-solving method when it comes to math. Don't get stressed if one of them doesn't make sense to you. Instead, shift your focus to what does make sense. Chances are high that you know more than you think you do.

Visualization

Visualization is the process of creating images in your mind's eye. Picture yourself as a successful, confident mathematician. Think about how you would feel and how you would behave. What would your work area look like? How would you organize your belongings? The more you focus on something, the more likely you are to achieve it. Visualizing teaches your brain that you can achieve whatever it is that you want. Thinking about success in mathematics will lead to acting like a successful mathematician. This, in turn, leads to actual success.

Focus on the Easiest Problems First

To increase your confidence when working on a math test or assignment, try solving the easiest problems first. Doing so will remind you that you are successful in math and that you do have what it takes. This process will increase your belief in yourself, giving you the confidence you need to tackle more complex problems.

Find a Support Group

A study buddy, tutor, or peer group can go a long way in decreasing math-related anxiety. Such support systems offer lots of benefits, including a safe place to ask questions, additional practice with mathematical concepts, and an understanding of other problem-solving explanations that may work better for you. Equipping yourself with a support group is one of the fastest ways to eliminate math anxiety.

Reward Yourself for Working Hard

Recognize the amount of effort you're putting in to overcome your math anxiety. It's not an easy task, so you deserve acknowledgement. Surround yourself with people who will provide you with the positive reinforcement you deserve.

Remember, You Can Do This!

Conquering a fear of math can be challenging, but there are lots of strategies that can help you out. Your own beliefs about your mathematical capabilities can limit your potential. Working toward a growth mindset can have a tremendous impact on decreasing math-related anxiety and building confidence. By knowing the symptoms of math anxiety and recognizing common misconceptions about learning math, you can develop a plan to address your fear of math. Utilizing the strategies discussed can help you overcome this anxiety and build the confidence you need to succeed.

Tell Us Your Story

We at Mometrix would like to extend our heartfelt thanks to you for letting us be a part of your journey. It is an honor to serve people from all walks of life, people like you, who are committed to building the best future they can for themselves.

We know that each person's situation is unique. But we also know that, whether you are a young student or a mother of four, you care about working to make your own life and the lives of those around you better.

That's why we want to hear your story.

We want to know why you're taking this test. We want to know about the trials you've gone through to get here. And we want to know about the successes you've experienced after taking and passing your test.

In addition to your story, which can be an inspiration both to us and to others, we value your feedback. We want to know both what you loved about our book and what you think we can improve on.

SCAN HERE

The team at Mometrix would be absolutely thrilled to hear from you! So please, send us an email at tellusyourstory@mometrix.com or visit us at mometrix.com/tellusyourstory.php and let's stay in touch.